CANADA AND THE BRITISH ARMY
1846-1871

A Study in the Practice of Responsible Government

BY

C. P. STACEY

O.B.E., C.D., A.M., Ph.D., LL.D., F.R.S.C.
Professor of History, University of Toronto
Late Director, Historical Section, General Staff, Canadian Army

REVISED EDITION

Published in association with THE ROYAL COMMONWEALTH SOCIETY *by*
UNIVERSITY OF TORONTO PRESS

Revised edition
© UNIVERSITY OF TORONTO PRESS 1963
Reprinted in 2018

SCHOLARLY REPRINT SERIES
ISBN 0-8020-7042-6
ISBN 978-1-4875-7250-1 (paper)
LC 64-7285

First published 1936 by Longmans, Green and Co. in the "Imperial Studies" Series of the Royal Empire Society (now the Royal Commonwealth Society)

Printed in Great Britain

*TO
MY MOTHER*

CANADA AND THE BRITISH ARMY
1846-1871

Canadian Illustrated News, December 2, 1871

THE BRITISH ARMY LEAVES QUEBEC
The 60th Rifles marching out of the Citadel, November 11, 1871

" An army maintained in a country which does not permit us even to govern it ! What an anomaly ! "
　　　　　　　DISRAELI to DERBY, September 30, 1866.

PREFACE

THIS essay is an outgrowth of a study of Fenianism in North America undertaken some years ago. In the course of that research my attention was strongly directed to the anomalous and unsettled condition of the military relations of Canada with the mother country at the time of the organization of the Dominion; and a very brief investigation revealed that an abundance of interesting and significant material bearing on this subject was easily available at Ottawa. I was thus encouraged to attempt to compile an outline of the salient features of the problem of Canadian military responsibility as it developed after the grant of responsible government, down to the time when Britain, weary of urging Canada to take up defensive obligations commensurate with the extent of her new political autonomy, determined to withdraw the great body of her troops and cast upon the Dominion the whole burden of its own local defence in time of peace.

On account of the heavy financial burden which the maintenance of colonial garrisons imposed upon the mother country, this question had great importance in the eyes of contemporaries; and it is a trifle surprising to find it so largely overlooked by more recent writers. While I do not wish to claim for it an importance which it does not merit, I trust that the suggestion made in this study—that the final abolition of the garrisons, by redressing the one great grievance of the British taxpayer against the colonies, contributed substantially to the revival of imperial enthusiasm in England—may be found to be not entirely without foundation.

PREFACE

It will be observed that in the pre-federative period this study deals almost exclusively with the Province of Canada. For reasons explained in the text, the question presented itself there in a much more extreme form than in the Maritime Provinces; and Canada was the laboratory where experimentation in the direction of a division of defensive responsibility between mother country and colony was most largely carried on. It will be noticed also that the matter is treated in increasing detail in the later years of the period concerned—those which saw the birth of the Dominion. During the decade 1861-1871, military affairs were of major importance in the relations of Britain and Canada; and this monograph, though not primarily designed with that object in view, may make a minor contribution to the study of the forces which were then at work to produce Canadian nationality.

To make proper acknowledgments to all those who have given me assistance and encouragement in this work would be impossible; but I can at least record in general terms my gratitude for the innumerable kindnesses received from the Department of History at Princeton University, and in particular from its Chairman, Professor T. J. Wertenbaker, during the time that this essay was in preparation. To Professor R. G. Albion, who directed my work, I find myself under especially heavy obligations, not only for the most helpful guidance and criticism which I received from him in general, but also for many valuable suggestions on particular points; his association with this research has done much to make the task a very agreeable one. I have also to thank Professor W. P. Hall for his kindness in reading the manuscript.

I owe a heavy debt to Dr. A. G. Doughty, C.M.G., and his staff at the Public Archives of Canada, Ottawa, where most of the material for this book was gathered. I am particularly grateful to Dr. J. F. Kenney, the Director of Historical Research and Publicity; he has given me invaluable help on many occasions, and his patience has been inexhaustible. I must also

PREFACE

express my sense of obligation to the staffs of the Princeton University Library; the Library of Parliament, Ottawa; the University of Toronto Library and the Toronto Reference Library; the New York Public Library; and the Library of Columbia University.

To Professor J. B. Brebner, of Columbia University, I have been greatly indebted for his constant interest in this project and for most useful criticism; while Professor James T. Shotwell, Director of the Division of Economics and History, Carnegie Endowment for International Peace, has placed me under a deep obligation by the encouragement he has given the work in its final stages. Finally, I must acknowledge the kindness of the Imperial Studies Committee of the Royal Empire Society in admitting the book to their series and generously defraying the major part of the cost of publication; and of the Carnegie Endowment for International Peace, which by granting me an honorarium for a related study has enabled me to meet the remaining expense.

It is, perhaps, scarcely necessary to add that the errors and omissions which will be found in these pages are my own peculiar contribution.

C.P.S.

THE GRADUATE COLLEGE,
PRINCETON, NEW JERSEY.
February 10th, 1935.

PREFACE TO REVISED EDITION

THIS little book was first published in 1936, in the series of Imperial Studies sponsored by what was then called the Royal Empire Society. I am deeply grateful to the Royal Commonwealth Society and the University of Toronto Press for making possible this new and somewhat revised edition.

On the evening of December 29, 1940, I stood at the corner of Queensway and Bayswater Road with a brother officer, who like myself had landed from Canada only four days before, and watched the flames of London's worst fire-raid rise above the City. My interest in the spectacle would have been even more painful than it was had I known that the publisher's stock of the original edition of *Canada and the British Army* was helping to feed the conflagration. The fact that it became, to this extent, a war casualty must be the justification for republishing this work of my younger days. I may also appeal to the fact that it is a humble contribution to the history of the era of Canadian Confederation, whose centenary we are preparing to celebrate. I am well aware that it would be desirable to make a more complete revision than has been attempted here. Examination of the sources in the Public Record Office, London, which were not consulted when the book was written, would certainly elicit new facts and would doubtless enable me to make a number of corrections. But I could not undertake so thorough a revision at the present time: and there has been enough continuing interest in the book to encourage me to hope that the republication of the original version, with several pages of additions and corrections, will be sufficiently useful to repay the effort and

PREFACE TO REVISED EDITION

expense generously devoted to it by the University of Toronto Press.

Following page 281 in this new edition, a brief selective bibliography has been added. It is chiefly composed of books and articles published since the book was written, but also contains some items that ought to have been included in the list of Authorities in the first edition. It has not been possible to incorporate in the section of Notes that follows the additional bibliography all the new facts found in the material now listed. But the topics of most of the works noted are rather incidental to this book ; and in general they contribute additional details rather than new interpretations. In these circumstances it has seemed sufficient to provide a list of these books and articles for the information of interested readers.

The section of Notes, each announced in the original text by an asterisk, amplifies or improves certain passages in the original edition of this book, and corrects various slips and errors that have been detected. Since the original index was rather inadequate, some additions to it are provided, the additions and corrections of this new edition being indexed at the same time. A number of errata in the text have been corrected.

In its earliest form this book was a dissertation presented to the Faculty of Princeton University in 1933. Revising it has brought back many memories of those pleasant pre-war days at Princeton. In sending it to the press a second time I record once more my gratitude for all the kindness I received there.

C.P.S.

DEPARTMENT OF HISTORY
UNIVERSITY OF TORONTO.
August 14th, 1962.

CONTENTS

CHAP.		PAGE
	PREFACE	ix
	PREFACE TO REVISED EDITION	xiii
I.	INTRODUCTORY: THE EARLY HISTORY OF IMPERIAL DEFENCE	1
II.	BRITAIN AND THE COLONIAL RELATIONSHIP AT THE BEGINNING OF THE VICTORIAN AGE	26
III.	PROBLEMS OF BRITISH MILITARY POLICY: COLONIAL RELIEFS AND HOME DEFENCE	52
IV.	CANADA UNDER RESPONSIBLE GOVERNMENT: THE MILITARY QUESTION DURING ELGIN'S ADMINISTRATION	64
V.	THE CRIMEAN WAR AND THE BEGINNINGS OF THE CANADIAN VOLUNTEER FORCE, 1854–1860	89
VI.	CANADA AND THE AMERICAN CIVIL WAR: THE EARLY PHASES	117
VII.	CANADA AND THE AMERICAN CIVIL WAR: THE DEEPEST SHADOW	147
VIII.	FENIANISM AND FEDERATION	179
IX.	CARDWELL CUTS THE GORDIAN KNOT	204
X.	THE END OF THE OLD ORDER	230
	AUTHORITIES	265
	NOTES ADDITIONAL TO THE TEXT	**285**
	INDEX	**289**

ABBREVIATIONS

C	..	" C " Series (Military Papers), in Public Archives of Canada, Ottawa.
C.D.Q.	..	*Canadian Defence Quarterly*.
C.H.R.	..	*Canadian Historical Review*.
E	..	" E " Series (Executive Council Records, etc.), Public Archives of Canada.
G	..	" G " Series (Governor-General's Correspondence), Public Archives of Canada.
G.E.C.	..	Grey-Elgin Correspondence, Public Archives of Canada.
M.P.	..	Papers of Sir John A. Macdonald, Public Archives of Canada.
P.P.	..	Parliamentary Papers, House of Commons (United Kingdom).
S.P.	..	Sessional Papers, Parliament of Canada (Province and Dominion).

CHAPTER I

INTRODUCTORY: THE EARLY HISTORY OF IMPERIAL DEFENCE

> "Great Britain is, perhaps, since the world began, the only state which, as it has extended its empire, has only increased its expense without once augmenting its resources. Other states have generally disburdened themselves upon their subject and subordinate provinces of the most considerable part of the expense of defending the empire. Great Britain has hitherto suffered her subject and subordinate provinces to disburden themselves upon her of almost this whole expense."—ADAM SMITH in *The Wealth of Nations*, 1776.

AMONG the innumerable special problems that make the government of a great colonial empire perhaps the hardest task ever faced by man's political science, there is none more obstinate than that of imperial defence; and nowhere has it presented itself in a more thorny guise than in the history of the British Commonwealth. To combine an adequate organization for the protection of the British Isles with arrangements for the preservation of numerous scattered colonies "against the envy of less happier lands" has not been a simple matter at any period since overseas possessions became prizes in the European game of diplomacy and war.

Merely to formulate effective military plans for such an object is not easy; and yet the matter cannot be dealt with upon a basis of military theory alone. The fact that defensive preparation entails large expenditure immediately projects it into other fields than strategy. At once to attain military efficiency and to apportion the resultant financial burden in a fashion just and acceptable both to the metropolitan community and the colonies is a problem that has heavily taxed the resources of British statesmanship, and it could scarcely be said of any epoch in the history of the Empire that the situation in this respect was then completely satisfactory. The greatest tragedy of British imperial history—the loss of the old American colonies—was the outcome of an inept attempt at solving this problem; and there have been few periods when it did not occasion some friction between dwellers at the centre of the imperial circle and those at various points of the circumference.

In the earliest days of the colonial empire, the defence of the dependencies involved the mother country in little trouble or expense. It never occurred to the English Government that royal troops should accompany and protect those of its citizens whom the love of gain, of adventure, or of civil or religious liberty pricked on to the establishment of colonies in America. True, these enterprises were undertaken with the approval of the Crown; the colonists retained the status of Englishmen, and were required to take an oath of allegiance before leaving England. This implied the acknowledgment by the Home Government of responsibilities towards them: notably that of defending them against foreign attack. The knowledge that to attack the colonies was, in effect, to attack England naturally served as a deterrent to aggression—no small advantage in that age of casual bloodshed. Yet the colonies were assumed to be capable of providing for their own ordinary local defence, such as might be required against Indian raids, and one of the settlers' first cares was usually the institution among themselves of some rudimentary military organization.[1] Inevitably, the efficiency of these local forces was low; but they were considered enough to relieve England from the necessity of maintaining colonial garrisons, which, indeed (as she possessed no real standing army) she could scarcely have provided in any case. The English Government's direct contribution to the defence of the colonies consisted in supplying some quantity of "powder and munition," and in the protection afforded their seaborne trade by the Royal Navy.[2]

Nevertheless, the increasing colonial activity of England during the Commonwealth and Protectorate, and after the Restoration, led naturally to the assumption of new responsi-

---

[1] Beer, *Origins of the British Colonial System, 1578–1660*, 16, 17 and n., 24. On early colonial militia legislation, see Osgood, *The American Colonies in the Seventeenth Century*, I, 292, 496–99, 506; II, 375 ff.

Full particulars concerning the more important works employed in writing this book are given in the list of authorities at the back. In footnotes, it has been thought proper to give the initials of authors, the place and date of publication, etc., only in the cases of books omitted from that list.

[2] Beer, *op. cit.*, 319–20. In the first days of royal government in Virginia, the province, then suffering heavily from Indian attacks, asked for a garrison from home. The request was not granted. (*Ibid.*, 320)

EARLY HISTORY OF IMPERIAL DEFENCE

bilities. The conquest of Jamaica perforce entailed the maintenance of a garrison there;[1] and a regular force was permanently established in New York after it was taken from the Dutch. New York, in fact, was unique among the old continental colonies in that it had an Imperial garrison stationed on its soil throughout the period during which it was under British rule. The four companies composing it were, however, not effective units; their history, we are told, " presents such a series of horrors, miseries, frauds, stupidities, and sheer neglects as is rare in either colonial or military annals."[2] Misery and neglect were in fact the rule rather than the exception among the garrisons maintained abroad by Britain in these early times;[3] yet the garrisons continued to multiply. In 1679, the colonial military establishment cost the mother country £12,816,[4] and reductions effected during the next few years proved only temporary. Despite the fact that English policy remained consistently opposed to assuming new military burdens in respect of the colonies, by 1737 the bill had risen to £52,754, quite apart from the great military stations of Minorca and Gibraltar, which themselves cost £162,956. The share of the continental colonies which later seceded was, it must be observed, only a small proportion of the total—a trifle over £10,000.[5]

This expansion was chiefly a result of the beginning of that long series of wars with France, fought out on both sides of the Atlantic, which were to have their issue in the extinction of French dominion on the western continent. And this emergency raised new problems of defensive policy for the British empire in America—those involved in organizing co-

[1] Fortescue, *History of the British Army*, I, 264.
[2] Pargellis, S. M., " The Four Independent Companies of New York," in *Essays in Colonial History Presented to Charles McLean Andrews* . . ., New Haven, 1931.
[3] Cf. Beer, *The Old Colonial System* . . . *Part I* . . ., I, 116–17.
[4] *Ibid.*, 115 n. Bacon's rebellion in Virginia (1676) appears to have been the first occasion on which troops of the British standing army served on the mainland of America, a mixed battalion of the Guards being included in the force sent out. (*Calendar of State Papers, Colonial, America and West Indies, 1675–1676*, pp. 460–61). Two companies of English troops remained in Virginia until 1682.
[5] Beer, *British Colonial Policy, 1754–1765*, 12 n. The mother country was disposed to give military aid on the mainland only to colonies which seemed especially exposed. Thus, in addition to New York, South Carolina and Georgia were garrisoned at different times, and Nova Scotia had a regiment of its own.

operation between the colonies and the mother country, and among the colonies themselves, against the common enemy.[1]

The English colonists were ill-prepared. Properly organized, they should have been able to overwhelm the Frenchmen in Canada without assistance from Britain, for in 1688 they outnumbered them twenty to one. But the English were divided among a dozen unmilitary and mutually jealous communities, whereas New France had the advantage of political unity and a government all but absolute, while in addition it was strengthened, from the beginning of the era of conflict, by the presence of a fairly considerable garrison of regular troops and the constant reinforcement of its population by disbanded soldiers. So efficient an organization was never achieved by the English. The despotic " Dominion of New England " set up under James II offered some hope in this respect (if in no other) ; but its collapse in 1689 left the northern colonies without any central authority to organize their efforts in the War of the League of Augsburg (remembered in the United States as King William's War), which broke out in the same year.

That war, and the War of the Spanish Succession which followed it, demonstrated the absurdity of this situation, which permitted each British province to make an independent decision as to how much aid (if any) it would give to a hard-pressed neighbour, and to what extent (if at all) it would comply with the requisitions of the mother country for troops to serve the common cause. Some colonies were active, some apathetic ; all, in general, were more intent upon avoiding the possibility of assuming burdens larger than those taken up by adjacent provinces than upon using their resources to the best advantage in the prosecution of the war.[2] And when armaments from England began to intervene actively in the colonial struggle, the results, at first, were discouraging ; the expedition against Quebec in 1711 is one of the gloomiest fiascos in British annals.[3]

---

[1] For a survey of the organization of imperial defence at this time, down to the outbreak of the Seven Years' War, see Pargellis, S. M., *Lord Loudoun in North America*, New Haven, 1933, chap. I.
[2] Osgood, *The American Colonies in the Eighteenth Century*, I, 81–93, 403–4, 451.
[3] *Ibid.*, 437–50 ; Fortescue, II, 255.

EARLY HISTORY OF IMPERIAL DEFENCE 5

The later stages of the long contest failed to produce great improvement in the machinery for organizing joint action on the British side. Though a sound scheme[1] was adopted for incorporating a colonial contingent in the British force which was sent against the Spanish West Indies (1740-41), this did not prevent recriminations between colonials and regulars;[2] and even the brilliant capture of Louisbourg in 1745 by a New England force aided by the Royal Navy was the result rather of good fortune and local enterprise than of proper intercolonial co-operation.[3] The obvious approach of the crucial phase of the struggle induced the Albany congress of 1754 to suggest a plan for the union of the British colonies under a central Grand Council, but the scheme was killed by colonial particularism, and a proposal for a union for military purposes, put forward by the Board of Trade, was not proceeded with. The only central authority in existence in the colonies when the Seven Years' War began was that implied in the ill-fated Braddock's appointment as commander-in-chief over all regular and colonial forces;[4] and he found the colonial assemblies as hard to deal with as ever.[5]

In the later years of this so-called French and Indian War, nevertheless, the presence of great Imperial armaments and the vigour of British policy as directed by Pitt led to colonial co-operation on an unprecedented scale, and large bodies of provincial troops were placed in the field.[6] It must be remembered, however, that about two-fifths of the colonies' expenditure in this connection was made good by Britain, and that their forces were equipped at English expense.[7] And the conquest of Canada was more the mother country's victory than theirs. The expeditions which overthrew the two great fortresses of Louisbourg and Quebec in 1758 and 1759 were

---

[1] Pargellis, *Lord Loudoun*, 13-14.
[2] Fortescue, II, 59-79; Osgood, *Eighteenth Century*, III, 497-501.
[3] *Ibid.*, 517-34; Pargellis, 7. Louisbourg was handed back to France by the Treaty of Aix-la-Chapelle (1748); but in the next year the British government founded on Chebucto Bay the city and fortress of Halifax, which served to check the threat from Louisbourg and was a great contribution to the security of New England. Brebner, J. B., *New England's Outpost* . . ., New York, 1927, 166-69.
[4] Beer, *British Colonial Policy*, 16-30; Osgood, *Eighteenth Century*, IV, 323-25, 340-42.
[5] *Ibid.*, 345-46; Pargellis, 35.
[6] Osgood, *Eighteenth Century*, IV, 403 ff., 416; Fortescue, II, 315.
[7] Beer, *British Colonial Policy*, 52-71; Osgood, *Eighteenth Century*, IV, 185.

almost wholly composed of regulars; and, above all, it was the Royal Navy that made these triumphs possible. England had ended the menace that had hung so long above her American dependencies; and in relieving them from the need for her protection she had severed the strongest link that bound them to herself.

The Peace of Paris left Britain in possession of an American realm stretching from Hudson Bay to the Gulf of Mexico. British statesmanship was faced with a supreme problem of imperial organization, in which the question of defence was a major element. There was the possibility of a war of revenge on the part of France; there were conquered territories to be held in subjection; and with the acquisition of the interior the Indian question was more pressing than ever, and garrisons were necessary for the "frontier" forts. The Imperial Government decided to meet the situation with an expedient which, while quite sound from the military point of view, proved to be ruinous politically: the installation in "North America and the plantations" of a regular garrison of 10,000 men, to be supported, in part at least, by the colonists.[1] The scheme was accepted by Parliament in March, 1763; and in the same year the events of the Pontiac War seemed to justify it by making the futility of the requisition system more obvious than ever.[2]

The expansion of the Empire necessitated a departure from the old policy under which almost no British troops had been maintained on the mainland of America; and if Imperial forces were to undertake, under the pressure of expediency, a great part of the ordinary local defence of the colonies, it did not seem at variance with the established colonial theory that the provincials should contribute to their support. Events since 1754 had seemed to demonstrate that it was hopeless to expect the various colonies to unite to tax themselves for this purpose; and now the ministry of George Grenville decided to cut the knot of difficulty with that sharp instrument, the supremacy of Parliament: they would tax the colonies for the maintenance of the troops.[3] The Revenue Act of 1764[4] declared, "It is just

---

[1] Beer, *British Colonial Policy*, 265 ff.; Alvord, C. W., *The Mississippi Valley in British Politics* . . ., Cleveland, 1917, I, 127–33. One-fourth of this force was to be in the West Indies.
[2] Beer, *British Colonial Policy*, 262–65.
[3] *Ibid.*, 271 ff. [4] 4 Geo. III, c. 15.

and necessary that a revenue be raised in your Majesty's dominions in America for defraying the expenses of defending, protecting, and securing the same." Next year came the Stamp Act,[1] dedicated to the same end.

There is no need to recall in this place the details of the struggle that ensued: how colonial opposition forced the modification of the first act and the repeal of the second; how Grenville in 1767 badgered the Grafton ministry, pointing to the burden borne by Britain for colonial defence; how Townshend provided as a panacea that disastrous budget which sought to defray the expense by external taxation enforced by new and efficient machinery,[2] and only produced renewed agitation in America. The history of the British Army entered a sad phase when in 1768 two regiments were sent to Boston to aid in enforcing the law, and were met by a town-meeting's declaration that a standing army could not be kept in Massachusetts without the consent of the province. By 1770 the idea of making the colonies pay for their own defence had been abandoned, but Britain still clung to the theoretical right of taxing them, and the political question raised by Grenville's expedient for meeting the expense of the colonial garrison would not down. The soldiers whose duty was to have been the protection of the colonists were soon to be devoted to a vain attempt at preserving by force of arms the subjection of those same colonists to the mother country.

The immediate origins of the American Revolution are thus to be found in an ill-starred essay at the solution of the old problem of imperial defence, which raised the questions of principle that in their turn led directly to the catastrophe. To quote the late Mr. G. L. Beer: "The question of defence was predominant throughout the transitional years from 1754 to 1765, and gives a certain unity to the period. . . . The controversies that led ultimately to the American Revolution, grew out of this military question, and in its narrower phase this movement was the direct result of the inherent difficulty of creating an efficient and equitable system of defence in a decentralized empire."[3]

[1] 5 Geo. III, c. 12. The two acts are to be found in Macdonald, W., *Documentary Source Book of American History* . . ., New York, 1926, 117-31.
[2] Townshend's act (7 Geo. III, c. 46) is in Macdonald, 143-46.
[3] *British Colonial Policy*, 314.

Having briefly considered the military problem as it presented itself in the history of Britain's earliest empire, we must now turn to its aspect in Canada, which became British in 1763 and was the largest unit in the scattered western domain which remained to Britain after the loss of the American colonies twenty years later.

Under the old *régime*, compulsory military service had been the rule in New France. The useful irregular forces of the colony[1] were organized locally by *captains of militia* chosen from among the upper ranks of the *habitants*. In addition to being military officers, these men performed a very wide variety of civil duties.[2] In the period immediately after the conquest, the British authorities made some use of them, but the legal difficulties in the way of employing Roman Catholics in office led to their commissions being allowed to lapse.[3] The old militia system continued to exist, but the existence soon became merely nominal.

It was natural that in a conquered country the victor should, for a time at least, rely chiefly on his own troops. In 1763 the Lords of Trade recommended the maintenance of a large force in Canada.[4] Four years later the garrison was a trifle more than 1600 strong, and the governor, then Guy Carleton, was urging the desirability of interesting the French-Canadians in the defence of the province.[5] In 1774 the force was much reduced by sending aid to Gage in Boston;[6] and when an American army invaded Canada in the following year, the French made almost no response to Carleton's call to arms. Nevertheless, he defended Quebec successfully; and, despite many alarms, Canada was not again invaded during the course of this war. Under the terms of an ordinance of 1777,[7] active

---

[1] On the military system of New France, see Thomas, H. M., "The Organization of National Defence in the French Regime," *C.D.Q.*, XI, April, 1934; and Sautai, M., *Montcalm au combat de Carillon*, Paris, 1909, 11-14.

[2] Sulte, B., "The Captains of Militia," *C.H.R.*, I, Sept., 1920.

[3] Burt, *The Old Province of Quebec*, 28, 92.

[4] Shortt and Doughty (eds.), *Documents relating to the Constitutional History of Canada, 1759-1791*, 143.

[5] Carleton to Shelburne, Nov. 25, 1767: *ibid.*, 282-85.

[6] Gage to Carleton, Sept. 4, 1774, and Carleton's reply, Sept. 20; *ibid.*, 583-84.

[7] The historical section of the General Staff [Canada], *A History of the Organization, Development and Services of the Military Forces of Canada from*

attempts were made to revive the militia, and a provision of this law permitting the impressment of vehicular transport at prices fixed by the commander-in-chief proved very objectionable to the Canadians.[1] It is probable that much of the strong dislike for military service which has manifested itself at subsequent periods among the French inhabitants of Canada had its beginning in the enforcement of the militia laws during the War of the American Revolution.

In 1782–83 the Treaty of Paris recognized the independence of the old colonies. Britain, however, retained the northern half of the continent—Newfoundland, Nova Scotia (from which a region settled by American loyalists was soon separated under the name of New Brunswick), and the great province of Quebec; as well as that vast and dubious hinterland over which the Hudson's Bay Company exerted its shadowy authority. The military situation of this smaller British America was much altered. The area to be guarded was greatly diminished; yet on the other hand the rise of the United States meant the presence of a greater immediate danger than had before existed. The new body politic had had its origin in a conflict with Great Britain which had left behind it an ominous heritage of distrust and hatred. For a century thenceforward, the organizers of British American defence made their plans almost exclusively against one contingency—that of war with the United States.

Their task was rendered difficult in the extreme by the disparity in population between the two sections of the continent. The result of the war had reversed the familiar circumstances of the long struggle betwen France and Britain in America. In those days the French of Canada had maintained an unequal contest with the much more numerous English colonists. Now the small French community, augmented by a proportion of English-speaking settlers (chiefly loyalists who had chosen, or been forced to choose, exile rather than submission to the new republic), was under the British flag; but the former English provinces, still retaining their numerical superiority, had become the chief menace to British dominion

the Peace of Paris in 1763 . . ., II, 204–07. This work contains many valuable documents for this period.

[1] Burt, *op. cit.*, 264 ff.

on the American continent. This disproportion in man-power, which time did not remedy, was to be the constant bugbear of Canadian defence ; and it could not but vitiate in some degree any attempt at drawing from the defensive practice of the first empire precedents which could be erected into a military policy adequate to the necessities of the American territories of the second. It was obvious that Canada, however loyal, could scarcely be successfully defended against the United States without abundant aid from Britain. These conditions, combined, presumably, with memories of the disastrous experiment of 1764–67, postponed for two generations any radical attempt on the part of the mother country to free herself from the burden of military expenditure in Canada. Even had she wished to repeat in that country the attempt at taxing the colonists, she could not have done so ; she had closed the door in her own face by a fruitless conciliatory gesture of 1778— an Act[1] renouncing the right of Parliament to raise revenue in the colonies. Only in the prosperous island dependencies in the West Indies was any genuine effort made at this period to obtain colonial contributions towards the cost of the military establishment.[2] On the mainland, the attack on the problem was postponed, as we shall see, until a day when great changes had come across the face of the Empire.

In the meantime, the force of circumstances ensured general acceptance for the principle that a respectable garrison should be maintained in British North America at imperial expense ; and although the force in the province of Canada was rapidly reduced after the war to a strength of less than 2000 men,[3] Pitt declared in Parliament in 1790 that " the exclusive protection of Canada and Nova Scotia, demanded . . . a larger military establishment than all our American possessions before the war, taken together."[4] Without examining too critically the exact truth of the statement, we may recognize in it the reflection of those new political conditions in North America which we have just described.

---

[1] 18 Geo. III, c. 12 ; see Lucas, *History of Canada, 1763–1812*, 267–68 *n*. The Act applied to North America and the West Indies.
[2] Manning, H. T., *British Colonial Government after the American Revolution, 1782–1820*, New Haven, 1933, 217 ff.
[3] General Staff *History of the Military Forces of Canada*, III, 39.
[4] *Parliamentary History of England*, XXVIII, 327–28 (Feb. 5, 1790).

From this time forward the strength of the garrison of Canada registers like a barometer the condition of Anglo-American relations. That condition may be said to have grown steadily worse after 1790—first on account of the controversy over the western military posts within the boundaries of the United States, which Britain had persisted in retaining despite the treaty,[1] and later on account of British interference with American shipping, arising out of the war which had broken out with revolutionary France. The mother country's annual expenditure for her American military establishment—it was estimated in 1800 at £260,000 for Upper and Lower Canada alone[2]—tended steadily to increase ; for, despite her difficulties nearer home, she contrived to strengthen the regular force in America as the tension there grew more severe. Including the garrisons in the Maritime Provinces, and excluding artillery and engineers, it rose from 3400 men in June, 1804, to 8000 in May, 1809. It must be remembered that the regular army of the United States was very small; its actual strength was only 2700 in 1810 and 6600 in July, 1812. Thus the British garrison in North America considerably outnumbered it.[3]

During the same period the militia of British North America was improved by the passage of new laws, differing from one another only in detail, in the four continental provinces.[4] The obligation to serve was universal; careful enrolments were made of the men of military age, and periodical musters held. Regimental officers were appointed to supervise this work. For training there was little provision : "the organization was administrative rather than tactical." The system had the advantage of costing almost nothing in time of peace, while nevertheless it made the whole man-power of the country available in emergency as material for the formation of fighting units under the direction and inspiration of the professional soldiers. It proved its value after the outbreak of hostilities with the United States in 1812.

[1] They were finally given up, after Jay's Treaty, in 1796.
[2] Milnes to Portland, Nov. 1, 1800 ; Egerton and Grant (eds.), *Canadian Constitutional Development*, 111–21. Upper Canada had been separated from the older section of the province following the Canada Act of 1791.
[3] Hamilton, C. F., "The Canadian Militia : Universal Service ", *C.D.Q.*, V : April, 1928 ; Upton, *Military Policy of the United States*, 92.
[4] The Upper Canada Act of 1808 is in Cruikshank, E., *Documentary History of the Campaign upon the Niagara Frontier in the Year 1812* [part I] (Welland, n.d.), 3–18.

The most significant fact in the story of the defence of Canada during this struggle is, however, the pre-eminence of the British regular. He supplied the leadership and professional skill; he trained the local forces and set them an example in the field; he bore the brunt in nearly every engagement, as the casualty returns show. It was his presence, with all that it implied, that gave the defenders the fighting-gauge over the amorphous masses of soldiery (chiefly militia) which the United States moved to the frontier in 1812, and which (despite their numerical superiority) came to grief so consistently in the campaign of that year. The matter is well summed up by Colonel C. F. Hamilton:

"Surveying the system as a whole, one is bound to think soberly of the oft-repeated assertion that it was 'the Militia' which saved Canada in 1812-15. That it was the zeal and valour of the native-born Britons of British America which saved Canada, is true enough. That the Regular troops who fought comprised far more British subjects born in British America than we generally realize, is not to be overlooked. That the Militia sprang to arms, marched to the frontier in their peace-time organizations and under their amateur officers, and beat off the invaders, is grotesquely untrue. It is necessary only to look at the figures. . . . It is to be borne in mind that the American invaders on the whole trusted to Militia troops marching direct from the place of assembly to the front, and that they effected amazingly little considering their numerical strength and resources. Indeed, they began to be formidable only when they began to rely more on regular troops. . . .

"The defence of His Majesty's American dominions was a highly scientific piece of work. It was effected, not merely by exceptionally high moral courage and leadership, not merely by hard fighting, but also by an organization which was exceedingly sound in relation to the circumstances of the time. It combined the skill and discipline of the Regular with the patriotism and bravery of a people armed and free."[1]

It must be noted further that it was not British soldiers only that preserved Canada, but British money also. The colonies in America, thinly-populated and poor, could contribute to the defence a quota of men, but little else. The men had to be drilled, clothed, fed and armed at the expense of the mother country, for the simple reason that there was no other way of doing it at all.

[1] "The Canadian Militia: Universal Service" (as above).

EARLY HISTORY OF IMPERIAL DEFENCE 13

The influence of the War of 1812 upon the later development of Canadian defensive policy was not altogether admirable from the military point of view. The too-easy, David-and-Goliath victories won over an enemy whose organization (at least in the earlier stages) was so faulty as to deprive him of the advantages of his superior resources, left behind them a confidence not justified by the facts, and not calculated to promote sound military measures. Furthermore, they left behind them a tradition of reliance upon the mother country. The War of 1812 passed into Canadian legend as the natural and unchanging example of sound defensive policy; the methods of a period when the British North American colonies were feeble backwoods communities incapable of effective action in their own defence still ruled the mind of the Canadian public half a century later, when they had so increased in population and prosperity as to be able to bear a large share of the burden of any military project. The war had taught the United States a lesson in military policy, but had had no such effect in Canada. Canadians, though not cherishing particularly friendly sentiments towards the United States nor feeling the confidence in that country's intentions that has come to their twentieth-century descendants, continued to believe that their own military responsibilities were adequately discharged by the maintenance on paper of an organization designed to afford at the outbreak of hostilities a large force of recruits without arms, uniform, or discipline. As in the neighbouring country at many periods, there was an overweening confidence in the military virtue of mere courage and patriotic feeling, and an almost complete lack of appreciation of the value of the trained professional soldier.

No fundamental change in the defensive arrangements of British North America resulted from the war. Britain continued to maintain a considerable regular garrison in the colonies. In 1819, it amounted to about 5800 rank and file. By 1835, it had been reduced to the strength at which it had stood before the commencement of the wars in Europe: in that year there were 2400 men in Canada and 2300 in the Maritime Provinces, including Newfoundland.[1] At the same

[1] *P.P.*, 1834, No. 570, vol. VI (First report of Select Committee on Colonial Military Expenditure), appendix III; *P.P.*,1835, no. 473, vol. VI (second report), appendices 5, 7, 8, and evidence pp. 42 ff.

time, the obligation of universal militia service was retained, and on one or more days in each year a muster was held. Almost the only cost of this force was that involved in keeping up a small administrative staff; in Upper Canada, where the legislature in 1816 made provision for the appointment of an Adjutant-General, this amounted only to £600 or £700 a year.[1]

The experience of the war was, however, reflected in a new interest at the War Office in the defensive possibilities of the Canadian frontier. The matter received the particular attention of the Duke of Wellington, who in 1819 drew up an extensive memorandum on the subject, recommending a fortification programme and the development of the internal waterways of the country—especially the improvement of the route from Montreal to Kingston by the Ottawa and Rideau rivers, which might render the defenders of Canada independent of the international section of the St. Lawrence.[2] Next year Britain undertook the construction of a citadel at Quebec and large improvements in the fort at Isle aux Noix in the Richelieu;[3] and in 1825 Wellington despatched to America a commission of officers charged with reporting upon the proper system of defence for the colonies there.[4] Their recommendations[5] followed the lines of the Duke's own previous ideas, and he proceeded to urge the government to put their scheme into effect forthwith;[6] but it was of such proportions as to take away the breath of civilian ministers. The total expense was estimated at £1,646,218, including the execution of the Rideau canal project. Very extensive fortifications were proposed for Halifax, Montreal, Kingston and the Niagara frontier, and lesser works for nearly a dozen other points.

[1] For the history of the militia at this period, see Hamilton, "The Canadian Militia: from 1816 to the Crimean War" (*C.D.Q.*, V: July, 1928).
[2] *Despatches, Correspondence, and Memoranda of . . . Arthur, Duke of Wellington . . . edited by his Son . . .*, I, 36–44. March 1, 1819. Cf. Holmden, H. R., (ed.), "Baron de Gaugreben's Memoir on the Defence of Upper Canada" [1815], *C.H.R.*, II: March, 1921.
[3] *P.P.*, 1828, no. 420, vol. V (Second report from Select Committee on Public Income and Expenditure), evidence of Hardinge, pp. 73 ff.
[4] See their instructions, *Despatches, Correspondence and Memoranda*, II, 436. Wellington at this time was Master General of the Ordnance.
[5] *Copy of a Report to his Grace the Duke of Wellington . . . relative to His Majesty's North American Provinces . . .* (dated Sept. 9, 1825. Lithographed). See Talman, J. J. (ed.), "A Secret Military Document, 1825," *American Historical Review*, XXXVIII: Jan., 1933. Cf. Sir J. Carmichael Smyth's *Precis of the Wars in Canada*. Smyth was chairman of the commission.
[6] *Despatches, Correspondence and Memoranda*, II, 573 (Dec. 6, 1825).

The British ministry hesitated to broach so costly a plan to the public. The Rideau canal was begun in 1826—and proved very much more expensive than the commissioners had anticipated.[1] Not until two years later did the fortification proposals go before Parliament, and then only in a much attenuated form, with the assurance that it was not intended to ask for more than £330,000 in all, to be expended at Halifax and Kingston.[2] Even this arrangement encountered severe criticism in the House of Commons.[3] Wellington, on the other hand, greatly regretted the mutilation of the plan, and in later years ministers actually feared to approach the old Duke on Canadian defence, because, as one of them explained, " he always harks back to a plan laid down by himself in 1826, the expense of which was so enormous that all Governments have deferred acting upon it."[4] Nevertheless, Canada received during this period the great citadels at Quebec and Halifax, the works at Kingston and Isle aux Noix, and the Rideau canal—all entirely at imperial expense.[5] This was one aspect of British policy which the Canadian radicals of the time, in their attacks upon the home government, chose studiously to ignore.[6]

Returns made for the select committee of the House of Commons which investigated the colonial military expenditure in 1834 and 1835[7] afford us convenient means for a survey of the imperial establishment in North America at that period. It consisted of 4,720 rank and file, very widely distributed. In Newfoundland there were 276 men, in Prince Edward Island 64, in New Brunswick (for which apprehension had lately been

[1] *P.P.*, 1828, no. 420, vol. V (Second report from Select Committee on Public Income and Expenditure), evidence of Hardinge, pp. 75-6. Their estimate (based on calculations of a Canadian civil engineer) was £169,000 ; but the officer sent out to do the work raised it to £474,000, and the actual ultimate cost was approximately £800,000. See Hill, H.P., " The Construction of the Rideau Canal, 1826-1832," *Ontario Historical Society Papers and Records*, XXII (1925).
[2] *Hansard*, new series, XIX, 1628 ff. (speech of Hardinge, July 7, 1828) ; and cf. *ibid.*, XX, 669-70 (March 2, 1829).
[3] *Ibid.*, XIX, 1629-32 : (speeches of Stanley, Maberly, and Baring).
[4] Stanley to Peel, Aug. 12, 1845 : Parker, C. S., *Sir Robert Peel from his Private Papers*, London, 1899, III, 216.
[5] The citadel at Quebec, originally estimated to cost £70,000, finally cost £236,540 (*Copy of a Report to the Duke of Wellington, appendix* A ; *P.P.*, 1831, no. 177, vol. VI (Ordnance estimates), p. 43).
[6] Dunham, A., *Political Unrest in Upper Canada, 1815-1836*, London, 1927, 27.
[7] See below, chapter II.

felt on account of the unsettled boundary separating it from the United States) 498 ; while Nova Scotia had 1,474—nearly all at Halifax. Canada had 2,408 men in (apart from tiny detachments) ten stations. At Quebec there were two infantry battalions, in addition to its quota of artillerymen, and Montreal, Kingston and Toronto each had one battalion, which supplied parties for lesser stations in the same area.[1]

Most of the witnesses examined by the committee with respect to Canada opposed any reduction of this force ; the Canadians' growing dissatisfaction with the form of their government, the Maine boundary dispute, and the ineffective character of the local militia, were all used as arguments.[2] The committee accordingly did not recommend any diminution of the garrison. It did, however, enjoin strict economy, particularly with respect to commissariat, barrack and ordnance expenditure ; and in 1836 some effort was made to meet its views by reducing the number of outlying stations. The inhabitants of Niagara and Amherstburgh petitioned against the withdrawal of the parties stationed in those places, asserting that the troops were necessary to support the civil authority. In reply[3] the Colonial Secretary enunciated an important principle :

" His Majesty cannot consent to devolve upon Great Britain the Burthen of affording that protection to the inhabitants of the Niagara and Western Districts which ought to be found in an efficient local Police."

Britain herself had but lately learned the advantages of a disciplined civil force of police, and no such force yet existed in Canada. When civil commotion occurred in the colony, it was customary (as it had long been in the mother country) to call upon the King's troops for aid to the civil power ; they were sometimes employed upon such unmilitary duty as the prevention of smuggling ;[4] and in Quebec and Montreal, and in some places in the Maritime Provinces, it was even usual for

---

[1] See the Select Committee's second report, *P.P.*, 1835, no. 473, vol. VI, appendices 4, 5, and 8. The first report is *P.P.*, 1834, no. 570, vol. VI.
[2] Second report, e.g., pp. 15-16, 43-44.
[3] Glenelg to Head, March 2, 1836 : Public Archives of Canada, C, 35, pp. 17-18.
[4] *Montreal Gazette*, Feb. 17, 1817 (in Innis, H. A., and Lower, A. R. M. (eds.), *Select Documents in Canadian Economic History, 1783-1885*, Toronto, 1933, 324).

EARLY HISTORY OF IMPERIAL DEFENCE 17

the regiments to supply guards for the gaols.[1] This situation was not to be completely rectified for years to come.

Events were preparing which were to make these petty economies appear a trifle ludicrous. The political grievances which had long been agitating the colonies (exacerbated in Lower Canada by racial antagonism, and in Upper Canada by the self-complacency of a governing clique) issued in armed rebellion in both these provinces in the autumn of 1837. For such an occurrence, it is obvious, the British government was not prepared. The regular force on the spot was very inadequate, and Lord John Russell all but admitted that the ministry were open to criticism on this score. The situation, in fact, might have been fatal, for with the St. Lawrence closed by ice Canada could not be effectively reinforced until spring. It is interesting to note that the government expressed less fear of the Canadian insurgents than of the possible raids of American filibusters disposed to fish in troubled waters.[2] The filibustering spirit was abroad across the border, as recent events in Texas had shown; and the anticipated frontier disturbances duly materialized, bringing with them a danger of war with the United States, arising out of the violation of American territory by a British force on the occasion of the cutting-out of the steamboat *Caroline* on the Niagara river. Though the rebellions themselves were suppressed with comparative ease, the situation called for the presence of a large military force in Canada; and Britain promptly provided it.

In 1838 reinforcements poured in until there were more than 13,000 regulars in British North America; where before there had been nine battalions of the line, there were now nineteen, in addition to two battalions of the Guards and a regiment of cavalry.[3] Moreover, an extensive local mobilization took place

[1] Select Committee second report, 1835: evidence of Maitland (pp. 24 ff.) and Kempt (pp. 44 ff.).
[2] *Hansard*, 3rd series, XL, 33 ff. (speech of Russell, Jan. 16, 1838). One battalion had been brought from Halifax to Lower Canada in the summer of 1837: Gosford to Glenelg, June 10, 1837 (see *Calendar of Durham Papers* in *Report* of the Public Archives of Canada for 1923, p. 269).
[3] *Hansard*, 3rd series, XLVI, 1146; LXI, 157; CIII, 967-8 (speeches of Howick, March 22, 1839; Hardinge, March 7, 1842; Fox Maule, March 16, 1849). (Unless otherwise stated, *Hansard* references hereafter are to the 3rd series.) For the infantry establishment in successive years, 1828-50, see *P.P.*, 1850, no. 662, vol. X (Report of Select Committee on Army and Ordnance Expenditure), appendix 10, p. 770.

C

at imperial expense ; a large number of corps were raised from the militia, trained with the aid of officers specially sent from England, and taken into British pay. The upkeep of this auxiliary force accounts for the enormous appropriations—£500,000 in 1838-39, £1,000,000 in 1839-40, £354,000 in 1840-41—approved by Parliament to meet the special expenses of the rebellion. Most of it was disbanded in 1839.[1] The need for keeping so many troops in Canada obliged the imperial government to increase the total strength of the British Army by more than 9,000 men.[2]

Early in 1839, Lord Durham's *Report on the Affairs of British North America* was presented to Parliament. This very celebrated document was composed at a time of domestic and foreign difficulties, when (as Durham himself had urged upon the Imperial authorities)[3] the maintenance of strong British forces in Canada was essential and unavoidable. The report, accordingly, avoided the subject of colonial military policy ; and what Durham would have regarded as a proper system of military relations, in a time of peace, between the mother country and a colony possessing a responsible government such as he recommended as the remedy for the political ills of Canada, remains largely a matter of speculation. He fully accepted, however, the obligation of the mother country to defend the colony against foreign enemies, and advanced this benefit derived by the colonists from the imperial connexion as an influence which would lead them to accept without objection their own subordination to the imperial legislature in those few matters—" the constitution of the form of government—the regulation of foreign relations, and of trade with the mother country, the other British Colonies, and foreign nations—and the disposal of the public lands ", which he considered proper exceptions to the general principle of local control.[4] It seems fairly apparent that in such a system of reciprocal advantages as he contemplated—a system quite different from that which

---

[1] Statements of Howick in introducing the army estimates in 1838 and 1839: *Hansard*, XLI, 786 ff., and XLVI, 1120 ff. For the appropriations, see *Annual Register* (Chronicle), 1839, p. 385 ; 1840, pp. 323, 343. For 1841-42 and 1842-43, the bill fell to £108,000 ; by 1843-44 it was down to £25,000.
[2] *Hansard*, XLVI, 1121-22.
[3] New, *Lord Durham*, 381.
[4] Sir C. P. Lucas's edition of the *Report*, Oxford, 1912, II, 281-82. Cf. I, 150.

ultimately grew up under the ægis of his reputation—the maintenance of military forces in British America at imperial expense would have been no anomaly; and he probably contemplated in this respect no departure from the traditional arrangement. Durham certainly appreciated the fact that a display of disciplined troops made for respect for British authority in Canada among citizens of the United States; and in his policy towards that country during his Canadian administration this element went hand in hand with a civility and cordiality towards Americans which were remarked as unusual in a British governor.[1]

In any case, the reinforcement of British North America in 1838 was fated to be more than a mere temporary measure. Even after a silly recrudescence of rebellion had been crushed that autumn, discontent inevitably continued to smoulder in Canada; even after the filibustering raids had been repulsed, there were attempts to disturb the peace of the frontier—as late as 1841 President Tyler was moved to issue a proclamation against such outrages. With the United States Government itself there were dangerous controversies. The Maine boundary dispute passed through a perilous stage in 1839; New Brunswick then called out militia to support the regular forces.[3] Two years later, the case of Alexander McLeod, who was arrested in New York State on a charge arising out of the *Caroline* affair, brought the two countries within measurable distance of war.[4] Fortunately, peaceable counsels prevailed, and the long boundary difficulty was ended at last by the Webster-Ashburton treaty of 1842. The settlement, though not to-day considered unfair, gave little satisfaction to either side; and it seriously embarrassed British military policy in America, for it meant that the only available winter communication between the ports of the Maritime Provinces and Quebec was by a very roundabout route, which moreover, from its position close to

---

[1] Durham to Glenelg, July 19, 1838: *Durham Papers* calendar, 63. Charles Buller's "Sketch of Lord Durham's Mission . . .", *ibid.*, 354. Cf. New, *Lord Durham*, 397–400.

[2] *British and Foreign State Papers*, XXX, 1365–66.

[3] 850 men were called out, and co-operated with the regular garrisons of New Brunswick and Canada to form a fighting front in the St. John Valley. Harvey to Glenelg, Feb. 18, 1839: Public Archives of Canada, C.O. 188, no. 200 (New Brunswick, despatches sent, vol. VII).

[4] See Watt, A., "The Case of Alexander McLeod": *C.H.R.*, XII: June, 1931.

the border, was exposed to interruption in time of war. But it served to ease the immediate tension, and Britain seized the opportunity to reduce her regular force in America by about 5,000 men.[1]

Even so, it was still twice as strong as before 1837, and its maintenance was a heavy burden. In 1843-44, Great Britain's military expenditure in the Canadas was £541,000, while the Maritime Provinces with Newfoundland cost £173,000 more.[2] The small and expensive outlying stations were back again, more numerous than ever—a necessary part of a system of defence against sporadic border threatenings. In 1840-41 a special regiment of the British Army, the Royal Canadian Rifles, was raised at imperial expense to man these border posts. Permanently localized in Canada, it did not require periodical relief, and thus eased the difficulty of one of Britain's perennial military problems. The chief object in forming it, however, was to check desertion, which had been a constant vexation to the military authorities in Canada, particularly at border stations. The new corps was recruited from solid old soldiers, many of them married, who were allowed to volunteer into it from other regiments. Such troops, it was believed, would not easily be tempted to desertion by the savour of immunity and high wages that drifted across from republican territory.[3]

The settlement of the Maine controversy had not ended the danger of collision with the United States. In 1845 a similar question on the other side of the continent caused a gust of apprehension, when the utterances of Democratic politicians seemed to indicate an American determination to possess the whole of Oregon, then jointly occupied by the United States and Britain. The British government, while disposed to regard this as " mere braggadocio,"[4] took no chances. Orders were given for the construction on the Great Lakes of vessels which

---

[1] The troops withdrawn were the two battalions of Guards, four battalions of the line, and the cavalry regiment. At the same time 2,300 local volunteers, who had been kept on service since the rebellion, were disbanded. (*Hansard*, LXVI, 1359 ff.: speech of Hardinge, Feb. 27, 1843).

[2] *P.P.*, 1849, no. 224, vol. XXXIV (abstract of colonial expenditure for 1843-44 and 1846-47), appendix (A).

[3] Lord Hill's memorandum, enclosed in Lord Fitzroy Somerset to Lt.-Gen. Sir R. Jackson, Aug. 27, 1840: *C*, 769 (" Royal Canadian Rifles, 1840-42 "), pp. 1-10.

[4] Stanley to Metcalfe (secret), April 17, 1845: *G*, 121.

EARLY HISTORY OF IMPERIAL DEFENCE 21

in case of need might be available as gunboats ;[1] steps were taken to strengthen the defences of Kingston ;[2] and in 1846 the civil office of Governor-in-Chief of British North America and the military one of Commander of the Forces were united in the person of the Peninsular veteran Lord Cathcart.[3] At this time, also, a detachment of some 350 British soldiers was sent (by way of Hudson Bay) to the western prairies. They occupied the Hudson's Bay Company's post at Fort Garry (now Winnipeg) from 1846 to 1848.[4] While this emergency lasted, further reductions in the British force in America could not be thought of. Nor was the external menace the whole story. Circumstances within the provinces were such as to render it impossible to reduce imperial expenditure and responsibility.

Durham's recommendation for Canada—a responsible government, administered according to the practice familiar in the United Kingdom—did not in itself terminate the political struggle in the colony. It still remained for the logic of events to convince the British Government that Durham's novel proposals were not too dangerous to be practical. This process consumed eight eventful years. Indeed, it was not easy for men accustomed to accept as axiomatic the Austinian theory of indivisible sovereignty to reconcile the responsibility of a colonial government to a local legislature with the maintenance of the unity of the Empire ; and Lord John Russell's long struggle with his reason and his conscience in the matter[5] must have been paralleled in the minds of many of his contemporaries. It is to be remembered, moreover, that the public life of the Canadas had been characterized by a crudity, turbulence and obstructiveness which did not make it easier for Englishmen to accept Durham's thesis that a greater degree of self-government was the natural panacea for the country's difficulties. In the circumstances, it is not surprising that conviction came slowly.

In 1840 the Imperial Parliament carried out one of Durham's recommendations by passing an Act reuniting the two Canadas ;

[1] Same to same, April 4, 1845 : *ibid.*
[2] Stanley to Master General of the Ordnance (confidential), Jan. 23, 1845: *ibid.* (copy).
[3] Grey, *Colonial Policy of Lord John Russell's Administration*, I, 206.
[4] Begg, *History of the North-West*, I, 266–69.
[5] Kennedy, *The Constitution of Canada*, 179–80.

and Durham's successor as Governor, Poulett Thomson, Lord Sydenham, inaugurated the new *régime* in the following year. Sydenham's theory of government envisaged co-operation with the leaders of popular opinion rather than automatic deference to that opinion. The Governor's sole responsibility, he would have argued, was to the Imperial Government, and he was in a definite sense the chief executive of the colony, charged with governing it for its good and the good of the Empire. To that end he worked with the popular majority whenever possible, but was not averse on occasion to taking independent ground as a benevolent despot. Before his early death he had done much to direct the energies of Canadian public men into a sorely-needed programme of practical legislation; but the success of his governmental system could scarcely have been more than transitory.

Under Sir Charles Bagot, who succeeded him, decided constitutional progress took place. Finding that the local ministry faced defeat in the legislature, he reconstructed it by admitting representatives of the French-Canadian national party (which Sydenham had ignored) and thus "united the voice of seven-eighths of the house of assembly" in support of it. His own illness left public business largely in the hands of the ministers, and responsible government seemed a fact accomplished. But there was to be one more setback. The next Governor, Sir Charles Metcalfe, could not believe that in surrendering the substance of government to a Canadian cabinet he would not be false to a trust reposed in him by the Crown. His determination to be Governor in fact as well as in name led to the resignation of Bagot's ministry, and in 1844 he found himself virtually leading a party—the party of reaction—in an election campaign of unexampled bitterness. By appealing to the sentiment of loyalty to the mother country he obtained a small majority; but the episode only emphasized the breakdown of the old order, and the impossibility of ruling Canada in a peaceful and creditable manner other than through a ministry acceptable to the popular branch of the legislature.[1]

[1] On this period of Canadian constitutional history, see Kennedy, *op. cit.*, chapters XII–XV; Martin, *Empire and Commonwealth*, 245–303; and Morison, *British Supremacy and Canadian Self-Government*. It has been suggested that Metcalfe's success in the elections of 1844 was due in part to disgust aroused by the peculiar violence of the reformers' attacks upon the Queen's representative.

EARLY HISTORY OF IMPERIAL DEFENCE 23

While these bitter political struggles lasted, it would scarcely have been fair to the Governors who were the instruments of Imperial policy to have removed the troops from Canada. Furthermore, it was quite clear that if the country was to be kept in a state of defence against the United States the expense, for the moment, would have to be borne by the Imperial Government. Although most Canadians would have been ready to resist invasion, it was impossible to enlist in a joint scheme of defence the co-operation of a legislature and people in great part dissatisfied with the British ministry's attitude towards the colony, and certainly useless to appeal to them to undertake the additional military expenditure which would be necessary if the imperial establishment was to be reduced without impairing the general efficiency of the defensive arrangements for Canada.[1] So the redcoat regiments stayed, gloomily performing the unpleasant duty of rendering aid to the civil powers in the savage riots which testified to the fierceness of the political passions of the day.[2] Many years later, Lord Elgin described to the House of Lords[3] the situation of the British troops as he found it in 1847 :

" They were scattered in small detachments all over the colony, and, as a matter of course, the whole duties of police devolved on them. Under these circumstances, it was quite impossible to induce the local Legislature to do anything towards the establishment of a local force ; and the military force was viewed with mixed feelings by the colonists—with favour on account of the expense [being] incurred by the mother country, and with great and not unfounded jealousy, because it was supposed to be maintained for imperial, distinct from colonial interests, and that its influence was used for the support of that party which had the favour of the Home Government for the time. Consequently there was little disposition on the part of the local administration to do anything to relieve the mother country from any portion of the burden on this account. . . ."

Elgin even found " that it was actually the practice to charge

---

[1] Note in this connexion the difficulties encountered by Metcalfe and Cathcart in their efforts to persuade their Canadian advisers to undertake an effective reorganization of the militia at the time of the Oregon crisis. Metcalfe to Stanley, May 23, 1845 : *G*, 460, p. 447. Cathcart to Gladstone, Feb. 25, 1846 : *ibid.*, p. 531. Cathcart to Grey, Dec. 27, 1846 : *G*, 461, p. 107.
[2] *C*, 316 and 317 (" Military Aid at Riots, etc.", 1800–1845 and 1845–1854).
[3] *Hansard*, CXLII, 684–85 (May 27, 1856).

with duties articles purchased by the money of this country and imported into the colony for the use of the troops maintained there." He added that he "sometimes mentioned this fact to Americans, but with all their appetite for the marvellous, they thought it so extraordinary that he could hardly get any of them to believe it."[1]

In these last days of the old colonial system, the whole Canadian situation might well appear intolerable to British statesmen. Turbulent and dissatisfied, the colony seemed a reproach to British policy in the face of the world, while at the same time the mother country was burdened with the whole huge cost of its police and defence—a cost which might at any moment be vastly increased by the outbreak of an American war. "It is a hard bargain enough," wrote Sir Robert Peel in 1844, " to have to give every advantage of connexion with the Mother Country, and to undertake the serious responsibility and charge of providing for internal tranquillity and for defence from external attack. . . . To be met at every turn by a captious and quibbling spirit, and above all to be denied the means of well governing the Province, of ensuring the independent and respectable administration of justice and the employment of honest and efficient Civil servants, will make the connexion too onerous a burden to be borne. We shall soon have to tell these factious people there is one limit to our concessions—We will not govern you in a manner discreditable to us or injurious to you."[2]

Change, indeed, was overdue, nor was the remedy now to be long delayed. But it was to proceed from minds more elastic than that of the conscientious but unimaginative Peel. Certain of his contemporaries were growing more and more disposed to give a real trial to the basic doctrine of the Durham report—

[1] This rather astonishing feature of the situation arose in part at least from a desire to protect the agricultural interests of the province against the practice of importing produce for the use of the troops from the United States (Metcalfe to Stanley, May 23, 1845 : G, 460, p. 449). The imposition of duty upon wines imported for the officers' messes also caused trouble (Cathcart to Gladstone, June 27, 1846 : G, 461, p. 52). Elgin finally obtained the necessary exemptions from the legislature in 1850. "It is gratifying to reflect," he wrote, "that henceforward the Gentlemen of H.M.'s army will be able to drink confusion to the Gov. Genl. and his administration in untaxed liquor" (Elgin to Grey, Aug. 2, 1850 : G.E.C.). Cf. E. Kylie in *Canada and its Provinces*, V, 133-34.

[2] Peel to Stanley, Feb. 2, 1844 : quoted in Morrell, *British Colonial Policy in the Age of Peel and Russell*, 64.

EARLY HISTORY OF IMPERIAL DEFENCE 25

that Canada could best be made a credit to British government by giving up the attempt at governing her from Britain. The unity of the Empire was no longer to depend primarily or even partially upon a system of institutional subordination; it was to be freely committed to those stronger ties that had been familiar to the comprehensive mind of Durham, and the bright imaginings of Edmund Burke. In that larger air (it did not seem altogether too much to hope) the colonies might grow into communities willing to take upon themselves some of the heavy responsibilities that hitherto had fallen upon the motherland alone: communities, perhaps, which would be to her a source, no longer of weakness and apprehension, but rather of strength in dark days.

In 1846 Peel put an end to the Corn Laws, and thereby destroyed the unity of the Conservative party, the basis of his own political power. The Whigs now came into office, under Lord John Russell. His was not a strong ministry: it tottered along from day to day, ever expecting to meet defeat at the next corner; but it was strong enough to save the colonies. Lord Grey went to the Colonial Office, determined to end the pitiful tragi-comedy that had been in progress in Canada; and within a year Durham's son-in-law was in Government House at Montreal, meeting the colony's problems in Durham's spirit and applying to their solution the rich resources of a penetrating intelligence, a compelling personality and a robust commonsense. A brighter day was dawning; and as the light broadened, Canadians were to find themselves dowered with the new liberties which they had desired. They were to find themselves faced, also, with new riddles of policy, whose solution was to be no simple matter.

CHAPTER II

BRITAIN AND THE COLONIAL RELATIONSHIP AT THE BEGINNING OF THE VICTORIAN AGE

" The colonies, army, navy, and church are, with the corn laws, merely accessories to our aristocratic government. John Bull has his work cut out for the next fifty years to purge his house of those impurities!"
RICHARD COBDEN to THOMAS DICK, Oct. 7, 1836.

THE successful revolt of the American colonies initiated a period of almost a century during which imperialism—as a belief in extending the overseas empire, or even in fostering the development, as an integral and permanent part of the Crown's dominions, of the distant regions already under its sway—had little honour in England.

True, the routine of administration went on in the dependencies that remained; huge and increasing sums of money were poured out by the mother country in the process; most striking of all, the territorial extent of the Empire steadily continued to grow. But these things were the results not so much of convictions and principles entertained at home, or of any comprehensive design on the part of government, as of the mere force of custom and the pressure of local circumstances in the colonies. Throughout the period there existed in England an active and pertinacious school of opinion, well represented in Parliament, which regarded colonial enterprises with disfavour and distrust, and which exercised on the views of the English people and their government an influence which attained its greatest strength during the first half of the reign of Queen Victoria.

The American War of Independence was indeed a catastrophe well calculated to produce a sense of disillusionment. Depriving England at a blow of the fruits of a century and a half of colonization, it left her (apart from her insular possessions) only the least considered elements in her former great American empire. It was easy to represent the late events as the natural consequence of an attempt at perpetuating political connexion between communities separated by thousands of miles of sea. What—it was said—was the use of squandering the national resources on further distant ventures which would necessarily end as the old colonies had ended: not only in severance, but also perhaps in bloodshed such as had produced an apparently insuperable embitterment between Great Britain and the United States?

The imperial idea, however, had to contend against adverse forces even more formidable in the long run than the mere natural discouragement generated by a deplorable failure of British policy and an unsuccessful war. The whole economic theory to which the old imperial system had mainly owed its prestige in England was crumbling before the advance of new doctrine. In the nationalistic scheme of things devised by mercantilist thinkers, the colonies had occupied a definite place: it was their function to supply the mother country with those forms of raw material which she could not herself produce, and thus render her independent of foreign nations, as well as to provide a market for her manufactures. It was a philosophy based primarily upon considerations of mercenary advantage for the mother country, though tempered by solicitude for national defence. But now the mercantilists' day was ending; and in their place was arising a new school of economists, not less devoted to the love of gain, but thinking in terms of the individual rather than of the nation. In the system which these men propounded, the colonies no longer enjoyed a special significance.

As the industrial organization of Britain widened in scope and increased in efficiency in the latter part of the eighteenth century, the leaders in the movement, seeking the largest possible profits, found themselves more and more opposed to the strict nationalistic regulation to which the mercantile system subjected their commercial operations. The ends of profit were best served by obtaining their raw material wherever they found it cheapest, and by selling their product in the market in which it commanded the best price—under whatever flags these conditions might be found. To the economic-minded British manufacturer it began to be intolerable that he should be obliged by government order to purchase from a British colony what he might be able otherwise to purchase more cheaply elsewhere, or for that matter that the price he paid for a colonial product should include the cost of transport in an English ship when it might have been carried more cheaply in a foreign bottom. He ceased to value his monopoly of the colonial market, for he argued that the superior efficiency of his methods would procure him that market (which after all was comparatively small) in any circumstances; and certainly he did not propose to allow the conditions of the colonial connexion to raise his costs of production to the point of imperilling his command of the world-market which was coming to be all-important to him.

It was not merely by restricting the manufacturer's purchasing that the traditional colonial arrangements seemed to threaten this. Taxation was a large factor in production costs; and the new industrialists, applying to the affairs of the nation the strict standards of their own counting-houses, made it their business to seek out extravagances in the national economy and demand of government an administration conducted on the most frugal principles. It was soon apparent that the colonial department was to be a special target for their shafts, and that it was by no means difficult to construct a plausible argument representing the colonies as costing the British taxpayer large sums every year and making him no tangible return whatever. Garrisons and war vessels maintained at his expense protected a score of countries scattered round the globe; yet these countries, it was said, were of no greater commercial value to Britain than if they had been utterly independent. Less so, in fact; for their influence prolonged the existence of a mistaken and unprofitable commercial system.

The new school of economic thought had other grievances against the colonies. Colonial competition had been a frequent occasion of war; and the most logical of the free traders were internationalists and pacifists. The colonial empire was constantly referred to as justifying the maintenance of large armaments, and the "economists" were more hostile to expenditure for this unproductive object than for any other. Finally, the rising class of industrial capitalists were prejudiced against the colonial system because it was a source of public employment for an aristocracy which they disliked and despised. Thus it came about that among the men who pulled down mercantilism there were few who were disposed to interest themselves in the welfare of the colonies as portions of the British Empire; while on the other hand there were many who, regarding them simply as anachronistic survivals of the discarded commercial organization, would gladly have seen the last of them.

These views attained their greatest currency under Queen Victoria, in the era when the preachers of free trade at last established their doctrine as the national canon; but they influenced the community from the time of the first assaults on the old order. The greatest document of the free trade struggle, and the most powerful inspiration of its later protagonists, was of course Adam Smith's *Wealth of Nations*, published in the year of the Declaration of Independence. Smith's classic attack on the old colonial system, his demonstration that monopoly was inimical both to British and colonial prosperity, need not be recapitulated here. It furnished his successors with a whole armoury of argument, and must be accounted a major contribution to that revolution in British colonial policy which they saw accomplished. Yet Smith cannot justly be called an anti-imperialist. He assailed the existing colonial arrangements, and went so far as to say that under such conditions Britain would be better off without the colonies; but nothing in his work suggests an animus towards colonial connexion in itself, or a conviction that under another system the colonies could not with mutual advantage remain joined to England. On the contrary, he produces a definite plan— colonial representation in the Imperial Parliament —for effecting this result.[1] His later disciples, however, in many cases disregarded or discounted this aspect of his work, and were prepared to abandon, not merely the particular scheme of colonial relations against which Smith's reason had revolted, but the colonies themselves.

---

[1] " Though the Roman constitution . . . was necessarily ruined by the union of Rome with the allied states of Italy, there is not the least probability that the British constitution would be hurt by the union of Great Britain with her colonies. That constitution, on the contrary, would be completed by it, and seems to be imperfect without it." (*Wealth of Nations*, Book IV, Chap. VII, Part III).

From Smith's time, in fact, the whole idea of colonial enterprise may be said to have been on the defensive against the criticisms of many reputable publicists. About the time of his death, Sir John Sinclair, in his *History of the Public Revenue of the British Empire*, not only gave thanks for the loss of the American colonies, but bitterly attacked " that source of future waste and extravagance," the new colonization project lately undertaken in Australia.[1] A few years later, the indefatigable English reformer, Jeremy Bentham, offered the National Convention in France what he considered the soundest possible advice, in a letter entitled *Emancipate Your Colonies*.[2] The Utilitarian political philosophers who were Bentham's followers, and the economists who owed so much to Smith, united their influence against the extension and perpetuation of the colonial empire, on the ground that it was both politically dangerous and economically unsound. Doubtless the educative agitation carried on by the Benthamite radicals had a beneficent influence upon the fortunes of the colonies in that it prepared the minds of the British parliament and public for the grant of colonial self-government; but it did not envisage the possibility of the Empire being transformed into a league of free states. Their writings suggest rather a complete separation, with the colonies freed from the enervating domination of the mother country, and the mother country herself freed from the burden of expense formerly borne on their account.

The nationalistic excitement of the great war with France, and the expansion of the Empire to which it led, failed to discourage these critics. After Waterloo they made their influence more and more widely felt, as standard-bearers in the fight for reform which then convulsed Britain; and the colonial system continued to receive its full share of attention. The article " Colony " which James Mill, the close associate of Bentham, contributed at this time to the *Encyclopædia Britannica*[3] serves to exhibit the vehemence of their opposition to this particular aspect of the old order. In it he demonstrates

[1] Third edition, London, 1803–04, II, 101. The first edition was published in 1785, the second in 1790, the year of Smith's death. New South Wales was founded in 1788.
[2] " Shewing the uselessness and mischievousness of distant dependencies to an European state." Written, 1793 ; first published, 1830. In Bowring, J., (ed.), *The Works of Jeremy Bentham*, Edinburgh, 1843, IV, 407–18.
[3] Supplement to the fifth edition : volume III (published 1819), pp. 257–73.

BEGINNING OF THE VICTORIAN AGE

the fallacy of "holding a colony for the benefit of its trade," using the arguments of Smith and the modifications of them lately circulated by Ricardo; derides the argument for the Navigation Laws founded on the importance of naval defence, and notes with pleasure that those laws now have "hardly any defenders" in Parliament; and concludes by stating, according to the views of his school, the reasons why nations persist in clinging to their colonies despite their uselessness. This passage reflects the passions of that time—the time of Peterloo :

"It ought never to be forgotten, that, in every country, there is ' a Few', and there is ' a Many '; that in all countries in which the government is not very good, the interest of ' the Few ' prevails over the interest of ' the Many ', and is promoted at their expense. . . . It is according to the interest of ' the Few ' that colonies should be cultivated. . . . There is not one of the colonies but what augments the number of places. There are governorships and judgeships . . . and above all, there is not one of them but what requires an additional number of troops, and an additional portion of navy—that is of great importance. In every additional portion of army and navy, besides the glory of the thing, there are generalships, and colonelships, and captainships, and lieutenantships, and in the equipping and supplying of additional portions of army and navy, there are always gains, which may be thrown in the way of a friend. . . .

"But besides all this, there is another thing of still greater importance. . . . The colonies are a grand source of wars. Now wars, even in countries completely arbitrary and despotical, have so many things agreeable to the ruling few, that the ruling few hardly ever seem to be happy except when engaged in them. . . . Of the proposition, that colonies are a grand source of wars, and of additional expence in wars; that expence, by which the ruling few always profit at the cost of the subject many; it is not probable that much of proof will be required."

These bitter declarations demonstrate how completely the prophets of a new order identified the colonies with that outworn fabric of society which they so ardently desired to destroy. The imperial system seemed to them simply one of the props of privilege; and this belief was probably a factor not less decisive than the economic arguments of Smith and Ricardo in determining their hostility to it.

The spread of liberal commercial ideas which Mill observed with such satisfaction was soon to have its effect upon imperial economic policy. In 1822 the " Wallace-Robinson code " of commercial legislation made the initial breach in the venerable façade of the Navigation Acts.[1] In the next year William Huskisson became President of the Board of Trade, and the way was open for further liberal enactments. Huskisson's liberalism, however, was not that of the radicals.[2] In 1825 he effected a sweeping reform of the Navigation Laws, ending the monopoly of colonial trade by permitting free intercourse between the colonies and such foreign states as would grant reciprocal privileges. But for imperial monopoly he substituted imperial preference—discriminating duties in favour of colonial produce in the mother country, plus a similar discrimination in favour of British produce in the ports of the colonies, and a limitation of trade within the Empire to British and colonial ships. His system was a halfway-house on the road to free trade, and the restrictions which it allowed to remain were the result of a vigorous imperialism. They were anathema to such reforming economists as J. R. M'Culloch, who could not abide any arrangement which might force the English to buy in a market other than the cheapest ; and the advent of preference made these men even more hostile than before to the colonial connexion.[3] The apparent contradiction between the advantages enjoyed by colonial produce in the home market and the heavy burdens imposed on the mother country for colonial defence began to be widely canvassed ; and though perhaps not many Englishmen would have echoed Sir Isaac Coffin (who in 1822 declared " It would have been a good thing for this country if Canada had been sunk to the bottom of the sea ; it cost us £500,000 per annum and did not make a return of 500 pence "),[4] many were coming to regard the colonies' connexion with England as difficult to justify from the

[1] Brady, A., *William Huskisson and Liberal Reform*, Oxford, 1928, 89–91 ; Walpole, *History of England from the Conclusion of the Great War in 1815*, II, 84–5.
[2] Brady, *op. cit.*, 132, on Huskisson's imperialism.
[3] *Ibid.*, chaps. V and VI. For M'Culloch's remarks on the last preferential duty to survive—the timber duty, which forced the importation from Canada of " a dearer and worse article " than could be obtained in the Baltic—see his *Descriptive and Statistical Account of the British Empire*, 4th edition (1854), II, 18.
[4] Brady, 122 : from *Hansard*, new series, VI, 1073.

BEGINNING OF THE VICTORIAN AGE 33

strictly material viewpoint which was more and more the fashion.

That viewpoint is reflected in Sir Henry Parnell's influential work *On Financial Reform*, published in 1830. Parnell (afterwards Lord Congleton) was an eminent if erratic member of Parliament, whose economic opinions were much respected. His survey of national finance was dominated by the new *laissez-faire* conceptions and by a conviction of the possibility of large retrenchment in the public services; and he pointed to the colonial system as an example of offence against sound policy in both respects. He especially detested the preferential principle. If the preferences were abolished, he argued, British products would still hold their own in the colonies by their superior cheapness; the English public would no longer pay " full two millions more for sugar and timber than they ought to pay "; and the colonies, given control of their own commercial policy, would be able and willing to meet the costs of their own defence.[1] But he would gladly have seen them completely independent, and pointed in particular to the cost of the Canadian garrison and fortifications as a dead loss to the British nation.[2]

Another member of Parliament had long been agitating for the twin causes of reform and retrenchment, and casting many a stone at the colonial system by the way. Joseph Hume, once a school-fellow of James Mill, had made a fortune in India and returned to enter public life in England. Mill introduced him to Francis Place, and as a result of the latter's influence he became a parliamentary spokesman of Utilitarianism.[3] As Place's mouthpiece he was largely responsible for that repeal of the Combination Laws which is so important a landmark in the history of trade unionism; but it was as a pertinacious critic of government expenditure that he was most familiar to his fellow-members of the House. The army estimates received his special attention, and more particularly that part of them relating to the colonies. During his first session he suggested the possibility of the colonies assuming this expense themselves;[4] and thereafter he never allowed the idea to sleep.

[1] Pp. 234-49.   [2] Pp. 253-57.
[3] Stephen, Sir L., *The English Utilitarians*, London, 1900, II, 2, 28, 57, 66 and *n*.
[4] *Hansard* (first series), XL, 240-46 (May 7, 1819), 268-72 (May 10).

D

He was a constant advocate of colonial self-government, one of the chief advantages of which he conceived to be that it would relieve the mother country of this burden. Over a long period of years, his lonely and persistent agitation kept the allied questions of military expenditure and colonial government before Parliament and the public.[1]

Early in Queen Victoria's reign there appeared in English politics a small group of men whose ideas were, in large measure, those which Hume had been preaching since 1819.[2] These were the members of the so-called " Manchester School," for the most part self-made men representative of the new industrial capitalism, who were destined to make the ideas of Adam Smith and the economists who followed him a ruling force in the policies of England. They were the complete embodiment of the radical slogan, since so famous, " peace, retrenchment, and reform "; in an age which seems to be rejecting their doctrines in nearly every particular, they are remembered as the most uncompromising advocates of the system of *laissez-faire* whom the British Parliament has ever known. " The gospel of free trade " is the popular phrase for their economic teaching; and indeed their various agitations were carried on in an evangelical spirit of conviction. Both economically and politically, they wanted a new England : they had the vision of a great free nation, in which the last privileges of aristocracy would have been swept away along with the remnants of the mercantile system ; a nation at peace with the world, its fighting services cut to a minimum and taxation reduced so that its factories might turn out even cheaper goods ; a nation selling those goods freely in every market (once all countries had accepted the new commercial revelation), vanquishing competition by superior efficiency, and entering upon a period of unexampled prosperity which could but increase with the passage of the rich and fruitful years.

The vision was not without very large elements of nobility ; it played an important part in the making of modern England ; and (if one may venture to moralize) it might still, perhaps, be

---

[1] For a hostile estimate of Hume, see Fortescue, *History of the British Army*, XI, 84–6.
[2] Cobden entered Parliament in 1841, Bright in 1843.

considered with advantage by the modern world. Yet its basis in the main was a thorough-going devotion to material profits; and it was in this balance that the Manchester men weighed the colonies particularly—and found them wanting. And although it is surely possible to make valid objection to their standard of values, within the limits of that standard it must be admitted that their argument was strong.

The "Little England" side of the Manchester leaders' ideas has often received surprisingly little attention. Perhaps the usefulness of much of the work they did has created about them an atmosphere of admiration inimical to extended treatment of such of their activities as did not prove to the ultimate taste of their countrymen. Writing in an age which accepts the imperial tie as a matter of course, recent historians have sometimes chosen simply to overlook their anti-colonial bias; but to contemporaries this was not the least familiar aspect of their philosophy.

Richard Cobden was the leader and inspirer of the group, at least in its earliest period; and a glance at his opinions will not come amiss. He had addressed himself to colonial questions long before his entry into Parliament. In his able pamphlet of 1835, *England, Ireland, and America* (first published simply as the work of "A Manchester Manufacturer"[1]), he argued, as he was to do throughout his career, against the extent of Britain's expenditure on her fleet and army, pointing to the much smaller establishments of the United States, which he indicated as her great commercial rival of the future. In particular he took exception to the cost of defending the colonies, and briefly raked the whole existing colonial system with a salvo of criticism. Laughing the preferential duties to scorn, he proceeded bitterly:

". . . If it could be made manifest to the trading and industrious portions of this nation, who have no honours, or interested ambition of any kind, at stake in the matter, that, whilst our dependencies are supported at an expense to them, in direct taxation, of more than five millions annually, they serve but as gorgeous and ponderous appendages to swell our ostensible grandeur, but, in reality,

[1] Republished in the various editions of his *Political Writings*, e.g., that edited by Sir Louis Mallet, London, 1878. For a discussion of Cobden's colonial ideas, see Dawson, W. H., *Richard Cobden and Foreign Policy*, London, 1926, chap. IX.

to complicate and magnify our government expenditure, without improving our balance of trade—surely, under such circumstances, it would become at least a question for anxious inquiry with a people so overwhelmed with debt, whether those colonies should not be suffered to support and defend themselves, as separate and independent existences."

The colonial connexion, said the Manchester Manufacturer, constituted in fact a genuine and immediate peril to Britain. " Spain lies, at this moment," he wrote, " a miserable spectacle of a nation whose own national greatness has been immolated on the shrine of transatlantic ambition. May not some future historian possibly be found recording a similar epitaph on the tomb of Britain ? . . . Three hundred millions of permanent debt have been accumulated—millions of direct taxation are annually levied—restrictions and prohibitions are imposed upon our trade in all quarters of the world, for the acquisition or maintenance of colonial possessions ; and all for what ? That we may repeat the fatal Spanish proverb—' The sun never sets on the King of England's dominions '." Here, two years before Victoria's accession, are the views of the genuine Victorian Little Englander. There were no limits to such men's ambitions for the expansion of British trade : the world could never be too large for the British merchant, and they were fain to think of him undoing his corded bales on every shore ; but from the responsibilities of government in far countries, with their horrid possibilities of swollen expenditure and foreign complication, they shrank as from the plague.

One of Cobden's earliest interests in Parliament was the war on imperial preference. In a debate of 1843 on a measure affording additional advantages in the home market to British West Indian sugar, he moved as an amendment :

" That in the opinion of this house it was not expedient that, in addition to the great expense to which the people of this country are subjected for the civil, military, and naval establishments of the colonies, they should be compelled to pay a higher price for the productions of the colonies than that at which similar commodities could be purchased from other countries, and that therefore all protective duties in favour of colonial produce ought to be abolished."

Once more, on this occasion, he scoffed at those who boasted of the vastness of the Empire : " Of what use was it, in the present condition of this kingdom, to point to a boundless extent of territory in America, when people were wanted as customers and consumers?"[1] This is the core of the matter. The search for "customers and consumers" was the primary concern of the Manchester School; and from this viewpoint independent Americans were as useful as loyal Canadians, in addition to being more numerous. And they did not have to be defended at English expense.

To the enormous annual expense of the colonial garrisons Cobden returned again and again. It was one of his most important points when, on February 26, 1849, he moved for a reduction of £10,000,000 in the annual expenditure of government;[2] and at the end of the same year he devoted to it a long and vigorous speech at Bradford.[3] Canada was then passing through a sad period of tumult, attributed by the protectionists (and with reason) to economic distress resulting from the loss of the preference on wheat which suddenly occurred when Cobden's Anti-Corn Law League won its victory in 1846. Cobden met the criticism with a counterblast. It was absurd, he said, to suppose that the great colonies would for ever remain dependent upon England; and he favoured treating them in the most liberal spirit, for that and other reasons:

". . . I would say to the colonies—' I will give you the fullest amount of self-government '; I would say also, on behalf of Englishmen, ' You must pay the price of self-government ;—you must pay for it, as the United States is doing with so much success, as is evidenced by her great prosperity ;—you must pay for your army, for your navy; you must pay for your civil and ecclesiastical establishments.' Why should they object ? "

Britain, Cobden pointed out, was maintaining at her expense in North America, to protect a population of two millions, a military force as strong as that maintained by the twenty million people of the United States. " I want to know," he asked, " why we should support a standing army at all in Canada ? Bear in mind, that the colonies do not pay one shilling of the cost! That is, to my mind, a fact which proves

---

[1] *Hansard*, LXX, 205–12 (June 22, 1843). Printed in pamphlet form under the title *Our Colonies* (Manchester, n.d.), with date misprinted as 1842.
[2] *Hansard*, CII, 1218–35; and in *Speeches of Richard Cobden . . . delivered during 1849*, 22–43.
[3] *Speeches . . . delivered during 1849*, 216–44.

the folly of the arrangement between yourselves and the colonies. . . . They don't even contribute for the priming of their muskets."

It might have been foreseen that the colonial military expenditure would ultimately become an object of serious attack. Official attention had been called to the matter as early as 1817 by the House of Commons Select Committee on Finance, which noted that the force then maintained in the colonies just acquired in the Napoleonic Wars was equal to that which in 1792 had held all the dependencies then possessed by Britain. In 1817 these new colonies (including the Ionian Islands) were occupied by 12,600 rank and file, while the older ones had 20,400 more. The Committee expressed a hope " that some means may be devised for rendering the foreign possessions of the British empire more efficient towards defraying the expenses of their own military protection, since their value to the parent state must be greatly diminished by their continuing a lasting drain on its resources."[1] The only effect of this recommendation seems to have been to afford Hume a good excuse for keeping the question alive.[2]

By the early 'thirties there was sufficient sentiment in Parliament on the subject to bring about the appointment of a Select Committee to investigate the colonial military expenditure itself. The Government were not hostile to the project, being confident that they could demonstrate that the expense was not greater than the necessities of the service required;[3] and their confidence was justified, for the Committee's two reports[4] showed great reluctance to interfere with the executive's distribution of the forces. Military witnesses opposed any reduction of the garrisons ; and in the end the Committee, while urging a policy of general economy and suggesting various minor expedients to this end, made no sweeping recommendations for retrenchment. The transaction is typical of the state of the question at this time. There was a growing consciousness among public men of the magnitude of the

[1] *Second Report from the Select Committee on Finance* (ordered to be printed, March 29, 1817 : *Annual Register*, 1817, pp. 320–337).
[2] *Hansard* (first series), XL, 268–72 (May 10, 1819).
[3] *Ibid.*, (third series), XXI, 963 (speech of Stanley, Feb. 28, 1834).
[4] *P.P.*, 1834, no. 570, vol. VI, and 1835, no. 473, vol. VI. The Committee began its work in 1834 and was reappointed in 1835.

burden of colonial defence, but no belief, among the majority, that contemporary circumstances really justified strong measures to alleviate it. The radicals who were determined to achieve economy even at the cost of the loss of the colonies still had to contend against a weight of conservative opinion, in great part inarticulate, which refused to listen to their arguments and was content to follow the ancient paths.

Nevertheless, public attention had been directed to the question and facts relevant to it had been recorded in parliamentary papers ; and anyone taking the trouble to consult those documents might find that for the financial year 1834-35 Great Britain's net expenditure for her colonies (including both military stations like Gibraltar and populous communities like the Canadas) amounted to £2,431,900—and that of this sum no less than £1,924,337 was occasioned by military charges. That is to say, roughly four-fifths of the whole cost of the overseas empire to the English taxpayer was accounted for by the expense of the colonial garrisons. In March, 1835, the Committee was informed, the effective soldiers of all ranks stationed in the colonies were 37,361 in number.[1] In 1838 (as we have already seen)[2] the situation was greatly aggravated by the rebellion in Canada, which necessitated an increase of imperial expenditure there which was neither small nor transitory. This was the state of affairs at the advent of the Manchester School, and these conditions provided its leaders with their heaviest shot for the bombardment of the colonial system.

The men of that party, however, were not alone in their objection to the existing defensive arrangements in the colonies. We must here take note of another political group in the England of that day—a group, like the Manchester men, small in numbers but strong in capacity and important in its ultimate influence. Among the so-called " philosophical radicals "—the liberal-minded young men who were followers of James Mill[3]— there were some who did not share the typical radical opinions on colonial questions, but who on the contrary combined with a healthy dissatisfaction with the existing colonial system a

---

[1] Second report, appendix no. 4. The statistics from the reports may be found, in great part, in the appendix to Martin, R. M., *History of the Colonies of the British Empire* . . . *from the official records of the Colonial Office*, 288 ff.
[2] See above, pp. 17-19.
[3] See Stephen, *The English Utilitarians*, III, 29 ff.

solid faith in the continued unity of the Empire. To this group of " colonial reformers " or " radical imperialists " belonged the great Lord Durham, the father of colonial responsible government; Charles Buller, who went to Canada as his secretary and shares in some degree the credit for the *Report*; Edward Gibbon Wakefield, another of Durham's Canadian retinue, and author of *A View of the Art of Colonization*; and Sir William Molesworth, an industrious member of Parliament who for many years exerted a salutary influence on colonial discussions in the Commons.[1]

These men were constant advocates of a liberal colonial policy, and persistent (and sometimes unfair) baiters of the Colonial Office, on which they poured biting ridicule for what they called its attempts at governing great communities on the other side of the world by edicts issuing from a clerk in a back room in Downing Street. But while arguing for true colonial self-government, they did not regard that measure as preliminary to independence; believing, on the contrary, that the goodwill bred by free institutions freely administered would be the strongest of imperial bonds, they looked forward to the permanent existence of the Empire as a free association of British countries under the Crown. It was a misfortune that these imperialist politicians were tragically short-lived. Durham died the year after his report was published, Buller in 1848; the only " colonial reformer " of eminence who remained active in Parliament after the decision to give real responsible government to the colonies had become effective was Molesworth, who lived until 1855, and received some extra-parliamentary assistance from Wakefield until the latter settled permanently in New Zealand in 1853.

In their basic views on British colonial policy, these radical imperialists were at the opposite pole from Manchester; yet on the purely military aspect of it the two groups found themselves agreeing as the new reign advanced. Molesworth was out of Parliament from 1841 to 1845, and when he appealed in the latter year to the electors of Southwark, colonial reform was one of the causes to which he pledged himself.[2] *Hansard*

---

[1] For a sketch of the group, see Williamson, *Short History of British Expansion*, 2nd ed., II, 51–57.
[2] Mrs. Fawcett, *Life of . . . Sir William Molesworth*, 246.

shows that he well redeemed the pledge during the succeeding sessions. He fought for genuine colonial self-government during the years when the final political struggle was being waged in Canada, though the particular measures he urged were not always those whose wisdom seems to have been approved by time; and he repeatedly attacked the expense of the colonial garrisons as being one of the weakest points of the imperial structure. The annual bill for colonial defence seemed to him an unquestioned evil and an injustice to the British taxpayer—but the evil and injustice were to be remedied by granting the colonies the fullest autonomy, and thus obviating the possibility (naturally present in British politicians' minds after the Canadian rebellion) of having to use imperial troops to coerce the colonists into acquiescence in imperial regulations. Increased freedom for the colonies, he declared, meant for the Empire, not disruption, but perpetuation:

"I maintain that if we govern our North American colonies as we ought to govern them, follow out rigorously the principle of responsible government, and leave them to manage their own affairs, uncontrolled by the Colonial Office, we may with safety diminish our military force and expenditure, and they will willingly continue to be our fellow-subjects."[1]

Making the essential distinction between settlement colonies and mere imperial military posts such as Gibraltar or Malta, he stated his idea of " the true colonial policy of Great Britain " in the simple formula, " self-government for true colonies, and no imperial expenditure except for military stations."[2]

Molesworth was well acquainted with the Manchester reasoning, and could put the materialistic logic of the matter before the House as cogently as Cobden himself. The commercial argument he summed up thus:

" In 1844 we exported to the United States produce and manufactures to the value of 8,000,000*l.*, an amount equal to the whole of our real export trade to all our colonial dominions, which we govern at a cost of 4,000,000*l.* a year; while the United States cost us for consular and diplomatic services not more than about 15,000*l.*

---

[1] Egerton (ed.), *Selected Speeches of Sir William Molesworth* . . ., 180. (Speech in Parliament, July 25, 1848.)
[2] *Ibid.*, 289. (Speech in Parliament, April 10, 1851.) For other utterances of Molesworth on the colonial military question, see *Hansard*, XCVII, 1169 ff.; CIII, 1007–11; CIX, 667–73; and CXV, 762–3 (speeches on the army estimates, 1848–51).

a year, and not one ship of war is required to protect our trade with the United States."[1]

He preferred, however, to present such calculations less as his own ideas than as those of " some persons who take merely a commercial and economical view of these questions "—persons to whom these facts furnished all-too-trenchant arguments for terminating the connexion with the colonies altogether.[2]

Sir William devoted himself particularly to mastering the statistics of colonial expenditure for presentation to Parliament. In 1848 he estimated Britain's total disbursements for colonial purposes at £4,000,000 annually, and accounted for £2,500,000 of this as direct military expenditure, while allotting £1,000,000 more for naval defence.[3] This last was a difficult matter to estimate, the more so as it was frequently argued that Britain could not have reduced her naval expenditure even if all her colonies had become independent.

Apart from this, however, official figures make it clear that Molesworth did not exaggerate. A parliamentary return[4] of Imperial expenditure in the colonies of all classes (always excepting, of course, India, which paid for its own defence, and so did not come within the scope of the problem) shows the total—civil, military and naval—for the year 1846-47 as £3,500,472. Of this, the net military expenditure accounted for £2,928,069, and naval expenditure £82,395. Civil expenses were £492,192. That is to say, approximately six-sevenths of the colonial expenditure was for the fighting services; and in point of fact the true proportion was larger, for the items listed as naval charges represented only the cost of shore establishments in the colonies; the much greater expense of maintaining squadrons in colonial waters was not included. The figures for the North American colonies (where by this period almost the whole cost of civil government was defrayed locally) show the situation in its most extreme form. The total imperial expenditure on account of the Province of Canada was £496,576. Of this, net civil disbursements were only £20,889, and naval costs £897; but the net military expenditure was £474,789—or some nineteen-twentieths of the total. In the Maritime

---

[1] Egerton, 179.   [2] Ibid., 276-7.   [3] Ibid., 155-8.
[4] P.P., 1849, no. 224, vol. XXXIV: General abstract of colonial expenditure for 1843-44 and 1846-47.

BEGINNING OF THE VICTORIAN AGE 43

Provinces (including Newfoundland) the total expenditure was £184,656, and the net military expenditure £170,464.

These statistics demonstrate how it came about that the cost of the colonial garrisons was the Achilles heel which the imperial system offered to the shafts of radical critics in England. And not the least disquieting feature of the case against them as presented by Molesworth was the fact that the bill was steadily increasing. It had risen from £1,761,505 in 1832 to £2,556,919 in 1843-44.[1] This was largely the result of the Canadian rebellion; but the increase did not end with the restoration of order in Canada, for, as we have seen, the total was up to more than £2,900,000 in 1846-47.[2]

It is interesting to note the proportion of the bill for colonial military defence to the whole cost of the fighting services and the size of the general national budget. In 1846-47 the whole sum expended for the army (including ordnance services) was £9,061,000. In that financial year, therefore, the army in the colonies accounted for nearly one-third of the whole military expenditure of Britain; and this is calculated without allotting to the colonies their share of the general dead-weight of army services, or making allowance for the number of troops necessarily kept on foot for the purpose of affording relief to colonial garrisons. On the other hand, it must be remembered that this includes all the colonies—the mere military stations as well as the populous provinces. The total national expenditure in 1846-47 was £50,944,000; thus (speaking once more in approximations) the military defences of the colonies were responsible for about one-seventeenth of it. More than half of the total—£28,078,000—went to debt services, however; so the proportion of the colonial bill to the expenditure for effective national objects was much higher. At this period, it is worth observing, the expenses of the army and navy together amounted to £16,864,000, or roughly eight-elevenths of the national expenditure apart from debt services.[3]

[1] Egerton, 156. These figures are for the net military expenditure, including ordnance and commissariat services.
[2] This latter increase was mainly the result of a Kaffir war which broke out at the Cape of Good Hope in 1846. In the interval between 1843 and 1846, moreover, troops were stationed for the first time in New Zealand, which had been annexed in 1840. See the detailed figures for the various colonies in *P.P.*, 1849, no. 224, vol. XXXIV, pp. 4-5, 10-11.
[3] The statistics of revenue and expenditure are from Page, W., *Commerce and Industry: tables of statistics for the British Empire from 1815*, London,

One aspect of the argument against the garrison system remains to be noticed. The colonial reformers' friendship for the colonies did not prevent them from stating their conviction that some elements among the colonists, regarding the presence of the soldiers simply as a road to riches, through the money spent locally by the men themselves and by the imperial government on their behalf, did all they could to prevent any withdrawal of troops. Molesworth used strong terms in referring to such people's " sinister interest " in the matter :

" These persons have made, or expect to make, large gains by contracts, jobs, and by the innumerable other modes of robbing the mother country. They rejoice on every increase of imperial expenditure. To them a Kaffir or a Maori war, or a rebellion, is a godsend. I have heard on good authority that in the Canadian rebellion the enormous gains of these persons were equal to the losses of the rest of the community, and that they have been heard to toast the good old times of the rebellion, and the speedy commencement of the next."

The Imperial expenditure, he thought, had corrupted the colonists until they lacked the self-reliance and self-respect of the men who had fought the Indians and the French in the Empire's early days.[1]

It would be very difficult to make accurate estimate of the influence of colonial greed on the military problems of the Empire at this period. Certainly it was an existent factor, and was loudly spoken of in connexion with New Zealand (where the settlers, coveting the Maoris' lands, were accused of fomenting wars, to be fought by imperial troops and made excuses for confiscations) and with the Cape, where commissariat and transport charges were always enormous items in the cost of the recurrent Kaffir wars ; and certainly also tales of this sort were calculated more than most to lead Englishmen into disgust with their colonial arrangements. In every society still in the pioneer stage, with cash scarce and business operations on a small scale, the expenditures resulting from the presence of a body of troops are necessarily a matter of local importance.

1919, 32, 38–9. It is difficult to decide exactly what constitutes a military station and what a " true " colony. P.P., 1849, no. 224, shows the total military expenditure for Gibraltar, Malta, Mauritius, Bermuda, St. Helena, and Hong Kong as about £570,500 for 1846–47 ; whereas British North America alone cost about £645,000 and the Cape of Good Hope £685,000.

[1] Egerton, 287–88.

In Canada, we have already seen Amherstburgh and Niagara, in 1836, petitioning against the withdrawal of their little garrisons;[1] and no doubt it was partly for these sordid reasons. But there is no evidence that such motives had great influence in determining the official attitude of Canada towards the Imperial troops. The soldiers' disbursements were of primary importance to the economic life of small towns where they might be stationed, but in the general affairs of such a province as Canada they were a comparatively minor consideration.

This purely mercenary side of the question was one on which Edward Gibbon Wakefield entertained particularly strong feelings. In March, 1851, he addressed to W. E. Gladstone (then out of office) a vigorous memorandum on the colonial garrisons, hoping to obtain his support for Molesworth, who was about to make one of his full-dress assaults on the subject in Parliament.[2] Of the native war then in progress in South Africa, he wrote, "I firmly believe that the war was *made*"; and he further declared that incendiary outrages on the Canadian border in 1839-40 had been winked at locally because their real object was the prevention of troop withdrawals. But he had other reasons for criticising the garrison system. He believed that real responsible government was impossible in a colony so long as Imperial troops were kept there for internal purposes, and went so far as to declare, with the dogmatic assurance characteristic of the colonial reformers, that there would never have been a rebellion in Canada if the arrogant ruling faction there had not been able to count upon the support of English soldiers. On the Canadian tumults of 1849 his comment was, "The local parties would be heedful and moderate, rather than reckless and violent, if there were no foreign troops to strike an unnatural balance between them."

We can now see that in 1851 these arguments were already becoming antiquated. Lord Grey—though the colonial reformers were unwilling to admit it—had already made responsible government a reality in Canada; and the events of 1849 had in fact been the death-struggle of the old oligarchy

[1] See above, p. 16.
[2] Knapland, "E. G. Wakefield on the Colonial Garrisons, 1851," *C.H.R.*, V. Professor Knaplund found this document among the Hawarden papers. Though Gladstone probably sympathized, he did not speak in the debate raised by Molesworth on April 10, 1851.

there which had claimed a monopoly of loyalty and believed itself the only party properly entitled to the support of Her Majesty's Government and Her Majesty's troops. When the British Government renounced the right to interfere in the internal affairs of the colony—and it had really done so, with respect to Canada, in 1847—the Imperial troops simply ceased to be regarded as a possible determining factor in colonial politics, and became merely a guarantee against foreign aggression and an ornament to garrison-towns; but the colonial reformers continued to use the supposed menace to local rights as an argument against the garrisons for years thereafter.

It is abundantly clear that—despite their wide differences of motive—colonial reformers and Manchester men stood shoulder to shoulder against the colonial military expenditure. Molesworth's imperialism did not make his insistence upon a reduction in the cost of the system a whit less firm than Cobden's. Cobden in fact took occasion to praise Molesworth's agitation,[1] and seconded his efforts in the House;[2] and old Hume, recognizing a recruit for his favourite cause, likewise rallied to his support in debate.[3] Molesworth seems to have been remembered after his death as the pioneer in forcing the colonial military question upon the attention of Parliament.[4] This was the result of his intensive agitation in 1848-51; but, as we have seen, he was very far from being the first to protest against the system. The fact is that all the various radical elements in the House of Commons and outside it united in urging upon the Government the necessity of colonial retrenchment. The strange alliance between imperialists and antiimperialists appeared in a declaration of Wakefield in his memorandum for Gladstone :

" I assert that if a Hume-Cobden imperial policy had prevailed at the time when the Troops were sent to New Zealand, all the main evils of New Zealand colonization, which the British Government will one day be heavily tasked to remedy, would have been avoided. I never thought to say as much for the Manchester School."

[1] Bright and Rogers (eds.), *Speeches by Richard Cobden* . . ., I, 486 (speech at Manchester, Jan. 10, 1849) ; cf. *Speeches Delivered during 1849*, 237 (speech at Bradford).
[2] See debate of April 10, 1851, in *Hansard*, CXV, 1364-1450.
[3] *Ibid.*, CIII, 1017-18 (March 19, 1849).
[4] Clode, *Military Forces of the Crown*, I, 15.

BEGINNING OF THE VICTORIAN AGE 47

The radical groups, moreover, possessed in this matter an ally outside Parliament whose influence was almost incalculable. It was just at this period that Emerson said of *The Times*, " No power in England is more felt, more feared, or more obeyed." This mighty engine now began to direct its thunder against the cost of colonial defence. In 1849 it was inclined on the whole to take sides against the radical critics ;[1] but in the course of the next year its opinions moved on ;[2] and by 1851 it was making brutal references to the pecuniary advantages accruing to colonial communities where troops were stationed. " It has often been calculated," it remarked in a leading article on the Kaffir war then in progress, " that Canada was enriched by her outbreak, and that the blood our soldiers shed was amply compensated by the money they circulated."[3] In this tone the leading journal of the British Empire continued to hammer at the question at intervals thereafter. In some of these devastatingly frank and bitter anti-colonial leading articles, it is perhaps more than merely fanciful to see the hand of Robert Lowe, that arch-Little Englander whose sour genius was during these years devoted to composition for *The Times*. Lowe had returned to England, after an unsuccessful political career in Australia, in 1850, and began to write leaders for the journal next year, at a date just previous to that of the one last quoted.[4] Those familiar with the acerbity of his views on colonial questions[5] may perceive his influence in the hostile attitude of *The Times* towards the overseas empire during the mid-Victorian era.

The fifth decade of the century was one of triumph for the economic theories of radicalism ; for it saw the ultimate acceptance in British commercial policy of the principles of *laissez-faire*. Peel's two free-trade budgets of 1842 and 1845 were followed in 1846 by that great victory of Manchester, the repeal of the Corn Laws ; and the removal by the Whigs in 1849 of the attenuated remnant of the Navigation Acts was a

---

[1] *The Times*, Feb. 27, 1849 ; cf. Jan. 19 and March 20.
[2] *Ibid.*, March 12, 1850.
[3] *Ibid.*, March 7, 1851. See Bell and Morrell, *Select Documents on British Colonial Policy, 1830–1860*, 519–21.
[4] Martin, A. P., *Life and Letters of . . . Robert Lowe Viscount Sherbrooke . . .*, London, 1893 : I, 401 ; II, 17, 23.
[5] See below, p. 125.

blowing of trumpets over the mangled corse of Protection. It was admitted that the transformation of England into a free-trading nation was due in no small measure to the educative agitation carried on by Cobden and his associates. More than ever, it was clear now that they were men to be reckoned with ; and their growing influence seemed to bode no good for the future of the colonial empire. Statesmen who did not share their indifference to the imperial tie realized the need of finding means of depriving their assaults upon the system of some of their force. We shall see this appearing very clearly during Lord Grey's tenure of the Colonial Office—in the apprehension with which both he and Elgin watch the actions of the Cobdenites, in Grey's constant fear of " economical " influences in the Commons, and very strikingly in his insistence upon a policy of frugality designed to forestall radical threats of retrenchment by more violent means.

Such apprehensions were the more natural as the advent of free trade had afforded the critics a new and powerful argument. The system which for two hundred years had obliged the British colonies to give special commercial advantages to the mother country was, at length, altogether a thing of the past. Henceforth the colonies were to be free to buy from, and sell to, whom they would, in any and all forms of commerce ; while their markets would be as open to the enterprise of foreign merchants as to that of those of the United Kingdom. Inevitably, this change was invoked as the best of reasons for Imperial economies. While the colonies had been forced to favour British trade, it was argued, it had been just, perhaps, to compensate them by defending them at British expense, but now that their commercial relationship to England was no different from that of foreign countries, commercially-minded politicians found it hard to justify saddling the British taxpayer with the cost of battalions in New South Wales or Canada West. One of many such was Robert Vernon Smith (afterwards Lord Lyveden), in whom the flame of imperial faith burned even more dimly than was usual in that age of doubt. The adoption of free trade, he said in 1849, had quite altered Britain's colonial relationships :

" We had given up the system of exclusive markets, and had no longer the interest we once had in extending our colonial interests.

BEGINNING OF THE VICTORIAN AGE 49

If, then, we had not the interest we once had, we had no longer any motive for extending to them further military protection, with certain exceptions. . . . He did not shrink from saying that whenever the colonies come into collision with us, either in interest or feeling, we must look forward to . . . a separation effected amicably. . . . He cautioned the House . . . against laying out money in military expenses, which could be of no avail when the day of separation came."[1]

Cobden himself declared that free trade had changed the whole system of colonial relationships—" and if it was folly before to garrison the Colonies, it was now downright insanity."[2] And it appears that the commercial argument was the decisive one in bringing *The Times* round to the radical point of view.[3]

Along with economic autonomy for the colonies came political autonomy, with the decision of Lord John Russell's government to instruct the Governors to accept in local matters the advice of colonial ministries possessing the confidence of the local legislatures. This was one more weapon, and a very formidable one, for the reformers' armoury. Canada, said Hume, now happily had responsible government; why, then, keep 7,000 troops there? And Molesworth remarked that " it seemed to him as absurd to pay for troops in the virtually independent colony of the Canadas, as it would be to pay for the military establishments in the independent colony of the United States."[4]

The great importance of the advent of responsible government as it affected this issue, however, was the fact that it afforded British ministers a line of reasoning which could be employed with the most complete propriety in urging the colonies to assume some of the burdens previously borne on their behalf by the mother country. It was not for Her Majesty's ministers to speak to the colonies in the huckstering tones which were possible for radical parliamentarians; it would have been undignified and impolitic for them to have stated bluntly to loyal colonists that Britain had defended them so long as she considered a monopoly of their trade essential

---

[1] *Hansard*, CIII, 1003-5 (March 19, 1849).
[2] *Ibid.*, CXV, 1440-41 (speech in support of Molesworth's motion, April 10, 1851).
[3] See its leading article of March 12, 1850.
[4] *Hansard*, CIII, 992, 1010 (March 19, 1849).

to her own material interest, but that monopolies having now been abandoned as unsound business, funds spent on colonial defence had become simply unproductive expenditure which must cease. Even when the star of imperialism was at its lowest, a British secretary of state would not have dared to deny that there were elements in the corporate life of the Empire other than those that could be represented upon a balance sheet in terms of pounds, shillings and pence. Certainly Lord Grey was not the man to take so narrow a view. But even Grey, a convinced imperialist, could without qualms present to the colonies the proposition that now, as a result of their own aspirations and the bounty of the motherland, they were the possessors of a new liberty; that the acquisition of new rights implied properly the assumption of new duties; and that the dignity of a free colonial community demanded of it a spirit of self-reliance which would not permit it to remain a burden upon the purse of a mother country which had renounced the right to interfere in its affairs.

To the task of convincing the colonies of the justice of this view, Grey now addressed himself; and the extent to which he and those who followed him might succeed in it was a matter of profound importance to the future of the Empire. In his day, we have seen, that whole future was clouded with a doubt. It was the day when Herman Merivale in his Oxford lectures dared only in a most apologetic fashion to advance the vision he had caught of a permanent union of British countries under the Crown—and felt obliged to recant in a second edition;[1] when Sir George Cornewall Lewis, putting sentiment from him, coldly weighed in the balance the material advantages and disadvantages of the imperial connexion, declared that it should be the concern of a dominant country to prepare its colonies for independence, and regretted that public opinion seemed as yet insufficiently enlightened to consent to such renunciations;[2] when pride in the colonial empire—which never became extinct[3]—was regarded by most of the exponents

---

[1] *Lectures on Colonization and Colonies.* See 1st ed., II, 292–93; and cf. 2nd ed., appendix to lecture XXII (p. 677).
[2] *Essay on the Government of Dependencies* (Ed. 1891), 233–34, 324. First published, 1841.
[3] An example of imperial enthusiasm contemporary with Merivale and Lewis is Martin's *History of the Colonies of the British Empire*: see p. v.

BEGINNING OF THE VICTORIAN AGE 51

of the new political economy as mere uninstructed enthusiasm which would yield in time to more advanced ideas. There were not many men who could, like Grey and Elgin, cut loose from the mercantilist economics of empire and at the same time retain a faith in the imperial ideal; imperialism and mercantilism had gone too long together.

If the unity of the Empire was ultimately to survive the prevalence of such views in the mother country, it could only be by virtue of a shift in the balance of imperial responsibilities commensurate with that which had taken place in the balance of imperial authority. It was necessary that it should be rendered impossible to represent to the people of England that while they had abdicated the supposed advantages of the old imperial connexion they nevertheless retained its burdens. So long as the colonial expenditures of Britain could be regarded as a material grievance to the British taxpayer, counterbalanced by no material advantage, so long would the foundations of imperial unity be insecure. This was clear by the middle of the nineteenth century, and British statesmen had already begun to grapple with the problem presented by the cost of the army in the colonies. Yet despite the manifold and weighty objections to it, the colonial garrison system as it then existed was destined to display a quite astonishing vitality. A full score of years were to elapse before it finally passed into limbo, leaving the way open for a new and freer imperial association.

CHAPTER III

PROBLEMS OF BRITISH MILITARY POLICY: COLONIAL RELIEFS AND HOME DEFENCE

> "With the exception of the few troops kept to defend and ornament the metropolis . . . the soldiers of England spent ten out of every fourteen or fifteen years in foreign climates, scattered a few hundreds together over the face of the earth; serving either amidst the snows of Canada or the pestilential exhalations of the two Indies; watching the convicts of Australasia, or guarding the rock-built fortresses of the Mediterranean; yet their discipline was admirable, and it was surprising how few complaints had been made of their conduct by a people with whom soldiers had never been popular."
> —SIR WILLIAM MOLESWORTH in Parliament, March 31, 1848.

WHILE English politicians complained of the expense of the colonial garrisons, English soldiers and military administrators found them a source of difficulty in other respects. In particular, they were plagued by the perennial problem of how to provide reliefs at decent intervals for the regiments on "foreign service," which could not be left abroad indefinitely.

The British Army's strength was small in proportion to its responsibilities; it was heavily taxed merely by the routine duties of its many stations, yet in addition it was frequently called upon for troops to deal with sudden emergencies which might arise in any part of the world. Under these conditions it was hard for the War Office, with the best of intentions, to reduce each regiment's share of foreign service to the amount which efficiency and humanity alike required; and men joining the army were compelled to spend the best years of their lives in exile, often in unhealthy climates. In 1834 the member of the Government who introduced the Army Estimates declared that "the English service was more severe, in times of peace, on account of our colonies, than that of any other European country in time of war."[1]

Humanitarian considerations—which acquired more and more prestige as the century wore on—dictated that even so

---

[1] *Hansard*, XXI, 974 (speech of Ellice, Feb. 28, 1834).

PROBLEMS OF BRITISH MILITARY POLICY 53

despised a class as the men who fought the Empire's battles deserved moderately decent treatment. And those inaccessible to such motives might be reached through the practical fact that if the conditions of the soldier's life were allowed to remain *too* hard, it was going to be increasingly difficult to fill the ranks. In the prosperity of Victorian England, there was some economic opportunity for the humblest; and the prospect of banishment on starvation wages was not likely to tempt her citizens to take the shilling. The danger was clear to the Secretary at War in 1848 : nothing, he said, so tended to render the service unpopular as " the extremely long periods for which regiments had been sent abroad, some to bad and some to better climes, but all in the condition of expatriation for fifteen, twenty, and even twenty-five years."[1] Such conditions could be alleviated in only two ways : either by increasing the army, so as to diminish the time each regiment had to spend on foreign service, or by reducing the number of garrisons abroad.

The question engaged the attention of the War Office at frequent intervals. In 1825 Lord Palmerston asked Parliament to increase the army by nearly 9,000 rank and file, purely for the purpose of providing better means of relieving troops on foreign service and generally protecting the outlying possessions of the Empire. He used the increase to augment the infantry regiments from eight companies to ten, of which in the case of regiments on foreign service four were to remain at home as a *dépôt*, available for replacing casualties and relieving officers and men invalided from abroad.[2] Two years later the Duke of Wellington, newly appointed Commander-in-Chief, found himself confronted with a proposal for a reduction of the army ; and he met it with a memorandum to the Prime Minister which dwelt at length on the problem of reliefs.[3]

There were in the army, he pointed out, 110 battalions of foot, including the Guards. Of these only 40 were stationed in Great Britain and Ireland ;[4] 20 were in India ; and the

---

[1] *Hansard*, XCVII, 1156 (speech of Fox Maule, March 31, 1848).
[2] *Ibid.*, new series, XII, 925 ff. Cf. Fortescue, *History of the British Army*, XI, 87–88.
[3] *Despatches, Correspondence, and Memoranda of . . . Arthur Duke of Wellington . . .*, IV, 106–18. Aug. 4, 1827.
[4] Even this number included nine temporarily stationed in Portugal.

remaining 50 were on other foreign stations. The difficulty of providing proper relief appeared in its most extreme form in the case of the battalions in India. "One of these," wrote the Duke, "has been twenty-two years in that country, three twenty-one years, three more twenty years, one fourteen years, and one ten years." At any given time, he observed, the proportion of the army absorbed by the service of distant stations was not merely the number of battalions required to garrison the several posts, but included also a number of units rendered for the moment ineffective, either because they were at sea on their way to or from foreign stations, or because they had but recently returned home and were engaged in recruiting and reorganizing. Allowing two years as the period required for the relief of a regiment in the East (from the date at which the relieving unit sailed from home to that at which the relieved one would have returned to England, been completed with men, and made fit for home service again),[1] and one year for reliefs on other stations, Wellington calculated that to relieve the 70 battalions abroad, each after ten years, meant that at all times nine battalions would be in transit or in, at best, a low state of efficiency. The force available in Great Britain, he showed, was barely equal to supplying these reliefs and garrisoning the points in the island whose occupation was indispensable, without affording any reserve whatever for emergencies; and the occurrence of the latter usually meant, in consequence, a cessation in the relief of troops abroad.

The Duke's natural conclusion was that the infantry of the army could not safely be reduced:

". . . Upon every occasion on which an attempt has been made since the year 1817 to reduce the force, a necessity has been found to exist immediately for augmenting it again at a large expense. . . .

"The reason is obvious. The empire is immense, and includes nearly every important post in the world, whether naval, military, or commercial. None of these posts are occupied even for defence, much less to be able to assist each other, even if they were within distance. Every service must be provided for in, and proceed from, Great Britain, and it is astonishing that we should be able to maintain seventy battalions on foreign service generally within the tropics, and twenty-eight (including twenty depots) in Ireland, with the small number that we have in Great Britain."

---

[1] The regiments in India had no *dépôts* in England.

The Canadian rebellion, followed by troubles in India and China, upset the whole routine of reliefs, just as Wellington had said would necessarily happen in such cases; and Sir Henry (afterwards Viscount) Hardinge, during his term as Secretary at War from 1841 to 1844, devoted himself to an attempt at improving the situation. He reminded Parliament that, although the principle that ten years' service abroad should be followed by five years at home had been laid down by Lord Liverpool's government years before, nevertheless there were still regiments in India that had been there more than twenty years, and that in all, in 1842, there were 32 or 33 regiments which had been abroad without relief for more than the ten-year period. Hardinge tried to alleviate the situation by making increased use of "colonial corps" paid by Britain but permanently localized in certain colonies and so requiring no relief, and by converting first six and finally nine of the *dépôts* at home into second battalions of their regiments and sending them abroad as reliefs. In 1844 he was able to boast that, though the Indian situation was still unsatisfactory, "there was not at present in the Colonies a single battalion which had been more than ten years abroad," and that there were now 36 battalions at home, whereas in 1842 there had been only 24.[1]

The need of keeping up a considerable force at home for no other reason than that it was necessary for the regular relief of the regiments overseas was of course used by ministers as a defence against the radicals' attacks on the size of the army. A notable example of this line of argument was that famous budget statement made by Peel on February 14, 1845,[2] which was one of the chief milestones marking the advance of free trade. In it he took occasion to glance at the military situation of the colonies, and pointed out that whereas in 1792 Britain had possessed only 22 dependencies, by 1820 the number had risen to 34 and by 1845 to 45. Noticing the anti-imperialist position, he rejected it (though not perhaps in terms of the strongest conviction). The forty-five colonies had to be

[1] For Hardinge's work, see his speeches on introducing the Army Estimates in *Hansard*, LXI, 155 ff. (March 7, 1842); LXVI, 1359 ff. (Feb. 27, 1843); LXXIII, 547 ff. (March 4, 1844). The force kept up at home, he said on the last occasion, "was not for the sake of maintaining a Standing Army, but to afford relief".
[2] *Hansard*, LXXVII, 455–97.

defended; and the infantry force available for this purpose (and all others) was 112 battalions of the line, plus the Guards. He reminded the House that the force maintained had in practice not proved sufficient to provide reliefs on the basis of giving the soldier one-third of his time at home, and observed that under these circumstances it seemed hopeless to think of reducing it.

" When I look to the system of relief . . . I am bound to say," he declared, " that I do not think it would be consistent with sound policy, or with economy, to propose—while you retain your vast Colonial empire—a reduction in the military establishments of the country." No franker statement of the relation between the extent of the British Empire and the strength of the British Army was ever made. The same attitude was taken by Peel's Whig successors. Fox Maule in 1848 informed the Commons that when regiments then on the way home from India arrived, there would not be a single regiment which had been on foreign service more than twelve years; but he reminded honourable members that the efficiency of the relief arrangements would be destroyed by any reduction of the army.[1]

The radicals were not slow to reverse this ministerial argument. If the colonial garrisons were the obstacle to reduction of the military forces, they said, then the obvious course was to do away with the garrisons. As Cobden put it:

" It has been shown that only one-third of our troops are permanently employed in this country, while two-thirds are maintained for the colonies. That is a system which requires a total change, and if you do change it you can no longer have any difficulty in making the reduction I call for."[2]

Both he and Molesworth[3] quoted the Peel statement, designed as an argument against any diminution of the force on foot, to prove that in fact such action was quite possible if the colonial military arrangements were reformed on the lines which they suggested.

To provide for the defence of the overseas empire was, and

[1] *Hansard*, XCVII, 1149 ff. (March 31, 1848).
[2] *Ibid.*, CII, 1218 ff. (Feb. 26, 1849).
[3] Cobden in the speech just cited; Molesworth on April 10, 1851 (*ibid.*, CXV, 1366).

is, only one side of the work of the British Army. It has also to secure the imperial metropolis against the possible hostility of European neighbours; and during the period of which we treat its preparedness for this service became a matter of increasing public concern.

In that tangled skein which is the history of Victorian Britain, there are few threads more interesting to trace than that of her reaction to the military activity of continental Europe during the era of national wars ending with the substantial establishment of the state system which endured well into the present century. Except in the case of the Crimean War, England's part in the successive European struggles of those crowded years was that merely of a bystander; but the bystander was shaken by repeated spasms of apprehension for her own safety, which, it seemed, might at any moment be seriously menaced by a turn of the continental kaleidoscope.

These fears were strongest during the existence of the Second Empire in France; but they had in fact begun before the rise of Louis Napoleon. This is not the place to chronicle at length the diplomatic relations of France and Britain. It is sufficient to recall that a gradual estrangement between the two countries came to a head in 1840–41, over the question of the status of Mehemet Ali, Pasha of Egypt. Britain held that his power should be restricted, and joined with Russia, Prussia and Austria in an agreement to protect the Sultan of Turkey against this rebellious vassal, leaving France, who had espoused his cause, completely isolated. War seemed probable; but the matter was smoothed over by the " Convention of the Straits " which received France back into the European concert by making her a party to the final settlement. The Anglo-French friendship was said to be completely restored, but the crisis left unpleasant memories behind it.[1]

The so-called *entente cordiale* was seriously strained in 1844 by the Tahiti incident, arising out of alleged outrages by the French against George Pritchard, the British missionary-consul. The war-spectre had arisen again before this matter was settled.[2] In the course of the crisis the Prince de Joinville, a son of King Louis Philippe and an officer in his navy, had

[1] See *Cambridge History of British Foreign Policy*, II, 170–82.
[2] *Ibid.*, 182–85; Walpole, *History of England from 1815*, IV, 502 ff.

published in the *Revue des Deux Mondes*[1] a striking paper comparing the French fleet unfavourably with that of Britain and demanding reform. This attracted much attention;[2] and Cobden in his trenchant pacifist pamphlet *The Three Panics*[3] (one of the most interesting accounts of the British attitude towards France during this period) expresses his belief that it prepared the way for the first great bout of fear which afflicted English minds in these troubled years. In 1846, finally, the *entente* was suddenly ended by the double Spanish marriage which simultaneously united the Queen of Spain to the Duke of Cadiz and the Infanta to another son of Louis Philippe, the Duc de Montpensier. This action, which raised the possibility of a French prince becoming King of Spain, was claimed by the British to be contrary to an Anglo-French agreement that the Infanta's marriage should not take place until the Queen had married and had children; and this "breach of faith" left Englishmen deeply suspicious of France.[4]

In these circumstances, those directing British policy began to examine the country's military resources. The Duke of Wellington, as Commander-in-Chief, was painfully aware of the smallness of the force available to defend the British Isles in the event of war.[5] In December, 1846, he pointed out to the new Whig government that while there were 101,200 infantry on the rolls of the army, only 39,605 were available at home; 2,160 were under embarkation orders, and 59,435 actually on foreign service. His deduction was that a further increase of the army (already augmented that year) was necessary if the country was to be considered safe.[6] The warning did not fall on inattentive ears. Earl Grey, Secretary of State for War and the Colonies, had himself written a paper, on the previous October 17, arguing that more attention should be paid to the

---

[1] Vol. VI (new series): issue of 14 Mai, 1844. *Notes sur l'état des forces navales de la France.*

[2] The *Revue* in its subsequent issue of June 30 remarked, "L'émotion produite en Europe par la Note sur l'état des forces navales de la France n'est pas apaisée encore."

[3] 1862: reprinted in his *Political Writings*.

[4] For this complicated matter, see *Cambridge History of British Foreign Policy*, II, 185–98; Walpole, IV, 515–28.

[5] On his anxiety from 1844, see Parker, *Sir Robert Peel from his Private Papers*, III, chap. VII.

[6] Wellington to Grey, Dec. 12, 1846: Public Record Office, W.O., 1/598. See Knaplund, "E. G. Wakefield on the Colonial Garrisons, 1851," *C.H.R.*, V.

PROBLEMS OF BRITISH MILITARY POLICY 59

force at home, and advising large reductions in the colonial garrisons. He suggested that the advent of steam communication made it England's wisest policy to defend her empire by maintaining a large reserve at home, whence it could readily be moved to any threatened point.[1] He now answered the old Duke by pointing out that the Treasury had lately been insistently urging economy upon the departments, and that an increase in the army was thus impossible; but he promised to effect the desired result by reducing the force abroad.[2] We shall soon see the attempts he made in this direction.[3]

About the same time, Sir John Burgoyne, the Inspector General of Fortifications, submitted to the Master General of the Ordnance certain *Observations on the Possible Results of a War with France, under our Present System of Military Preparations*;[4] and this led Lord Palmerston to address to his colleagues in the Government a *Report on the Defence of the Country*[5] which declared that the British Empire existed only on the sufferance of other nations. Burgoyne's paper, however, was destined to have wider repercussions. He sent a copy of it to Wellington; and the Duke returned a lengthy acknowledgment stating in strong terms his conviction of the defencelessness of England. This communication (which Wellington certainly considered confidential) was given wide private circulation without his knowledge; and at the beginning of 1848 it reached the newspapers.[6] Everyone in England now knew that her greatest soldier thought the country criminally unprepared against the perils of the time; the Press echoed his apprehensions;[7] and panic ensued.

When Parliament met the matter was taken up at once. Lord John Russell stated his intention, despite the existing

---

[1] Biddulph, *Lord Cardwell at the War Office*, 39.
[2] Grey to Wellington, Dec. 21, 1846: W.O., 1/598; Knaplund, as above.
[3] See chapter IV, below.
[4] Published in Wrottesley, G. (ed.), *The Military Opinions of General Sir John Fox Burgoyne*, 1–23.
[5] Published in Wrottesley, G., *Life and Correspondence of Field Marshal Sir John Burgoyne, Bart.*, I, 436–44.
[6] Maxwell, *Life of Wellington*, II, 365. The whole transaction is fully described in Wrottesley, *Life of Burgoyne*, I, 444 ff., where Wellington's letter is reprinted. The letter can also be found in the *Spectator* of Jan. 8, 1848, which copied it from the *Morning Chronicle* of Jan. 4, where it had first appeared.
[7] See, e.g., *Spectator*, Jan. 15, 1848, and Molesworth's protest in the next number.

commercial depression and the decreased revenue, of renewing the income tax at an increased rate, in order to improve the fighting forces.[1] This was a bitter pill; the Manchester men raged against these warlike preparations. Then, while the Government's plans were still being discussed, came news of revolution from France: and Louis Philippe and his most eminent supporters (Joinville among them) appeared seeking asylum in England. This enabled the Government to abandon its expensive programme; and the panic of 1848 came to an end.[2]

However, it was only the first of a series which was to last for a quarter of a century; and the second was not far behind. On December 2, 1851, Louis Napoleon effected in Paris the *coup d'état* which destroyed the Second Republic. Britain regarded this event with deep apprehension. *The Times* was soon warning her that:

"When Louis Napoleon has accomplished his mission of 'tranquillizing France', two necessities will press upon him—to employ the energy and reward the devotion of an enormous army, and to gratify the national passions of a people whom he has deprived of its national rights."[3]

Other journals went even further;[4] and although alarmist statements were reprobated by the leaders of both parties in Parliament, Russell nevertheless introduced a new Militia Bill. His government succumbed to an attack upon this measure by Palmerston (lately dropped from the ministry for his too-hasty recognition of the new *régime* in France and desirous of a "tit for tat with John Russell"), but the incoming Derby cabinet promptly introduced another Bill permitting the raising of 80,000 men; and the versatile Pam supported it energetically.

The argument for this Bill turned upon the smallness of the force available for the defence of England. The Home Secretary

---

[1] *Hansard*, XCVI, 921 (Feb. 18, 1848).
[2] On these episodes, see Cobden, *The Three Panics*; Wrottesley, *Life of Burgoyne*, I, 474–82; Walpole, *History of England from 1815*, IV, 338–42. It is worth recalling that domestic causes added to British anxieties in 1848; that summer Irish discontent actually led to rebellion. On the dangers inherent in the possible combination of foreign war and Irish insurrection, see Grey to Elgin, Aug. 10 (G.E.C.).
[3] *The Times*, Dec. 12, 1851.
[4] e.g., *Spectator*, Dec. 6, 1851.

assured the House of Commons that even if all available men were withdrawn " from the manufacturing districts, from the central depots, from the metropolis itself, from most of your fortified arsenals," still it would not be possible to bring to bear upon any one point twenty-five thousand men; and the reason was simply the diffusion of strength resulting from the extent of the Empire:

" The very greatness of your Empire . . . is, in one sense of the word, a source of weakness; for no question can there be that the extent of it multiplies the opportunities and means of attack, while it diminishes, at the same time, the means of defence."[1]

Again the radicals seized the opportunity presented by the Government's use of this argument; Cobden made it the occasion of one of his most vigorous utterances on the subject:

" Has it never occurred to the right hon. Gentlemen . . . that the taxation to maintain the vast police forces by sea and land for this enormous territory is paid altogether by the people of these little specks of islands, Great Britain and Ireland? We draw no revenue from Australia, from Canada, or from the Cape of Good Hope; and let hon. gentlemen opposite be quite sure that, a few months hence . . . the Members . . . will be inquiring . . . whether free trade is not to be carried out to its logical consequences in regard to such a country as Canada with its 2,000,000 of inhabitants, whose average condition economically speaking is superior to that of our own people, with a more absolute self-government than is enjoyed by any of the States of the neighbouring federation—with a perfect control over its own waste lands, and which actually put a prohibitive duty upon your paupers from Ireland, diverting your emigration in one year to New York? . . . I say, make your colonies, from which you get no revenue, protect themselves, and then you will no longer have the argument in favour of such a proposal as this, that your Army—your Army of 100,000 men—is scattered."[2]

Hume and Bright spoke in much the same sense. The Bill, however, duly passed.[3]

On September 14, 1852, the Duke of Wellington died; and this event, recalling as it did the long agony of 1793-1815, intensified the panic feeling. Only three days separated the

[1] *Hansard*, CXX, 270-71 (speech of Spencer Walpole, March 29, 1852).
[2] *Ibid.*, 308-09.
[3] Walpole, *History of England from 1815*, V, 39-41.

Duke's funeral from the plebiscite which approved the institution of the Second Empire in France; and Englishmen shivered, for a Bonaparte reigned again as Emperor in the Tuileries. " People began again to talk of invasion, and before Christmas the alarmists had more complete possession of the field than at any previous time."[1] Cobden's attempts at checking the hysteria led to immoderate attacks upon himself.[2] An echo of this controversy, in which the radical pacifists fought in vain against the apprehensions that were sweeping the nation into ever greater armament expenditures, comes to us across the years in Tennyson's *Maud* :[3]

> " Last week came one to the county town,
> To preach our poor little army down,
> And play the game of the despot kings,
> Though the state has done it and thrice as well :
> This broad-brimmed hawker of holy things,
> Whose ear is crammed with his cotton, and rings
> Even in dreams to the chink of his pence,
> This huckster put down war ! Can he tell
> Whether war be a cause or a consequence ? "

In one respect England was already rejecting the doctrines of Manchester. She refused to embrace the policy of unilateral disarmament which bulked so large among them; on the contrary, from this time we find the size of her establishments, and her expenditure upon them, steadily increasing under the pressure of conditions abroad. Cobden and his colleagues might regretfully recall the days when Englishmen distrusted standing armies and relied upon a " constitutional force " of half-trained militia; but England in 1852 stood on the brink of a maelstrom created by the clash of nationalities on the continent nearby, from which she could not divorce herself. The nations of Europe were passing into the modern era of competitive armaments, and she was drawn in their wake.

She was, in fact, entering a period in which the most pressing problem of imperial military policy was not to be the defence of distant colonies, but that of her own shores against her heavily-armed continental neighbours, whose intentions so

---

[1] *The Three Panics.*
[2] e.g., *Spectator*, Feb. 12, 1853.
[3] This passage was regarded as an attack on Bright, but Tennyson, in his notes, writes, " I did not even know at the time that he was a Quaker."

often seemed dubious. Henceforth she was to be more acutely conscious than ever of the difficult dualism of her position as being both a European state, threatened by the contingencies of continental politics, and an imperial power burdened with distant obligations involving a perilous diffusion of her strength. Repeated alarms forced on the attention of Englishmen the fact that only a small proportion of the army which they paid was really available to defend their homes; and it was clear that increased security for England could be obtained only by augmenting the already considerable burden borne by the taxpayer for military purposes, or by finding means to bring home a large number of the troops stationed in the colonies. The constant pressure exerted by the continental situation can never be forgotten in considering the colonial military problems of Britain as they presented themselves during that troubled age.

CHAPTER IV

CANADA UNDER RESPONSIBLE GOVERNMENT: THE MILITARY
QUESTION DURING ELGIN'S ADMINISTRATION

" If I were vindictive, which I trust I am not, I could imagine no greater curse for my worst enemy than to be Sec. of State for Colonies or Gov. of Canada in these times."
—ELGIN to GREY, December 19, 1849.

WITH the advent of Lord Grey as Colonial Secretary in 1846, a new phase of imperial history begins; and new problems arise as mother country and colonies apply themselves to the task of working out the practical implications of colonial responsible government. The new polity was inaugurated in the colonies in the right English way; its basis was nothing more formal than a letter of instruction from the Colonial Office to a Governor. In North America, at least, it was not the result of Act of Parliament; and above all, it was accompanied by no formal attempt whatever at explicit definition of the respective rights and duties of Great Britain on one side and the colonies on the other under the new arrangements. *Solvitur ambulando*: it was for those who put colonial autonomy into practice to reach, on these matters, such understandings as they could.

Grey himself, however, was not without definite views on the proper nature of the new relationship. He was both an imperialist and a strong free-trader. He believed it to be the duty of the Whigs to clear away the last relics of commercial monopoly from the colonial system, and believed moreover that the abolition of monopoly made it possible and desirable to put an end, almost entirely, to imperial interference in the internal affairs of the most advanced colonies. The first object was attained during his administration by sweeping away most of the remains of the preferential system, and repealing the Navigation Acts; the second, of course, by the concession of responsible government. This was not all. It was another cardinal point in Grey's belief,

" that when this Country no longer attempts either to levy a commercial tribute from the Colonies by a system of restriction, nor to interfere needlessly in their internal affairs, it has a right to expect that they should take upon themselves a larger proportion than heretofore of the expenses incurred for their advantage."[1]

As has already been demonstrated,[2] the cost of the garrisons overshadowed all other items of Imperial expenditure in the colonies; and Grey desired to reduce the proportion of the army serving in the colonies, not only because the anti-imperialists (as he knew well)[3] were making this expense an argument for abandoning the colonies altogether, but because of the threatening continental situation. He was charged with responsibility for both the War and Colonial Offices; and it was difficult to see how he could defend England against continental enemies with an army, not only much smaller than theirs to begin with, but which could muster considerably less than half its strength for the defence of the United Kingdom. We have already seen that in October, 1846, he wrote a memorandum urging the strengthening of the force at home at the expense of the colonial garrisons, and that he met Wellington's apprehensions for England with the same proposal.[4] This was even before the steps had been taken which were to mark the advent of responsible government in the North American colonies.[5] There are no grounds for saying that Grey granted responsible government to the colonies merely because he hoped that to do so would relieve the mother country of expense and set free additional troops to defend her shores; but there is no doubt whatever that in his mind the two things went together, and that he envisaged the assumption of larger responsibilities by the colonies as an important result of the concession.[6]

[1] Grey, *The Colonial Policy of Lord John Russell's Administration*, I, 18. The opening pages of this book (Grey's apologia for his much-abused administration) are an exposition of his general colonial theory.
[2] See above, pp. 42–3.
[3] *Colonial Policy of Russell's Administration*, I, 10.
[4] See above, pp. 58–9.
[5] The chief landmark in this respect is Grey's dispatch to Harvey in Nova Scotia, of Nov. 3, 1846.
[6] In justice to Conservative colonial policy, it is proper to remark that it was consistent, in that, while less friendly to autonomy than that of the

Finally, it is worth while to remember, in assessing the motives of Grey's policy, that the Whig ministry lacked a majority in the House of Commons. In these circumstances the radicals were an element of some importance in the party balance, which it was desirable to conciliate ; and to this group no cause was dearer than colonial retrenchment.

One of the Whigs' earliest acts with respect to Canada was in fact to take steps for a reduction of the military force there. They came into power at the end of June, 1846, at the same moment that the Oregon controversy was settled at last ; and on August 1 a private dispatch[1] went to Lord Cathcart, asking his opinion whether " in the altered state of our relations with the United States " it might not be expedient to withdraw two or more battalions and reduce the number of outlying detachments. Cathcart discouraged the proposal ;[2] but the Government persevered, and in the course of the next year the establishment of infantry of the line in Canada was cut from ten battalions to eight—that is, from 5,400 rank and file to 4,320.[3]

There was one part of the Empire where Grey was convinced there could be no logical argument against drastic reduction ; and there he put his doctrines into rapid and vigorous execution. This was Australia—which had no formidable native tribes to contend with, and no powerful foreign neighbours. The month after composing his memorandum on the colonial garrisons, he informed the Governor of New South Wales that Maori troubles necessitated reinforcing New Zealand, and instructed him to

incoming Whigs, on the other hand it seems definitely to have accepted a higher degree of defensive obligation towards the colony on the part of the mother country than was agreeable to Grey. This appears in the matter of fortifications. On Sept. 16, 1845, Stanley informed Metcalfe that of the three forms of precaution required in Canada—fortifications, the preparation of a naval force, and the provision of an efficient militia—the two first were the province of the mother country (G, 122, pp. 99–116 : confidential). When Grey came to the Colonial Office, and discovered that the Conservatives had had in hand a considerable programme of colonial fortifications, he ordered the stoppage of all projects on which work had not actually begun, on the principle that " the fortifications to be paid for by this country ought to be confined entirely to those which are required . . . for purposes interesting to the whole empire " (Evidence before Select Committee on Army and Ordnance Expenditure : P.P., 1849, vol. IX, no. 499, ans. 7281). No further fortification projects were undertaken in Canada until the later stages of the American Civil War.

[1] C, 35, pp. 250–56.   [2] Draft of reply on back of the dispatch.
[3] P.P., 1850, no. 662, vol. X : appendix 10. This was in addition to the Royal Canadian Rifles.

send thither the whole force easily disposable in the colony.[1] At the same time he made it clear that, while Britain would provide protection against foreign attack, the maintenance of internal order in the colonies was henceforth no duty for Imperial troops, and that the colonists would have to supply police or other forces for that purpose, to replace the regulars, whose numbers would in future be greatly reduced. A considerable correspondence took place without Grey receding an inch from this position. When New South Wales argued that Sydney had as good a right to be fortified at English expense as Halifax or Quebec, he replied that the latter were far more exposed; if Sydney was to have forts the local legislature would have to pay for them. In 1849 he gave notice that thereafter the cost of providing quarters for Imperial troops in New South Wales would have to be met by the colony. The only force to remain there was to be a detachment at the capital, while Melbourne, the capital of the new province of Victoria, was to have a similar one. If the Australians desired to retain a larger force, they would be expected to provide the pay and allowances of the additional men.[2]

This seems clear evidence of what Grey and his colleagues considered the proper attitude towards colonial defence; and had they felt free to do so they would certainly have acted similarly towards all the larger colonies. But Maori troubles in New Zealand and Kaffir troubles at the Cape tied their hands; while in North America special conditions created by the new British commercial policy and by the proximity of the United States, and vigorously presented in the letters of the very able Governor-General whom Grey had appointed, prevented action for some years, in spite of the anxiety of the head of the Colonial Office to effect additional economies. The absorbingly interesting private correspondence of Grey and Elgin, now preserved at Ottawa, affords us full information on the state of the question there.

[1] Grey to Fitzroy, Nov. 24, 1846: *Colonial Policy of Russell's Administration*, I, 353. The Australian colonies had not yet received responsible government, which in fact was not introduced there until some years after Grey left the Colonial Office.

[2] Grey to Fitzroy, several dispatches, 1846–50 : *ibid.*, I, appendix B. Also in *P.P.*, 1861, no. 423, vol. XIII. The dispatch of June 21, 1850, on the fortification question, is in Bell and Morrell, *Select Documents on British Colonial Policy*, 129–30.

When Elgin[1] arrived in Canada, early in 1847, to inaugurate the new *régime*, he found the colony passing through a ruinous commercial crisis which seemed directly attributable to imperial legislation. In 1843 the Canada Corn Act had given Canadian wheat and flour a great advantage in the home market, and in consequence all available Canadian capital had been attracted to the businesses of wheat farming, milling and forwarding. Then, in 1846, there came, with terrible suddenness, the repeal of the Corn Laws, involving the loss of the preference and the ruin of the trade. On one side, Canada faced disaster as a result of the Imperial Parliament's shifting policy; on the other, it was represented to her that the United States, free from such influences, was as prosperous as ever. It was a dangerous moment for the British connexion, and economic distress combined with political discontent presented to Elgin a task that would have daunted a lesser man.

These circumstances, however, did not prevent Grey from raising the question of military expenditure almost immediately. A complaint from Elgin that the expenses of his position were a heavy drain upon his purse brought from the British Government the opinion that while it was certainly desirable that the imperial treasury should take over from the province the responsibility for paying the Governor's salary, in order to raise it to a sum better befitting the dignity of his office, nevertheless it was not possible for it to do so unless the province at the same time relieved the mother country of part of the cost of its defence.[2] And in the spring of 1848 a dispute over the expenses incurred in relieving the destitute and fever-stricken Irish, fleeing from the famine, who had flowed into the colony in the previous summer, led Grey to declare :

" I confess I think that now the Canadians have self Govmt. so completely granted to them they ought also to pay all its expenses including military protection, the only exception being the Governor

---

[1] There are a number of lives of Elgin, of which Morison, *The Eighth Earl of Elgin*, is the best for present purposes. Walrond, *Letters and Journals of James, Eighth Earl of Elgin*, is very useful. There are excellent estimates of Elgin's work in Canada in Morison, *British Supremacy and Canadian Self-Government*, and in Martin, *Empire and Commonwealth*.

[2] Grey to Elgin, Sept. 30 and Nov. 18, 1847: *G.E.C.* References, not otherwise particularized, to communications passing between Grey and Elgin, are from this correspondence. As it is arranged chronologically, page references are not given.

General's salary wh. for many reasons shd be charged upon this Country (if we were relieved from the other expenses of the Colony) . . ."¹

To Elgin, labouring to lay in Canada the foundations of a state devoted alike to the British system of constitutional government and to permanent connexion with Britain, these ideas seemed just one more peril added to the many which his conception had to encounter; and to Grey, whom he respected and trusted, he did not hesitate to speak plainly. " I cannot conceal from you," he wrote, " that I consider the line of argument which you adopt . . . a dangerous one in the present temper of men's minds."² A colony whose frontiers marched with those of a powerful and prosperous republic could not be handled without gloves. If Britain chose to make the conditions of British connexion burdensome to Canada, the colony was by no means forced to accept them—there was always an alternative ready to hand:

" In this respect the position of Canada is peculiar. When you say to any other Colony ' England declines to be longer at the expense of protecting you ' you at once reveal to it the extent of its dependence and the value of Imperial support. But it is not so here. Withdraw yr. protection from Canada, and she has it in her power to obtain the security against aggression enjoyed by Michigan or Maine—about as good security I must allow, as any which is to be obtained at the present time."³

And yet it was against the United States, and the United States alone, that Canada under the existing conditions required defence.

Elgin was quite prepared to admit that " very weighty reasons " could be adduced in favour of requiring the colony to pay part of the cost of defending it :

" I am . . . of opinion that the system of relieving the Colonists altogether from the duty of self defence is attended with injurious effects upon themselves. It checks the growth of national and manly morals. Men seldom think anything worth preserving for which they are never asked to make a sacrifice.

" My view, therefore, would be that it is desirable that a move-

---
¹ Grey to Elgin, March 22, 1848.
² Elgin to Grey, March 2, 1848. A whole succession of letters deal with these matters and there is considerable repetition.
³ Elgin to Grey, April 26, 1848. Quoted in Walrond, 130-32.

ment in the direction which you have indicated should take place, but that it ought to be made with much caution.

"The present is not a favorable moment for experiments. British Statesmen, even Secretaries of State, have got into the habit lately of talking of the maintenance of the connexion between Great Britain and Canada with so much indifference, that a change of system in respect of military defence incautiously carried out might be presumed by many to argue on the part of the Mother Country, a disposition to prepare the way for separation."[1]

Moreover, despite the fact that a period of calm in Canadian politics had followed Elgin's prompt acceptance as ministers of the leaders of the reforming party when that party defeated the previous ministry at the polls, there were endless possibilities of trouble latent in the circumstances of the time. A revolution was in progress in France, and Ireland was threatening rebellion; and it was almost too much to hope that these events would not have echoes among Canadian radicals of French and Irish stock.[2] And still more of Elgin's worries emanated from the United States.

That country had just emerged victorious from the Mexican War, and was reported to be in a highly aggressive mood.[3] The American Irish, represented by an organization called the Irish Republican Union, were active in attempting to foment discontent in Canada, while at the same time talking invasion. Elgin was obliged to take actual military measures to combat this menace, and he showed his confidence in the influence of the sincere and liberal policy which he had pursued by authorizing the Commander of the Forces to take the whole regular garrison of Montreal to the frontier if need arose, leaving the Canadians themselves to maintain the peace of the city.[4] The presidential canvass, accompanied by the usual manifestations, which took place in the United States in the summer of 1848, added to the tension.[5] This was one of the very few occasions when military force played any considerable part in Elgin's scheme of things. In general, his prescription against internal disorders was self-government, granted in all frankness and honesty; and he realized that far the best means of averting

[1] *Ibid.* [2] *Ibid.*
[3] Elgin to Grey, March 27, Aug. 16, 1848.
[4] Elgin to Grey, July 18, 1848; cf. June 11, 1849. And see confidential dispatch, Elgin to Grey, Sept. 7, 1848: G, 461, pp. 280–84.
[5] Elgin to Grey, June 1, 1848.

UNDER RESPONSIBLE GOVERNMENT 71

foreign attack was to cultivate the friendship and respect of the United States.[1] But for a moment in 1848 he was almost a fire-eater :

" As to any aggressions from without I shall throw the responsibility of repelling them on Her Majesty's troops in the first instance. This is the service wh. we profess to render to our Colonists without charge to them. It is well that they should see this benefit resulting from the connexion and I shall be disappointed indeed if the military here do not give a very good acct. of all Yankee & Irish marauders notwithstanding the swagger of the cutthroats from Mexico."[2]

Certainly the situation of Canada, in 1848, was not so secure that sound policy could have been said to permit a reduction of the garrison. And unquestionably the feature of the situation which weighed most heavily on Elgin's mind was the economic difficulties of the colony. Summed up, his argument against Grey's proposed economies amounted to this : " I am pursuing in Canada a policy designed to build up a nation permanently devoted both to British connexion and to British parliamentary government. I believe that this can be done, if I have moderately good luck and am allowed a few years of peace in which my policy can take effect.[3] But in the meantime I am fighting against odds—the turbulent heritage of this colony ; hostility in the neighbouring country ; indifference in England, and its effect in Canada ; most of all, the fact that the country is in a state of commercial prostration attributed to the policy of the mother country. Under these circumstances, to threaten to withdraw the Imperial troops and force Canada to assume the burden of her own defence is to make my task just so much harder, and may very probably be the last straw which will ruin everything. If Britain believes the perpetuation of her connexion with this great colony to be desirable, she must be prepared to pay a price for it : and the price is the cost of the Canadian garrisons during this dangerous period of transition."

[1] See, e.g., Elgin to Grey, Aug. 16, 1850, on the friendly reception of two hundred visitors from Buffalo in Toronto.
[2] Elgin to Grey, Aug. 16, 1848.
[3] Elgin to Grey, Nov. 1, 1850 : " Whether we shall be able to carry on the war here long enough to allow the practises of Constitutional Govt. and the habits of mind which they engender to take root in the Provinces, may be doubtful. I hear that Mr. Cobden is writing to Gentlemen in America begging them to annex us as soon as possible, so perhaps he will not give us he necessary time."

Thanks to Elgin's incisive arguments, and to the fact that the Colonial Secretary, however frightened of the House of Commons, was ready to admit their force, Britain paid the price. Poor Grey was sorely harassed by the attacks which Manchester men and colonial reformers alike, not to speak of Tory diehards, directed against his policies ;[1] his situation, as " the great mark for every section of opposition,"[2] was not enviable. But his faith in the judgment of the great politician whom he had sent to govern Canada, and his own devotion to the imperial ideal, gave him strength to meet the storm. He met Elgin's first remonstrances with the assurance :

" About the Military protection of these Colonies I agree almost entirely with you, & in my letter to wh. you allude you will find that I took a distinction between what *ought* in reason to be the arrangement & what *can* be so. Practically I quite concur with you that all that is possible is to get the Colonies to *contribute* towards their own defence & that even this must be attempted very cautiously."[3]

Nevertheless, the continued agitation in the Commons forced him to broach the subject again and again in one form or another ; and Elgin continued to be cool to his proposals, including one for laying upon Canada the cost of barracks for the troops stationed there.[4]

The fact is that while Elgin was primarily aware of the circumstances in Canada which made the proposed economies a danger to the success of his own work, Grey was becoming more and more convinced that the growing resentment in England against the expense of the colonies constituted in itself a serious threat to the continued unity of the Empire, and that in the interests of that unity some concessions to the agitators were essential. In reporting a new representation from Cobden on the subject, he wrote to Elgin :

" To proceed indeed as Cobden and his friends wd. wish wd. be to abandon the greater part at all events of our Colonies wh. I am old-fashioned enough to believe wd. be a national misfortune, & what is more a misfortune to the civilized world but to avert this I am

---

[1] Cf. Morrell, *British Colonial Policy in the Age of Peel and Russell*, chap. XIX : " Lord Grey and the Colonial Reformers."
[2] Grey to Elgin, Dec. 13, 1849.
[3] Grey to Elgin, May 18, 1848. Cf. same to same, Dec. 29, 1848.
[4] Elgin to Grey, Dec. 6, 1848.

UNDER RESPONSIBLE GOVERNMENT 73

sure it is necessary to adopt the policy of cautiously proceeding to throw more of the Military expenditure upon the Colonies."¹

In consequence of this conviction, during 1849 a number of minor measures were taken to reduce the cost of the Canadian military establishment. The last of the local forces raised after the rebellion were disbanded, despite protests from both Elgin and the military authorities in Canada.² A small saving in the cost of the staff was effected when the office of Commander of the Forces in British North America was abolished and the North American command divided into two—Canada forming one section and the Maritime Provinces the other.³ Lack of barrack accommodation at Montreal—and the fact that the Colonial Secretary feared to approach the Commons with a supplemental estimate for £12,000 to provide it⁴—led to a decision to withdraw a battalion thence, unless the local government cared to supply quarters; and as (in view of the recent serious rioting in that city on the occasion of the Rebellion Losses Bill crisis) the local government was anxious for the troops to remain, Elgin prevailed upon them to meet the cost. But he warned Grey against considering this a precedent for future action.⁵ Finally, when Elgin was obliged to send a detachment of regulars to Mica Bay (on Lake Superior) where a party of Indians had raided one of the mining establishments lately set up there,⁶ Grey seized the opportunity to insist that the expense of thus dispatching troops to aid the civil power should be met by the province. When some members of the Canadian Parliament "made a row" about this, Elgin sent to the Legislature, along with the dispatch directly involved, an extract from one of Grey's confidential dispatches pointing out the clear duty of the colony to provide for its own internal police; and this, he thought, "did good."⁷

---

¹ Grey to Elgin, Aug. 22, 1849. Cf. same to same, Jan. 10, 1850.
² Grey to Elgin (confidential), Nov. 14, 1848; same to same, July 27, 1849; G, 451, pp. 399, 535. Elgin to Grey, Jan. 29, 1849.
³ Grey to Elgin, June 14, 1849; cf. Maule's evidence before the Select Committee on Army and Ordnance Expenditure (*P.P.*, 1850, no. 662, vol. X: p. 106). ⁴ Grey to Elgin, June 1, 1849.
⁵ C, 1281, p. 95: Rowan to FitzRoy Somerset, Oct. 31, 1849; cf. C, 523, p. 245. Elgin to Grey, Dec. 19, 1849; partially quoted in Walrond, 132. Grey's dispatch to Elgin, of June 20, 1849, on the intention to remove the battalion, is in G, 451, p. 522.
⁶ Elgin to Grey, Nov. 23, 1849: G, 461, p. 384; cf. C, 1305, p. 81.
⁷ Grey to Elgin, Jan. 4, 1850: G, 532, p. 6. Elgin to Grey, Sept. 27, 1850 (this letter is misplaced in the Grey-Elgin Correspondence; it is in

These were small matters; the great grievance—the cost of the regular garrison of Canada—remained untouched. For some time, however, Elgin had been evolving a policy which he thought might satisfy the " economists " in England without irritating the Canadians. We have already observed that the presence of the troops played no part in his plans for the government of Canada—he would simply have considered a *régime* requiring such support a hopeless failure; now the expedient which he proposed was simple—to reduce the lmperial force in the country, but not to require Canada to undertake any additional expenditure in consequence. This was his view as early as 1848:

> " I would not ask the legislature to vote money for militia, or the towns to keep up barracks, because I think you would lose more in moral than you would gain in physical force by making such proposals—at the present time. But I would quietly, and sans phrase, remove the troops altogether from some points—reduce them in others, and aim at the eventual substitution of a Major General's command for that of a Lt. General in Canada."[1]

Grey seemed a trifle surprised at Elgin's readiness to part with his battalions[2] (a readiness, it may be noted, which the military staff in Canada did not share).[3] He did not really close with the suggestion until the beginning of 1850, when he wrote to say that the time now seemed ripe for a reduction, but that he needed Elgin's support in convincing the Duke of Wellington of its expediency. Sending an official communication requesting advice on the subject, he remarked privately, " In answering this you may tell me that a much more moderate number of Troops concentrated in some of the principal ports [? posts] will suffice and we will act upon your recommendation."[4]

Letters of Lord Elgin, 2 (1848), p. 65). *Journals of the Legislative Assembly of the Province of Canada*, Session 1850, pp. 215–16.

[1] Elgin to Grey, Dec. 6, 1848; cf. same to same, Dec. 19, 1848.

[2] Grey to Elgin, Dec. 29, 1848. He did send a confidential dispatch requesting Elgin's official views and instructing him to consult the Commander of the Forces. The latter simply declared that the garrison was too weak already. (Elgin to Grey, Jan. 29, 1849; cf. C, 1304, p. 262.)

[3] Elgin to Grey, Dec. 19, 1849: " If you wait till Domesday you will never get a military man here to agree to such a course."

[4] Grey to Elgin, Jan. 10, 1850; cf. same to same, Jan. 11 (confidential): G, 532, p. 10.

Unfortunately, events in Canada during the intervening months had considerably weakened the Governor-General's own conviction of the possibility of reductions being made without ill effects. In October, 1849, the famous " Annexation Manifesto " had been issued in Montreal. This document (the product of the temporary difficulties of the merchants of that city) prescribed as the remedy for Canada's ills " a friendly and peaceful separation from British connection, and a union upon equitable terms with the great North American Confederacy of sovereign states ". In arraying plausible arguments for cutting the painter, it did not overlook the new attitude of Britain towards colonial defence, which, it declared, was evidence of her desire to cast off the colonies :

" We would premise that towards Great Britain we entertain none other than sentiments of kindness and respect. Without her consent, we consider separation as neither practicable nor desirable. But the colonial policy of the parent state, the avowals of her leading statesmen, the public sentiments of the empire, present unmistakable and significant indications of the appreciation of colonial connection. That it is the resolve of England to invest us with the attributes, and compel us to assume the burdens, of independence is no longer problematical. The threatened withdrawal of her troops from other colonies—the continuance of her military protection to ourselves on condition that we shall defray the attendant expenditure, betokens intentions towards our country against which it is weakness in us not to provide."[1]

The manifestants, it will be observed, were a trifle ahead of the facts ; the small economies lately effected scarcely justified in themselves such sweeping statements. But as we have seen, they could quote plenty of utterances of the English radicals to support their assertions. When reports of Cobden's Bradford speech in which he made such a resounding attack on the colonial military expenditure[2] reached Canada early in 1850, a leading annexationist newspaper placed extracts from it in juxtaposition with the passage just quoted from the manifesto, and remarked, " Events are doing for us more than we could expect to do for ourselves."[3]

[1] The text of the manifesto is to be found on pp. 106–14 of Allin and Jones, *Annexation, Preferential Trade, and Reciprocity*, the best account of the whole movement.
[2] See above, p. 37.
[3] *Montreal Herald*, Jan. 22, 1850. See Elgin to Grey, Jan. 28, 1850.

The Governor-General seems to have regarded this chain of events as justifying only too fully his previous apprehensions of the dangers to the connexion between Britain and Canada which might lurk in an economical policy. At any rate, he now replied to Grey in two dispatches (one public and one confidential)[1] which distinctly discouraged reduction. In the former he recalled the filibustering tendencies of Americans, and pointed out that it was prudent to reduce the force just in proportion to the extent to which the British government felt that, by exerting influence at Washington or by other means, they could guarantee to the Canadians security against external aggression. But he also referred to the prevalent opinion that England was about to adopt the policy of disallowing the claims of the colonies to her protection, an opinion diligently circulated, he said, by annexationists and protectionists. "As the people at large," he added, "are apt to judge of the intentions of Government from its acts, I do earnestly hope that should H.M.'s Govt resolve to reduce still further the force stationed in this Province, the measure may be carried out so gradually and with such precautions as to furnish as little as may be grounds of misgiving and alarm to the faithful subjects of the Queen, or of encouragement to those who seek the dismemberment of the Empire."

The confidential dispatch stated that while the Governor-General agreed with the doctrine that the colonies should be responsible for their own internal security, he saw reasons for applying it in Canada with some reserve. One was the contiguity of the United States, where any faction in Canada disaffected to Britain could count on finding support; it might be just and politic, he suggested, for Britain to afford to "the supporters of order in the Colony" an advantage to offset this. He also pointed to the peculiar racial problems of Lower Canada, where French and English were dwelling together "under conditions of equilibrium which could never have been established but for the presence on the same scene of a directing and overruling power", and declared his belief that "the sudden withdrawal of Britain's moderating control, whether as the result of annexation or of a change of Imperial Policy would

---

[1] Both dated Feb. 9, 1850. *G*, 461, pp. 402, 407.

be followed at no distant period by a serious collision between the races ".

Privately, Elgin apologized for not going further in these communications, but explained that he could not give advice contrary to his own convictions " and to the opinions of every class of persons in the Colony except the annexationists ". He repeated that he thought it safer " to economize by withdrawing troops than by asking the Colonists to assume fresh burdens ", and while he could not advise a reduction, he would do his best to " keep up the spirit of the Colonists " if one were carried out.[1] A little later, in a more cheerful mood, he suggested other reasons for keeping troops in Canada :

" I suppose your economists at home do not deign to take into consideration the good effect which Regiments in Canada produce on the American mind. The general notion on the other side of the line being that we are utterly effete, I really believe that the Yankees are much edified by witnessing the manœuvring of a well-disciplined British Regt. Nothing certainly delights them so much. They always come back from the Reviews saying ' Wall nothing can whip the Britishers on a field day '. I have no doubt that these spectacles and the civilities they receive from the officers raise us greatly in their estimation and tend insensibly to promote the interests of peace."[2]

Grey took the blow well ; though (as usual) he looked towards the next session of Parliament with trepidation, he assured Elgin that he hoped " if the H. of Commons does not run wild " to make no further reductions except in the staff.[3] But he continued to remind him of the growing tendency of English opinion towards " the rejection of any burthen whatever on account of our Colonies ".[4] During 1849 and 1850 the operations of a House of Commons Select Committee on Army and Ordnance Expenditure (including among its members Cobden, Hume, Molesworth and Vernon Smith) supplied one more straw to show how the wind blew.[5] And though Grey

[1] Elgin to Grey, Feb. 11, 1850.
[2] Elgin to Grey, Oct. 25, 1850. Elgin may have been thinking particularly of the visit of the Buffalo people to Toronto in the previous August, when the visitors attended a review of the 71st Regiment : Toronto *Examiner*, Aug. 14, 1850.
[3] Grey to Elgin, April 12, 1850.
[4] Grey to Elgin, April 19, 1850.
[5] The Committee made two main reports : *P.P.*, 1849, no. 499, vol. IX, and 1850, no. 662, vol. X. Their final report is in *P.P.*, 1851, no. 564, vol. VII.

made a determined effort to disarm criticism by pointing out to the Committee the economies already effected, and the reasons which made it desirable to proceed slowly with respect to Canada[1]—though Fox Maule, the Secretary at War, and Lord John Russell, the Prime Minister, refused, in debates on the army estimates, to accept the validity of the radicals' extreme demands[2]—it was perhaps fortunate that as the months passed the affairs of Canada began to take a turn favourable to the possibility of retrenchment.

For one thing, the prosperity of the colony was definitely returning,[3] and in consequence the annexation movement was rapidly becoming merely a memory, as those Canadians who kept their patriotism in their pocket-books began to find themselves in better circumstances. To add to this, the provincial politicians afforded the Home Government a definite opening. Canada too had had a retrenchment movement. A Select Committee on Finance sat in the summer of 1850, and its investigations (largely conceived in a partisan spirit) had led the ministry to give " a kind of pledge " that it would bring the Governor-General's salary—the amount of which, as paid by the province, had been an object of criticism—under the consideration of the imperial authorities. It was proposed in fact to give them a broad hint that it would be well if the imperial treasury were to undertake the payment of the salary —thus preventing it from being a football of Canadian politics ; this despite the fact that an Act had been passed only four years earlier fixing the civil list salaries at the existing rate for the Queen's lifetime.[4]

Reporting this affair privately to Grey, Elgin told him, " I think you have an opportunity which should not be lost if you are resolved on making considerable reductions in Imperial expenditure here ". He suggested that the Imperial Government should look favourably on the proposal that it should pay the salary, but that it should explain that this new burden could not be undertaken without reductions of the other heavy

---

[1] See particularly his evidence in the 1849 report of the Committee, pp. 470 ff.
[2] *Hansard*, CIII, 967, 1915–17 (March 19, 1849).
[3] See the trade statistics in *Colonial Policy of Russell's Administration*, I, 271 n. 1848 had seen the nadir of the depression.
[4] Elgin to Grey, July 5, 1850.

UNDER RESPONSIBLE GOVERNMENT 79

charges borne by Britain on account of Canada; and he repeated his earlier proposal that two or three posts only should henceforth be held by British troops, the colonists being informed that soldiers required elsewhere would have to be accommodated at their expense. " I know," he wrote, " that the gravest objections will be raised to this proposal by the military authorities—and I should be well pleased if it were possible to leave things on their present footing—but if a change be inevitable, now is the time in my judgement to make it. For every £1 you advance you may save from £10 to £20 and the colonists cannot but feel that they have brought the mischief on themselves."[1]

Just at the end of 1850 Elgin duly forwarded his Executive Council's report on the civil list, expressing the hope that "some arrangement" might be made to remove the Governor-General's salary from the control of the provincial legislature.[2] A few weeks later, Grey translated his suggestions into action, in the form of a monumental dispatch, dated March 14, 1851, announcing to Canada a change in imperial military policy.[3]

In this document he examined the whole situation of the colony at length, and warned it that the time had come for the assumption of larger responsibilities. The British Government, he said, was ready to make the Governor-General's stipend a charge upon the Imperial treasury, but could only send this recommendation to Parliament " as part of a general measure for placing the fiscal relations of the Mother-country and the colony on a footing adapted to the greatly-altered circumstances of the present time, as compared to those under which the existing arrangement of those relations has grown up." He proceeded to argue from Canada's new political rights:

"Canada (in common with the other British provinces in North America) now possesses in the most ample and complete manner in which it is possible that she should enjoy it, the advantage of self-government in all that relates to her internal affairs. It appears

---

[1] Elgin to Grey, Dec. 11, 1850.
[2] Elgin to Grey, Dec. 31, 1850, enclosing council minute of Dec. 20: *P.P.*, 1851, no. 141, vol. XXXVI (Correspondence relating to the Civil List and Military Expenditure in Canada).
[3] In *ibid.*; also in *P.P.*, 1861, no. 423, vol. XIII, appendix 16, and in *Colonial Policy of Russell's Administration*, I, 258–66; cf. G, 532, pp. 252–62.

to Her Majesty's Government that this advantage ought to carry with it corresponding responsibilities, and that the time is now come when the people of Canada must be called upon to take upon themselves a larger share than they have hitherto done, of expenses which are incurred on this account, and for their advantage. Of these expenses, by far the heaviest charge which falls upon this country is that incurred for the military protection of the province."

In throwing a large share of military responsibility upon the colonists, Grey maintained—the argument was a favourite of his—that the ministry "would merely be reverting to the former colonial policy of this country"—to that of the days of the first empire; and he declared that this policy would have been applied to Canada earlier but for the "season of commercial depression", now happily past.

The dispatch made it clear that Britain still fully acknowledged the responsibility of defending the colonies against any foreign attack. Presumably remembering Elgin's anxieties, Grey took care to dissociate himself from those who seemed to look towards dismemberment of the Empire.

"Regarding Canada as a most important and valuable part of the empire, and believing the maintenance of the connexion between the mother country and the colony to be of the highest advantage to both, it is far from being the view of Her Majesty's Government that the general military power of the empire is not to be used in the protection of this part of Her Majesty's dominions. But, looking to the rapid progress which Canada is now making in wealth and population, and to the prosperity which she at this moment enjoys, it is the conviction of Her Majesty's Government, that it is only due to the people of this country that they should now be relieved from a large proportion of the charge which has hitherto been imposed upon them for the protection of a Colony now well able to do much towards protecting itself."

As regarded the actual measures to be taken, Grey informed the Canadian government that in future, except for a certain number of enrolled pensioners who were to be settled in the province, "the troops maintained in Canada should be confined to the garrisons of two or three fortified posts of importance, probably only Quebec and Kingston." With the local militia properly kept up, he felt, this would be sufficient to provide security while the existing friendly relations with the United States continued. If, unfortunately, a war should occur with that power, then great sacrifices and exertions would be required of both mother country and colony.

The barracks and other buildings vacated by the Imperial troops would be made over to Canada if she were willing to keep them up in case of their being required at a later time. It was further intimated that the Home Government desired that the cost of maintaining the canals, built by England " at a very heavy cost, chiefly with a view to the military defence of the Province," should now be taken over by the local authorities. In case the Canadians desired to retain imperial forces for local purposes at any of the stations whose abandonment was envisaged in Grey's plan, such forces would be readily supplied " if the actual cost thus incurred were provided for by the Province ".

The dispatch also announced the readiness of the British Government to apply to Parliament for a guarantee for a loan to assist in the construction of a railway between Halifax and Quebec, a great scheme then pending.[1] " I hope," wrote Grey to Elgin, " I shall have made the intended reduction of our Military Expenditure more palatable by coupling it with proposed assistance towards the railroad."[2]

In England, this dispatch served the purpose of enabling the Government to meet the attack on the colonial garrisons which Molesworth launched in Parliament on April 10, 1851. (Charles Adderley rather rudely suggested that the appearance of Molesworth's motion on the paper had hastened Grey's resolution to announce a new policy.)[3] Molesworth presented his case with much cogency,[4] supported by Cobden as well as by Adderley, who was later to be the heir of the Molesworth policy. Having to some extent cut the ground from under their critics' feet, the ministry did not choose, nevertheless, to admit the full force of the radicals' argument. The debate was a clash between, on one side, the *doctrinaires* of Colonial Reform and Manchester, demanding the prompt and sweeping translation of theory into practice, and, on the other, the ministers, acting

[1] The Conservative government which succeeded Russell's in 1852 was not satisfied with the conditions, and the scheme fell through ; the line was not built until after the creation of the Dominion.
[2] March 13, 1851.
[3] *Hansard*, CXV, 1419. (Adderley afterwards became Lord Norton.)
[4] This speech (already cited above, pp. 57–61) is in Egerton, *Selected Speeches of Sir William Molesworth*.

in something of the spirit of responsibility which we have seen exemplified in Elgin's letters to Grey—not denying the possibility of salutary change, but fully conscious of the difficulties that resulted from the variance of local conditions in the units of a world-wide empire. Russell was at pains to be polite to Molesworth. " I should agree with him," he said, "if, instead of saying that we were altogether to withdraw our military force from a certain class of colonies which it is difficult to define in any way, and impossible to define in a resolution, he had said that there were some colonies in which our military garrisons were too great, and in which the people themselves might furnish sufficient militia to suppress any internal disturbances, and to maintain internal tranquillity."[1]

To one tried reformer, at least, Grey's dispatch seemed a very important event. The ex-rebel, William Lyon Mackenzie, had returned by permission from the United States to Canada, and had re-entered Parliament there. On hearing of his return, old Joseph Hume, who had befriended him in his agitation of twenty years before, wrote to him recalling the fashion in which they had then been rebuffed when they ventured to demand the reforms in colonial government which had since been so fully conceded. " It is better late than never," he concluded ; " and the Despatch of Earl Grey, of the 14th of March, 1851, to the Earl of Elgin, must be taken as the close of the struggle."[2]

This laboured dispatch may be said to have been the theoretical basis of imperial military policy in Canada for years afterwards. It was repeatedly referred to as the classic statement of the official position ; but to put its principles wholly and permanently into practice was another thing. We shall see how successive governments, striving to do so, were thwarted by those innumerable incidents requiring military intervention which are the nemesis of empire. It was twenty years before Grey's ideas could be said to have been fully realized ; and by that time conditions were again greatly altered, and the form in which his principles were then put into action was a more extreme one than he had contemplated in 1851.

[1] The debate is in *Hansard*, CXV, 1364-1450.
[2] The letter is dated April 21, 1851. Elgin encloses it, as a clipping from the Toronto *Examiner*, in his letter to Grey of August 16, 1851.

Let us turn to consider the reception of the new policy in Canada. Elgin himself would have preferred to have had the thing done less ostentatiously, and anticipated that the dispatch would occasion " some tall talking here when Parliament meets ". And he disliked the reference to the possible contingency of war with the United States: " sufficient for the day is I think its own evil ". But he was quite certain that, whatever came of the proposed changes, " there never is likely again to be so favorable an opportunity for attempting them ".[1]

The dispatches on the civil list and military expenditure were published in Canada early in May, the newspapers in general printing them in full;[2] and the public received them with more calmness than the Governor-General had expected. A few weeks later he was able to tell Grey:

" I am glad to say . . . that the publication of the Despatches has not in so far as I can judge been attended with any bad effects. The Clear Grits rather approve of your course about the Troops. . . ."[3]

The comments of the provincial Press showed, one journal remarked, no marks of surprise and but few of regret.[4] The notes of criticism that sounded were those of partisan journals that disliked the Governor-General or his ministers; and even these do not seem to have taken much exception to the principles of military policy newly enunciated.[5] The Toronto *Examiner* (which flaunted the motto " Responsible Government and the Voluntary Principle " and did not realize how complete was the bloodless victory this cause had already won) still remembered the struggles and disappointments of the recent past. Not the least significant feature of the withdrawal of the garrisons, in its eyes, was the fact that this seemed a guarantee that Britain would never attempt to resume a policy of coercion in Canada. (As for the loss of imperial expenditure in the province, the *Examiner* impolitely observed that this would be made good by the advantage to public morals result-

[1] Elgin to Grey, April 23, 1851.
[2] e.g., *Examiner*, May 7, 1851.
[3] Elgin to Grey, May 31, 1851. The " Clear Grits " were the radical liberal group in Upper Canada.
[4] *Examiner*, May 21.
[5] e.g., Montreal *Transcript*, April 22, May 6, 1851. On the former date it declared that police duty was " no part of the business of soldiers ".

ing from the soldiers' departure.) It admitted (after some preliminary reluctance) that no just exception could be taken to Grey's propositions:

"Whether viewed in the light of political economy, or as a question of national policy, the proposed reduction of troops in Canada cannot be reasonably condemned: in the one case it is an act of justice to the over-taxed people of England; in the other, there is exhibited a generous reliance on the unbought affections of the people—the best guarantee for the continuance of the connection with the parent state. . . . The time has arrived when the affections of the people constitute the only secure defence of the British Colonial empire. Earl Grey, with the profound sagacity of a statesman, has penetrated the mystery; and with a boldness and a magnanimity that contrast favourably with the childish fears of some of his colleagues, he announces his determination to commit the fate of the empire to that conservative element. Let not Canada oppose a policy so just and humane, so bold, liberal, and magnanimous."[1]

The fact was that Canada, in the circumstances of 1851, was simply not interested in military affairs. The existing friendly relations with the United States made defence a matter of small moment to a people whose trend of thought, except when forced into military channels by the existence of some actual and immediate menace, had always been thoroughly unmilitary. The individuals composing both the English-speaking peoples of North America were far more interested in advancing their own prosperity than in devoting money and energy to the apparatus of national defence; and this was especially true of the Canadians, whom the protection of the mother country had always relieved from the necessity of thinking for themselves in such matters, and to whom high military policy was a closed book. Their quiet acceptance of the new condition of things justified Elgin's advice to Grey in favour of a reduction of the imperial force unaccompanied by any attempt to force Canada to undertake expenditure for military purposes. Such an attempt would assuredly have led to difficulties, for in the absence of immediate danger the Canadians would certainly have maintained that there was simply no need for an expensive military organization in their country.[2] As it was, the

[1] *Examiner*, May 21, 1851; cf. May 7.
[2] The *Examiner*, for instance, urged the complete absence of danger as one reason justifying Grey's policy.

way was open for easing the burden of the British taxpayer without in the least endangering the unity of the Empire.

Grey now proceeded to put the new policy into effect, though without undue haste. On the last day of the month in which he wrote his dispatch, the effective strength of all ranks in Canada was 6,106 ; one year later it had been reduced to 4,960.[1] By that time, however, Grey himself was no longer in office. His unreluctant retirement ended the long partnership with Elgin, in which, like some pair of batsmen at cricket who thoroughly understand each other, they had played such a cautiously fruitful game. He had known much frustration, and not least in the matter of the military expenditure whose reduction was one of his chief aims. True, he had attained his object in Australia, and made gratifying progress in Canada ; but trouble elsewhere annihilated the effect of these successes. The outbreak of a new war at the Cape necessitated a great augmentation of the force there,[2] and an increase of some 3,000 men in the general strength of the Army.[3] But the state of things would have been much worse but for the reductions effected on more peaceful stations. When the new Conservative ministry began to take stock of the colonial situation in 1852, Elgin was able to point out that within the past two years the force in Canada had been reduced by at least 1,400 men, and eight minor stations abandoned.[4] Only slight further reductions were made in the course of the next year, and in point of fact the troops continued to garrison several other posts besides Kingston and Quebec.[5]

Reductions were also made in the Maritime Provinces ; the strength of the Nova Scotia command in officers and men was reduced from 2,697 to 2,026 during 1851–52.[6] There, however, no such careful efforts were made to lead the provinces in the

[1] *P.P.*, 1861, no. 423, vol. XIII, appendix 1.
[2] From 5,050 on Mar. 31, 1851, to 9,096 on Mar. 31, 1852 : *ibid.*
[3] Speech of Major Beresford, moving army estimates, March 19, 1852 : *Hansard*, CXIX, 1304–6.
[4] Elgin to Pakington, Oct. 27, 1852 : *G*, 462, p. 139. The stations were Three Rivers, Sorel, Chambly, Laprairie, Brockville, Amherstburgh, Chatham, and Penetanguishene.
[5] The British Government never put into effect Grey's scheme for paying the Governor-General s salary. The Whigs fell before Grey could carry out the whole scheme of arrangements which he had in mind.
[6] *P.P.*, 1861, no. 423, vol. XIII, appendix 1.

direction of undertaking larger responsibilities as we have seen in Canada. For this there were several reasons. Canada, with a garrison two or three times as large as that of the Maritimes, had lately been a much more serious problem from the point of view of expense. Moreover, it was much larger, wealthier and more populous than Nova Scotia and New Brunswick put together, and by so much the more capable of a measure of self-reliance. Finally, the British force in the lower provinces consisted in great part of the garrison of Halifax. This great naval base was universally considered a very valuable unit in the general scheme of imperial defence—important, like Bermuda or Gibraltar, for imperial purposes apart altogether from its function in the local defence of British North America. No one thought of abandoning it as an Imperial station.[1]

It may be noted here that Canada never took advantage of Grey's offer to increase the force in the colony beyond that considered necessary by the British government, provided the local legislature paid the extra expense. Apart from the colony's general lack of conviction of the need for armed forces, familiarity with the history of Canadian nationalism would lead one to expect that a Canadian government, when unable to avoid making appropriations for defence, would prefer to expend them, not on (so to speak) the temporary rent of regiments which an emergency elsewhere might call away, and which in any case would be subject to the orders of the Home Government and its officers in Canada, but rather on organizing local forces over which its control would be complete. Moreover, a comparatively large force of half-trained militia can be kept up for the cost of one battalion of regulars. This was the system that Canada ultimately preferred to adopt.

In Australia it was otherwise. After the gold discoveries of 1851, the colonies there asked for an imperial reinforcement, presumably to aid in ensuring order among the mixed population attracted to the diggings. Their request was granted, but only on the condition that they should pay " all the expenses except arms and clothing ".[2] In 1858, New South Wales spent £23,493 on British troops, and £6,394 on forts and barracks,

---

[1] See Grey's evidence before the Select Committee on Army and Ordnance Expenditure—1849 report, q. 7887, p. 528 ; 1850 report, q. 8600, p. 667.
[2] *Hansard*, CXXX, 1291 (speech of Sidney Herbert, Feb. 24, 1854).

while Victoria spent under the same heads £35,323 and £1,350 respectively, as well as £3,727 on local forces.[1]

After the fall of Grey, Elgin (who remained in Canada until the end of 1854) continued to advise a moderate and cautious military policy. Early in 1853 he wrote to the Duke of Newcastle, who had lately become Colonial Secretary, pointing to the progress lately made and adding:

" If further reductions are to be made, let them be effected in the same quiet way without parade or the ostentatious adoption of new principles as applicable to the defence of colonies which are exposed, as Canada is by reason of their connection with Great Britain, to the hazard of assaults from organized powers. . . .

" Do not ask England to make unreasonable sacrifices for the Colonists, but such sacrifices as are reasonable, on the hypothesis that the Colony is an exposed part of the empire. Induce her if you can to make them generously and without appearing to grudge them. Let it be inferred from your language that there is in your opinion nothing in the nature of things to prevent the tie which connects the Mother-country and the Colony from being as enduring as that which unites the different States of the Union, and nothing in the nature of our very elastic institutions to prevent them from expanding so as to permit the free and healthy development of social, political, and national life in these young communities. By administering colonial affairs in this spirit you will find, I believe, even when you least profess to seek it, the true secret of the cheap defence of nations. If these communities are only truly attached to the connection and satisfied of its permanence (and, as respects the latter point, opinions here will be much influenced by the tone of statesmen at home), elements of self-defence, not moral elements only but material elements likewise, will spring up within them spontaneously as the product of movements from within, not of pressure from without. Two millions of people, in a northern latitude, can do a good deal in the way of helping themselves when their hearts are in the right place."[2]

Elgin might have boasted that during the past seven years the policy of sacrifice and forbearance which he had urged upon the Colonial Office had enabled him, in the face of the powerful hostile influences of economic depression and violent political partisanship in Canada, and widespread indifference in England, to establish the connexion between Britain and the colony on

[1] P.P., 1861, no. 423, vol. XIII, appendix 14.
[2] Walrond, 133 : exact date not given.

a firmer basis than it had ever rested on before: that of free constitutional government. At the same time he had contrived to relieve England, not by any means of the whole financial burden she had borne on account of the colony, but of a respectable proportion of it.[1] It was true that this economy had been effected merely by England doing less, without Canada doing more. That great province, in a fair way towards becoming a nation, still confined its legislative contribution towards its own defence within the singularly narrow limits of an annual militia grant of about two thousand pounds.[2] It remained to be seen whether Canada would justify Elgin's confidence that, with the development of that national spirit which he considered no whit inconsistent with her position in the British Empire, she would come naturally to a conviction of the appropriateness of more substantial efforts. Self-government had not yet produced self-defence; yet the time was at hand when the colony would take its first hesitant steps in that direction.

[1] For the year ending March 31, 1847, Britain's total expenditure in the Province of Canada was £496,576, of which military expenditure was £474,789. For the year 1853, the total imperial expenditure was £332,224; of this all but about £21,000 was for military purposes, and even of this residue more than £8,000 was for "naval charges". *P.P.*, 1849, no. 224, vol. XXXIV, pp. 8-11; 1859, session I, no. 240, vol. XVII.

[2] The grant in 1849 was £2,043; in 1854, £2,280: *P.P.*, 1851, no. 141, vol. XXXVI, and Canadian supply act 18 Vict., cap. 4. Most of the militia expenses, however, were met by the revenue from fines for non-attendance at musters: C. F. Hamilton in *Canada and its Provinces*, VII, 393.

CHAPTER V

THE CRIMEAN WAR AND THE BEGINNINGS OF THE CANADIAN VOLUNTEER FORCE, 1854-1860

> " It may be said that . . . the line which separates the duty of the Mother Country and that of the Colony is vague and undefined. It would be singular if it were otherwise; for the present relation of Great Britain to her freely governed Colonies is, I believe, new and unprecedented in the history of the world, and political duties and relations can only be rendered definite by experience and practice."
> —SIR EDMUND HEAD to LABOUCHERE, February 8, 1858.

THE European settlement of 1815 was not, perhaps, a particularly good one; but at least it served to prevent a general conflict between great powers for forty years. When Napoleon III became Emperor of the French in 1852, men began to fear that this comfortable era (already sadly shaken by the revolutions of 1848) was nearing its end. Almost immediately, clouds were seen gathering in the Near East; and 1854 found a desperate war in progress between Russia and an alliance headed by Great Britain and France. This war was to have repercussions even among the peaceful folk of the British Provinces beyond the Atlantic, to whom Constantinople and the Hellespont—once only antique and outlandish names far off in time and space—suddenly became curiously important and familiar as Canadian newspapers chronicled the struggle of redcoat and Russian on the shores of the Black Sea.

The war did not come suddenly. Hostilities seemed probable for the best part of a year previous to their actual outbreak on March 27, 1854[1]; and their approach naturally led Britain to accelerate the reduction of her garrisons abroad in order to have as large a force as possible disposable in Europe. In February, Sidney Herbert, Secretary at War in Aberdeen's ministry, was able to tell the House of Commons that during

---

[1] This was the date of the declaration of war by Britain and France; hostilities had already taken place between Turkey and Russia.

its short life that Government had withdrawn 5,000 men from British North America, the West Indies, and the Cape.[1] The regulars in the North American Provinces had been reduced during the past year from 7,000 to 5,600 in number, almost entirely at the expense of the garrisons in Canada.[2] But far more sweeping cuts were soon to come. England was discovering that her scattered little army was a very inadequate instrument for intervention in an European war. It was with difficulty that she scraped together 30,000 men for the Crimean expeditionary force, and with greater difficulty that she found soldiers to fill the gaps in the ranks caused by enemy shot and by the rigours of the winter before Sebastopol. She might count herself fortunate that profound peace in North America gave her the opportunity of withdrawing her regiments thence; and she made the most of it.

Before the actual invasion of the Crimea had begun, it was decided to bring home from Canada three more regiments of infantry and three companies of artillery. Thereafter the force remaining in the province would consist only of one regiment of the line and two companies of artillery, in addition to the Royal Canadian Rifles. The latter were to be stationed at Kingston, with two companies detached to Montreal; the whole of the remaining troops were to garrison Quebec. All other stations were to be evacuated. These arrangements, it was explained, were in accordance with the policy announced by Grey in 1851.[3]

No time was lost in carrying them out. By the end of the fiscal year 1854-55 there were only 1,887 Imperial troops in Canada, while in the Maritime Provinces (where the axe had likewise fallen) there were 1,086, apart from 311 in Newfoundland. The troops in all the British Colonies then totalled 39,637, as against 45,848 two years earlier. Reductions on the Canadian scale had not been possible elsewhere: the Cape, for instance, retained 6,000 men throughout the war in Europe, and (owing to the serious disturbances at the gold diggings late in 1854)

---

[1] *Hansard*, CXXX, 1290 (Feb. 24, 1854).
[2] *P.P.*, 1861, no. 423, vol. XIII, appendix I.
[3] Sir George Grey to Elgin, Aug. 11, 1854: *G*, 146, p. 104. Cf. Newcastle to Rowan, " April " (?), 1854, in *P.P.*, 1861, no. 423, vol. XIII, appendix 16. The departments of War and the Colonies were separated in July, 1854.

a battalion was actually added to the force in Australia, though at local expense.[1]

The good feeling of the population of British North America facilitated the reductions there. There was ample evidence of the colonists' interest in the success of British arms. In both Nova Scotia and New Brunswick the legislatures assured the Imperial Government that the defence of their provinces might if necessary safely be entrusted to the local militia.[2] In the wealthier inland province, feeling was no less actively loyal; and it found expression in important new departures in defensive organization.

As the troops were drawn off from Canada, the question arose of the disposal of the buildings and other Crown property at the stations vacated, and the provincial executive council decided to undertake the task of upkeep. There were settled in Canada several hundred " enrolled pensioners " sent out in Lord Grey's time and given small grants of ordnance land on condition of holding themselves in readiness for service in case of need.[3] Of these men 150 were now taken into provincial service and placed on permanent duty in detachments in the barracks vacated by the regulars. In their decision to undertake the small but unprecedented expenditure involved, the ministry may have been encouraged by a hint lately dropped that it was likely that the Imperial Government would make over to Canada the considerable areas of military lands surrounding the stations no longer occupied.[4]

Larger enterprises were in the air. With the province almost completely stripped of troops, some substitute seemed necessary —the more so as its police organization was still rudimentary.

---

[1] *P.P.*, 1861, no. 423, vol. XIII, appendix 1. *Hansard*, CXXXVI, 1546 (speech of Frederick Peel, introducing army estimates, Feb. 19, 1855).

[2] *P.P.*, 1855, cd. 1871, vol. XXXVI : Despatches from governors of British colonies transmitting addresses and resolutions on the subject of the war with Russia. Continued in cds. 1888, 1940, 1983, and no. 63, in the same vol.

[3] Cf. *G.E.C.*, Grey to Elgin, Dec. 29, 1848 ; Mar. 23 and Nov. 30, 1849 ; Mar. 8, 1850. The men were settled on the reserves at Niagara, London, Toronto, Amherstburgh and Penetanguishene (Head to Herbert, Mar. 17, 1855 ; confidential. G, 462, p. 304).

[4] Elgin to Sir G. Grey, Oct. 11, 1854, with letter of Col. Tulloch and council minute of Sept. 29. The appropriation for the pensioner force was £1,700 for the last months of 1854, and £7,927 for 1855. Apparently Grey mentioned the ordnance land proposal in a dispatch of Sept. 15, 1854, which has not been found. It had been spoken of to Tulloch, by the Duke of Newcastle. (G, 462, p. 276.)

In October, 1854, the provincial ministers, acting on a memorandum written by the premier (Sir Allan MacNab), decided to appoint a commission of three eminent Canadians and one Imperial officer to report upon " the best means of reorganizing the militia of Canada " and improved police arrangements. From this measure Lord Elgin expected excellent results ;[1] there now seemed good hope of the appearance in the colony at no distant time of that spirit of active self-reliance whose rise he had so confidently foretold. Before the commissioners reported, however, Elgin himself had left the province. He was succeeded by another admirable public servant, Sir Edmund Head, formerly Governor of New Brunswick. Elgin had long since communicated some of his ideas on Canadian government to Head ;[2] and the latter's dealings with military policy, we shall see, are in many respects reminiscent of his predecessor's.

It must be noted, nevertheless, that a change was taking place in the situation of the Governor-General. Elgin's had been a time of transition, when he had been able to use the prestige of his office and the force of his personality and great abilities in educating Canadians to the practice of the constitutional system which his administration introduced. But, that system once established, the position of the Queen's representative in Canada becomes more and more analogous to that of the Queen herself in England : he exercises influence rather than power. Generally from this time it is with the Canadian ministers that the domestic policies of the colony originate, and invariably they make the controlling decisions. The Governor-General's most important function is that of a *liaison* officer between the colonial government and Whitehall. He is frequently charged with the difficult and thankless task of influencing Canadian policy in accordance with the desires of the ministry at home ; and in this respect no matter engages his attention more constantly, and none demands the application of greater tact, than the perennial problem of military defence.

In February, 1855, the militia commission submitted a

[1] Elgin to Grey, Oct. 14, 1854 ; with MacNab's memorandum and council minute of Oct. 13. *G*, 462, p. 280.
[2] Elgin to Lord Grey, Nov. 1, 1850 : *G.E.C.*

report[1] which justified Elgin's confidence in its members' capacity. It suggested comprehensive plans for the development of the local forces of Canada. The basis of the scheme was the retention and improvement of the old militia (quaintly called the "sedentary" force); but its great innovation was the institution of a small and separate force of volunteers, which would differ from the older body in being, even in peacetime, uniformed and armed, and required to carry out a prescribed course of training. The object clearly was to maintain the ancient system of universal service as the essential element for the successful defence of the province against a foreign power, but to provide in addition a disciplined force of greater immediate availability, capable of dealing with sudden minor emergencies.

The new force, the commissioners suggested, should be composed of proportions of cavalry, artillery and rifles, to amount only to a little more than 4,000 men in all. It was to train for ten consecutive days a year (except the artillery, who were to do twenty days); and officers and men were to be paid while performing this service. As for the "Sedentary Militia", the report recommended that the battalions should not be required to assemble except at one annual muster, but that special pains should be taken to ensure that their enrolment on paper was complete and up-to-date. It was urged that arms, accoutrements and ammunition for 100,000 men should be obtained and kept in the province for the purpose of equipping this force in emergency—a provision never carried into effect.[2] The commissioners pointed out that (apart from such initial items as the cost of arms and armouries) the expense of the whole scheme which they proposed would not exceed £24,000 annually—although one regular regiment of the line of 953 officers and men cost £43,000.[3]

A Bill embodying the report's recommendations was pre-

[1] *Report of the Commissioners Appointed to Investigate and Report upon the Best Means of Re-organizing the Militia of Canada, and upon an Improved System of Police*, Quebec, 1855.
[2] It was struck out of the Militia Bill in the committee stage. (*Globe*, Toronto, April 18, 1855).
[3] The commission also made what seem admirable recommendations for a centralized provincial police system; but a Bill based upon them met with a hostile reception in the legislature and was withdrawn. G, 462, pp. 475-6; cf. Dent, J. C., *The Last Forty Years*, Toronto, 1881, II, 347.

sented to the provincial Parliament at once. It provided that the " Active Militia " or volunteers should not exceed 5,000 in number, and made special provision for using them in support of the civil power. It was to be in force for three years only.[1]

The Bill did not pass without a struggle. At the second reading, a strong attack was made upon it by the advanced Liberals of the opposition. L. H. Holton, a member for Montreal, moved the " six months' hoist ", and was seconded by A. T. Galt (afterwards Sir Alexander Galt), another eminent member from Lower Canada. A group of Upper Canadian Liberals supported them—among them George Brown (the proprietor of the influential Toronto *Globe*), and M. H. Foley. The latter made a particularly bitter attack on the Bill as being alien to the feelings of the country.[2] This opposition was the result of a number of influences: party feeling; the province's long immunity from the need of providing for its own defence, and the consequent slowness of Canadian politicians to recognize military considerations upon which they had never had to reflect before; perhaps, also, the influence of radical and pacifist thought in England. True, the measure was a very modest one by comparison with the sums that Britain expended every year on her colonial military establishment; but it was a complete novelty in Canada, and to ask a legislature whose defensive appropriations had amounted to only £2,000 annually to increase them to £25,000 seemed a considerable new departure. It is doubtful whether, without the patriotic enthusiasm engendered by the existing war, the Militia Bill of 1855 could have passed.

As Britain looked about her for means of obtaining troops to replace those perishing in the Crimea, various suggestions were made for raising men in Canada.[3] Head advised the home government to deal cautiously with proposals emanating from individuals; success in such an enterprise, he insisted, would depend upon the attitude of the local government, which

---

[1] The act is 18 Vict., cap. 77.
[2] Memorandum of John A. Macdonald, Pub. Arch. Can., *M.P.*, " Militia and Defence," I, p. 3. *Globe*, March 28, 30, April 12, 19, 23, 1855. Holton's motion was lost by 75-25; the final vote on the Bill was 57-33.
[3] Head to Russell (confidential), April 27, May 12, 1855: *G*, 462, pp. 320, 325. Head to Molesworth, Aug. 15, 1855: *ibid.*, p. 366. Head to Herbert (confidential), March 16, March 28, 1855: *ibid.*, 304, 311.

CRIMEAN WAR AND VOLUNTEER FORCE 95

would have to be fully consulted before the attempt was made.[1] He broached the matter to Sir Allan MacNab, who drew up a memorandum on the possibility of raising a regular regiment in the colony with the aid of a promise of grants of lands as a reward for service. This scheme, in which Head took much interest,[2] did not prove acceptable to MacNab's colleagues. Clarifying their position, the ministers expressed their readiness to help British recruiting by promising grants of land to actual settlers (being British subjects) whom the Imperial Government might send out in the course of the next ten years ;[3] but they showed no enthusiasm for the project for raising Canadian troops, stating that they feared that recruiting for the regular service might interfere with that for the new volunteer force. They gave further reasons :

" The Committee are also impressed with the conviction that a large and lawless party exists in the U.S. unfriendly to Great Britain and desirous, if possible, of depriving her of her North American Colonies. Should the War be protracted, or the course of events render it necessary to employ the whole Military force of the Empire in the East, the Committee have too much reason to believe that attempts similar to those from time to time made on Cuba, and in the years 1838-1839 on Canada would be made by the party alluded to."

Under these circumstances, the ministers declared, they could not " advise the withdrawal from the Colony of those upon whose services we should have to rely for the maintenance of British Supremacy therein, in the event of the War extending to our own Borders ". They did not object, however, to Britain exercising her undoubted right of recruiting in the province by voluntary enlistment.[4]

Clearly, the memory of 1838 died hard ; and that there was some justification for fears of a recrudescence of filibustering will be demonstrated in a later chapter. The ministers' anxiety

---

[1] Head to Herbert (confidential), March 28, 1855 ; to Russell (confidential), April 27, 1855 : *ibid.*, pp. 311, 320.

[2] He suggested that the corps might be called the " 100th or Royal Canadian Regiment "—an anticipation of the actual name and number given the unit raised three years later. Head to Russell, May 12, 1855 : *ibid.*, p. 330.

[3] Head had feared that a previous suggestion that the province appropriate lands to assist recruiting for the Foreign Legion which Britain was raising would be unpopular in Canada. *Ibid.*

[4] Two minutes of council, enclosed in Head to Russell, June 1, 1855 : *ibid.*, p. 340. The whole attitude of the Canadian Government on the enlistment question seems obscure and equivocal.

over the possible withdrawal of a large portion of Canada's fighting population, however, seems a trifle ludicrous when it is considered that Head's idea was to attempt to raise only one regiment, at least in the first place. Yet the amount of active military spirit in the province was extremely small ;[1] an appeal for recruits for a regiment for foreign service might have brought forward a very large proportion of those men in the country who had military interests or experience, and the loss to the native defensive strength would have been greater than the mere numbers involved. The argument reminds us that in organizing even the little force of volunteers then contemplated Canada was making an unprecedented experiment, the success of which did not seem certain.

The idea of raising troops in Canada was not dropped at once ; but many difficulties were seen in the way besides the local Government's misgivings. Recruiting, it was thought, would not be easy in a country where even unskilled labourers earned a dollar a day ; accounts of the sufferings of the troops in the Crimea had a dampening effect on Canadian ardour ; finally, the Imperial authorities themselves interposed a major obstacle by stipulating that, except for old soldiers, enlistment would have to be for ten years.[2] So, for the time, the scheme languished.

With the organization of the new Canadian forces going forward, the local Government showed a desire that the suggested transfer of the ordnance lands to its own control should take place as soon as possible—in order that the revenue from them might defray the new expenditure, or (perhaps) that the transfer might at least aid the ministers in defending the new policy against criticism in Parliament by pointing to the lands as a compensatory *quid pro quo*. The Colonial Secretary now definitely made the offer of the lands in a dispatch which discussed the whole question of the military relations of colony and mother country.[3] He proposed no change of principle.

---

[1] It found expression only in the maintenance by individual efforts of a very few voluntary units such as the Montreal Fire Brigade, described as " a species of infantry battalion " (*Canada and its Provinces*, VII, 395).

[2] Head to Molesworth, Aug. 15, 1855 ; to Labouchere, Jan. 3, 1856. *G*, 462, pp. 366, 413. Cf. Head to Panmure (confidential), June 8, 1855 : *ibid.*, p. 348.

[3] Published in *P.P.*, 1861, no. 423, vol. XIII, appendix 16, and misdated " August, 1854." It was evidently written in the spring of 1855.

CRIMEAN WAR AND VOLUNTEER FORCE   97

The Imperial authorities still undertook to defend any part of the Queen's dominions that might be menaced by a foreign power, and they would maintain in Canada, as before, the force necessary to occupy the most important posts, " so as to form a nucleus for the defence of the Province " ; but for all beyond this they proposed to rely on " the loyalty and military spirit " of the Canadians. The military lands at the posts no longer occupied by the regular troops would be handed over to Canada ; and it was observed that while those not important for military purposes were to be made over unconditionally, the Imperial Government would regard with much satisfaction the appropriation of the revenue from them to internal defence.

The Canadian Parliament lost no time in passing an Act[1] permitting the Governor-in-Council to agree with the British Government for the transfer. The preamble declared that Her Majesty's faithful subjects in the province, " well knowing that the strength of the Empire would, in case of need, be put forth to defend any part of it against aggression ", were " willing to take upon themselves the maintenance of peace and order within the Country " ; and the Act provided that moneys derived from the transferred lands should be kept account of and credited in deduction of expenses incurred by the province for military or police purposes. In the summer of 1855, a delegation of Canadian ministers visited England to arrange the details ; and one of them, Colonel Taché, was also charged with purchasing the arms and accoutrements " absolutely indispensable " for equipping a portion of the new volunteer force not exceeding half of the whole number authorized.[2]

Before the volunteers were fully organized, the spectre of possible conflict with the United States rose once more. In 1855 the British Government made attempts at obtaining recruits in that country which the American authorities regarded (not without reason) as contrary to international usage and their

[1] 18 Vict., cap. 91.
[2] Minute of council enclosed in Head to Russell, June 4, 1855 : G, 462, p. 344. No appropriation for the new force appears to have been made during 1855. The supply act (18 Vict., cap. 90) provides only £2,285—about the usual sum in former years—for the militia. It also provides, however, £91 for the transport of troops in aid of the civil power, £7,927 for the pensioner force, and £2,000 for compensation to pensioners in lieu of the lands they would lose by the transfer.

H

own municipal law; and a series of diplomatic exchanges culminated, in May, 1856, in the dismissal by the United States of Mr. Crampton, the British minister, and three consuls.[1] The two countries were also at odds over the interpretation of the Clayton-Bulwer treaty of 1850 regarding their interests in Central America. With hostilities apparently threatened, Sir Edmund Head in Canada turned his attention to the means of domestic defence. By the New Year of 1856 the volunteer force was making progress, but the want of arms was a serious problem. As usual, the difficulties with the United States had arisen at the worst possible season; the St. Lawrence was sealed by ice, and the arms purchased by Taché in Europe could not be brought in.[2]

By the time of Crampton's dismissal various precautions were unostentatiously in train. Small arms were being moved into Canada West. The "flank companies"[3] at the ends of the Welland Canal had been armed, to secure that work against any sudden enterprise. The guard of pensioners in Fort Mississauga at the mouth of the Niagara was doubled, and another guard placed in the fort at Amherstburgh. The Adjutant-General's office was deluged with letters "offering services and requesting arms".[4]

This emergency caused, moreover, a sudden augmentation of the diminished regular garrison of British North America. Before the dispute reached its most dangerous stage, the war in Europe was over. Britain, after her humiliating difficulties, was victorious; and what is more, her army in the Crimea was at last in a highly healthy and efficient state.[5] Hungry Russians and ragged Frenchmen tried to conceal their envy as Sir William Codrington's prosperous brigades moved through the precise evolutions of the grand reviews with which the British forces beguiled their last months in the East; ministers in England,

---

[1] See Brebner, J. B., "Joseph Howe and the Crimean War Enlistment Controversy," *C.H.R.*, XI; *P.P.*, 1856, cd. 2080, vol. LX; Rhodes, J. F., *History of the United States from the Compromise of 1850* . . ., II, New York, 1906, 186–88; Bemis, S. F., (ed.), *The American Secretaries of State and their Diplomacy*, New York, 1928, vol. VI, chap. VII.
[2] Head to Labouchere, Jan. 11, 1856: G, 462, p. 416.
[3] The portions of a sedentary militia battalion which it had been customary in some cases to keep in a state approaching military efficiency.
[4] Head to Labouchere (confidential), March 28, 1856: G, 180 B ("Secret and confidential despatches, 1856–66").
[5] Fortescue, *History of the British Army*, XIII, 224–27.

CRIMEAN WAR AND VOLUNTEER FORCE 99

hearing of the condition of the troops, found themselves " regretting that we had not opportunity to use them ".[1] Under these circumstances, and with Palmerston Prime Minister, some military demonstration in America was to be expected. Two months before Crampton's departure from Washington, Palmerston wrote to Lord Panmure, his Secretary of State for War, on the need for sending troops thither. " This American dispute," he wrote, " may, and most likely will, end in smoke ; but we must be prepared for the case of its ending in gunpowder smoke, and as Peace is now signed, and our troops are disposable, we should be greatly and justly blamed if we lost a day in properly reinforcing the garrison of our North American Colonies."[2]

It was decided to dispatch at once from the Crimea five infantry regiments and a reinforcement of artillery, while Lieutenant-General Sir William Eyre went out to take command of all the troops in America.[3] The office of Commander of the Forces in British North America was thus revived.[4] Panmure's view of the situation was as cheerfully simple as his chief's : " The fact is we have denuded N. America too much, and Jonathan is bumptious ; but our hands are empty if he wants a trial, and I think he would come second-best off."[5] However, the Government, anxious that the movement " should not appear as a menace in any way ", took some pains " to avoid ostentation ".[6] The fact remained that the five regiments moved to Canada very expeditiously ; and with them went 10,000 rifles, camp equipage for 10,000 men, and four million rounds of ball cartridge, to be added to the stores there.[7]

These preparations were challenged in the House of Lords by a voice which carried much authority—that of the Earl of Elgin.[8] Protesting against the growing British impression that

[1] Codrington to Panmure, April 19, April 26, 1856 ; Panmure to Codrington, May 12 : Sir G. Douglas and Sir G. D. Ramsay (eds.), *The Panmure Papers*, London, 1908, II, 197, 211, 225.
[2] Palmerston to Panmure, March 30, 1856 : *ibid.*, II, 172.
[3] Panmure to Palmerston, March 30, 1856 : private. *Ibid.*, 173.
[4] Cf. above, p. 73.
[5] Panmure to Codrington, March 31, 1856 : *ibid.*, 174.
[6] Panmure to Codrington, April 4, 1856 ; to the Queen (cabinet minute), April 25 : *ibid.*, 179, 204.
[7] The last of the troops embarked the first week in May : Codrington to Panmure, May 6 (*ibid.*, 220). Labouchere to Head (confidential), May 3 ; cf. Head to Newcastle, May 25, 1861 (confidential), in *G*, 180 B, p. 98.
[8] *Hansard*, CXLII, 673 ff. (May 27, 1856).

the United States was unfriendly, he declared his belief that there had never been a time " when the substantial interests which bind the two countries together were so manifold and so important, and when the differences between them were so trifling and puerile ". But his chief concern was with the relation of the new military movements to colonial policy.

Some weeks before, he recalled, he had questioned Panmure in the House on the reinforcements for Canada. The minister had replied that the Government simply intended " to send back to British North America a certain number of regiments, which were taken from the garrisons of those provinces at the commencement of the war."[1] This statement, said Elgin, might indicate that the late reductions were merely the result of accidental or temporary circumstances, whereas in fact they had been the result " of a policy deliberately adopted and steadily and consistently carried out ", and would have been effected even if the war had not occurred. The Government's new course, he feared, " might have a tendency to arrest the work now in progress, which promised, if perseveringly carried out, to render those colonies in time to come a support instead of a burden to the Empire ". With the British force in Canada reduced to a minimum, and the Canadians organizing forces of their own, much seemed to have been accomplished ; and he was ready to resist any retrograde policy—" because he thought that it would be unjust towards the mother country, and also because, although it might be a boon to the colonies, in the first instance, it would be a boon followed by a speedy reaction, and would put an argument in the hands of those who were disposed to denounce our colonies as burdens ".

Elgin realized that the best assurances of security for British North America were, first, the cultivation of a relationship of mutual esteem and respect between its inhabitants and those of the United States, and between the American and British Governments, and, secondly, the cultivation among the colonists of what he loved to call " national and manly morals ".[2] He had advised caution in imposing new burdens on Canada, but now that circumstances had enabled progress to be made he was not disposed to look back. It can have given him little

[1] *Ibid.*, CXLI, 1142-43 (April 18, 1856).
[2] Cf. above, p. 69, as well as the speech in the Lords here referred to.

CRIMEAN WAR AND VOLUNTEER FORCE

comfort when Panmure merely declared that the garrison was not to be larger than in 1853, and that no change in policy was intended.[1] Apparently the advantages resulting from the Crimean War were to be lightly thrown away.

Palmerston's Government, however, had not altogether overlooked the labours of Grey and Elgin. The Colonial Secretary had already addressed to Sir Edmund Head a dispatch expressing the hope that the arrival of the reinforcement would not be misinterpreted in Canada.[2] The principles affirmed by Grey in 1851, he said, still stood. The vigour of the new Canadian militia organization was their best justification; and "although the regular soldiers in Canada may be more or fewer at any particular time, the policy of Her Majesty's Government continues the same, and they desire to place their main dependence on the well-proved loyalty and courage of Her Majesty's Canadian subjects to repel any hostile aggression, should the occasion ever unfortunately come, although in that event Her Majesty's Government would not fail to give to the Province the full support of the whole power of the British Empire."

The volunteer force had, indeed, proved popular in Canada. During the summer of 1856 Head reported creditable progress in its organization, and mentioned the first instances of the volunteers being called upon to support the civil power.[3] Interest in the force was reflected in an Act passed in that year to permit the formation of unpaid units in addition to the paid ones authorized by the Act of 1855.[4] This Act, however, was fiercely criticized by the opposition in the Provincial Parliament, which maintained that *all* the corps should be unpaid. W. H. Merritt, a member famous for projects of economy in the Manchester manner, opposed the " reckless manner ".in which the volunteers were paid (a rifleman could draw five shillings for each of his ten days of annual drill); and George Brown considered it a bad precedent for Canada to begin to spend money on her own defence:

---

[1] *Hansard*, CXLII, 691–94. Lord Grey supported Elgin.
[2] Labouchere to Head, May 2, 1856: *P.P.*, 1861, no. 423, vol. XIII; appendix 16.
[3] Head to Labouchere (confidential), June 21, 1856 (G, 180 B); July 19, 1856 (G, 462, p. 528).
[4] 19 Vict., cap. 44.

"If they began this year with the sum now before them, next year it would be much more. . . . This was the commencement of the system, and he voted against it now as a protest against the whole thing. . . . They had government troops coming, enrolled pensioners, and river police at Montreal and Quebec, and now a paid militia. . . . The whole thing was unnecessary. . . ."

When the Government argued that the expense of the system would be covered by the revenue from the ordnance lands, the opposition was sceptical (and the event justified their scepticism).[1] When Antoine Dorion, leader of the *Rouge* radicals of Lower Canada, moved an amendment opposing payment of the volunteers, 36 members voted for it, against the Government's 53.[2]

The appropriation finally made for the militia in 1856 amounted to £25,145, of which £10,000 was for the purchase of arms, accoutrements, and ammunition.[3] This was in addition to provision for the pensioner force (which, however, was not to be continued on duty). We have seen what a novelty this new expenditure was, and how strongly the opposition had resisted it. Yet in the same year the regular military establishment in the province of Canada cost the mother country £280,312.[4] The little volunteer force represented a first step by the colony towards the creation of an independent defensive organization; but the omens did not indicate that further progress would be easy or rapid, and certainly the prospect had not been improved by the advent of the large reinforcement so light-heartedly sent from England in the spring of 1856.

This year saw the completion of the transfer of the ordnance lands.[5] Nearly all the lands and buildings at the various stations which had at one time or another been held by imperial troops were handed over to the province. The exceptions were chiefly at Quebec, Montreal, and Kingston. The lands transferred were situated in forty-three different localities; their total area was in the neighbourhood of 60,000 acres, the greater

---

[1] Council minute, April 7, 1865 (State Book A.B., p. 279), points out that the rents and profits (including Rideau Canal) have not equalled expenses.
[2] Macdonald's memorandum, *M.P.*, "Militia and Defence," I, 3 ff. Toronto *Globe*, June 10, 1856.
[3] Supply Act, 19–20 Vict., cap. 86.
[4] *P.P.*, 1859 (session I), no. 240, vol. XVII.
[5] Effected by the Provincial Act 19 Vict., cap. 45. The first schedule of the Act recites the lands retained by the Imperial Government, the second those transferred. They are not final in all details.

CRIMEAN WAR AND VOLUNTEER FORCE 103

part being made up of one large parcel at Sorel. Among the items were the works and barracks at Chambly, St. Johns, Isle aux Noix, Prescott, London, and Toronto, in addition to the Rideau and Ottawa canals with their adjuncts.[1]

With the return of more normal relations with the United States in 1857, the Home Government began once more to think of economy. When Head was informed that it was proposed to withdraw one regiment from Canada, he made no objection.[2] Shortly, however, a plan of a different sort was broached. General Eyre had complained that there was in Canada no horsed artillery unit; and the Colonial Secretary asked Head's views on a suggestion that the expense of mounting one should be defrayed by the province.[3] Head, " at the risk of speaking freely ", discouraged the scheme in a long dispatch that might have been written by Elgin.[4] He wrote:

" Many persons in the Colony on the whole well affected to England and attached to their allegiance would be apt to reason as follows :—

" ' We have been lately threatened with a war with the United States. On what ground was this war likely to occur ? Would it have been in defence of Canadian interests properly so called ? No —what do we care for Central America or Cuba ? As regards our own internal tranquillity, or defence against mere marauders, the Volunteer artillery are likely to be more than we shall want. The chances are that any quarrel between the United States and England will originate in matters not concerning us. Under any circumstances, we should have to bear a heavy loss in destruction of property & trade—Is it unfair that we should expect Great Britain, who conducts negociations committing us, to furnish troops to protect us against foreign Aggression ?

" ' We admit to the fullest extent our obligation to keep the peace within our own Territory, but if we are to horse the Royal Artillery,

[1] For an interesting private letter of Head to Sir William Eyre on this subject, Dec. 22, 1856, see Public Archives of Canada, S series, Internal Correspondence, Miscellaneous, 1856 and 1857. Head observes that " Mr. Gladstone and his colleagues " seem to have adopted the idea that the separation of Canada from Britain is only a matter of time, questions " the consistency of the course taken in the cession of the Ordnance Lands, unconditional and sweeping as it is, with the ' solidarité ' of defensive interests between England and Canada," and remarks upon the difficulty of obtaining funds for military purposes from Canadian ministers.
[2] Labouchere to Head, Jan. 19, 1857: *G*, 153, p. 87. Head to Labouchere, Feb. 8, 1857: *G*, 463, p. 34.
[3] Labouchere to Head, with enclosures, March 13, 1857: *G*, 153, p. 183.
[4] Head to Labouchere, April 1, 1857: *G*, 463, p. 49.

may we not as naturally feed all troops employed in Canada ? We should not mind doing even that, if we were ensured against all wars except those the origins of which concerned ourselves. . . .' "

" On the whole therefore," Head concluded, " if the question be, Shall a Field Battery of the Royal Artillery be sent to Canada, subject to the condition that the Provincial Government will horse it ? I should say that the Battery is no doubt desirable, but it may be bought too dear, and I think the effect of asking the Provincial Government to horse a Battery of the Queen's Artillery, would do more harm morally, than its presence on the spot would make up for."

A year later, Head gave a similar exposition of the situation for the benefit of the Conservative Government which had succeeded Palmerston's, and which now proceeded to suggest the possibility of the Canadian Government's defraying the cost of hiring buildings for the accommodation of troops at Quebec and Montreal.[1] Head replied bluntly[2] that if he referred the suggestion to his ministers the result would be very doubtful, and that if they did take it to the assembly it was probable that that body would refuse to sanction the outlay. The Canadian impression, he said, was that when the imperial authorities retained the military properties at Quebec, Montreal and Kingston it was on the principle that these places were to be garrisoned at Imperial expense. He added :

" The payment of a portion of the expenses of these garrisons involves the admission of the principle that the whole might be required at any time. If the whole were required, I think the Colonial Legislature would run all risks and dispense with the troops —in other words, they would place the colony in a position almost defenceless in time of war.

" As a matter of course, the discretion of leaving the North American Colonies in this position rests at any time with Her Majesty's Government."

There is no escaping the implications of this, the considered opinion of an able official who had spent ten years among the people of British North America. If England's dominant interest is economy, let her economize by decreasing her American military establishment ; but let her beware how she

[1] Stanley to Head (confidential), May 18, 1858 : *G*, 157, p. 191.
[2] Head to Stanley (confidential), June 7, 1858 : *G*, 180 B, p. 62.

CRIMEAN WAR AND VOLUNTEER FORCE 105

seeks to lay new burdens on her colonists there. If the defensive organization maintained in the provinces is to be cut on a pattern drawn in England, then England must pay for it. To attempt to make British Americans devote their revenues to military objects of whose importance they themselves (rightly or wrongly) are not convinced, will do the Empire in the end more harm than good.

In the course of 1857, another distant emergency arose to strain the military resources of the Empire. In May the great Mutiny broke out in India. Now the army (just reduced after the Crimean augmentations) had again to be increased. Regiments were hastily sent from England to the East, and new battalions raised to take their places. Canadian sympathies were actively enlisted for the British cause. As early as August the Kingston volunteer battery offered its services, either for India or for active duty in the province to release British troops who might be needed there ;[1] other volunteer corps soon followed suit ;[2] and a whole succession of suggestions were made for raising new regiments in the colony—including more than one for the enlistment of negroes.[3] The volunteers' offers met with a cold reception at the Horse Guards, rather to the disgust of the Colonial Secretary ;[4] the military authorities had no use for volunteers of any kind, English or Colonial.[5]

The project for raising regular troops, however, was a different matter. The Commander of the Forces thought it feasible ; and Head entered into the scheme with enthusiasm, stipulating again, however, that nothing should be done without consulting his council.[6] Early in 1858 proposals from England received the council's approval ; and in the spring enlistments began for the 100th Royal Canadian Regiment of Foot. By the middle of May it was complete, 1,027 strong, with Colonel Baron de Rottenburg, the provincial Adjutant-General, who had played a great part in organizing the volun-

---

[1] Eyre to Labouchere, Aug. 23, 1857 : *G*, 463, p. 88.
[2] Eyre to Labouchere, Sept. 7, 1857 : *ibid.*, p. 91.
[3] Eyre to Labouchere, Sept. 7, Sept. 18, Oct. 3, 1857 ; Head to Labouchere, Nov. 21, 1857 : *ibid.*, pp. 91, 92–3, 93, 98.
[4] Labouchere to Palmerston, Sept. 23, 1857 ; Palmerston to Panmure, Sept. 25 : *Panmure Papers*, II, 432–33.
[5] Duke of Cambridge to Panmure, Oct. 2, 1857 : *ibid.*, 439.
[6] Eyre to Labouchere, Sept. 7, 1857 ; Head to Labouchere, Nov. 21, 1857 : *G*, 463, pp. 91, 98.

teers, as its Commander.[1] Head regarded the raising of a colonial regiment for general service as an important precedent, writing :

"Great Britain is, as it were, placed in the centre of a circle ; every man who emigrates to Canada or Australia has hitherto ceased to be available for any Military purpose other than the defence of the single and distant point on the circumference which he may have adopted as his new home.

"But if a Regiment for General Service can be, from time to time, drawn from one of these outlying points, it will be so much gained ; the population, not of Great Britain and Ireland, but of the whole Empire may contribute in some degree to the Military strength of the whole. . . ."[2]

Certainly the raising of the Royal Canadians was an episode of some note in the military history of the Empire. The sacrifices made for the imperial interest, however, were purely those of individuals. The regiment was organized, equipped, and paid at English expense, and became a unit of the regular army different from the others in no particular except the distant origin and peculiar speech of its members. Within a few years, in fact, it ceased to draw recruits from Canada, and when the regiments of the army were territorialized it was allotted to a district in Ireland. But as the Prince of Wales's Leinster Regiment (Royal Canadians) it still remembered its beginnings, and wore the maple leaf through the wars in South Africa and France, until, with other Irish regiments, it fell a victim to governmental economy in 1922.

The policy of stripping the colonies of troops, resorted to during the Crimean War, did not appear in Canada to a similar extent during the Mutiny. The Duke of Cambridge opposed the idea very strongly, insisting that the Canadian garrison should not be reduced below two battalions, (in addition, apparently, to the Royal Canadian Rifles)[3] ; and the total garrison of British North America does not seem to have fallen below 4,500 men in 1858,[4] though the seven line battalions that

[1] Head to Labouchere, Jan. 13, March 8 and 9, 1858 ; to Stanley, May 15 : *ibid.*, pp. 111, 129, 130, 155.
[2] Head to Stanley, May 1, 1858 : *ibid.*, p. 142. Cf. Head to Stanley, May 31, 1858 (*ibid.*, p. 161) ; and on the raising of the regiment see Whitton, *History of the Prince of Wales's Leinster Regiment (Royal Canadians)*, I.
[3] Cambridge to Panmure, Sept. 25, 1857 : Verner, *Military Life of George, Duke of Cambridge*, I, 162 ; cf. I, 211.
[4] *P.P.*, 1861, no. 423, vol. XIII, appendix I.

had been there after the reinforcement of 1856 had been reduced to four.

As the time approached for the expiration of the Canadian Militia Act of 1855, those who desired the permanence of the new volunteer organization were not without misgivings. Despite the apparent popularity of the force, the opposition's hostility to it had no whit declined, as a vigorous attempt to strike out the appropriation for it demonstrated in 1858.[1] The Governor-General showed his own anxiety in a dispatch of February of that year, addressed to the Colonial Office but really designed to be sent to the legislature with a view to forwarding their education in the matter of defence.[2] Stressing the desirability of maintaining and improving the existing organization, he called attention yet once more to the fulness of Canadian self-government, and proceeded to affirm his belief that the possession of some organized means of self-defence was essential to the complete political development of any community. He recalled that Canada in the past had on occasion been threatened, not with that open war which would call forth the united force of the Empire to repel it, but with lawless attacks by citizens of the neighbouring country:

"No country and no colonial community can be said to enjoy a complete political existence, or to be properly organised in itself, unless it possess within itself the power of meeting and putting down external aggression of this irregular kind on the part of foreigners, or internal tumult amongst its own people. . . .

"I cannot therefore for a moment imagine that Canada would desire to lower her own standing in the world by abandoning a military organization such as would serve to attain the objects which I have described. To think this would be to suppose that the Province sought its own humiliation, and was anxious to diminish, rather than gradually to increase the completeness of its political existence."

These arguments made little practical impression; Head's apprehensions of an attack by Parliament upon the efficiency of the active force were realized in 1859. The Act then passed, "To amend and make permanent the Laws relating to the Militia of this Province",[3] retained the volunteer principle, but

[1] Macdonald's memorandum, *M.P.*, " Militia and Defence," I, 3 ff.; *Globe*, June 2, 1858.
[2] Head to Labouchere, Feb. 8, 1858: *G*, 463, p. 119.
[3] 22 Vict., cap. 18.

was inspired by an economical spirit so extreme as to be greatly injurious. It must be remembered that there was reason for economy. The effect of the severe financial crisis of 1857 had been aggravated in Canada by crop failures; the colony's deficit in 1858 was more than $1,100,000.[1] But it was unfortunate that the provincial defences should have been so harshly served just at this time. The new Act slightly reduced the authorized strength of the paid force; and it provided that pay should be given to only a portion of the strength of the units,[2] while at the same time the annual drill period was practically cut in half. The office of Adjutant-General was abolished, only to be revived in case of emergency. The act was naturally unpopular with the volunteers; and as the appropriations declined (they were cut from $102,968 in 1858 to $69,430 the next year)[3] the strength, enthusiasm, and efficiency of the force declined with them.[4]

Economy in the militia organization was not the only result of the commercial depression following 1857. Canada was now mistress of her own commercial policy, free to adopt what expedients seemed good to her for repairing the deficiency in the revenue; and in 1859 Alexander Galt, the new Inspector-General of Finances, decided that the only remedy was an increase in the tariff on manufactured goods.[5] The Canadian tariff had shown an upward trend since 1841, watched with suspicion by the exporters of England. Now the new increase provoked an outburst of criticism from English free-traders, who resented it not merely as an injury to English trade, but also as a piece of impudence on the part of a dependency: thus to abandon the new gospel which the mother country was in the very act of preaching to every nation seemed to them an act of positive impropriety. The merchants and manufacturers of Sheffield thought it "indecent and a reproach", and said so in a memorial to the imperial government begging it to interfere. The Duke of Newcastle forwarded this document to

[1] *Canada and its Provinces*, V, 177–78
[2] Commanding officers, however, were authorized to divide the whole sum due to the company among a greater number.
[3] Supply acts 21 Vict., cap. 83, and 22 Vict., cap. 13.
[4] *Canada and its Provinces*, VII, 398–99; Denison, *Soldiering in Canada*, chap. V; cf. Colonel Eardley-Wilmot's report on the artillery, Oct. 31, 1861: copy in *M.P.*, "Militia and Defence," I, 11.
[5] Skelton, *Life and Times of Sir Alexander Tilloch Galt*, 270–73.

CRIMEAN WAR AND VOLUNTEER FORCE 109

Canada with a dispatch remarking that, while the Queen would probably not be advised to disallow the Tariff Act, he nevertheless felt it his duty to express his regret at its nature. Galt replied in a celebrated memorandum in which, apart from economic arguments, he read the Colonial Office a lecture on the nature of responsible government :

" Her Majesty cannot be advised to disallow such acts, unless her advisers are prepared to assume the administration of the affairs of the Colony, irrespective of the views of its inhabitants.

" The Imperial Government are not responsible for the debts and engagements of Canada, they do not maintain its judicial, educational or civil service, they contribute nothing to the internal government of the country ; and the Provincial Legislature, acting through a ministry directly responsible to it, has to make provision for all these wants ; they must necessarily claim and exercise the widest latitude as to the nature and extent of the burthens to be placed upon the industry of the people."[1]

This outspoken exposition the Imperial Government made no attempt to refute ; and the episode remains a notable milestone upon the road that has led Canada to legislative equality with the mother country. But Englishmen were not slow to point out that the colony was far readier to assert national rights than to assume national responsibilities. In particular, they called attention to the military situation. England might " contribute nothing to the internal government " of Canada ; but she kept her troops there to protect the colonists, and spent more than £250,000 annually for that object, while the province contributed towards its own defence only a small fraction of that sum, and had in fact almost halved its exiguous expenditure in the same session that produced the tariff act. Here was grist for the mill of those who opposed the Imperial military expenditure in the colonies. That the military protection which Britain afforded them might fail even to purchase for her products free entry to their markets was a hardship which the earlier critics had not anticipated. Molesworth had thought of the garrisons as ensuring that advantage, though he thought the price far too high ;[2] one wonders what he would have said to Galt's tariff, had he lived to see it. And, naturally, as Canada

---

[1] *Ibid.*, 328-31. The documents are in Egerton and Grant, *Canadian Constitutional Development*, 348-51.
[2] Egerton, *Speeches of Sir William Molesworth*, 175-77.

began to tend towards protection she deprived herself of her last hope of any shred of sympathy from the high-priests of free trade, the men of the Manchester school. To find the colonies, still defended at imperial charge despite their long agitation, actually raising barriers against the trade of the country that paid the bill, seemed to them the last straw.

The Imperial Government, we shall see, refrained from making any official use of the argument which the new fiscal policy afforded against the maintenance of troops in Canada at English expense. Private individuals were not obliged to be so nice. From this time the contradiction between the acceptance of English protection and the taxing of English goods was in many mouths. The Canadian tariff of 1859 was in fact a large nail in the coffin of the garrison system; but it was to be ten years and more before the lid was screwed down above the corpse.

. . . .

The year 1859 saw England in the throes of another military panic. Hostile feelings towards France had been revived by incidents following Orsini's attempt upon the life of the Emperor, which had been planned in England ;[1] Parliament showed its peevish determination to have no truckling to France in defeating Palmerston's Conspiracy to Murder Bill; and the succeeding Conservative ministry announced increases in naval expenditure. As Franco-Austrian tension grew, so did English anxiety; the idealistic element in Napoleon's Italian policy went unrecognized. Then, in April, France and Austria went to war. The English Press demanded more attention to national defence ;[2] a volunteer system was spoken of; and on May 9 *The Times* published certain verses whose authorship was, perhaps inadequately, concealed by the modest signature " T." :

> " Form, be ready to do or die !
>   Form in Freedom's name and the Queen's !
> True, that we have a faithful ally,
>   But only the Devil knows what he means.
>   Form ! Form ! Riflemen form !
> Ready, be ready to meet the storm !
>   Riflemen, riflemen, riflemen form ! "

[1] See *Spectator*, Jan. 30, 1859, for the outbursts of French army officers.
[2] e.g., *Times*, April 28 ; *Spectator* and *Saturday Review*, April 30.

They formed obediently. Three days later the War Office authorized the enrolment of volunteer corps,[1] and organization meetings began to be held throughout the country. Thus suddenly began the English volunteer movement, which to the Cobdenites seemed an unholy aberration. By 1861 the volunteer army was 160,000 strong.[2]

Palmerston was in power again before 1859 was out, and an exaggeration rather than a diminution of panic feeling followed. There was a very large increase in the navy estimates next year,[3] and £2,000,000 was voted for beginning a great scheme of dockyard fortifications, admittedly inspired by fear of France.[4] The effect of Cobden's negotiation of an advantageous commercial treaty with Napoleon's government was offset by the French annexation of Savoy and Nice; and apprehension continued until British attention was suddenly diverted to America by the *Trent* affair in the autumn of 1861. In that crisis the Emperor showed himself friendly to Britain, and the panic thus came to an end.[5] It had served the purpose, not merely of bringing the volunteer force into being, but also of perpetuating the increase in the regular army which had been produced by the Indian Mutiny.[6]

Inevitably also, by directing attention to the problems of home defence, it had revived the question of the colonial garrisons. It did not immediately produce sweeping reductions (though the force in British North America was pared down to little more than 4,000 men),[7] but it did occasion a searching inquiry into the situation. In 1859 the Secretary of State for War (General Peel) complained officially of the "difficulty and embarrassment" caused to his department by "the absence of any fixed and recognized principle for the guidance of the

---

[1] *Times*, May 13.
[2] Walpole, *History of Twenty-Five Years*, I, 320. For the growth of the volunteer force see also *P.P.*, 1871, no. 171, vol. XXXIX.
[3] Walpole, *op. cit.*, I, 326; cf. *Hansard*, CLVI, 962 (Feb. 13, 1860).
[4] Speech of Palmerston, *Hansard*, CLX, 22 (July 23, 1860).
[5] Walpole, I, 275; Cobden, *The Three Panics*.
[6] Cf. Fortescue, XIII, 530. The British force permanently maintained in India was much increased after the Mutiny.
[7] *P.P.*, 1861, no. 423, vol. XIII, appendix 1. There was a slight temporary increase after the end of the Mutiny; but from 1859 the force in Canada so far as infantry was concerned was only one line battalion, plus the Canadian Rifles, whose strength had been augmented. *Hansard*, CLXI, 1409; CLXII, 2194 (speeches of Chichester Fortescue and T. G. Baring, March 5 and May 17, 1861).

Secretary of State in determining the numerous questions of military expenditure which are continually arising in most of the colonies." In consequence a departmental committee consisting of representatives of the War Office, the Colonial Office, and the Treasury was convened to consider the matter.

Its investigation showed that during the financial year 1857-58 there had been in all the colonies more than 47,000 Imperial troops; that the British exchequer disbursed that year for colonial military defence £3,590,000, while the colonies' own total expenditure for that purpose was £378,000; and that while some colonies made large contributions to the upkeep of Imperial forces, others preferred to spend money on local organization, and still others spent no money on defence at all. Thus, Victoria spent £94,000, chiefly on the Imperial troops, while the English expenditure there was only £44,000; Canada devoted £40,000 to defensive objects, most of which went to the upkeep of the volunteer force, whereas the Imperial bill in that colony was £261,000; and in Nova Scotia and New Brunswick, where Great Britain spent £191,000, the only local military expenditure the committee could find amounted in all to £432!

To the War Office and Treasury representatives,[1] this diversity was highly objectionable. Their report vigorously criticized the whole garrison system, as being both burdensome and inefficient; the proper system, they said, would be one based on "local efforts and local resources". The only ground which they recognized as constituting a valid claim on the part of the colonies to defensive aid from Britain was the latter's complete control of foreign policy. They divided the colonies into just two classes—imperial stations like Gibraltar, and others; and with regard to the latter class, they declared, "the system of defence should be founded on two simple principles, colonial management, and joint contribution at a uniform rate". The colony was to decide the amount of armament required; the Imperial Government was to bear a fixed proportion of the cost —perhaps half.

As might have been expected, the representative of the Colonial Office[2] dissented from this over-simplification and

[1] J. R. Godley and G. A. Hamilton, respectively.
[2] T. F. Elliot.

CRIMEAN WAR AND VOLUNTEER FORCE 113

objected very strongly to the idea of imposing a single rate of contribution upon colonies of vastly diverse situations. With regard to North America in particular, he observed that, in the special circumstances of the colonies there, the principles laid down by Grey eight years before seemed quite acceptable.[1]

Before this committee had reported, the question of the garrisons had been aired once more in the House of Commons. Hume and Molesworth were now no more; but Charles Adderley made the question his own, and took up the cudgels in the old style, declaring that the scattered garrisons weakened England without strengthening the colonies.[2] As usual, the Government admitted the force of many of the criticisms, but urged the need of cautious procedure.[3] The departmental committee was spoken of; and Adderley did not rest until, in the following year, he obtained the Government's consent to lay its report before Parliament.[4] Then he made it the text of a demand for sweeping reforms.[5] Again ministers admitted that the existing situation was not ideal; but they refused to consider putting into effect the majority report's idea for a " Procrustean rule ", which they regarded as " very simple but quite impossible ".[6]

More than one member suggested that the whole problem should be referred to an impartial select committee of the House.[7] The Government at first was not disposed to assent,[8] but in 1861 the demand, renewed by Arthur Mills,[9] received so much sympathy that Palmerston, while gruffly observing that the Government saw no profit in the suggestion, did not oppose it.[10] Mills accordingly became chairman of a committee " to inquire and report whether any, and what, alterations may be advantageously adopted in regard to the Defence of the British Dependencies, and the proportions of cost of such Defence as

[1] *P.P.*, 1860, no. 282, vol. XLI: Report of committee on expense of military defences in the colonies.
[2] *Hansard*, CLV, 391–97 (July 25, 1859).
[3] *Ibid.*, 404 (speech of Sidney Herbert).
[4] *Ibid.*, CLVI, 2220–21 (March 5, 1860) and CLVII, 1637–42 (March 30, 1860).
[5] *Ibid.*, CLVIII, 1826–33 (May 31, 1860).
[6] *Ibid.*, 1836–40, 1855–56 (speeches of Chichester Fortescue and Herbert).
[7] *Ibid.*, 1840–41 (Arthur Mills); *ibid.*, CLIX, 331–32 (H. C. E. Childers, June 12, 1860).
[8] *Ibid.*, CLIX, 332 (speech of Herbert).
[9] *Ibid.*, CLXI, 1400 ff. (March 5, 1861).
[10] *Ibid.*, 1419–21.

now defrayed from Imperial and Colonial funds respectively ". The Committee fell to work, but before its monumental report was completed the shadow of a new emergency was arising in the West ; and a consideration of this document may best be reserved for a place in our account of the British reaction to the American Civil War.

. . . . . .

From the point of view of their significance in connexion with the problem of imperial defence, the events of 1854-60 in Canada seem to reveal somewhat conflicting tendencies in the colony's life.

That there was a sturdy (and, apparently, growing) imperial sentiment among the colonists was undoubted. Watching with the deepest feelings the fortunes of Britain as she played her part on the world-stage, they had begun to manifest some signs of a willingness to share those fortunes. The individual offers of service in the Crimean and Indian crises, and the ease with which the Royal Canadian Regiment was raised, seemed to indicate such a development. Hitherto (as Head had observed) Britons removing to the colonies had seemed cut off from the possibility of sharing in the mother country's defence in time of peril.

" We n'er shall tread the fancy-haunted valley
    Where 'tween the dark hills creeps the small clear stream—
In arms around the patriarch banner rally,
    Or see the moon on royal tomb-stones gleam. . . .
Come foreign rage—let discord burst in slaughter—
    Then O for clansmen true, and stern claymore !
The hearts that would have giv'n their blood like water
    Beat heavily beyond the Atlantic roar."

Now there were stirrings of a new consciousness of unity. Another great imperial emergency at this period might have brought the mother country active assistance from the colonies. Actually, such an emergency was not to arise for forty years ;[1] yet the Queen lived to hear the lyre strike out a robust strain very different from (if hardly more melodious than) the romantic regret of the *Canadian Boat Song* :

[1] In 1878, when war with Russia was threatened, tentative arrangements were made for raising a division of 10,000 Canadians. See General MacDougall's memorandum of Feb. 27, 1882, in *M.P.*, " Militia and Defence," II, 169.

"Southern Cross and Polar Star,
Here are the Britains bred afar;
Serry them, serry them, fierce and keen,
Under the flag of the Empress-Queen. . . ."

The spirit that sent Canadian contingents to South Africa in 1900, and Canadian armies to France in 1914, may, perhaps, be identified as moving in the colony even in the days of the Crimean War.

On the other hand, the official attitude of the Canadian government is a rather different story. It is true that these years saw it take its first steps in the organization of independent military forces. In organizing the volunteer force, even on so small a scale, it recognized a new principle and broke definitely with the inert past. Yet we cannot shut our eyes to the slightness of the effort, judged by comparison with the sums spent in the colony by Britain; we may not disregard the fierceness of the opposition which even these modest projects aroused, nor the fact that the mother country, in suggesting that the colonists undertake new responsibilities, offered them the ordnance lands in compensation. There was ample justification for the caution which experienced governors urged upon the Colonial Office in these matters; for Canadian politicians were only in very small degree accessible to considerations of military policy.

The long tradition of Imperial protection had its effect—not so much perhaps in a conscious casting of the burden of defence upon Great Britain as in a failure to recognize the need for defensive preparation. The same economical attitude which in the United States appeared in the determination of Congress to tolerate only a very small army, was in evidence in the Canadian Parliament; but it was intensified by the fact that the colony had grown up behind the mother country's shield. The facts of hard experience had not impressed upon its legislators the desirability of applying some portion of the country's revenues and energy to military preparation in time of peace. Pioneer communities are in general both short of cash and extremely self-confident; and Canada was no exception. With a small and often embarrassed revenue, it was not easy for her to see the source from which funds for large armaments might be obtained, and her people, remembering her preservation in the face of great odds in 1812, forgot how altered conditions had shifted the military balance against her since those days.[1] Above all, they felt—apparently—a confidence in the martial prowess of a patriotic people (even a people untrained and unaccustomed to military life) which history does nothing to justify. Least of all the history of Canada: for, as we have seen, the defence in 1812-14 had succeeded simply because it was conducted by trained regular troops against an enemy who, superior in numbers and equal in courage, was inferior in the disciplined cohesion that comes of training and experience. In a period when war between the United States and Great Britain was a great deal less " unthinkable " than it has since become—when at intervals, in fact, it seemed more than probable—the reluctance of Canada to spend money on the preparations which alone could preserve her if the worst came to the worst is an interesting phenomenon.

That the colony stubbornly insisted upon receiving from Britain the fullest political privileges, and nevertheless was particularly slow in assuming the burden of military expenditure which the mother country had carried on her behalf so long, was thus not the result of mere selfishness. Canadians were convinced that their happiness and prosperity were bound up with those privileges; but few of them entertained a conviction of any such intimate relationship between their country's welfare and the state of her military preparations—whether the latter were made at English or at Canadian expense. Partly (though not altogether) because Britain had so long relieved them of the need for considering such matters, military affairs played almost no part in their scheme of things. We shall soon see that even in the presence of imminent danger Canada undertook defensive precautions with notable reluctance.

---

[1] Although the populations of both countries had grown enormously, the British regular garrison of Canada was now smaller than it had been before 1812, and was considerably inferior even to the regular army of the United States which it had formerly equalled in strength. And the growth of modern communications and the disappearance of the forests deprived Canada of the isolation which had been a great source of her defensive strength in 1812.

CHAPTER VI

CANADA AND THE AMERICAN CIVIL WAR: THE EARLY PHASES

"Now, during the American war the Parliament of this country passed an Act by which it declared that it was illegal to tax the colonies. I am afraid that it would be very difficult to pass an Act declaring it illegal for the colonies to tax us."
SIR GEORGE LEWIS in Parliament, February 17, 1862.

To consider the history of Canada apart from that of the United States of America is not possible, though Canadian writers have sometimes bent to the task with laudable determination. At no time has British North America been able to regard happenings south of the border with complete detachment, and least of all at the great crises of the Republic's growth. The American Revolution was one of the greatest events in Canadian history, if for no other reason than that it gave Canada her English-speaking population; and the American Civil War is of no less significance, for the fierce heat which it generated played a major part in welding the diverse elements of British America into a Dominion and a nation. The complete story of the reactions of the provinces to that terrible struggle has not yet been told;[1] but here we must make some attempt at evaluating at least its effects upon the military policy of the Colonial Governments and of the Empire as a whole.

In the spring of 1861 the "irrepressible conflict" between northern free states and southern slave states, which the anxious care of American statesmen had postponed so long, burst at last into open flame. On April 12, Beauregard's guns opened against Fort Sumter; three days later, President

---
[1] Much material is collected in Macdonald, *Canadian Public Opinion on the American Civil War*. It is rather surprising that Adams, *Great Britain and the American Civil War*, almost completely overlooks the Canadian aspects of British policy, and makes no mention even of the border incidents such as the St. Albans raid. The same is true of Jordan, D., and Pratt, E. J., *Europe and the American Civil War*, Boston and New York, 1931.

Lincoln called for volunteers to defend the Union; and thereafter for four years there was no peace in North America. With this battle of giants in progress close to her American frontier, Britain took stock of the means immediately available for defending that frontier against the menaces latent in such a situation; and the inventory was not impressive. So far as the Imperial regulars were concerned, there were in British North America at the end of March, 1861, less than 4,300 effectives of all ranks, of whom only 2,200 were in Canada, where of course the danger was greatest.[1] As to local resources, there were in Canada something less than 5,000 volunteers, uniformed, armed, and partially drilled. The Maritime Provinces now had volunteers also, having emulated the movement of 1859 in the mother country; in Nova Scotia, New Brunswick and Prince Edward Island together, their numbers amounted to about 5,000.[2] Behind these little forces stood the man-power of the provinces, organized on paper in a fashion that made them available in emergency, but in the meantime left them without arms, uniforms or training, and therefore without any immediate military value whatever.

Only a fortnight after the news from Sumter reached them,[3] the Imperial Government took steps to improve this unsatisfactory situation by reinforcing the garrison of Canada. First one regiment was sent;[4] two more, and a field battery with the new Armstrong guns,[5] followed—rather dramatically, for the Government chartered for the purpose the largest steamship of that day, the *Great Eastern*, which took the whole force in one voyage.[6] Adderley immediately raised in the House of

---

[1] *P.P.*, 1861, no. 423, vol. XIII, appendix 1. Small detachments were stationed at this time in two distant regions of British North America. In 1857 about 100 men of the Royal Canadian Rifles were, at the request of the Hudson's Bay Company, which offered to pay the cost of transport and rations, stationed at Fort Garry (now Winnipeg) and remained there until 1861 (see C, 364). A little later about 150 of the Royal Engineers were sent to British Columbia, where they did very useful work in forwarding the development of the colony until the detachment was disbanded in 1863. Half of the cost of this force was defrayed locally: see *P.P.*, 1863, no. 112, vol. V, p. 5; cf. Howay, *The Work of the Royal Engineers in British Columbia, 1858 to 1863.*
[2] *Canada and its Provinces*, VII, 413 ff.
[3] *Hansard*, CLXII, 2194 (May 17, 1861).
[4] Newcastle to Head, May 31, 1861: G, 165, p. 444.
[5] Newcastle to Head, June 21, 1861: *ibid.*, 480.
[6] Fortescue, *History of the British Army*, XIII, 547; cf. Butler, *Annals of the King's Royal Rifle Corps*, III, 246.

Illustrated London News, January 22, 1859

PRESENTATION OF COLOURS TO THE 100TH REGIMENT, SHORNCLIFFE, ENGLAND, JANUARY 10, 1859

The "first public act" of the young Prince of Wales (afterwards King Edward VII) was this presentation to the 100th (The Prince of Wales' Royal Canadian) Regiment of Foot, the first regiment to be raised in a British colony for general service

REINFORCEMENTS FOR CANADA AT THE TIME OF THE TRENT AFFAIR
The Guards crossing Westminster Bridge, London, on their way to embark, December 19, 1861

Illustrated London News, December 28, 1861

Commons the question of the expense involved ;[1] and later the government's action was criticized as likely to arouse apprehension in the United States.[2] Disraeli, it is interesting to observe, objected to it also on the ground that it was calculated to " damp the ardour " of the people of Canada, and prevent their taking active measures on their own account.[3]

The Government's explanation was that Sir Fenwick Williams, commanding in British North America, had asked for reinforcements, and that they had sent them, not from fear of the hostility of the United States Government, but because of the possibility of lawless filibustering incursions by discharged soldiers when the war came to an end.[4] Palmerston's private view of the utility of an increased regular force in Canada was characteristic ; it would serve, he thought, to " keep the United States Government in check, to give spirit and confidence to our own people in the provinces, and to take the best chance for the continuance of peace ".[5] In any case, the new departure had thwarted the ten-year-old economy policy once more, just as in 1856, when Palmerston had taken a similar attitude ;[6] and it was to be many a long day before the garrison of Canada fell again to the strength at which the outbreak of the American War had found it.[7]

The provincial ministers demonstrated their own sense of the dangers of the situation by pointing out to the Imperial Government the desirability of augmenting the small supply of arms available in Canada before winter closed the St. Lawrence ; their suggestion was that 100,000 stand of arms and a proportion of artillery should be sent out and stored in the colony, to be distributed only in case of emergency. As Head remarked, they did not offer to pay the expense of transport ;[8] but they

[1] *Hansard*, CLXIII, 937 (June 11, 1861).
[2] *Ibid.*, 1516-21 (June 24, 1861) : speech of Sir James Fergusson.
[3] *Ibid.*, 1523-27.
[4] Report of Select Committee on Colonial Military Expenditure (*P.P.*, 1861, no. 423, vol. XIII), p. 236 : evidence of Herbert.
[5] Palmerston to Newcastle, Sept. 1, 1861 : Ashley, E., *The Life of . . . Viscount Palmerston* . . ., London, 1876, II, 226.
[6] See above, pp. 98-9.
[7] Head discouraged a suggestion made at this time that the colony might pay the expense of sending out heavy guns for which Williams had asked (Newcastle to Head, Aug. 21, 1861 : G, 166, pp. 216-29 ; Head to Newcastle, Sept. 9 : G, 463, p. 496.)
[8] Head to Newcastle, Sept. 23, 1861 : G, 463, p. 501.

did suggest that the arrival of the arms would " encourage the Legislature at its approaching Session to organize an efficient force to be drawn from the ranks of the Sedentary Militia ".[1] The Imperial Government replied on October 23 that as the last ship sailed for Quebec on November 5, there was not time to send further stores that autumn, but that 25,000 rifles and some guns would be shipped early in the spring.[2] They soon regretted that they had not taken the request more seriously.

In November, 1861, Sir Edmund Head was succeeded as Governor-in-Chief of British North America by Viscount Monck. The latter had scarcely had time to look about him when he was confronted with one of the most dangerous crises that ever threatened Canada. On November 8, Captain Wilkes, of the U.S.S. *San Jacinto*, acting on his own responsibility, stopped the British mail-packet *Trent* in the Bahama Channel and took from her by force two Confederate diplomatic agents. The main facts of the ensuing controversy are familiar : the explosion of anger in England, the silly exultation in the United States ; the harsh British demand for an apology and the release of the prisoners, toned down by the dying Prince Consort before its dispatch ; the weeks of suspense while notes travelled across the Atlantic ; the wise decision of Lincoln's Government to hand over the captives and thus save the Union from the deadliest peril that faced it during the whole course of the war. We must examine the military measures taken in Britain and in Canada to meet the danger of war in the days when the issue hung in the balance.

The news of the seizure reached England just before the end of November,[3] and feverish naval and military preparations began at once : " We shall soon *iron the smile* out of their face," wrote the Secretary of State for War.[4] On the edge of winter, with the hand of frost already on the St. Lawrence, which was the only safe and rapid highway for men and material from the Atlantic to Quebec, an Imperial army equipped for war, and accompanied by stores to equip a Canadian army that did not

---

[1] Council minute, signed by John A. Macdonald, Sept. 23, 1861 : *E*, State Book W, p. 367.
[2] Newcastle to Head, Oct. 23, 1861 : *G*, 166, p. 309.
[3] *The Times*, Nov. 28.
[4] Lewis to Twisleton, Dec. 5 : Lewis (ed.), *Letters of . . . Sir George Cornewall Lewis*, 406.

yet exist, had to be dispatched from England in wild haste. The season was mild, and it was hoped that the first transports might fight their way up the river as far as Rivière du Loup (whence there was rail communication with Quebec and Montreal) or at least as far as Bic. There was more than a touch of drama in their race for the St. Lawrence; but luck was against them. Only one—the *Persia*—got up to Bic; and even she had to hoist anchor and run for it with 100 soldiers and all the heavy stores still aboard, and leaving her boats behind. The other vessels were all forced to turn back to Halifax.[1]

In consequence, the troops had to be moved overland to Canada through New Brunswick. The " snow road " by Lake Temiscouata was put in shape, and the reinforcements were soon passing along it in sleighs in successive detachments.[2] The Madawaska Road, as it was called, lay close to the American border, and the Imperial Government desired to open a second and safer line by the Matapedia, reaching the St. Lawrence at Métis. The Canadian Government had already been engaged on this project, and appropriated considerable sums for its completion during the succeeding years.[3]

The size and composition of the expeditionary force sent at this time to British America indicate what a serious view the British Government took of the situation. It included two battalions of the Guards (as in 1838) and an unusually large proportion of the technical arms. As given to the House of Commons, the catalogue of the whole reinforcement (including the forces sent in the summer, before the *Trent* difficulty arose) is impressive : 16 batteries of the Royal Artillery, 4 companies of the Royal Engineers, 11 battalions of foot, a large body (2 battalions) of the Military Train, and staff and detachments.

[1] The Commander-in-Chief's journal of the events in Verner, *Military Life of George, Duke of Cambridge*, I, 317–19 ; Monck to Newcastle, Dec. 27, 1861 (*G*, 464, p. 53). For the voyage of the lame duck *Melbourne*, with the staff aboard, see Wolseley, *The Story of a Soldier's Life*, II, 103–10. The officers she carried took the military labels off their baggage and travelled to Montreal by rail through the United States.

[2] Verner, I, 319 ; Wolseley, II, 111–15 ; numerous documents in *C*, 1671 and 1343. Between Jan. 11 and March 9, a force of 6780 all ranks, with 18 guns, passed into Canada by this route (Gen. Doyle to Chief of Staff, Montreal, March 12, 1862; *C*, 1671, part I, no. 32).

[3] Newcastle to Monck, Dec. 28, 1861 : *G*, 166, p. 511. Appropriations in the Canadian supply acts are as follows : 1862, $49,100 ; 1863, $15,000 ; 1864, $20,000 for that year and $40,000 for 1865. It was completed in 1867.

The total strength was 706 officers, 13,730 men, and 207 horses.[1] Bermuda was reinforced at the same time. On January 8, news of the American decision to surrender the Confederates reached England; and the Government decided to suspend troop movements to Canada.[2] However, the troops that had been sent remained there; and spring, returning to the St. Lawrence, found about 18,000 British regulars doing duty in British North America.[3] This time the Imperial authorities' desire to keep the colonial garrisons at a low figure had been thwarted with a vengeance.

In Canada also, the weeks of the crisis had been a time of anxious activity. Warned by the British minister at Washington, Lord Monck, in close conjunction with his executive council and the commanding general, took hasty defensive measures. Williams had batteries thrown up at Toronto and Kingston, armed with the heaviest guns available, to protect those places against " any sudden attack ". With the council's concurrence, arrangements were made for calling out 38,000 of the sedentary militia, as well as for largely increasing the number of volunteers.[4] The ministers asked that 100,000 infantry uniforms should be sent from England, to be issued in case the sedentary force should have to be placed on duty; all the barracks and lands in the hands of the local authorities were offered as accommodation for the regulars;[5] and finally, a provincial portfolio of defence was for the first time created, John A. Macdonald, Attorney-General for Canada West, being designated " Minister of Militia Affairs ".[6]

[1] *Hansard*, CLXV, 396 (statement of Lord Clarence Paget, Feb. 17, 1862). Confidential printed War Office *Lists* dated Jan. 3, 1862 (copy in C, 1671, pt. III), show the force in British North America on Dec. 1, 1861, as 7,407 all ranks, and the total after the reinforcement as 18,582 all ranks; the total increase ordered during the Trent difficulty was therefore 11,175. It appears, however, that the transport *Victoria*, with 570 men of the 96th Regiment on board, was forced to put back to England, and these men never reached America; the rest of the regiment, 340 strong, arrived on the *Calcutta* in February, 1862, and were sent home in the *Adriatic* in April : see documents in C, 1343.
[2] Verner, I, 318.
[3] *P.P.*, 1870, no. 254, vol. XLII, gives the total on April 1 as 17,599 effectives of all ranks.
[4] Monck to Newcastle, Dec. 19, 1861 : G, 464, p. 47. Action was suspended after the end of the *Trent* crisis (Monck to Newcastle, Feb. 2, 1862 : *ibid.*, p. 109).
[5] Council minute, Dec. 27 (E, State Book W, p. 621); Monck to Newcastle, Dec. 27 and 28, 1861 : G, 464, pp. 53, 65.
[6] Council minute, Dec. 28 : E, State Book W, p. 634.

The Government's determination was only a reflection of the attitude of the public; for when the danger was realized, "a patriotic wave swept the whole country ".[1] This feeling was not least in evidence in French Canada, where the Roman Catholic clergy were active in encouraging their parishioners to generous exertion.[2] Applications poured in for permission to organize additional volunteer corps, and many were accepted.[3] Whereas, before the *Trent* episode, General Williams had observed in the volunteers an apathetic attitude,[4] now at drill the ranks were full, and officers and men of the sedentary militia, anxious to acquire proficiency, were found taking part.[5] The warmth and obvious sincerity of Canadian feeling encouraged Lord Monck to believe that the next session of the legislature would see the passage of a law authorizing the organization of a really powerful provincial force.[6] In the meantime, the volunteers drilled assiduously, and the people of the Canadian cities lavished hospitality upon the Imperial redcoats whom fortune had suddenly thrown down among them in such numbers. Colonel Garnet Wolseley found life in Montreal very pleasant:

"We had very successful garrison theatricals in the winter, and many were the sledge expeditions we made into the neighbouring country. Altogether, it was an elysium of bliss for young officers, the only trouble being to keep single. Several impressionable young captains and subalterns had to be sent home hurriedly to save them from imprudent marriages. Although these Canadian ladies were very charming, they were not richly endowed with worldly goods."[7]

Victorian England demanded that romance should rest on solid foundations.

. . . .

Before the *Trent* affair came to upset the world, Mr. Mills's Select Committee of the House of Commons had delivered its report[8]—the most important single document in the long

[1] Landon, "The Trent Affair of 1861," *C.H.R.*, III; cf. Denison, *Soldiering n Canada*, 50-51.
[2] Landon; cf. Monck to Newcastle, Feb. 2, 1862 (G, 464, p. 109).
[3] Monck to Newcastle, Dec. 27, as above.
[4] Mentioned in Newcastle to Monck (confidential), Dec. 18, 1861 : G, 166, p. 491.
[5] Monck to Newcastle, Jan. 7, 1862 : G, 464, p. 77.
[6] Monck to Newcastle, Feb. 2, 1862, as above.
[7] Wolseley, II, 115-16.
[8] *P.P.*, 1861, no. 423, vol. XIII : Report from the Select Committee on Colonial Military Expenditure. Dated July 11, 1861.

series of events which was to lead at last to the evacuation of the self-governing colonies by the imperial army. The Committee, despite Palmerston's cold water, had taken itself seriously. It had called important witnesses, and they had spoken out; and the general trend of their evidence was definitely hostile to the garrison system.

The chief exceptions to this trend were found in the remarks of witnesses connected with the Colonial Office, who (more aware than others of local difficulties and variations in the colonies) stressed the progress already made, and the dangers of treating the matter in a dogmatic spirit. The Colonial Secretary himself, the Duke of Newcastle, took this attitude. Speaking of North America, he said that he could not possibly recommend any reduction of the force there below the very low figure at which it stood early in 1861, and emphasized that while the American Colonies were unwilling in time of peace to devote to military preparations sums from their small revenues which might be used for peaceful development, they had always been ready to come forward when war was threatened.[1]

Representatives of the fighting services and the War Office were not so ready to concur in the existing arrangements; they were too well aware of dangers at home. Rear-Admiral Sir Charles Elliot, for instance, affirmed that he could not see the object of a military occupation of the Canadas—though Halifax was a different matter.[2] J. R. Godley, Assistant Under-Secretary of State for War, the author of the majority departmental report of the previous year, spoke with great assurance in support of his ideas, remarking that he had never seen a foreign criticism of Britain's resources which did not mention " as the main element of our weakness " the need of protecting scattered colonies.[3] The Secretary of State for War, Sidney Herbert (Lord Herbert of Lea), summed up the military argument against the existing dispersion of Britain's resources. " I think," he said, " that the necessity for the distribution of our forces in the last few years is much altered. I should accumulate all the forces that it is possible to accumulate

---

[1] Qp. 2993, 2982. Cf. the evidence of T. F. Elliot and Herman Merivale.
[2] Qq. 1008, 1125–26, 1133.
[3] Q. 2093. Godley said that the plan he urged had been originated by Sir William Denison, a former Australian Governor (qq. 2067–68).

at home, and keep as few men as possible in the colonies."[1]

The way the wind blew, however, appeared perhaps most obviously in the evidence of two eminent politicians who were both less interested in the abstractions of military and colonial policy than in their results at home, particularly with respect to the tax-rate. Robert Lowe and W. E. Gladstone (the latter at this time Chancellor of the Exchequer) spoke in dissimilar terms, but their words led to the same conclusion.

Robert Lowe (afterwards Lord Sherbrooke) was one of the most extreme Little Englanders—eleven years later he greeted a newly-appointed Governor-General of Canada with the remark, "Now you ought to make it your business to get rid of the Dominion "[2]—but his bitter tongue never had freer play on colonial subjects than in his remarks before this committee. The colonists, he said, were always glad of the presence of troops : " The upper classes think that it makes society more agreeable ; the young ladies are frantic upon the subject, and people who keep public-houses are always glad to see our soldiers."[3] But a garrison was only " an opiate to put the Colony to sleep ", and every British soldier in the colonies prevented 100 colonists from taking up arms and drilling.[4] Probably, however, it was Lowe's small faith in, or desire for, the continued unity of the Empire, that chiefly determined his views ; for he also remarked :

" I cannot help looking forward to a period which may arise when some of those Colonies may wish to separate from the Mother Country. The presence of troops and garrisons in those Colonies would form on such an occasion a formidable obstacle in the way of an amicable separation. . . . Instead of taxing them as our forefathers claimed to do, we, in the matter of this military expenditure, permit them in a great degree to tax us ; I hope we are above the vulgar notion that the mere extent of territory over which our flag waves is any increase to our strength."[5]

Mr. Gladstone's views were more politely expressed. (Indeed, his public utterances on imperial questions were in general

---

[1] Qq. 3552–54. Herbert died shortly afterwards, and was succeeded at the War Office by Lewis.
[2] Lyall, A., *The Life of the Marquess of Dufferin and Ava*, London, 1905, I, 286.
[3] Q., 3409–10.
[4] Qq. 3368, 3405.
[5] Qq. 3333–34.

quite consistent with the modern conception of the British Empire as a free association of nations, and with the permanence of the bond on that basis;[1] although colonials who sought in his acts some practical encouragement to that Imperial spirit to which his words paid homage were apt to encounter disappointments.) But he had, at bottom, no more use for the garrison system than Lowe. From the Exchequer point of view, he remarked that the whole contribution of the colonies to their own defence was quite insignificant as compared with the cost to Great Britain.[2] It was to the enervating effect of the existing situation upon the colonies themselves, however, that he paid most attention; and he expressed the conviction that without learning self-defence they could never attain true nationhood:

"I would almost venture to say, without speaking of cases in which the circumstances are altogether peculiar, that no community which is not primarily charged with the ordinary business of its own defence is really, or can be, in the full sense of the word, a free Community. . . . I am satisfied that they never can be altogether what they ought to be until they learn, and desire, to bear a principal part of the burden of their own defence."[3]

A significant feature of the evidence was the number of references made to the Canadian tariff. Gladstone spoke of it as "so adverse . . . to the relations between the mother country and the Colony, that I earnestly trust as a matter of propriety, of decency almost, it will in some manner disappear."[4] There was a rather sharp exchange on the subject between the Duke of Newcastle and J. A. Roebuck, a member of the committee, who represented in Parliament that town of Sheffield whose merchants' representations on this very matter had received such short shrift from Galt.[5] The Duke—generously, considering what he too had suffered from Galt—made the best case he could for the colony, and added that he did not believe in putting the colonial empire to the tests of the counting-house: "it is extremely difficult to argue those questions upon principles of business, and it is a very small

---

[1] Cf. Knaplund, *Gladstone and Britain's Imperial Policy.*
[2] Q. 3779.
[3] Qq. 3781, 3786. Cf. qq. 3791, 3842. These views recall Elgin's "national and manly morals": see above, p. 69.
[4] Q. 3790.   [5] Qq. 2995-97. Cf. above, pp. 108-9.

ground to take."[1] Nevertheless, Cobden and his friends had been arguing those questions on just that basis for more than twenty years; and Newcastle was soon to be reminded of the prevalence of these ideas in some quarters by a memorial of the Manchester Chamber of Commerce, which called his attention both to the height of the Canadian tariff and to the results of the Select Committee's investigation, remarking, " It appears that our pecuniary liabilities in respect of our colonies should be diminished at least in a corresponding ratio with the Legislative Independence which has of late years been conceded to them ".[2]

The Committee's report, formulated with this great mass of evidence before it, was moderate in tone, but none the less decided. Dividing the colonies (as the departmental committee had done) into two classes,[3] it postulated that the responsibility for the purely military stations was Imperial. With regard to the colonies proper, it agreed that, as the Colonial Office had insisted, local discretion was necessary—but apart from this, it declared, " it appears to your Committee that the responsibility and cost of the military defence of such dependencies ought mainly to devolve upon themselves."[4] They made special suggestions for increased local exertion in New Zealand and South Africa, and for a reduction of Imperial troops in Australia; on North America they made no definite recommendation. It would be well, they observed, not to enter into negotiations with the colonies on the proportion of imperial aid in time of peace, but rather to follow the example of Lord Grey in simply announcing to them the terms on which it would be afforded. It had been felt that negotiation might lead to recrimination.[5] The Committee's final word shows the influence of the apprehensions lately entertained for the safety of England:

" In conclusion, your Committee submit that the tendency of modern warfare is to strike blows at the heart of a hostile power;

[1] Q. 3021.
[2] Enclosed in Newcastle to Monck, March 29, 1862: *G*, 167, p. 153.
[3] The total military expenditure for 1859–60 was divided almost equally between the two: in the " imperial garrisons, convict settlements, etc.", there were 20,910 troops and the cost was £1,509,000, while in the " colonies proper " there were 20,657 troops and the cost was £1,715,000 (p. iv).
[4] p. vi.
[5] Evidence of Newcastle, q. 3026.

and that it is therefore desirable to concentrate the troops required for the defence of the United Kingdom as much as possible, and to trust mainly to naval supremacy for securing against foreign aggression the distant dependencies of the Empire."[1]

Clearly, the military situation in North America as it existed early in the summer of 1861 had not struck the Committee as constituting a just cause of complaint, considering the close proximity of a powerful foreign nation plunged in civil war, and the fact that the garrison had been kept at a very modest strength during the past two years. The Province of Canada still cost the mother country £200,000 a year for defence,[2] but the situation had been much worse in the past; and of the £150,000 spent in the Maritime Provinces, two-thirds was for the Imperial naval base at Halifax.[3] But the whole condition was changed by the reinforcements that were hurried to America at the end of 1861.

In February, 1862, the bill for the reinforcing operation came in, and it was of considerable size. The supplementary Navy Estimates included £234,000 for the transport of the whole force sent in the summer and autumn; this, with £40,000 to go on the next year's estimates, represented the whole cost of that service.[4] The similar estimates for the Army amounted to £609,000, but the Commons was warned that more was to come in the general estimates.[5] Little objection was raised to the amount, but significant interest was manifested, in the course of the debate, in the question of the future cost of British American defence. W. E. Baxter, member for Montrose, asked whether this was to be a permanent burden on the British taxpayer, and reminded the Government once more of the height of Canada's tariff.[6] Adderley made no objection to the reinforcement, and reiterated his belief in the high value of the colonies to England; but he thought that it would be fair to ask the Canadians " in future to tax themselves some-

---

[1] P. vii.
[2] In 1859–60, £206,264 : committee report, appendix no. 5.
[3] In 1859–60, £149,495 for Nova Scotia and New Brunswick : *ibid*. The Committee observed that 1,300 men and £100,000 were for the fortress of Halifax.
[4] *Hansard*, CLXV, 394–97, 402–03 (speeches of Lord Clarence Paget, Feb. 17, 1862).
[5] *Ibid*., 404–08, 410–13 (speeches of Sir G. Lewis, Feb. 17, 1862).
[6] *Ibid*., 387–89.

CANADA AND AMERICAN CIVIL WAR 129

what more as Englishmen were taxing themselves at home for their security ".[1] Sir George Lewis, replying for the Government, showed much sympathy for this point of view.[2]

A fortnight later,[3] the House of Commons for the first time expressed a formal opinion on the principles of colonial defence. Arthur Mills, anxious that his Committee's work should produce some tangible result, brought in a resolution :

" That this House, while it fully recognizes the claim of all portions of the British Empire on Imperial aid against perils arising from the consequences of Imperial policy, is of opinion that Colonies exercising the rights of self-government ought to undertake the main responsibility of providing for their own internal order and security."

Both he[4] and his seconder[5] explained that their aim was not to weaken the Imperial tie, but to strengthen it. The pertinacious Baxter, complaining that the resolution did not go far enough, moved to amend it by adding the words, " and ought to assist in their own external defence ".[6] The amendment was accepted. It could hardly have been resisted, for Mills's motion had been so mild in tone as to be of little practical value ; we have seen that the Canadian legislature, at least, had formally recognized its full responsibility for internal order six years before.[7] The ministry smiled on the motion,[8] and though Sir James Fergusson objected to the Canadian tariff being dragged into the debate,[9] and one colonial in the House—T. C. Haliburton, the creator of Sam Slick—thought the whole movement inopportune,[10] the feeling of honourable members was clearly almost unanimous in its favour, and it passed with no thought of a division.

This resolution of March, 1862, has frequently been noted as marking an epoch in the development of Imperial military relationships.[11] Too much stress has, perhaps, been laid upon

[1] *Ibid.*, 408–10.
[2] *Ibid.*, 410–12.
[3] On March 4, 1862.
[4] *Ibid.*, 1032–38.
[5] C. Buxton, M.P. for Maidstone : *ibid.*, 1038–44.
[6] *Ibid.*, 1044–48.
[7] See above, p. 97.
[8] *Ibid.*, 1053–55 (speech of Chichester Fortescue).
[9] *Ibid.*, 1056–57. Baxter had again mentioned the tariff.
[10] *Ibid.*, 1057–60.
[11] e.g., in Todd, *Parliamentary Government in the British Colonies*, 392–93, and in Keith, *Responsible Government in the Dominions*, III, 1248–49.

K

it. For fifteen years, the Imperial Government had been striving to put into effect just the principles which it embodied; nor did its passage produce an immediate result in the shape of a reduction of Imperial expenditure and an increase of colonial exertion. Nevertheless, it is important as a formal expression of the discontent with the garrison system which we have observed as manifesting itself, over a period of many years, in the House of Commons, and as an evidence that that discontent had grown to be almost universal. It might have been confidently declared, from that moment, that the garrisons in the self-governing colonies were doomed; and though in fact seven years were to pass before the death sentence was finally pronounced, this was merely the period required for the slow strangulation of the old colonial military system by the pressure of the sentiment represented in the Commons' unquestioning acceptance of Mills's resolution.

. . . .

It was not to be long before English dissatisfaction with the general colonial situation crystallized in violent denunciation of one particular colony—the Province of Canada. We must now relate the events that produced this result.

Both Lord Monck and his ministers, it has been remarked, intended and anticipated that in 1862 the provincial Parliament would pass a new militia law—one in keeping with Canada's dangerous situation, designed to produce a large force of drilled men. In January, accordingly, a strong commission, headed by John A. Macdonald and including among its members three of the four men who had served on the similar commission of 1855, in addition to Colonel Daniel Lysons, a distinguished regular officer, was appointed to report on the organization of the provincial forces.[1] On March 15 they submitted their findings, recommending a very extensive programme.[2]

The province, they declared, with its very long frontier and its relatively small population, could not be defended against the great strength of the neighbouring country without an

---

[1] *M.P.*, " Militia and Defence," I, 30 : letter to Macdonald, Jan. 28, 1862, notifying his appointment.

[2] *Report of the Commissioners Appointed to Report a Plan for the Better Organization of the Department of the Adjutant General of Militia, and the Best Means of Reorganizing the Militia of this Province, and to Prepare a Bill thereon.* . . . Quebec, 1862.

active force of 50,000 men and a reserve of the same number, in addition to a strong body of regulars and a gunboat flotilla on the lakes. They suggested that this force should consist in the principal towns of volunteers, and in rural districts of " regular militia " raised from the men on the rolls of the sedentary force by voluntary enlistment so far as possible and thereafter by ballot.[1] The commissioners had grasped the fact that the volunteer system, useful in the towns, was less practicable in the country, where the population could not readily assemble for periodical evening drills. The proposal therefore was that the " regular " units should be assembled for a considerable training period once a year at the most convenient season, while the volunteers would be allowed to perform part of their training by such evening parades. The total estimate for the annual cost of 50,000 men, including clothing, ammunition, and pay for a 28-day training period, was $1,110,000.[2] This was about one-tenth, or a trifle more, of the provincial revenue, and about equal to the cost of the reduced regular establishment which Britain had maintained in Canada before the outbreak of war in the United States.[3]

In a purely military view, it seems difficult to criticize this scheme adversely. The recent Anglo-American crisis had left bitterness behind it on both sides, and another such incident might at any moment bring on hostilities. The war in the United States had attained titanic proportions. The Union army was acquiring cohesion and efficiency, and it was of enormous size : at the end of 1861 there were already available about 700,000 men.[4] Facing the possibility of conflict with such forces, the Canadian Commissioners realized the military absurdity of relying only upon the small portion of the population who choose to prepare to defend their country by joining the volunteers. The volunteer force had grown since the *Trent* affair ; the Government had authorized its increase to 25,000 men, and by the spring of 1862 it amounted to about 12,000 effectives ; while the Maritime Provinces brought the volunteer

[1] If two-thirds of the men on the rolls of the sedentary company desired it, the choice might be made by selection by the company-commander.
[2] *M.P.*, " Militia and Defence," I, 110.
[3] The best discussion of the military aspect of these proposals is Hamilton, " The Canadian Militia : from 1861 to Confederation," *C.D.Q.*, VI.
[4] Shannon, F. A., *The Organization and Administration of the Union Army, 1861–1865*, Cleveland, 1928, I, 46–47.

strength of British North America up to about 20,000 in all.[1] But this was no force to resist the Northern states ; and the commissioners, remembering that there were half a million men of military age in the Province of Canada, had naturally fallen back upon the old universal-service militia.

Nevertheless, the attempt to revivify the old principle failed utterly. The publication of the scheme occasioned a tumult of criticism in the opposition Press, with the Toronto *Globe* leading the attack. " For a country like Canada ", this journal declared, " with a heavy debt, a large annual deficiency and the prospect of a fourth increase of taxation in four years—it seems to us totally indefensible."[2] This argument was given point when the public accounts for 1861 were published and revealed a deficit of $1,476,000, which the *Globe* declared would have been more truly stated as $2,579,000.[3] And not the least damaging criticism the proposals received was from the volunteers, who seem, in many cases, to have considered primarily the " vested interests " of the small existing force, forgetting that the new scheme's sole object was to provide an army capable of defending the frontiers of Canada against a powerful enemy—such an army as the existing volunteer force certainly was not.[4]

In May the Government brought into the legislature a Bill based on the report.[5] John A. Macdonald introduced it, and his speech and those of other ministers showed that they realized the strength of the opposition. He represented it as " an enabling bill ", permitting, but not obliging, the Government to put the commission's recommendations into full effect. It would be for Parliament to decide, in passing upon the annual estimates, whether funds would be appropriated for the whole scheme. Pressed for details of the expenditure the ministry would actually recommend, Macdonald made only tentative suggestions.[6] The opposition both in Parliament and the Press made the most of this indecision ; the *Globe* observed

---

[1] Hamilton, as above.
[2] *Globe*, April 10, 1862.
[3] *Ibid.*, April 28, 1862.
[4] Letters from volunteer officers (including printed circulars), April 15–28, 1862 : *M.P.*, " Militia and Defence," I, 67–83. On criticisms of the scheme, cf. Col. D. Lysons' *Parting Words on the Rejected Militia Bill*.
[5] Copies of draft bill, *M.P.*, " Militia and Defence," I, 20.
[6] *Globe*, May 3, 1862. Full report of speech, *ibid.*, May 9.

that the ministry were as much afraid of the bill as if it had been an infernal machine.[1]

Four days after the first debate, Galt spoke more definitely of the Government's intentions. For 1862 they proposed to call out only 30,000 men in all, and for only fourteen days. The year's expense would be about $500,000. He admitted that the Government had had no communication with England as to the possibility of her supplying arms for the force. He urged that, even though the House might not desire to make any appropriation for drill that year, still the Bill should be passed so that the organization might be proceeded with.[2] But the Assembly were as deaf to this as they had been to Macdonald's final appeal:

" I think we should as much as possible avoid mingling up this measure with the consideration of what England will do for us. . . . In case of war with the United States, England will undoubtedly be willing . . . to expend her last farthing and her last man in our defence. But . . . still it is plainly and obviously our duty to provide a large and efficient force for the purpose of fighting upon our own soil, for our own possessions, our own privileges and our own liberties."[3]

On May 20 the second reading was put to a division; and the Bill was defeated, by 61 to 54.[4] Next day the Government resigned.

The immediate cause of the defeat was the defection of fifteen French-Canadian supporters of the ministry. The general hostility of the people of French Canada towards military preparation in time of peace has never been more strikingly demonstrated. The French Press had been particularly vociferous against the bill; the government organ in Montreal, commenting bitterly upon " cette *sainte* croisade contre le bill de milice ", collected a fine anthology of the reasons given for rejecting it, ranging from that of *L'Ordre*, that " un mois peut suffire pour former de bonnes troupes ", to the ingenious observations of *Le Journal de St. Hyacinthe* upon the utility of the proposed Canadian force: ". . . et comment croire, nous le demandons, que l'Angleterre qui depuis

---

[1] *Ibid.*, May 5.   [2] *Ibid.*, May 7.   [3] *Ibid.*, May 9.
[4] *Ibid.*, May 21; Monck to Newcastle, May 30 (G, 464, p. 219); Skelton, *Life of Galt*, 340-41; Pope, *Memoirs of Sir John Alexander Macdonald*, I, 236-37.

tant de siècles a tenu tête aux plus puissants empires de l'Europe ait besoin de 50,000 hommes pour conserver le Canada ? "[1] It must be said, however, that while the Upper Canadian supporters of the ministry had all remained faithful, the debates had shown that the French-speaking members were far from having a monopoly of hostility to the principles of the Bill.

Other reasons had operated against the scheme's chances of success. One of the chief was the general unpopularity of the Government. This Conservative ministry headed by Macdonald and George E. Cartier had been in power since 1858, and indeed the same group of men had controlled the Government (except for a brief period in 1858) since 1854. By 1862 the basis of their domination was crumbling.[2] They were adepts in the lesser and meaner arts of politics, and dissatisfaction with their methods had become formidable ; the *Globe* alleged that, knowing they could not survive the session, they had elected to fall in an odour of sanctity on the Militia Bill.[3] The most unpleasant evidence on the subject is that of the Governor-General in a private letter to the Colonial Secretary :

" There is a general and, I am sorry to say, well-founded distrust of the administration of the public money here, and I am quite sure that this consideration had as great an effect in bringing about the adverse vote on the Militia Bill as the magnitude of the sum proposed to be devoted to its objects."[4]

The ministers, moreover, had invited defeat by their mismanagement of the Bill in Parliament. Finally, an unhappy personal failure occurred at the crisis. John A. Macdonald, by all odds the ablest politician in the Canadas and the dominant figure in the ministry, was overtaken by one of his periodical lapses from sobriety, and was absent from the House for a week before the vote on the measure which he was sponsoring.[5]

All these things played their part. But it can hardly be doubted that, in addition, the Militia Bill was, at best, not popular in the country at large. The *Globe* announced that the

---

[1] *La Minerve*, May 13, 1862.
[2] Skelton, 341, 355.
[3] *Globe*, May 21.
[4] Monck to Newcastle, May 23, 1862: Martineau, *Life of Henry Pelham, Fifth Duke of Newcastle*, 310.
[5] *Ibid.*

men who defeated it were as favourable to "a proper reorganization" of the militia as the ministry, but that they voted against the Bill because "it was too cumbrous and too costly, and because they could not entrust the carrying out of its provisions to the hands of the present men."[1] Yet the fact that no Bill providing for a militia scheme approaching the proportions of that of 1862 was ever afterwards proposed seems clearly to indicate a conviction in the minds of Canadian politicians that this project had gone further than the public opinion of the country was prepared to follow. Lord Monck's declared confidence that its principles would be accepted at a later time[2] was doomed to disappointment.

Of the reasons for the small popularity of the scheme, the necessary increase in taxation was certainly one. Nor can it be doubted that the strong savour of conscription about the project was highly prejudicial to its chances. We have seen that the ancient principle of universal service had been preserved in successive militia laws down to this time. But, practically speaking, it had been preserved in the laws alone, and latterly the volunteer idea had superseded it in the popular consciousness.

There seems, moreover, to have been widespread doubt as to whether the circumstances of the time really demanded such heroic measures. The *Globe* assured its readers that there was probably less danger of a collision with the United States in 1862 than at any time since 1776, adding:

" If the Ministry think that they can induce the people of Canada to lie upon their oars for the next ten years, waiting for a war which will never come, they are greatly mistaken. Make the militia efficient. Drill and arm the volunteers, and then let the business of the country go on. We are not afraid of the Americans provoking a war; we are not afraid of them if they do provoke it."[3]

The explanation of the colony's apparent apathy, in fact, was neither lukewarmness towards the British connexion (there was less doubt on that point in Canada than in Britain herself), nor a spiritless reluctance to make sacrifices for the preservation of the province's national existence. It was, first, a lack of conviction of the serious probability of war, and, secondly, a

[1] *Globe*, May 21, 1862.
[2] Monck to Newcastle, June 17, 1862: G, 464, p. 241.
[3] *Globe*, March 12, 1862.

failure to appreciate the gravity of Canada's situation in the event of war occurring. The *Globe* apparently believed that the militia could be made " efficient " without any great expenditure ; it believed that if the United States—a country possessing a dozen times the population and resources of British North America, and which moreover had now become a first-class military power—should turn its forces against the provinces, the invasion could be defeated without the aid of the advantages which previous preparation would confer upon the defence. The proximity of a devastating war of continental proportions had, so far, failed to make any great impression upon the old Canadian belief that it was time enough to begin preparing for war after war had begun.

There seems no reason whatever for believing that in case of hostilities Canada would not have made strenuous exertions, and indeed the spirit shown during the *Trent* crisis seems to indicate what her reaction would have been. Attention may be drawn to the situation in the Dominion in 1911-14, which presents in some respects a parallel. The Liberal and Conservative parties, it will be remembered, then agreed officially in acknowledging that it was Canada's duty to bear a larger share than formerly of the burden of Imperial naval defence ; but whereas the former demanded a separate Canadian fleet-unit, the latter were in favour of a contribution of vessels to the Royal Navy. The Conservatives came into power in 1911, as a result of an election fought mainly on another issue, and introduced a Navy Bill, which was promptly defeated by the Liberal majority surviving in the upper house ; and there Sir Robert Borden left the matter. That it was allowed to rest so is evidence that the naval projects were not the result of a demand from Canadian public opinion. The upshot was that when the Great War broke out Canada had still made no effective preparations against the catastrophe. Yet in the course of the conflict she raised more than 600,000 men ; she lost almost exactly the same number killed in action as the United States, which has twelve times her population ; her troops were reckoned among the most effective on the Western Front ; and when the war was won she allowed her defence forces to sink back to their old level of insignificance. This chain of events is surely illuminating.

England in 1862, however, was in no mood to make allowances. She saw that she had concentrated 18,000 soldiers in the North American Provinces to defend them against probable invasion ; that maintaining these forces there cost the British taxpayer not far short of £1,000,000 annually ;[1] and that in the face of these facts the representatives of the Canadian people had refused to spend even $500,000 in assisting to defend the country. That this should produce deep dissatisfaction in Britain was only natural ; yet it seems hard to justify the peculiar violence of the " shrill blast of objurgation " (the phrase is Goldwin Smith's) which was now directed at the unhappy colony.

The Times led the hunt. " The late Parliament of Canada ", it declared on June 6, " has shown itself signally wanting in those instincts of liberty which urge a free people to fly to arms on the least surmise of danger from foreign enemies " :

" It is to us inconceivable that 3,000,000 of civilized people can watch the explosions of the great American volcano without realizing to themselves the fact that the fiery flood which is desolating so large and so fair a portion of the earth's surface may come even to them, and, were it not for what we have seen, we should have thought it equally impossible for them to perceive this danger without taking every measure in their power to anticipate and prevent its approach. The only solution that can be offered for so strange a fact is that Canada has learnt to trust to others for the performance of services for which weaker and less wealthy populations are wont to rely exclusively on themselves. . . .

" Let not the Canadians deceive themselves by supposing that these things only threaten them because they are a dependency of the British Crown, and that the moment that link is broken the danger of invasion is destroyed with it. . . . Let not the Canadians, on the other hand, believe that they have in their present connexion with Great Britain a sufficient protection against invasion without taking any trouble to defend themselves. Such an opinion is founded on a mistake both of our power and our will. . . . If we had the power it is quite certain that we should not have the will. Opinion in England is perfectly decided that in the connexion

[1] *P.P.*, 1870, no. 80, vol. XLIX. For 1862-63 (the first financial year in which the force was in Canada throughout) the total cost of Canada to the British taxpayer was £718,343, and of Nova Scotia and New Brunswick £252,455. We have seen that military defence accounted for almost the whole bill. In 1860-61 Canada had cost only £166,415, and the Maritimes £133,933.

between the Mother Country and the Colony the advantage is infinitely more on the side of the child than of the parent. . . . We cannot even obtain from this very colony of Canada, reasonably fair treatment for our manufactures, which are taxed 25 per cent. on their value to increase a revenue which the colonies will not apply to our or even to their defence. There is little reciprocity in such a relation. . . . If they [the Canadians] are to be defended at all, they must make up their minds to bear the greater part of the burden of their own defence. This will be the case if they separate from us. This will be the case if they remain by us. . . . To us the exposure of Canada to foreign invasion is a secondary matter; to Canada herself it is life and death. Let her arm by all means, but let her arm, not for our sake, but for her own."

Six months before, Canada had been in high favour with the British public on account of her attitude in the *Trent* crisis. Now that enthusiasm was suddenly " damped, blighted, and extinguished ".[1] Journals more moderate than *The Times* were moved to admonish the Canadians in stinging terms. The *Spectator*, for instance, though slow to attack the colony,[2] ultimately came to the point of declaring, " it is, perhaps, our duty to defend the Empire at all hazards; it is no part of it to defend men who will not defend themselves ".[3] Perhaps the pinnacle of abuse was reached in a letter addressed to the *Daily News*, from Montreal, by a person calling himself " Hochelaga ", who may perhaps have been a British officer. Arguing for separation of mother country and colony, he declared that the militia and volunteers of Canada were not intended to have any existence except on paper:

"They are both a sham—a bait for more British troops—a pretence for demanding Imperial aid for railways, roads, arms, clothing—anything in the shape of money or money's worth, and to augment or to prolong, in any way, the Imperial stake in the Provinces. To aid in the deception, Bills may be brought in and rejected, and new ones framed, and every sort of administrative hocus-pocus gone through; but the only Bills which have a real meaning are those which John Bull will have to pay, for neither sous nor cents will be contributed by either Province; and there will be neither men nor supplies except such as are paid for out of Imperial funds."[4]

[1] *Spectator*, Aug. 23, 1862.
[2] *Ibid.*, June 7, 1862.   [3] *Ibid.*, July 26, 1862.
[4] *Daily News*, July 23, 1862; appendix II, in Goldwin Smith's *The Empire*.

CANADA AND AMERICAN CIVIL WAR 139

Whatever justification there might be for indignation against Canada's refusal to take the same view of her situation that the people of England did, there was none for such stuff as this.

More than one school of theorists on colonial policy made capital out of the situation. The inevitable Adderley had lately published a pamphlet advancing his views on colonial defence. Now he issued a new edition of it[1] with embellishments drawn from the recent events in Canada, which he regarded as demonstrating the soundness of his position. He had been accused, he said, of encouraging thoughts of separation by urging Canada to bear her proper share of the burden of her own defence; but it was his view, on the contrary, that thus alone might separation be averted; for " Canada and England cannot long remain together on terms of disadvantage to either ". The existing arrangement, he said, not only smothered Canadian self-reliance, but " its own inadequacy to supply the defence which it has crushed, offers to an aggressive and insolent neighbourhood . . . an opportunity for humiliating England ".

At the same time, another writer, of greater ability but narrower views, was drawing different conclusions from the same facts. Goldwin Smith, Regius Professor of Modern History at Oxford, was one of the most uncompromising of radical anti-imperialists; and now in a series of letters to the *Daily News*[2] he devoted himself to the thesis that the late occurrences merely proved how anomalous was the whole relation of Canada to Britain. A strong advocate of Anglo-American friendship, in a time when such folk were few, he regarded Canada's membership in the British Empire as a serious obstacle to the realization of that ideal. " For Canada, and for Canada alone," wrote Smith, " we stand always on the brink of a war with the great Anglo-Saxon Republic, our best mart, and, if we were not compelled to stand in the path of her advancing greatness, our closest and surest ally."[3] The

---
[1] *Letter to the Right Hon. Benjamin Disraeli, M.P., on the Present Relations of England with the Colonies.* New edition. *With a preface on Canadian affairs.* . . . Adderley addressed himself to Disraeli on account of the latter's opposition to sending troops to Canada in the summer of 1861.
[2] Reprinted under the title *The Empire.*
[3] *The Empire*, 131.

Canadians' refusal to raise troops merely showed that "their interests and feelings in the matter are different from ours ".[1] The sooner the connexion with Britain was severed, the better for all three communities concerned.

While these various points of view—agreeing only on the degeneracy of the Canadians[2]—were being aired in the Press, inevitably the matter was also aired in Parliament. When Newcastle was questioned in connexion with it, he suggested extenuating circumstances for the Canadian legislature's action, but added that he could not help regarding it as "most inopportune and most unfortunate."[3] Lord Carnarvon suggested that if the recent acts of her legislature really represented the feelings of Canada, "it became our serious duty to consider whether it was right to leave the flower of the English army in a position of acknowledged peril in order to defend a country which would not contribute either money or men to its own defence ".[4] Lord Ellenborough, too, was perturbed by the dangerous situation of the British troops in Canada.[5] Curiously enough, the classes in England which had been loudest in their ridicule of the North's attempts at raising an army and of the *débâcle* of Bull Run were now equally loud in proclaiming the difficulty of defending Canada against that same army.[6]

It was in the Commons, however, that the storm broke most fiercely. It was Adderley, naturally, who raised it. His tone was unusually bitter, and he suggested that " the embarkation of the first British regiment for the purpose of returning from Canada to England, would make Canada take a very different view on this question " ;[7] but it remained for Roebuck, once a radical and a liberal—who was soon in a speech at his constituency of Sheffield to rejoice that the American union had been split in two, and express the hope that it would shortly be split in five—to use the most brutal language :

[1] *Ibid.*, 127.
[2] Cf. Smith, *ibid.*, 122 : " *The Times* . . . first said that Canada was a useless and perilous possession. Then it reviled me for saying the same thing in milder words. Then it said the same thing itself again."
[3] *Hansard*, CLXVII, 627–29 (June 16, 1862).
[4] *Ibid.*, CLXVIII, 479–85 (July 18, 1862), [5] *Ibid.*, 493–94.
[6] *The Times* itself is the great example. It was quite capable of referring to the Northern states as " this insensate and degenerate people " (see the *Spectator's* comments on this pleasant phrase, July 12, 1862) and nevertheless informing Canada (as in its leader of June 6, 1862) that Britain's resources were not equal to the defence of Canada against them.
[7] *Hansard*, CLXVIII, 843–49 (July 25, 1862).

" My opinion is, that the people of Canada have been led to believe that we consider them of such wonderful importance that we shall undertake any expense to maintain dominion over them. What I want them to understand, and what I want our Government to make them understand, is that we do not care one farthing about the adherence of Canada to England. . . . The only chance of benefit we ever expected from our colonies was perfect freedom of trade. What has Canada done in that matter ? The Canadians have laid 20 per cent upon the introduction of all English manufactures into their country, thereby following the bad example of their friends on the other side of the St. Lawrence.

". . . The very veto of the Crown is entirely ignored, and that which we ought to have done—namely, protect the manufacturing interests of England—we have ceased to do. I say, therefore, we are now bound to look after the interests of our constituents, and I shall be the very last man to lay one farthing of expense upon the poor people of Sheffield in order to maintain the independence of the rich people of Canada."[1]

This outburst at least had the effect of drawing protests from certain members against addressing the colony " in language of contumely and insult ".[2]

Even the members of the Government, while deprecating such immoderate utterances as this, spoke with unusual frankness. Lewis rejected the Adderley scheme of withdrawing troops from Canada, but showed that his views had not changed since he wrote the *Government of Dependencies* :

" I, for one, can only say that I look forward without apprehension —and, I may add, without regret—to the time when Canada might become an independent State ; but I think it behoves England not to cast Canada loose, or send her adrift before she has acquired sufficient strength to assert her own independence."[3]

Finally, the Prime Minister spoke ; and his great position made his words the most stinging of all. " Generally speaking ", he said, " it may be said that we are proud of the conduct and bearing of our Canadian fellow-subjects ; but on the present occasion I certainly feel no such sentiment ".[4]

Canadians visiting England in the summer of 1862 found their country unpopular. George Brown was among them ; he

---

[1] *Ibid.*, 853-55. On the Sheffield speech, *Spectator*, Aug. 16, 1862.
[2] Speech of Viscount Bury, *ibid.*, 864-67 ; cf. those of T. Baring and Sir M. Farquhar, 860-62, 862-64.
[3] *Ibid.*, 855-60.   *Ibid.*, 872-76.

received a number of invitations to speak in public, but declined them all. " I have no idea ", he wrote, " of *defending* Canada before the English people, and *defence* is the only possible attitude at this moment."[1] At no other juncture in history has Great Britain been so bitter towards her greatest colony.[2]

The outburst in Britain naturally produced irritation in Canada. Canadian newspapers objected particularly to the attitude of *The Times*; the *Globe* observed that there would have been no talk of war but for the mischief-making of English and American newspapers, " of which *The Times* was the worst because the most influential ".[3] The veteran Joseph Howe took up the cause of Canada—a province not his own—first on the public platform[4] and a little later in a pamphlet[5] in answer to Adderley's, which expressed the Canadian point of view perfectly. It dwelt on Canadian loyalty, past and present, and on the fact that Canada was committed by British foreign policy, though she had no share in forming it ; and in the confidence which it expressed in the usefulness of the untrained militia of British North America we may see the roots of the colony's whole attitude on defensive matters. The letter showed, in fact, that Howe did not in the least appreciate the gravity of the military problem of the day ; and in this he was typical of the people and statesmen of British America in 1862.

On the fall of the Macdonald-Cartier Government, Lord Monck had entrusted the formation of a new ministry to John Sandfield Macdonald, instead of to M. H. Foley, who was considered the titular head of the Liberal opposition.[6] Monck's primary interest was in defence. He was now handing over the government to the party which since 1855 had fiercely resisted

[1] Brown to Holton, Sept. 3, 1862 : Mackenzie, *Life and Speeches of Hon. George Brown*, 202. Cf. Pope, *Memoirs of Sir John Macdonald*, I, 242, and the comments of the *Saturday Review* (Oct. 6, 1862) on Galt's speech at Manchester explaining the Canadian position.

[2] The interest in this controversy is reflected in Russell, *Canada : its Defences, Condition, and Resources*, chap. XII and *passim* ; Sala, *My Diary in America in the Midst of War*, 130–41 ; and Trollope, *North Amercia*, chap. VI.

[3] *Globe*, June 18, 1862. For this journal's attitude, see Underhill, " Canada's Relations with the Empire as Seen by the Toronto Globe, 1857–1867," *C.H.R.*, X.

[4] In a speech at Niagara, Sept. 18, 1862 : Chisholm (ed.), *Speeches and Public Letters of Joseph Howe*, II, 372–83.

[5] Reprinted in *ibid.*, II, 383–410.

[6] *Globe*, May 22, 1862 ; Kennedy, *Constitution of Canada*, 270 ; Pope, *Memoirs of Macdonald*, I, 242–43.

CANADA AND AMERICAN CIVIL WAR 143

the extension of the province's military responsibilities, and he probably believed that the militia would have a better chance with Macdonald than with Foley, who had been one of the bitterest assailants of the volunteer force from the beginning. Macdonald, with the aid of L. V. Sicotte, of Lower Canada, had no difficulty in forming an administration ;[1] but almost nothing was done for the development of the provincial forces during the remainder of the session. The Militia Act of 1859 was amended[2] in the direction of augmenting the volunteer force and treating it more generously. The aggregate of paid volunteer corps, however, was not to exceed 10,000 officers and men. The Commander-in-Chief (the Governor-General) had authority to increase the unpaid force as might be expedient ; and the appointment and payment of drill instructors was authorized. The appropriation for the militia was $250,000— three times as much as the previous year's.[3]

The end of the session of 1862 thus left the province with nothing in the way of an indigenous defensive organization except the little volunteer force, whose actual strength increased by the New Year to something over 18,000.[4] Monck, full of disgust, told the Colonial Secretary privately that his new ministers were nothing but " parish politicians ".[5] But the Imperial authorities did not make Canadian lassitude an excuse for relaxing their own exertions for the defence of the province. Though the first Bill's rejection caused a temporary suspension of the shipping of supplies to Canada,[6] J. S. Macdonald's exiguous Militia Act was sufficient excuse for Monck to ask for additional arms,[7]—and for England to send them ; 40,000 rifles and 48 guns were now added to the imperial stores in Canada.[8]

At the same time, however, the Colonial Office attempted to bring the parish politicians to a truer sense of the measures which Canada's situation demanded. On August 21 the Duke of Newcastle addressed to Monck a solemn dispatch[9] stating

[1] Pope, *Memoirs of Macdonald*, I, 243. Foley joined the ministry.
[2] By 25 Vict., cap. 1.
[3] Supply act, 25 Vict., cap. 3.
[4] Monck to Newcastle, Jan. 9, 1863 : G, 464, p. 375.
[5] Monck to Newcastle, Aug. 4, 1862 : Martineau, *Life of Newcastle*, 310.
[6] Newcastle to Monck, June 14, 1862 : G, 168, p. 43.
[7] Monck to Newcastle, June 10, 1862 : G, 464, p. 225.
[8] Lugard to Elliot (copy), July 30, 1862 : G, 168, p. 185.
[9] G, 168, p. 230. Published in *S.P.*, 1867–8, no. 63. p. 3 ; also in *P.P.*, 1862, cd. 3061, vol. XXXVI.

his conviction of the inadequacy of the new ministry's military policy. In the event of war, " what would be required would be a large army " ; it was, he thought, essential to have not less than 50,000 drilled men in readiness. The tone of the dispatch was moderate ; it took its stand on the firm ground of military necessity. " That the population is ready," wrote the Duke, " no one will venture to doubt ; that it cannot be competent, is no less certain, until it has received that organization, and acquired that habit of discipline, which constitute the difference between a trained force and an armed mob." He disclaimed " both the right and the desire " to interfere in Canadian politics ; but he strongly expressed the hope that Parliament would soon be called and that the winter would not pass without new and effective militia legislation being enacted.[1]

Monck referred this dispatch to his ministers, not pressing for an immediate answer, as they had so recently come into power ; but when October came without their having produced any defensive scheme, and two members of the ministry in whose absence nothing important could be decided were about to sail for England, the Governor-General, in a brusque note to Sandfield Macdonald, demanded that they should formulate their views without delay.[2] The result was a minute of council, dated October 30,[3] which rejected Newcastle's suggestions in the most definite terms.

The defeat of John A. Macdonald's Militia Bill, the ministers affirmed, had been " the result, not of party combinations, but of a deliberate conviction that its principle was unadapted to the occasion, that the more striking of its features were obnoxious to the Province, and that the financial resources available for military purposes were unequal to the outlay that would have followed the enactment of the Bill " ; and it further declared that in recent elections " embracing more than

---

[1] In the same dispatch, Newcastle made the interesting suggestion that, even without a political union of the North American Colonies being effected, it might be possible to bring about a union of their defensive organizations. Monck found, however, that both the Lieutenant-Governors of the Maritime Provinces and his own ministers in Canada thought this scheme impracticable ; and there were serious constitutional difficulties in the way. See Whitelaw, *The Maritimes and Canada before Confederation*, 180–84.

[2] Monck to J. S. Macdonald, Oct. 24, 1862 : copy in Monck to Newcastle, Nov. 15, 1862 (separate) : G, 464, p. 349.

[3] Published in *S.P.*, 1863, no. 15, and again in 1867–8, no. 63; also in *P.P.*, 1862, cd. 3061, vol. XXXVI.

one-third of the people of the Province ", not a single candidate, so far as they knew, had " ventured to declare himself in favour of a measure so extensive as that which was prepared by the late Government, and is now again recommended by His Grace." Compulsory service was very definitely rejected, and the volunteer system declared to be the only one possible in time of peace. The ministers exalted their own small measures for improving the volunteers.

Finally, they laid great stress upon the point so often made —that Canada had no voice in the foreign policy of the Empire, and that if war came it would not be through any act of hers ; and they urged the special circumstances of Canada as giving her large claims upon Britain for defensive aid, whatever might be done in less exposed colonies. Their most curious argument, perhaps, was that in case of war Canada would be the Empire's battleground and would suffer devastation ; this fact, which surely might have served as an argument for exertions on their part to prevent the horrors which they depicted, they used instead to support their contention that Canada should not be called upon to engage in large military projects.

This episode may be regarded from either of two points of view. On the constitutional side, the attitude of the Sandfield Macdonald Government appears simply as contributing one more stone to the rising edifice of Canadian autonomy. In the words of Professor Kennedy :

" The great point was that Canada in receiving responsible government had reached a place where Canadians, not British, were going to decide the policy. . . . All that had happened was that Canadians were untying another legal and formal knot in the bands of empire. Responsible government had brought the right to tax as the people liked, and it had brought the right to provide defence as the people liked."[1]

This was the light in which Joseph Howe saw the matter at the time. " I will take my stand," he said, " upon this broad principle, that whether the one Bill or the other [John A. Macdonald's defeated Bill, or the weak measure later passed by Sandfield Macdonald] was the better, the House of Lords and the House of Commons are not to be the judges—the Parliament

[1] *Constitution of Canada*, 277-78.

of Canada is to judge and the Parliament of Canada alone."[1]

To this there was no answer. It must, however, be pointed out that the total effect of this manifestation of manly independence was very much reduced by the insistence of the ministers' memorandum upon Britain's duty of defending Canada. That document admirably exemplifies the dominant fact that disengages itself from the whole long train of events which has been here related : that Canadian statesmen were far readier to assert Canada's rights as a free community than to acknowledge the responsibilities which such a community might be expected to assume.

From the purely military point of view, on the other hand, the Canadian cabinet had not a leg to stand upon. Colonel Hamilton sums the matter up quite adequately :

"Sandfield Macdonald and his colleagues discuss the responsibilities of the people of Canada—the dire nature of threatened calamity—the inadvisability of provoking hostilities—the readiness of the people to fight should war actually occur ; and overlook the consideration—surely of importance—that if war were to come with their country insufficiently prepared, their country would be beaten, perhaps conquered. John A. Macdonald and his commission had asked the question : If war does occur, what force shall we need ? Sandfield Macdonald discusses everything but that."[2]

Both positions are perfectly sound. There is no doubt that the Canadian Government failed lamentably to appreciate the military needs of the moment ; there is equally little doubt that it was useless for the Imperial authorities to attempt to push them into measures of whose expediency they, and the people of Canada at large, were not convinced. The facts of the case were those which had been so clear to Head and Elgin. If Canada was to be responsible for her own defences, the plans and extent of those defences would have to be decided by the representatives of the Canadian people. If England desired that the defences of Canada should follow a pattern drawn according to English views of military necessity, then England herself would have to pay the piper.

[1] From the Niagara speech : *Speeches and Public Letters*, II, 379. Cf. Smith, *The Empire*, 128.
[2] "The Canadian Militia : from 1861 to Confederation," *C.D.Q.*, VI.

NOTE.—*Scarcely any confidential dispatches for the year 1862 are to be found at Ottawa ; while of the private correspondence of Monck and Newcastle nothing survives (it would appear) but the tantalizing fragments printed in Martineau's "Life of Newcastle."*

CHAPTER VII

CANADA AND THE AMERICAN CIVIL WAR:
THE DEEPEST SHADOW

" The United States of America are now a military power, and have demonstrated their capability of raising and equipping in a short space of time an enormous mass of troops, and of bringing them to bear on any part of their enemy's frontier . . . and late operations in the western rivers of this continent have shown that they also possess the power of rapidly extemporizing a powerful fleet, adapted for lake warfare."
—REPORT OF THE COMMISSIONERS APPOINTED TO CONSIDER THE DEFENCES OF CANADA, 1862.

IN the spring and summer of 1862, while General McClellan was fighting his bloody and unsuccessful Peninsular campaign in front of Richmond, and Stonewall Jackson's " foot cavalry " were plaguing certain bewildered Union generals in the Shenandoah Valley, a group of British experts were conducting a severely unostentatious survey of the defensive possibilities of the Canadian frontier. They examined every possible avenue of attack, from New Brunswick to Lake Superior, taking careful note of the positions where those avenues might best be blocked by an army acting on the defensive, and of the points where fortifications might serve a good purpose. Their report was to the effect that Canada could be amply secured, provided their recommendations were carried out.

Unfortunately, the recommendations (like those of the commissioners of 1825) constituted a very large order.[1] With regard to troops, in the first place, their opinion was that (including reserves and an allowance for casualties) the province required for its defence a force of 150,000 men, and that other measures were useless until it adopted a system calculated to produce a large drilled force. A second necessity was the

[1] *Confidential. Report of the Commissioners Appointed to Consider the Defences of Canada.* 1862. (W.O. 33, vol. II, pp. 1901–72 ; photostat copy in Public Archives of Canada.) The commission consisted of three military officers (with a fourth as secretary), a naval officer, and an eminent Canadian civil engineer.

enlargement of the canals; for though the Rush-Bagot convention forbade any effective naval armament on the Lakes in time of peace, it was pointed out that in war everything would depend upon establishing a supremacy in the beginning upon Ontario and Erie, and this could best be done by making it possible for armoured vessels to make their way up from the sea. Finally, the commissioners (though especially warned to reduce their prescription in this respect to a minimum)[1] produced a vast scheme of permanent fortifications, which they estimated would cost (including £400,000 for new dockyards on Lakes Ontario and Erie) £1,611,000. The chief items were improvements at Quebec and elaborate defences for Montreal, which, though " the principal strategic point in the province ", was an open town; but there were also large projects for Sarnia, London, Guelph, the Niagara frontier, Toronto, Kingston, Prescott, and other places in Upper Canada.

This report serves to emphasize the British professional conviction (which was growing with the growth of American military power) of the extreme difficulty of defending Canada. Its recommendations were doubtless perfectly sound, from the abstract military point of view; but their enormous expense ruled them out of the field of practical politics. Under the conditions of 1862, it was useless to approach the Canadian Government with any such scheme, and equally useless to approach the House of Commons in England.

In December, Lord Monck again urged his ministers to make provision for raising a really important Canadian force, using the commissioners' opinions as an argument;[2] but Sandfield Macdonald and his colleagues were not moved. Contemplating their 18,000 volunteers with tranquil pleasure, they had no intention of truckling to the Imperial authorities' desire for a drastic militia law. Parliament did not meet until February, 1863; and in May the Government were defeated on a want-of-confidence motion. Monck granted them a dissolution, and the session and the parliament came to an end without the defence question being faced.[3]

---

[1] Memorandum of Instructions, Report, appendix no. 1 (p. 39).
[2] Memorandum of Dec. 17, 1862, quoted at length by C. F. Hamilton, *C.D.Q.*, VI, Jan., 1929.
[3] Pope, *Memoirs of Macdonald*, I, 244–49. At this time the Ministry was completely reorganized, Sicotte being dropped in favour of A. A. Dorion.

In the meantime, almost the whole of the Imperial force concentrated in British North America during the *Trent* crisis remained there.[1] Their officers enjoyed Canadian hospitality (though the Guards, in Montreal, appear to have felt that the provincials accorded them less than the deference properly due to their station in the Army List)[2] and watched with deep interest the progress of the great struggle across the border. Though the Army of Northern Virginia suffered its first serious check at Antietam in September, 1862, the balance of victory still inclined towards the South. Fredericksburg in December, and Chancellorsville in the following May, seemed to indicate that the event might justify those critics (listened to with satisfaction by large classes in Canada, as in the mother country) whose hostility to the Northern cause led them to predict a speedy realization of Southern independence. But July of 1863 brought different intelligence. In the west, the Confederate stronghold of Vicksburg fell, and within a few days the Mississippi was Union water from Minnesota to the Gulf; in the east, Pickett's men surged across the fields at Gettysburg to a glorious failure, and Lee retired southward, beaten. The fortunes of the potential enemies of Canada were in the ascendant; and still she had taken no effective measures for defence.

The general election produced no great change in the position of parties.[3] In August, Sandfield Macdonald's Government again met Parliament; and now at long last they passed into law an improved code of militia legislation, comprised in two Acts. The first,[4] referring to the militia proper, sought to provide means of readily obtaining, in emergency, the services of the most available men on the rolls, through a "Service Militia" forming a sort of first-line. A careful enrolment of the whole militia was to be followed, in 1864 and at three-year intervals thereafter, by the taking of a ballot to form, from the men first liable for service, such a number of "service battalions" as the Governor-General (acting, naturally, on his ministers' advice) might appoint. These might at any time be ordered out for six days' annual drill; and they were to be

---

[1] 15,468 effectives of all ranks on April 1, 1863, as against 17,599 a year before: *P.P.*, 1870, no. 254, vol. XLII.
[2] Russell, *Canada : its Defences, Condition, and Resources*, 138.
[3] Pope, *Memoirs of Macdonald*, I, 250–53.
[4] 27 Vict., cap. 2 : "An act respecting the militia."

officered by men who had undergone a course of qualification to be provided by schools of military instruction whose establishment, in connexion with regular battalions stationed in the province, was authorized by the Act. Not less than $100,000 was to be appropriated for this latter object.

The second Act,[1] relating to the volunteers, gave authority to increase the force up to 35,000 men. All (except the officers) were to be supplied with uniforms and arms;[2] none were to be paid, but there were to be prizes for efficiency, and allowances for general purposes to efficient battalions. The supply Act passed in the same session showed a new generosity; it appropriated $462,000 for the militia and volunteers, in addition to a credit of $121,000 unexpended from the 1862 vote, and $15,000 for the Matapedia road.[3]

While these Acts did not go so far as he would have desired, Monck transmitted them to the Home Government with satisfaction, commenting particularly on the excellent spirit in which Parliament had approached the matter at a time of great party bitterness.[4] Small though these preparations were in relation to the magnitude of the menace, niggardly as they seemed when compared with the great expense incurred by Britain for the defence of the province, nevertheless much had been accomplished. A great gulf separated the Canada of 1863, spending half a million dollars of her yearly revenue on defence, from the colony which eight years before had thought ten thousand enough for that object. Even the recalcitrant Sandfield Macdonald ministry had done more than might have been anticipated.

It is convenient to sum up in this place the progress made in the next year or so as a result of these Acts. As regarded the Service Militia, the Government in the spring of 1864 decided to enrol battalions to the extent of 88,000 men, exclusive of officers.[5] The preliminary enrolment was soon completed in Upper Canada, but in Lower Canada difficulties were encountered which Monck (charitably, perhaps), attributed

---

[1] 27 Vict., cap. 3 : "An act respecting the volunteer militia force."
[2] The force, however, was armed with rifles loaned by the Imperial Government, as permitted by War Office regulations dated March 27, 1862.
[3] 27 Vict., cap. 1.
[4] Monck to Newcastle, Oct. 16, 1863 : G, 464, p. 510.
[5] Monck to Newcastle, April 6, 1864 : G, 465, p. 80.

to that section's less perfect municipal machinery.¹ These overcome, the ballot was taken at the end of the year.² In at least one parish³ of the lower province, this ceremony caused disturbances necessitating the employment of volunteer units to assist the civil power. Monck's ministers disappointed him by failing to call out at least a portion of the Service force for the six days' drill permitted by the statute; it remained on paper. The Governor-General observed that the progress made, " if not quite satisfactory ", was yet sufficient to afford encouragement for the future.⁴

Especially encouraging was the working of the arrangements for the training of officers. Two military schools opened in March, 1864, immediately proved popular, and Canadians pressed forward to seek certificates of qualification.⁵ So pleased were the ministers with the results of this innovation, that they decided to appropriate funds in 1865 for four more schools.⁶ The debt of the local militia organization to this instructional system, conducted with great goodwill by the Imperial regulars, is incalculable. The province paid generous allowances to the regular officers and soldiers thus employed;⁷ but the cost of the battalions which were the framework of the schools was still paid by England.⁸

As for the volunteer force, under legislative encouragement it increased gradually in numbers and efficiency. In the spring session of 1864, Parliament authorized the payment of non-commissioned officers and men for a training period up to sixteen days in length.⁹ That summer, the effective strength of the force was 21,700;¹⁰ still small, it was yet five times what it had been before the outbreak of the war across the border.

¹ Monck to Cardwell, Sept. 2, 1864: *ibid.*, p. 150.
² Monck to Cardwell, March 17, 1865: *ibid.*, p. 302.
³ Château Richer: cf. council minute, Feb. 4, 1865, *re* payment of expenses, *E*, State Book A.B., p. 82. The episode suggests that if the original Militia Bill of 1862 had passed, it would not have been easy to enforce it in Lower Canada.
⁴ Monck to Cardwell, Sept. 2, 1864, as above.
⁵ *Ibid.*
⁶ Monck to Cardwell, Jan. 30, 1865: *G.* 465, p. 267.
⁷ Scale of pay enclosed in Monck to Newcastle, Oct. 16, 1863, as above.
⁸ On these schools, see C. F. Hamilton, in *C.D.Q.*, April, 1929.
⁹ 27-28 Vict., cap. 10, sect. 4.
¹⁰ Monck to Cardwell, Sept. 2, 1864, as above. Although the statute allowed 35,000 men, the Ministry had authorized an establishment of only 25,000. Certain inefficient corps had lately been removed from the roll.

During the same years, substantial progress was made in the Maritime Provinces, and more especially in Nova Scotia. We have seen the beginnings of the volunteer movement there, some years later than the one in Canada. But after 1862 the Nova Scotia volunteers began to be subordinated to the general militia organization. In this province the whole force was called out, in 1863 and succeeding years, for five days' training; 34,800 men were so trained in 1863.[1] They were, however, neither armed nor uniformed. This made the organization very economical; its cost rose from $11,500 in 1861 to a little over $20,000 in the years that followed, while in 1865 expenditures on equipment raised it to $95,000. New Brunswick trained its volunteers, some 1,700 strong; Prince Edward Island had a similar force of about 750, and later called out the whole militia for training after the Nova Scotian fashion.[2] None of these colonies, however, was in a position to carry on experimentation on the Canadian scale.

The history of the Canadian military organization during 1863 and 1864, we have just seen, indicates in the local government and legislature an increasing willingness to burden the provincial revenue with military expenditure. The situation which produced these results remains to be examined.

After Gettysburg, the Southern Confederacy was standing more than ever on the defensive, against foes whose material advantages became more and more apparent, and whose fighting qualities even *The Times*, which once had delighted to refer to " the swift-footed veterans of Bull Run ", could no longer deride. The prospect of Union victory—a victory which would leave the United States equipped with an enormous army which it might perhaps be disposed to use to satisfy its resentment against Britain—was no longer merely visionary; and in Canada certain public men—eminent among whom was the eloquent Irishman, Thomas D'Arcy McGee—were warning the public that the colony should be armed against possible calamity.[3]

Other influences emphasized the danger. Before the war

[1] *Report of Adjutant General of Militia for 1863* (Nova Scotia). The volunteer strength that year was 2,300.
[2] *Canada and its Provinces*, VII, 413–20.
[3] See *The Albion* (New York), Aug. 22, 1863, on " the powerful arguments wherewith Mr. McGee is plying the public ear ".

had lasted long, Canadian cities began to be flooded with "Southern refugees and Northern copperheads"[1] bent on injuring the Union cause. The presence of such people occasioned constant anxiety to the provincial Government, who were determined (the fact is clear enough) to do their utmost to maintain strict neutrality and give no just offence to the United States.[2] In the latter part of 1863, definite difficulties began. A plot to free the Confederate soldiers in a prison camp at Johnson's Island and attack the city of Buffalo was frustrated in November by a timely warning sent by Lord Monck to the American Government;[3] but this did not end the Southern intrigues.

The year 1864 dawned on a feeling of growing uncertainty. The United States was fortifying the border;[4] Lord Lyons reported from Washington that there was talk of abrogating the convention prohibiting naval armaments on the Lakes,[5] which soon grew into a motion in the House of Representatives.[6] This, for the moment, came to nothing; but the British found Mr. Seward's replies to Lyons's representations in the matter rather unsatisfying,[7]—the more so as a 165-foot "revenue" gunboat was building for the United States at Buffalo.[8] Lord Monck had already suggested that the British Government place on the Lakes (where it had no naval force whatever) the tiny vessels which the convention permitted, urging that they would be sufficient to check Confederate filibustering schemes. The suggestion was not entertained.[9]

In the meantime the Canadian political kaleidoscope had shifted again. The Sandfield Macdonald ministry fell in March, 1864; and a Conservative government, nominally headed by

[1] *Globe*, March 26, 1866.
[2] No complete examination of Canadian neutrality in 1861–65 exists; but the main facts may be gathered from *S.P.*, 1869, no. 75—an exhaustive compilation of the official correspondence.
[3] *S.P.*, 1869, no. 75, pp. 75–80.
[4] Newcastle to Monck, Jan. 16, 1864 : *G*, 171, p. 35.
[5] Lyons to Russell, Jan. 12, 1864, enclosed in Newcastle to Monck, Feb. 14 : *ibid.*, pp. 85, 89.
[6] Lyons to Russell, June 20, 1864, enclosed in Cardwell to Monck (confidential), July 16, 1864 : *G*, 172, p. 115.
[7] Lyons to Russell (two dispatches), July 15, 1864, enclosed in Cardwell to Monck (confidential), Aug. 22 : *ibid.*, p. 227.
[8] Cardwell to Monck, June 4 and July 16, 1864; report of British consul at Buffalo, June 16 : *ibid.*, pp. 5, 115, 129.
[9] Monck to Newcastle, March 19 and 31, 1864 : *G*, 465, pp. 45, 58. Cardwell to Monck (confidential), April 30, 1864 : *G*, 171, p. 311.

Sir Etienne Taché, but actually by John A. Macdonald, was formed to enjoy a short season of power and demonstrate by its difficulties that the political union of the Canadas effected in 1841 had ended finally in an insuperable deadlock of groups and parties.[1] The new ministry had to face renewed difficulties in the military relations of the province with the mother country.

The regular garrison of Canada had been reduced since the *Trent* affair, but only very gradually. When John A. Macdonald returned to office there were still some 11,000 troops in the province, in addition to about 3,500 in the Maritimes.[2] Now, however, the Home Government decided to make a considerable reduction. The two battalions of Guards, along with one battalion of the Military Train, were ordered back to England. The reasons given for this action were, first, that it was desirable to reduce the large expenditure for the hire of accommodation for the troops; secondly, to give the Commander in Canada a chance to concentrate his scattered forces; and finally, to make it possible to form a brigade of Guards for service elsewhere abroad in case of need.[3] It was well understood that this referred to the situation on the continent, where Denmark was trying to defend herself against Austria and Prussia. Those powers had shown scant respect to the protests of Britain, whose available forces, it was pretty clear, were not equal to intervention.

The Canadian Government immediately protested,[4] declaring that it was important that the force in the province should not be reduced while the war in the United States continued. In the hope of retaining " these magnificent Troops " in Canada, the ministers offered to recommend to Parliament an appropriation to meet the cost of barrack accommodation. Clearly, Canadian politicians were becoming increasingly apprehensive for the safety of the country. Nevertheless, the Guards and the Military Train departed, and by the next spring the Imperial force in Canada was down to 8,200 officers and men.[5]

[1] Pope, *Memoirs of Macdonald*, I, 255-57.
[2] *P.P.*, 1870, no. 254, vol. XLII.
[3] *Hansard*, CLXXV, 522 (speech of Lord Hartington, May 22, 1864); cf. *ibid.*, 633 (May 26, 1864).
[4] Council minute, June 13, 1864: *E*, State Book A.A., p. 77. The ministry fell on the following day.
[5] *P.P.*, 1870, no. 254, vol. XLII. The fashion in which at this period, the

The actual reduction, however, caused less dismay in the colony than the proposed disposition of the troops that remained; for the War Office had informed General Williams that the Government thought it desirable to do away, as far as possible, with outlying stations, and concentrate the troops " in two principal masses at Quebec and Montreal ".[1] This decision was well advertised in a debate in the House of Commons raised by Adderley, who devoted himself on this occasion to the thesis that it was " inexpedient that detachments of British troops should be stationed upon exposed posts on the Canadian frontier unless adequately supported by Canadian forces ". Troops so placed, he argued, could not even be withdrawn in case of sudden war " without disaster or disgrace ". He even suggested that it would be fair to concentrate the regulars at Quebec, " leaving the Canadian troops to defend all the rest of the frontier " ![2]

Many persons in England, in fact, were falling into something akin to panic at the idea of the danger of " disgrace " at the hands of superior numbers which they thought confronted the imperial force in Canada. Lord Robert Cecil (afterwards Lord Salisbury and Prime Minister) said of the possibility of war with the Northern States :

" That was a very serious danger ; but if the Canadians did not choose to make preparations . . . it was their affair and not ours. If the result of the neglect and delay, after the warnings they had received, should be that their country was overrun, then, although of course the people of England would be sorry . . . yet he did not think we could cast any great blame upon ourselves for the result. But the terrible thing would be if any considerable body of British troops were surrounded and made prisoners. . . ."[3]

The Times subscribed to the same doctrine, suggesting that nine or ten thousand British troops might actually serve as a bait " to allure the American army across the great Lakes ", and adding :

" We view with some anxiety the policy which leaves so rich a prize within the grasp of a nation which external losses and internal

uncertainty of the situation in America hampered Britain's action in Europe, and *vice versa*, has been too little studied.

[1] Lugard to Williams, May 25, 1864 : copy in Correspondence of the Governor-General's Secretary, 11,316.
[2] *Hansard*, CLXXVI, 373-78 (June 27, 1864).
[3] *Ibid.*, 382.

revolution, financial ruin and social disorganization, may at any time drive upon the most desperate enterprises."[1]

The spectacle of those elements in English society which had been outspokenly scornful of and hostile to the Northern cause now sinking into what can only be described as a blue funk at the apparent prospect of the war which their own attitude had done so much to provoke is not edifying.

That these feelings were not without their influence among ministers was indicated by Cardwell's reply to Adderley, which (though he dwelt at some length on " the improved spirit of Canada ") took in the main the form simply of quoting the orders which had gone out for the concentration in the St. Lawrence valley.[2]

When the orders reached Canada, they drew no protest from Sir Fenwick Williams. During Lord Herbert's time at the War Office, he recalled, a similar proposal had been made, and he had advised against it on the ground that it would discourage the Canadians' apparent disposition to take active defensive measures ; but he did not now intend to renew these representations :

" The Canadian Parliament and People (it is confessed on all sides) have not redeemed the promises which their position of danger at first called forth . . . they seem to look on their coming dangers with the eye of a Child, under the protection of a Parent who is *bound to fight*, whilst they pursue their ordinary business, or agitate themselves by fruitless party politics and parliamentary Conflicts. Yet Upper Canada will witness the withdrawal of the Queen's Troops with regret and mortification. . . . I only trust it may lead them to reflect and seriously to set about the organization of a *Militia*, for certes, a few *Volunteers*, neither can or will defend Canada."

Williams, however, urged that Kingston should be retained as an Imperial station.[3]

Lord Monck, on the other hand, strongly opposed the War Office plan. Concentration, he said, would be wise in case of war, but with the aid of the provincial railways and telegraphs

---

[1] *The Times*, June 29, 1864.
[2] *Hansard*, CLXXVI, 378–81. Cardwell had become Colonial Secretary in succession to the Duke of Newcastle, who had resigned in April and died six months later.
[3] Williams to Sec. of State for War, June 13, 1864 : Corr. Gov. Gen'l's Secy., 11,316 (copy).

it could be effected in a week at most, and he saw no need for taking the step while peace endured. Moreover, the infantry battalion at Toronto was employed as a military school, and its withdrawal would cause the breakdown of the militia instructional system in Upper Canada. Finally, he pointed out that fortification projects were in the air, and that whereas in their present state of feeling the Upper Canadians might be well disposed towards such schemes, " if they saw the whole of H.M. troops quartered in the eastern section of the Province and the demand were made upon them for contribution towards the expense of fortifications to be erected solely with a view to the security of Quebec and Montreal " they might hold different views.[1]

At the time when Monck expressed these opinions, he was lending a hand towards constructing the strongest government that Canada had known for many a long day. The Taché-Macdonald cabinet had fallen on June 14. " In three years four Ministries had been defeated, and two general elections had failed to break the deadlock which threatened to make all government in Canada impossible."[2] Every circumstance of the province's situation now counselled heroic measures ; and, thanks to the patriotism of George Brown, the Upper Canada Liberal who had so long been the bitter foe of John A. Macdonald, they were possible. By June 24, a coalition ministry had been formed by the co-operation of these two : a ministry pledged to the special mission of settling the existing difficulties by applying the federal principle, not only to the two sections of Canada, but to the whole of British North America, which they hoped to unite as one great country under the Crown.[3] It was the beginning of a new era.

Finding that the War Office, in the face of Monck's protest, adhered to the concentration scheme (the only concession made was to allow a battalion to remain temporarily at Toronto),[4] the new Government added their representations to the Governor-General's. Such a policy, they said, would necessarily

[1] Monck to Cardwell (confidential), June 16, 1864 : *ibid.*
[2] Pope, *Memoirs of Macdonald*, I, 257.
[3] Trotter, *Canadian Federation*, 66–81 ; Kennedy, *Constitution of Canada*, 293–97.
[4] Hartington to Elliot, July 6, 1864 : copy in Cardwell to Monck, July 19, 1864 (G, 172, p. 143).

cause alarm and discouragement in the western peninsula, for it would be taken as indicating that that section could not be defended in case of war. Declaring their belief that Canada could still be defended as efficiently as during the War of 1812, the ministers earnestly advised that the soldiers should be left where they were, " nothing being more effective in stimulating Military Spirit, and noble emulation in the hearts of youth than the presence of troops, with whose past career so numerous and such glorious recollections are connected."[1]

The ministers had good reason for affirming that the people of Upper Canada distrusted the proposal to remove the troops from among them. A fortnight earlier, the Governor-General had received a memorial, signed by some seventy gentlemen of the Toronto district, protesting against the scheme. The signatories included nearly every prominent person in that section of the province, and the document itself was an able and dignified exposition.[2] It had been prompted by the recent debate in the House of Commons, which (it observed) seemed more likely to encourage American attack than to serve any useful purpose. The military situation in Canada, the memorialists truly declared, had been misrepresented. A large invading army (such as alone could make the venture) could not be collected and moved against the province without there being ample warning to permit the concentration of the British forces; whereas it was to be feared that the withdrawal of the troops at this moment would discourage the growing military activity of the Canadian people.

But they did not scruple to say further that the withdrawal would inevitably be construed as showing a pusillanimous spirit in the Home Government:

"When the reasons . . . suggested as justifying the change are examined by those who know the actual facts here, men will begin to ask whether other unexpressed reasons have not in reality prevailed; and to fear that if in a time of present peace prudential considerations are deemed sufficient to induce the withdrawal of the

---

[1] Council minute, Aug. 26, 1864 : *E*, State Book A.A., p. 243.
[2] Corr. Gov. Gen'l's Secy., 11,392. Among the signers were the Anglican and Roman Catholic bishops, the Chief Justice and the Chancellor of Upper Canada, the Mayor of Toronto, the leading university dignitaries and the chief militia officers. The memorialists explained that they had chosen to present their case privately rather than engage in a public agitation which might have led to abusive utterances and shaken Canadian confidence in Britain.

troops, they would look in vain for their presence in Upper Canada in the time of actual war. . . .

". . . If the apprehension of present danger be with some Statesmen a sufficient reason for leaving the most populous, the most fertile, and the most extensively cultivated portion of Canada without a British Soldier, what policy have we to anticipate when all the Country west of Montreal, perhaps even of Quebec, is virtually in the power of the enemy . . . ? With such a possible future before them would not the Canadians be justified in concluding that they would soon hear from these same Statesmen, the language which an eminent Historian tells us the Romans used when they withdrew from Britain. They 'informed the Britons they must no longer look to them for succour, exhorted them to arm in their own defence, and urged that as they were now their own Masters it became them to protect by their own valour that independence which their ancient lords had conferred upon them'[1] . . .

". . . Your Memorialists . . . must declare that their alarm at this partial withdrawal of Her Majesty's Forces is the more lively because they fear it will be regarded as the first step to an end to which no consideration can reconcile them, and which, if it happen, they must view as an unmitigated calamity. They may be told coldly if not insultingly that 'Canada can no longer rebel for this simple reason that she has nothing to rebel for'[2]; their loyalty may be again, as it was said to have been years ago, an embarrassment in dealing with this Province; or it may be a matter of contemptuous surprize to some whose only idol is a cold blooded utilitarianism. It nevertheless continues to exist in undiminished force,—and it will not be the least painful part of what the People of Canada may be called upon to undergo that they should be treated as Outcasts from the Country which they have ever called their 'Home'."

This singularly authoritative presentation of Canadian opinion not only serves to demonstrate that the people of Canada (though probably never so ready as Englishmen to believe in the likelihood of the United States wantonly attacking the province) were becoming more and more apprehensive as the American war proceeded, but it also presents in very definite fashion the primary reason which led them, in this age when anti-imperialism was so prevalent in England, to mistrust any proposal for a withdrawal of troops from the colony. Such a withdrawal, they feared, might be only the

---

[1] The passage is, of course, from David Hume's *History of England*.
[2] Adderley had used this expression in the recent debate.

prelude to a complete separation from the mother country; and the circumstances of the time inevitably suggested to Canadians that there were people in England who would have regarded such separation as a happy release from the threat of a struggle with the American republic.

The memorial was not without effect. A copy appears to have reached the Duke of Cambridge, the Commander-in-Chief; and he forthwith recommended to the Secretary of State for War that General Williams, in conjunction with the Governor-General, should be allowed to distribute his force as he thought best, having always due regard to the means of rapid concentration and the availability of local support.[1] The ultimate upshot was that Upper Canada was *not* evacuated. The only station of importance abandoned was London; and even it was soon reoccupied in order to open a military school there.[2]

Encouraged perhaps by the advent of the coalition ministry, vowed to great projects, in Canada, and pricked on by the dangers of the American situation, the Imperial Government now ventured to propose that the time had come for mother country and colony to discuss the defence problem in all its aspects and concert effective measures of co-operation. The Colonial Secretary made the suggestion in a dispatch[3] which remarked that, whatever the support to be afforded by Britain in emergency, the defence of Canada would "ever principally depend upon the spirit, the energy and the courage of her own people". He enclosed for confidential consideration a new report on the defences of Canada, lately made to the War Office by Lieutenant-Colonel W. F. D. Jervois,[4] of the Royal Engineers. In the light of this report and that of 1862, it was suggested, the Home Government would welcome "full and frank communication" with the Canadians, and desired to know what measures the Colonial Government believed should be taken, and how much expense they were prepared to incur. Cardwell added :

---

[1] Cambridge to Lord de Grey, Sept. 9, 1864: Verner, *Military Life of George, Duke of Cambridge*, I, 360–61. There seems little doubt that this is the memorial alluded to.

[2] Lugard to Williams, Feb. 21, 1865: in Cardwell to Monck, March 4 (G, 173, p. 220).

[3] Cardwell to Monck (confidential), Aug. 6, 1864: G, 172, p. 205.

[4] Afterwards Sir William Jervois and Governor of New Zealand.

" In any assistance towards a system of defence which Her Majesty's Government could recommend to Parliament, the two primary objects must be—first, an adequate protection for British Troops in Canada ; and, secondly, a secure communication with the Naval Forces of Great Britain.

" It is obvious that Quebec is the position which best fulfils these conditions. But Her Majesty's Government have no wish to confine your attention and that of your Advisers to any one point, however important. It is their desire that the whole subject of the defence of Canada should be considered in a comprehensive spirit."

When the Imperial Government was informed how much Canada was prepared to expend, the dispatch concluded, they would be able to decide how much assistance towards the defensive scheme they would ask from Parliament.

Colonel Jervois, a very capable officer, had visited Canada, the Maritime Provinces, and Bermuda during the autumn of 1863.[1] It is worthy of remark that he had also traversed the Northern States, and had specifically investigated the new and formidable works with which the American Government had lately been at pains to protect its seaports. His report, like that of the commissioners of 1862, was dominated by the enormous recent increase in American military power ; and it called attention to the now increasing likelihood of Union victory. It was the more calculated to disturb the mental comfort of Canadian ministers in that they might clearly perceive in it the origin of the late concentration proposal. Jervois argued that the western part of the province *could not be defended* without a naval superiority on the lakes. On Huron and Erie it was useless to hope for such a superiority ; on

[1] *Report on the Defence of Canada and of the British Naval Stations in the Atlantic. By Lieut.-Colonel Jervois. . . . Part I. Defence of Canada. War Office, February, 1864.* A photostat copy of this report is at the Public Archives of Canada, which also possesses one of Jervois's supplementary *Report on the Defence of the British Naval Stations in the North Atlantic ; together with Observations on the Defence of New Brunswick, &c.*, (Jan. 25, 1865). The latter report recommends large programmes of fortification at Halifax and Bermuda. Jervois apparently conceived British strategy in a possible Anglo-American war as consisting of defensive action on the Canadian border (founded on fortified positions at Quebec and Montreal) and offensive action against the American Atlantic coast by fleets based on Halifax and Bermuda. The army estimates for 1865–66 adopt his suggestions, and initiate programmes to cost £190,000 for the Maritimes and especially Halifax (replacing an earlier estimate of £100,000, under which work was already in progress) and £260,000 for Bermuda (later increased to £375,000) : *P.P.*, 1865, no. 60, vol. XXXII. For the Quebec programme, see below, p. 171.

Ontario, he believed, it could only be assured by enlarging the Ottawa and Rideau canals to permit the passage of ironclads from the sea. Failing this action, he urged that the comparatively small forces available in Canada should be concentrated to defend the really vital strategic centres of the country—the districts essential to the maintenance of communication with England. " It is submitted ", he wrote, " that before the actual commencement of hostilities, the whole of the Queen's troops should be brought into Lower Canada (upon which . . . the main attack would be directed), and that, excepting perhaps 1,000 men for garrison and other duties, they should in the first instance be concentrated at or near Montreal. . . . Objections would, of course, be raised to the Western districts being thus left in the possession of the enemy, but we should gain strength by this system of concentration ; whereas the enemy, if he thought it worth while to make a serious attack on that part of the country, would be expending considerable resources upon operations which would not lead to the attainment of his object."[1] If Montreal was fortified and Quebec strengthened, Jervois believed that a successful defence could be conducted in the St. Lawrence valley.

Word soon arrived that the author of this disquieting document was coming back to Canada to advise the local Government ;[2] and apparently Monck's ministers decided to postpone a definite answer to Cardwell until they had consulted him. They had other considerations to occupy their minds, for the great project of British American union was advancing. Preparations, first for the conference of the provinces at Charlottetown, which met in September, attended by all the most important members of the Canadian Government, and then for the definitive conference at Quebec, were the great work of the moment. Those whose primary interest was the defence of British North America could not grudge the time thus spent, for that the union of the provinces was a measure of the highest importance to that object required no demonstration.

[1] *Report*, p. 12.
[2] Elliot to Monck, Aug. 27, 1864 ; Cardwell to Monck, Aug. 31 and Sept. 2 : *G*, 172, pp. 240–41, 259, 267. For Jervois's instructions, *C*, 482, p. 185 (Lord de Grey to Jervois, " August ").

CANADA AND AMERICAN CIVIL WAR 163

Before the Canadian cabinet finally grappled with the defence question, developments occurred to render it still more urgent. First, and most important, the Confederate sympathizers in Canada, reinforced now by official agents of the Southern Government, embarked upon a determined campaign of enterprises against the Union.[1] On September 20 a party of Confederates from Canada seized two steamers on Lake Erie and (after abandoning a projected attack on the U.S.S. *Michigan*) attempted to destroy them.[2] Soon afterwards, a scheme to employ a vessel named *Georgian* or *Georgiana* in undertakings against the United States on the same lake was frustrated by the Canadian authorities, who also found that warlike stores for such use had been manufactured in Guelph, Canada West.[3] And finally, on October 19, twenty Confederates raided St. Albans in Vermont, robbed the banks, killed one citizen, attempted to burn the town, and escaped across the border to Canada.[4]

The Canadian Government, though well disposed to prevent and punish such outrages, and urged to do so by the Imperial authorities,[5] was hampered both by the prevalence of Southern sympathies in Canada and by legal technicalities in the courts. The grave perils of the situation appeared in the panicky defensive activity of the American population along the border,[6] the truculent attitude of the Secretary of State,[7] and the menaces of the New York Press.[8] The situation entered its worst phase after the hasty and unjustified release of the St. Albans raiders by a Canadian magistrate.[9] " This Canadian

[1] See Headley, *Confederate Operations in Canada and New York ;* and for reminiscences of an eminent Canadian sympathizer (who, however, does not tell all he knows), Denison, *Soldiering in Canada*, chap. VI.
[2] Headley, 248-53 ; S.P., 1869, no. 75, pp. 80-84.
[3] Headley, 253-55 ; S.P., 1869, no. 75, pp. 87-97 ; Monck to Cardwell, Nov. 25, 1864 : G, 465, p. 205.
[4] Headley, 256-63 ; S.P., 1869, no. 75, pp. 117-39.
[5] Cardwell to Monck, Dec. 3, 1864 : G, 172, p. 397.
[6] See *Annual Report of the Adjutant General of the State of New York* . . ., Albany, 1865, I, 19-28, 51-56, 67-68.
[7] Seward to Lyons, Nov. 3, 1864 : S.P., 1869, no. 75, p. 138.
[8] See, e.g., *New York Herald*, Nov. 1 and Nov. 9.
[9] On the ground that action had been taken under the wrong statute. The prisoners were allowed to go before warrants for their re-arrest could be prepared, and the money taken from the St. Albans banks was returned to them. The Canadian Government suspended the magistrate, C. J. Coursol, apprehended such of the raiders as could be found and opened new proceedings against them ; while the money, which was not recovered, was made good by the provincial treasury.

business ", wrote Henry Adams from the American Legation in London, " is suddenly found to be serious, and the prospect of Sherman marching down the St. Lawrence, and Farragut sailing up it, doesn't seem just agreeable."[1] The United States Government showed its feelings by imposing stringent passport regulations along the border,[2] and by giving notice for the abrogation both of the Reciprocity Treaty of 1854 and of the convention limiting naval forces on the Great Lakes.[3]

The Canadian Government was thoroughly alarmed. On December 16 (immediately after the release of the St. Albans prisoners) orders were given for the organization of an efficient detective force to act against the promoters of disturbance on the western frontier,[4] and the cabinet decided to call out 2,000 men of the volunteer force for permanent duty to ensure the neutrality of the border.[5] The cost of these troops was estimated at $80,000 a month ;[6] those who have noted the reluctance of Canadian ministers at previous periods to undertake military expenditures can judge of the gravity which the international situation had now assumed in their eyes. Furthermore, as soon as Parliament met, an Act was obtained " for the prevention and repression of outrages in violation of the peace on the frontier of this province ", authorizing the summary deportation of suspected aliens, and the summary detention of suspected ships.[7]

Another difficulty, later to become serious, had begun to raise its head at this time. The Irish-American militant society known as the Fenian Brotherhood had grown in importance in the course of the war.[8] It was known to have ramifications in Canada ; and when in November of 1864 an Irish society believed to have Fenian connexions held an armed demonstra-

[1] To C. F. Adams, Jr., Dec. 30, 1864 : Ford (ed.), *A Cycle of Adams Letters, 1861–1865*, II, 238–9.
[2] Monck to Cardwell, Jan. 13, 1865 : S.P., 1869, no. 75, p. 32.
[3] Cardwell to Monck, Feb. 11 and 18, 1865 : G, 173, pp. 136, 190. The United States had given notice for abrogating the naval agreement immediately after the St. Albans raid ; it took effect on Nov. 23, 1864, and was ratified by a joint resolution of Congress, approved on Feb. 9, 1865 (*Congressional Globe*, 2nd Session 38th Congress, Appendix p. 159). This notice was later withdrawn the Reciprocity Treaty, on the other hand, duly came to an end in 1866.
[4] Council minute, E, State Book A.A., p. 516 ; cf. S.P., 1869, no. 75, p. 64.
[5] State Book A.A., p. 518 ; cf. S.P., 1869, no. 75, p. 65.
[6] State Book A.A., p. 568 (council minute, Dec. 28, 1864).
[7] Copy in S.P., 1869, no. 75, p. 69 ; in Monck to Cardwell, Feb. 9, 1865.
[8] See *The Albion*, Nov. 14, 1863, for an early account of its activity.

CANADA AND AMERICAN CIVIL WAR 165

tion in Toronto,[1] the country became decidedly alarmed, and there were a number of ludicrous panics in rural districts of Upper Canada.[2]

And in the south the Confederacy, still fighting doggedly, was crumbling before the relentless Union attack. Sherman was moving towards the coast, driving home the wedge that was to destroy the Southern nation, and incidentally giving to the world an admirable demonstration of the horror of modern war. Soon, street-boys in Northern cities would be singing a new song :

> " So we made a thoroughfare, for Freedom and her train,
> Sixty miles in latitude, three hundred to the main ;
> Treason fled before us, for resistance was in vain
>   While we were marching through Georgia."

Canadians might consider the possibility of the hard-bitten Union armies appearing upon the border with the intention of paving just such another bloodstained pathway across the fields of Canada ; and that Freedom whose progress from Atlanta to the sea had been attended by Sherman's bummers was a lady whose closer acquaintance few of them desired. Reasons were not lacking, indeed, to make the closing months of 1864 the darkest period of the war for Canada. In this atmosphere of deepening gloom, her statesmen sat down to consider measures for her defence.

On October 10 the " Fathers of Confederation " assembled at Quebec, determined to lay the foundations of a new nation.[3] The same week the Canadian ministers met Colonel Jervois ;[4] and the result was a request from them for answers to a succession of questions relating to the military situation of the province and Jervois's views upon the means of improving it. On November 10, in consequence, he submitted a second *Report on the Defence of Canada*,[5] comprehending means of

---

[1] *Globe*, Nov. 7, 1864.
[2] *Ibid.*, Dec. 19 and 20, 1864.
[3] For the stress on the defence question in the discussions, see Doughty (ed.), " Notes on the Quebec Conference, 1864," *C.H.R.*, I ; especially the remarks of Cartier.
[4] *P.P.*, 1865, cd. 3434, vol. XXXVII : *Letter to the Secretary of State for War with reference to the defence of Canada, by Lieutenant-Colonel Jervois*. . . .
[5] There are copies in M.P., " Militia and Defence," II. The letter of Wm. McDougall, the provincial secretary, to Jervois, of Oct. 18, with the ministers' queries, is printed as a preface.

defending the whole province. While agreeing in many respects with the report of the commissioners of 1862, this was a more realistic document, for Jervois refrained from throwing projects of fortification about the map in the manner of those gentlemen. Fortifications were, it is true, the basis of his scheme, as being the only means of solving the special problem of Canadian defence: "How to enable a comparatively small force to resist one which will be superior in numbers, and, in the first instance at all events, to a large part of it, in efficiency." He thought them particularly applicable, because the Canadian climate would permit large-scale operations for only about half the year, and he believed that such sieges as would be necessary for the reduction of his projected fortresses would almost certainly be interrupted by winter before attaining success. But he insisted upon the elaborate fortification of only three positions: Quebec, Montreal, and Kingston.[1] Whereas the report of 1862 had proposed to spend £1,611,000 for fortifications alone[2] (and it seems certain that the actual cost would have been very much more), Jervois's entire scheme, allowing £300,000 for the cost of gunboats, and very large sums for the purchase of land for the works and the cost of armament, was estimated at £1,754,000.

The sum was enormous; but Jervois's exposition encouraged the hope that it would purchase genuine security. He recognized the greatness of the menace, and yet was confident that it could be combatted successfully by measures taken in good time:

"If preparation for war were postponed until a period when hostilities were seriously threatened, no steps that could then be taken either by Great Britain or by Canada herself would be of any avail. Effective resistance to the invasion of Canada . . . can alone be made by adopting a permanent basis for defence.

"By means of the measures recommended in this paper, Canada, aided by Imperial troops, would be enabled to resist American aggression with success; and who shall say that, thus tiding over the time of her dependence and comparative weakness, she may not, united with the other provinces of British North America, at length

---

[1] Much smaller and cheaper works were also recommended for Toronto and Hamilton, but they were of subsidiary importance. Those at the three points named were declared indispensable.

[2] Apparently this did not include the cost of buying the land.

become a great and powerful nation which may hold her own against the world!"[1]

This was a note calculated to appeal to Canadian politicians at a time when doubts of the defensibility of Canada were beginning to be openly expressed in England.

Less than a week after the presentation of this report, the ministers drew up their answer to Cardwell's request for their views on the whole defence question.[2] It was certainly not conceived in the largest spirit, for it dwelt at length on the duty of England to play a major part in the defence of Canada, which the ministers considered " essentially an Imperial question ". It expressed anxiety over the fact that " the tone of public opinion " in England seemed to indicate a tendency to regard the matter as almost exclusively one for Canadian consideration, and some concern over Cardwell's remark that the two primary objects of Imperial assistance would be the protection of the British troops in Canada and the maintenance of communication with the fleet. The ministry went so far as to ask baldly the views of the Imperial Government as to how many regular troops would be maintained in the colony while the danger of war endured, the number " which might be depended upon should hostilities break out ", and " the means by which the expenses of war could be defrayed ".

The Confederation proposals, it was further pointed out, while promising more comprehensive defensive arrangements for the future, were at the moment something of an embarrassment; for if Canada now entered into large obligations for the future, such obligations might be invoked as an argument by the opponents of union in other provinces. The ministers, therefore, proposed to postpone permanent agreements on the whole question until after Confederation. Yet they felt that " the urgency of the existing circumstances " necessitated an immediate understanding on the most pressing matters. The fortification of Montreal seemed chief of these; and the Canadians proposed, pending final adjustments (and they felt that " the greater part " of the cost of the whole programme of works should be borne by the mother country), that they should apply to their Parliament for an appropriation to

[1] *Report*, p. 14.
[2] Council minute, approved Nov. 16, 1864: *E*, State Book A.A., p. 427.

construct the Montreal works, provided that Great Britain would undertake the construction of those at Quebec and supply the armaments for both. They asked, moreover, that, in order to avoid increasing the cost to Canada unnecessarily, the Imperial Government should guarantee a loan designed to meet her share. And they undertook to accompany the fortification scheme, before Parliament, with an appropriation of $1,000,000 for the militia.

These were not ungenerous proposals, for Jervois had estimated the cost of the Montreal defences, apart from armament, at £443,000. They serve to show that the Canadian Government was now distinctly apprehensive of war; Monck called attention to the contrast between these offers and past practice.[1] As for the protestations of Britain's duty to Canada with which they were surrounded, these were the product of the fear that, in the face of the American danger, a tendency was abroad in England towards the repudiation of such responsibilities. The Adderleys and Little Englanders, in Parliament and the Press, had done their work well, and the concentration proposal of the previous spring had given point to Canadian fears. George Brown visited England just at this time, and though he found Canada's reputation quite rehabilitated by the Confederation scheme, and hoped that the Canadian fortification proposals would be accepted, he watched the trend of British opinion with some dismay. To his colleague Macdonald he wrote:

" I am much concerned to observe . . . that there is a manifest desire in almost every quarter that, ere long, the British American colonies should shift for themselves, and in some quarters evident regret that we did not declare at once for independence. I am very sorry to observe this, but it arises, I hope, from the fear of invasion of Canada by the United States, and will soon pass away with the cause that excites it."[2]

The British answer[3] to the Canadian ministers' proposals did little to counteract this impression. The Imperial Government readily agreed to postponing final decisions until after Confederation, and in fact suggested that the whole negotiation should be so postponed, any measures taken in the meantime

---

[1] Monck to Cardwell (confidential), Nov. 16, 1864 : *G*, 180 B, p. 147 (draft).
[2] Dec. 22, 1864 : Pope, *Memoirs of Macdonald*, I, 273-74.
[3] Cardwell to Monck (confidential), Jan. 21, 1865 : *G*, 173, p. 77.

being on the separate responsibility of the two governments. Cardwell added :

" It must be distinctly understood that in waiving this discussion Her Majesty's Government give no assent to the proposals made by your Advisers. They reserve to themselves entire freedom as to the terms on which any engagements may hereafter be contracted between the Government of Her Majesty and the Government of the future Confederation."

Under these circumstances, the Home Government did not think it desirable to enter upon the discussion of the forces to be supplied by England and Canada respectively and the manner in which a hypothetical war might be financed.

Still more discouraging, however, was the fact that (although Monck had hinted broadly that it might be worth while to accede to the Canadian conditions)[1] the request for a guarantee for a loan was refused :

" Her Majesty's Government think it would be very inexpedient to accompany the proposal to Parliament of a Vote for the Defences of Quebec with a proposal to guarantee a loan for the defence of Montreal. Considering the great importance of that place to the defence of the whole Province,—and the very moderate sum which the proposed works are estimated to require,—they think a very bad effect would be produced by making that proposal."

It might have been argued that in an Imperial partnership for defensive purposes, the mother country might well consider it part of her contribution to lend the support of her unequalled credit to her impecunious colonies. Canada's bonds had been depressed in the market by the danger of her situation, and she could have floated a loan on her own credit only at a most disadvantageous rate ; while on the other hand she had never failed to meet her obligations, and the possibility of the suggested guarantee ever leading to the outlay of a penny from the Imperial treasury seemed slight. But the Imperial Government apparently lacked the courage to face the House of Commons and its distaste for expenditure for colonial defence with the proposal ; and its failure to do so naturally tended to strengthen the Canadian ministers' doubts.

It is difficult, in fact, to avoid the conclusion that at the beginning of 1865 the relation of Canada and the mother country

[1] Monck to Cardwell (confidential), Nov. 16, 1864 : as above.

was not much better than one of mutual suspicion. Canada, uncomfortably conscious of the growth of anti-colonialism in England, had actually felt the need of a promise in black and white that the Imperial forces would not fail her in the hour of need; and England, on the other hand, had felt the need of protecting herself with quasi-legal formulas against the possibility of being drawn by colonial importunities into the assumption of responsibilities not nominated in just such a bond.

The British position, however, was not purely negative. Along with the refusal of the guarantee went the announcement[1] that the Imperial Government intended to proceed at once to the improvement of the defences of Quebec, at its own expense. No attempt was made to conceal the object of this: it was to provide the regular forces in Canada with a secure position in which in case of war they could hold their own until reinforced. This was a direct intimation that, under existing circumstances, the outbreak of war would see all the Imperial troops in the colony concentrated at Quebec. The Colonial Office accompanied it with an expression of hope that Canada would (despite the refusal of the guarantee) proceed at once to strengthen Montreal, and offered to supply the armament for the forts there.

At the beginning of February, 1865, the Canadian Government increased the number of military schools from two to six.[2] The same week came another rude reminder that the war in the South was drawing to a close; for an attempt at peace negotiations was made in a conference at Hampton Roads between Lincoln and the Confederate Vice-President, Stephens. The attempt was, on the Southern side, based in part at least on a proposal that North and South should unite against a third party in defence of the Monroe Doctrine.[3] The third party proposed was, actually, France in Mexico; but the mere rumour that the negotiations dealt with the Monroe Doctrine caused consternation in England.[4] Incidentally, it pushed the

---

[1] Cardwell to Monck, Jan. 21, 1865: *G*, 173, p. 67 (a public dispatch of the same date as the confidential one just referred to).

[2] Council minute, approved Feb. 1, 1865: *E*, State Book A.B., p. 74. Cf. above, p. 151.

[3] Stephens, A. H., *A Constitutional View of the Late War between the States* . . ., Philadelphia, etc., 1870, II, 600–601.

[4] C. F. Adams to his son, Feb. 17, 1865: *Cycle of Adams Letters*, II, 256–57.

Canadian Government's five-per-cent bonds, which at the New Year had stood at 88, down to 80 on the London market.[1]

It was just at this time that Cardwell's dispatches reached Canada ; and on their heels came news of events in England which increased the Canadian chagrin. The Imperial Parliament reassembled on February 7, and the Government immediately let it be known that they intended to ask a vote of £50,000 for the fortification of Quebec, the first year's instalment of a total of £200,000 to be spent for this object. At the same time they laid before Parliament Jervois's report to the Secretary of State for War on his second mission to Canada, which immediately attracted much public attention.[2] Lord Lyveden soon raised the matter in the House of Lords, declaring that the report " showed—not to use any equivocal expression—the utterly defenceless state of Canada ".[3] Lord Derby accused the Government of having done too little for the defence of the colony ;[4] and the whole tone of the debate bespoke an agitated and uncertain frame of mind. It had at least the effect of eliciting from the Government declarations that if Canada was attacked, England would go to her defence[5]—a point on which, *The Economist* significantly observed, there had been some doubt.[6] But there was also strong insistence upon Canada's obligations ; the Secretary of State for War said, " We take a share of the expense upon ourselves. We ask them [the colonists] to take the larger share ".[7] The effect of the declarations that Canada would be defended was offset by the advertisement of the prevalence of a conviction that it was in fact indefensible.

Doubts and heart-searchings were, indeed, current in the highest quarters. Gladstone, the Chancellor of the Exchequer, had " objected strongly to fortifying Quebec ", and had waged a hard battle in cabinet with the majority of his colleagues, who were, as Palmerston told the Queen, " looking to the probability that, whenever the Civil War in America shall be

[1] *The Times*, Jan. 2, Feb. 18, 1865.
[2] *Ibid.*, Feb. 15, 1865. *Annual Register*, 1865, p. 52. For the projects undertaken at the same time at Halifax and Bermuda, see above, p. 161.
[3] *Hansard*, CLXXVII, 416–22 (February 20, 1865).
[4] *Ibid.*, 425–30.
[5] *Ibid.*, 434–38 and 430–32 (speeches of Russell and Granville).
[6] *Economist*, Feb. 25, 1865.
[7] *Hansard*, CLXXVII, 425 (speech of Lord de Grey).

ended, the Northern States will make demands upon England which cannot be complied with, and will either make war against England or make inroads into your Majesty's North American possessions which would lead to war."[1] And on February 12 the Queen had recorded in her journal an interview with Sir Charles Wood, in which they spoke of

"America and the danger, which seems approaching, of our having a war with her, as soon as she makes peace; of the impossibility of our being able to hold Canada, but we must struggle for it; and far the best would be to let it go as an independent kingdom, under an English Prince! But can we stave this off, and who could be chosen?"[2]

It was perhaps fortunate for the Canadian ministers' peace of mind that they did not know of these things.

There were, however, plenty of public manifestations of the same fears to worry them. In March the defence of Canada was the subject of two full-dress debates in the House of Commons (the second on a motion to strike out the appropriation for Quebec) in which wide differences of opinion became evident and very large statements were made. When criticized for failing to undertake the works earlier, the Government replied that they had not felt justified in coming to Parliament for appropriations "as long as Canada made no exertions", but that the improved spirit shown there during 1864 had made it their duty to give aid.[3] But where some members claimed that the aid was belated, others declared that it was useless to take steps to defend a country which was indefensible. Robert Lowe led this school, declaring in a characteristic speech that Britain should find other and more favourable ground on which to fight the United States. "In my opinion", he said, "nothing would be so strong an incentive in America to war with this country, as the notion that they could catch a small English army, and lead it in triumph"; and he urged that every Imperial soldier should be withdrawn from Canada at once.[4] He was not alone in his counsels of despondency. Major Anson's words were among the most striking:

[1] Jan. 20, 1865: *Letters of Queen Victoria*, second series, I, 248-49.
[2] *Ibid.*, 250.
[3] *Hansard*, CLXXVII, 1565-70 (speech of Cardwell): March 13, 1865.
[4] *Ibid.*, 1578-85.

"He maintained . . . that it was perfectly and utterly impossible for this country to dream of defending Canada for one moment. . . . For every gun that England brought . . . the Americans could bring ten; for every gunboat we put upon the Lakes and the St. Lawrence, they could put ten, and more too, if they chose to try it. . . . If the Canadians wanted a standing army, let them raise it for themselves, and let them rest content with the maritime and other efficient aid which England could render them. England certainly was not called upon by her honour to send troops to fight in Canada, especially when all knew that it was hopeless."[1]

One salient fact impressed observers of these debates. "The tone of silly bravado"[2] which certain politicians had been accustomed to use towards the United States, and which had done so much harm, was no longer heard. There was universal respect for Northern military power. Richard Cobden's comment was bitter, but hardly unjust: "The alteration of tone is very remarkable. It is clear that the homage which was refused to justice and humanity will be freely given to success."[3]

The Government's position was difficult. It took a pacific tone towards the United States—this was the easier as the passport system had just been discontinued, and the notice for the abrogation of the Rush-Bagot convention withdrawn;[4] it refused however to have anything to do with the ideas of Lowe,[5] and the House backed it up, sustaining the Quebec appropriation by 275 to 40;[6] and nevertheless it reiterated that the defence of Canada "must rest partly on the mother country, but mainly and principally on Canada herself".[7]

The effect in Canada was certainly to shake rather than to strengthen public confidence. If the Imperial Government had declared its intention of assisting in the defence of Canada, it

---

[1] *Ibid.*, CLXXVIII, 116–19 (March 23, 1865).
[2] *Economist*, March 18, 1865.
[3] Morley, *Cobden*, II, 468 (Cobden to Bright, March 15, 1865). Cobden fell a victim to his desire to oppose this vote " for guaranteeing three or four millions of North Americans living in Canada, etc., against another community of Americans living in their neighbourhood"; travelling to London in bitter weather, he was prostrated on his arrival, and died on April 2. *Ibid.*, 470–72.
[4] *Hansard*, CLXXVIII, 160–64 (speech of Cardwell); cf. CLXXVII, 1565–70.
[5] *Ibid.*, CLXXVII, 1633–37 (speech of Palmerston).
[6] *Ibid.*, CLXXVIII, 175 (the sponsor of the attack upon it, G. W. P. Bentinck, finding his motion supported by some members from motives not his own, sought to withdraw it; but the House insisted on a vote).
[7] *Ibid.*, 160–64 (speech of Cardwell).

had nevertheless surrounded the declaration with qualifications seeming to indicate that the assistance might be only measured and partial ; and the numerous assertions that the colony could not be defended blended with the obvious apprehension of immediate war which dominated the discussions to produce a most disturbing atmosphere. The disquieting aspect of the whole military situation, as it appeared both in America and in England, was naturally reflected in the session of the Canadian Parliament, dedicated mainly to the question of Confederation, which began in January of 1865.

The debates clearly showed the members' sense of the critical juncture at which the affairs of the province had arrived. One sentence of George Brown's speech for federation summed up the causes for anxiety—no comforting catalogue :

" The civil war . . . in the neighbouring republic ; the possibility of war between Great Britain and the United States ; the threatened repeal of the Reciprocity Treaty ; the threatened abolition of the American bonding system for goods in transitu to and from these provinces ; the unsettled position of the Hudson's Bay Company ; and the changed feeling of England as to the relation of great colonies to the parent state ;—all combine at this moment to arrest earnest attention to the gravity of the situation, and unite us all in one vigorous effort to meet the emergency like men."[1]

The American menace in its various manifestations was repeatedly canvassed. On March 13, J. H. Cameron gave frank expression to the current anxieties, declaring that it was Canada's duty to make large defensive preparations and Britain's duty to support her—in particular by guaranteeing her debentures. As matters stood, the United States felt that Canada was at their mercy :

" To-day they impose an obnoxious passport system upon us, and to-morrow they relieve us from that source of annoyance. . . . Next we hear of their intention of placing a force of gunboats on the lakes, and then we hear that the intention has been abandoned. What are all these fair promises they indulge in . . . but blinds of their real purpose ? Does anybody believe that it is not in their hearts to do all those things with which they threaten us, and is it not our duty to be prepared to meet the consequences of their

[1] *Parliamentary Debates on . . . the Confederation of the British North American Provinces*, 114.

threats being carried into execution ? . . . I think it would be a good thing if we were a little more aroused in this country by the events that are transpiring about us, and that the people of England should become a little more in earnest, so that the people of the United States should not fall into the habit of regarding the British lion . . . as a stuffed lion. I sometimes wish the British lion would roar "—(*laughter*)—" as it has roared in times past. . . ."[1]

These views were becoming typical. Apprehensions regarding the attitude of the United States were general, and with them went a growing discontent with the apparent timidity of the mother country.

How were these ghosts to be laid ? An amended offer by the Canadian Government, which held out some hope that Canada would undertake the western fortifications as well as those at Montreal, provided that Britain would make the gunboats of the Royal Navy available for Lake Ontario and would guarantee an issue of debentures to pay Canada's share of the scheme,[2] had met with no more encouragement from Cardwell than the earlier one.[3] And finally, to fill the cup to overflowing, bad news came from New Brunswick. The Government there had appealed to the electorate prematurely, and Confederation had been decisively rejected.

The Canadian ministers now resolved upon a bold attack on the accumulated difficulties. As a *beau geste*, to strengthen their hands in dealing with the mother country, they passed a special supply act providing $1,000,000 " for the permanent defence of the country " ;[4] and they decided to dispatch to England forthwith the strongest possible delegation from the Colonial Government, to obtain an understanding with the Imperial authorities. The delegates were to confer with the British ministry on the means of speedily effecting Confederation, on " the arrangements necessary for the defence of Canada, in the event of war arising with the United States, and the extent to which the same should be shared between Great Britain and Canada ", on the abrogation of the Reciprocity Treaty, on the question of the Hudson's Bay Company's

[1] *Ibid.*, 966–69.
[2] Council minute, Feb. 3, 1865 : *E*, State Book A.B., p. 76 and at back.
[3] Cardwell to Monck (confidential), Feb. 24, 1865 : *G*, 173, p. 194.
[4] 28 Vict., cap. 3. It also appropriated $330,000 for the maintenance of the volunteer force still on active duty on the frontier.

territories, "and, generally, upon the existing critical state of affairs by which Canada is most seriously affected."[1]

On the eve of the delegates' departure, Lord Monck submitted to his ministers a solemn memorandum designed to influence their action.[2] He advised against representations such as that of the previous November in which they had demanded from England a categorical assurance concerning the aid which she would lend in case of war;[3] for such requests were inimical to the maintenance "on a sound and kindly basis" of the connexion with the mother country. He shrewdly added, striking a chord to which the Canadians were especially responsive:

"There exists in England an able, active and energetic, though not numerous, party who desire to Sever the connection between England and her Colonies. Nothing could be more calculated to strengthen the hands of Men holding such views than an attempt on the part of Canada to compel England by *express Contract* to render herself liable for indefinite expenditure as the price of the continuance of the connection.

". . . The nature of the connection gives already a guarantee for the exertion of the power of Great Britain in defence of the Colony more binding than any mere written agreement, and with that obligation the Provincial Government may safely rest content."

As for the question of the proportional division between the two countries of the cost of peacetime preparations, Monck laboriously computed that, if the province paid the cost of the whole Jervois programme (exclusive of the works at Quebec, the gunboats and the fort armaments) and spent $1,000,000 annually on the militia, it would still be spending much less, in proportion, than was devoted to defence by the United Kingdom—whether the comparison was calculated on a basis of population, of relative wealth (taking as an index the aggregate value of imports and exports), or of the proportion of defensive expenditure to annual revenue devoted to civil purposes.

The ministers' reply[4] still showed a certain recalcitrance. They declared that no safe deduction concerning the ability of

[1] Council minute, March 24, 1865 : *E*, State Book A.B., p. 197.
[2] Misplaced in *M.P.* : "Railways," I, 44 ; dated March 21, 1865.
[3] Above, p. 167.
[4] Council minute, March 27, 1865 : *E*, State Book A.B., p. 205.

a country still in the pioneer stage to bear taxation for warlike purposes could be drawn from the amount borne by Great Britain, which was very differently situated. At the moment, moreover, crop failures, the derangements caused by the war nearby, and not least " the diminished confidence in the future of this Country, greatly caused by the remarks of the public men and press of Great Britain ", had thrown Canada into " a period of temporary but serious depression ". Once more the council referred to Britain's control of foreign policy. It was clear that (as indeed was far from unnatural in the circumstances of the day) they would insist that the mother country should continue to take the leading part in the defence of Canada. They added, however:

"But the Committee accept most heartily the principle of contribution to the cost of defence, and the people of Canada will not shrink from any burden that on a candid examination may be found to be justly theirs, and within the reach of their ability."

Shortly before the delegation sailed, John A. Macdonald committed to paper his own private dissatisfaction with the situation in England:

"The indiscreet publication of Col. Jervois' report in England has at present caused a panic in Western Canada, as it shows the defencelessness of most of our provinces, unless protected by permanent works; and the wretched debate in the House of Lords has not diminished the dread of forcible annexation, and abandonment by Great Britain. Fancy the British Empire, for the purpose of defending Canada and the British flag from an impending war, voting £200,000 in all, to be expended at £50,000 a year! Any war with the United States must occur within two years, and by that time a hole may be made in the mud opposite Quebec, and the foundation of a single redoubt laid. In order to shame them we carried the vote for a million dollars, to be immediately expended, and we go home with that sum in our hands."[1]

The delegation consisted of Macdonald, Brown, Cartier and Galt. The two last-named sailed a week before the others, who embarked on April 12. By that time they knew that the

---

[1] Macdonald to Col. Gray, of New Brunswick, March 27, 1865: Pope, *Memoirs of Macdonald*, I, 280-81. It had been explained by the British Government that £50,000 was the largest sum that could be laid out to advantage at Quebec in the first season's operations.

terrible drama so long in progress south of the border had at last reached the anticipated catastrophe. Three days earlier, General Lee had surrendered at Appomattox. The Southern Confederacy was no more ; and the United States of America, now for the first time in its history the greatest military power on earth, would soon have its hands free to deal with the problems of external affairs.

CHAPTER VIII

FENIANISM AND FEDERATION

> "We look to Confederation as the means of relieving this country from much expense and much embarrassment. . . . We appreciate the goodwill of the Canadians and their desire to maintain their relations with the British Crown. But a people of four millions ought to be able to keep up their own defences."
>
> —*The Times*, March 1, 1867.

WE have had frequent occasion to remark that, with regard to the future of the Empire, mid-Victorian Englishmen were in general men of little faith. Long before 1865, pessimism on this score was a decidedly familiar phenomenon. Yet it was, probably, during the years immediately following the American Civil War that the anti-imperial spirit had its greatest acceptance in England; it was then that the spectre of separation walked at noonday. To the old explanations—the commercial and political independence of the colonies, combined with their continued (and costly) dependence upon the mother country for defence—there was now added, in the particular case of Canada, another motive: the idea that this colony was the Achilles heel of England—the joint in her armour through which the sword of the resentful American republic might reach her.

In April, 1865, while the delegates of the Canadian Government were sailing towards England in hope and fear, a member of the House of Commons was putting the final touches to a book which admirably represented these opinions. Viscount Bury's *Exodus of the Western Nations*[1] reads strangely to-day. Six nations, said Bury, had taken part in the "exodus" from Europe towards the west; and the colonies of all of them had come in the end to independence. Was it to be supposed that this was not the result of the natural order of things? The

---

[1] London, 1865: 2 vols. The preface is dated April 13, 1865. Bury later became seventh Earl of Albemarle.

present situation of British North America was anomalous and therefore dangerous : it was virtually independent, yet nominally a subject state. Let some cause of quarrel arise between the legislatures, " each armed with supreme authority ", sitting on opposite sides of the Atlantic, and separation, accompanied by a rupture of friendly relations, would follow.[1] Such a quarrel might arise on any one of several topics ; but the events of 1862 were appealed to as evidence that the defence question was especially dangerous.[2] So long as Canada remained a colony, Bury observed, the obligation of Britain to defend her was undoubted. If, however, she ceased to be such, the United States would, probably, no longer desire to attack her.[3]

The remedy for these dangers, in his view, was to arrange " now, while it may yet be done in peace, without reference to any immediate subject of dispute ", the relationship of friendly alliance which was to be substituted for the existing connexion ; and he was ready with " articles of separation ".[4] In this fashion, he thought, it would be possible to arrange the parting between Canada and the mother country in such a way as to ensure permanent peace between them.[5]

Bury, like many another Englishman of his time, looked about him and saw no solid basis for Imperial unity to replace that purely authoritarian one which had lately vanished, unregretted, with the passing of the old colonial system. Mere loyalty and goodwill seemed but insecure foundations on which to build a polity ;[6] few men dared to believe that a free partnership could successfully be substituted for the old relationship of authority and obedience. And in 1865 there still remained upon the Imperial scene a legacy of the earlier age which seemed a serious obstacle to the development of a relation which might be a source of pride and strength to both sides, and of grievance to neither : the colonial garrisons. Bury himself put it plainly :

" One by one, the last rags of the commercial system have been torn away. We receive no tribute ; we expect no commercial

[1] I, 25–28.   [2] II, 466 ff.
[3] Bury postulated (as article IX of his proposed treaty of separation) a declaration that Britain would use her utmost efforts to defend the new nation in case of foreign attack ; but he apologized for the apparent danger to Britain latent in this provision by the above explanation.
[4] II, 459–63. He acknowledged a debt in this respect to Henry Thring's *Suggestions for Colonial Reform*, London, 1865.
[5] II, 493–94.
[6] Cf. the second ed. of Merivale's *Colonization and Colonies* (1861), p. 677.

advantage in the ports of our own colonies that we do not hold by merit and not by favour ; yet we undertake the burden of defending them against attack. It is on this ground that certain politicians exclaim against colonies ; that they denounce them as a useless expense, and would do away with them altogether."[1]

It was becoming steadily clearer that this anachronism would have to be done away with if the Empire was to escape the disruption which Bury foretold.

The Anglo-Canadian conferences in London[2] began on April 26 and 27 with two informal interviews of Cartier and Galt with Cardwell which merit considerable attention. Cartier was charged with explaining the Canadians' views on the Confederation question, which consisted mainly of a request for Imperial aid in convincing the Maritime Provinces. Considering the intimate connexion between the union proposal and the defence of the colonies, he said, they "thought that the Imperial Government, who were charged with the responsibility of the defence of the Empire, might properly exercise a very great influence through a decided expression of their views". He urged also that the conduct of the Lieutenant-Governors in both Nova Scotia and New Brunswick had been adverse to the scheme's chances of success, and that it was desirable that Imperial policy should be represented by officers friendly to the project.

Galt then took up the question of defence. He told Cardwell that the Canadian Government's views had changed since their suggestion, in the previous November, that the main issues should be left until after Confederation ; and his memorandum of his statement is worth quoting :

" . . . Events which had transpired on the American Continent & especially the irritation which had been created by the Raids from Canada had latterly convinced the Candⁿ. Govt. that the Measures for the Defence of the Provinces were much more urgent :—and upon the vote of N.B. proving that some delay must necessarily take place in the consummation of the Union, the Canadian Govt.

---

[1] *Exodus of the Western Nations*, I, 18.
[2] There are numerous memoranda relating to these discussions in *M.P.*, " Visits to England," I, 80 ff., with very full notes of the first two days' interviews, pp. 86 ff. and 106 ff. Galt's informing letters home are in Skelton, *Galt*, 377–86.

had come to the conclusion that it was their duty at the earliest possible moment to have a full and frank explanation with H.M. Govt. in the hope of being able to establish the relations which ought to subsist upon such a basis as would remove the present feeling of uneasiness which existed both in Canada & Gt. Britain on this subject.

" The Canadian Govt. were quite prepared to admit that Colonies possessing the population and wealth of Canada might fairly be required to assume a larger share of responsibility for their own Defence. That the desire and belief of Canada was, in seeking a Union, not in any way to weaken the connection with the Mother Country, but rather to remove those causes which now afforded many parties in England arguments for asserting that the connection was mutually disadvantageous. . . .

". . . It was urged that without undertaking to say whether implicit credence should be given to the amicable professions of the Amer$^{n.}$ Govt. it was perfectly plain that if those professions were insincere, the most frightful calamities must be entailed upon the American Colonies and especially upon Canada . . . and that therefore it was much better to take every possible precaution . . . rather than to incur the fatal consequences which would inevitably follow the possible and unexpected occurrence of hostilities with the U.S.—*Having these views, the C. Govt. had felt it their duty to regard the question of Defence as one of imminent necessity and paramount importance ; and that so far from confining it to the consideration of the works suggested by Col. Jervois, they were obliged to urge such measures as if war were immediate & certain.* It appeared to them that Defensive Works could only be fully available after a considerable lapse of time and that meanwhile either the danger of war would have passed away, or hostilities would have actually broken out :—that Canada was fully satisfied that in the event of war, everything wd. be done by Great Britain that could be done,—that no assurance on this point was therefore asked for, but that in the case of Canada unless preparation were meantime made, no subsequent exertions could ever redeem the disasters that would have fallen upon the people of that Province. It was therefore with the view of urging such preparation and of establishing the relative contributions of the Mother Country and of the Colony, that H.M. Govt. were now approached."[1]

This introduction needs no elucidation. The apprehension

[1] " Memorandum of Interview with Mr. Cardwell on 26th April, 1865 " : *M.P.,* as above. The italics have been supplied. Note the compliance with Monck's recommendation against asking an express and categorical assurance of aid.

of danger from the United States, a growing influence in Canadian councils since 1863, had now reached its climax. The contrast of the tone of this memorandum with the complacency of Sandfield Macdonald's Government in 1862 is curious to contemplate.

The ministers suggested, Galt went on, that while the fortifications were being constructed a very considerable force of the militia should be called out and trained, and that munition factories should be established in Canada. An increase in the regular force was also suggested, and naval defence, both on the Lakes and the seaboard, indicated as requiring attention. As to the distribution of expense :

" The principle which the Can: Govt. thought shd. govern was that all the Expense of the regular Forces beyond that which was required for their maintenance on the Home Station shd. be regarded as a portion of the Defence of the Colonies & that all the Expenditure within the Colonies in connection with the Militia, the fortifications, and the provision of the Munitions of war should be considered to belong to the same Class, & shd. be borne equally by the colony & Gt. Britain."

At the same time, Canada proposed to construct a railway between Halifax and Quebec, and improve the canals connecting the Great Lakes and the ocean. These works, useful both for defensive and commercial purposes, would, it was felt, reconcile Canadians to the scheme as demonstrating that " the views of the Government were not wholly directed to the mere question of defence ", while by providing a ready passage to the sea for the produce of the Western States they might induce those communities to use their influence for peace.

Canada, Galt observed, would require the aid of Imperial credit in raising the funds necessary for this enormous programme ; and he assured Cardwell that the additional taxation which was necessary " would not be imposed through additional Customs Duties ". When Cardwell asked for some unofficial estimate of the cost of the whole scheme, Galt replied that the Canadians thought it best to fix a maximum, in the expectation that the actual outlay would be much less, and went calmly on to say that in their opinion, " the joint expenditure . . . of the Imperial Government, and that of the Colony, would be from eight to ten millions sterling ". The works of communication (whose expense Canada would assume, subject to an Imperial guarantee) would cost, probably, five millions more. Galt expressed the hope that after three years, with the forts built and a large body of militia trained, the Imperial Government would be able to reduce the regular force and in fact " place the Colony in a position of self-defence ".

One feature of these proposals which was sufficient in itself to make it impossible for any British ministry to accept them was the suggestion that in the joint account Britain should be credited, not with the whole cost to her of the regular troops in Canada, but only with the small sum represented by the excess of their cost there over that on the home station. Signifying as it did that the Imperial Government would probably have to pay part of the cost of training the provincial militia, this proposal (which would have been hard to defend at any time) was, in the prevailing temper of Parliament, simple nonsense. This, however, should not blind us to the fact that the Canadians' proposals did represent a readiness on the part of the colony to make very great financial sacrifices ; for they amounted to a declaration that it was prepared to spend, if circumstances demanded it, sums aggregating £9,000,000 or more for defence and allied objects.[1]

Cardwell must have gasped as Galt produced his figures. His reply was that " he thought the magnitude and nature of the proposals would take both the Government and the British people somewhat by surprise ; and that he had hoped that the views of the Canadian Government would have been confined to the construction of the fortifications, as he thought it would be very difficult to justify the assumption by the Imperial Government of any part of the expense of drilling the Canadian Militia " ; he hoped the Canadians would consider the matter fully before official conversations commenced.[2]

After the arrival of Macdonald and Brown, interviews began with a committee of the Imperial cabinet, punctuated by lavish

---

[1] How far were these proposals designed merely as a gesture to impress the Imperial authorities ? The contrast with the more niggardly tone of the ministers' reply to Monck's memorandum, written just before they left Canada (above, pp. 176–7) suggests that they can scarcely have expected to be taken at their word in this matter. Even at the lowest valuation, however, this episode still seems highly significant.

[2] " Unofficial and confidential memorandum of an interview with Mr. Cardwell on the 27th April " : *M.P.*, as above.

entertainments in honour of the Canadian delegates, and a famous expedition to Epsom for the Derby (it was *Gladiateur's* year, and Macdonald won a pool of twenty guineas on him).[1] From the beginning, it was clear that there was no hope for any such grand joint design as the Canadians had sketched. When negotiations had been in progress for some time, Galt wrote home in discouragement :

"Our business here proceeds slowly. . . . It seems to me as if the Statesmen of England had lost many of the high qualities which used to distinguish them, they seem so timid and hesitating, but at the same time I must admit that the question is surrounded with difficulties. . . .

"You must say nothing about it to anyone, but I have the conviction we shall effect nothing satisfactory to our own people. It is very grievous to see half a continent slipping away from the grasp of England with scarcely an effort to hold it. If the worst comes to the worst we shall at any rate be relieved from all danger of war, as the United States will not quarrel with us."[2]

One of the earliest acts of the Canadians was to refer to the pessimism concerning the defensibility of Canada which had found expression in Parliament, and to ask for a report on the subject from the highest authorities. This, when obtained, fully endorsed the soundness of Jervois's opinion that successful defence was quite possible, if the measures which he had recommended were adopted. Much emphasis was placed on the importance of making preparations towards providing a naval force for Lake Ontario.[3]

On this basis the Canadians proceeded to make their official representations. Their attitude was that the danger was immediate—that war would come soon or not at all ; and they urged, in consequence, the immediate adoption of a complete system of defence. They offered to construct all the fortifications required west of Quebec (subject to the Imperial guarantee, and provided the latter was authorized during the session of

---

[1] This historic episode is particularly well documented : see Pope, *Memoirs of Macdonald*, I, 283–84 and cf. *M.P.*, " Visits to England," I, 155 ; and Skelton, *Galt*, 383–86.
[2] Galt to his wife, May 25, 1865 : Skelton, 381.
[3] *Confidential. Memorandum by the Defence Committee on the Report of Lieutenant-Colonel Jervois.* . . . (dated May 17, 1865) : 3 copies in *M.P.*, " Militia and Defence," II, 43 ff. This committee included the Duke of Cambridge, Sir John Burgoyne, and other distinguished soldiers and sailors.

Parliament then in progress), to undertake at their own cost (if likewise aided by a guarantee) the improvement of the inland navigation, and to train their militia to the satisfaction of the War Office provided the cost was not more than $1,000,000 annually. The attitude of Upper Canada, they considered, made it essential that any fortification programme adopted should be a complete one, protecting that part of the province as well as Montreal. They particularly insisted on immediate action on the guarantee :

"If the enabling Act be not obtained in the present Session, it is clear that the works west of Quebec cannot be commenced until next year, and not until all danger of war will perhaps have passed away. In such case we shall consider it better that no expenditure west of Quebec be undertaken until after Confederation."[1]

An engagement for the next year, they explained, would merely embarrass the Confederation project's chances of success without affording any immediate security.[2] They also stated that it was necessary that they should be able to inform their legislature that they had received "satisfactory assurance, that, at the moment war breaks out, England will have prepared an adequate naval force for Lake Ontario"; otherwise, they believed, no vote for fortifications could be carried.[3]

On both these points they met a refusal from the Imperial ministers. The latter declined to give the guarantee until after the Canadian Parliament had authorized the fortifications, nor would they commit themselves to any definite undertaking as to gunboats for the Lakes; they were quite prepared to accept the postponement of the whole fortification scheme until after Confederation.[4] And, though the Canadians declared that they would have greatly preferred the immediate execution of the whole project,[5] this was what was done. The final arrangement provided, however, that in the event of Canada deciding to undertake the works on her own responsibility, before Confederation, any communication to that effect would be

[1] Canadian memorandum of June 2 (private) : *M.P.*, "Visits to England," I, 121. Cf. also memorandum of May 26, *ibid.*, 114.
[2] Memorandum of June 3, *ibid.*, 126.
[3] Memorandum of June 2, as above.
[4] British memoranda, *ibid.*, 110, 120.
[5] Their dissatisfaction appears in their memoranda of May 26 and June 3, as above; also in undated pencil draft in Macdonald's hand, *ibid.*, 133.

received by the Imperial Government "in the most friendly spirit"—that there would be good hope, that is, of the necessary guarantee.

The conference's agreements—drawn with watchful care[1] in the form of a dispatch from the Colonial Office to Monck[2]—thus led to no augmentation of the physical resources for the defence of Canada; even the all-important works at Montreal were for the present to remain on paper. The mountain of the first Canadian proposals had been delivered of a very small mouse. Both parties to the conversations had been hampered by political considerations: the Canadians by, on one side, the fact that nothing less than a complete defence scheme, in which Upper Canada could not be represented as slighted in favour of Lower Canada, could be sure of passing their legislature, and on the other by the consideration that the Maritime Provinces, already dubious about joining Canada, might be still more so if the latter's future were heavily mortgaged for defensive works; the English by the hostility of Parliament to military expenditure in the colonies.

Yet, from a moral point of view, something had been gained. The dispatch chronicled the fact that the Canadian ministers had "expressed unreservedly the desire of Canada to devote her whole resources, both in men and money, for the maintenance of her connection with the mother country", and that the Imperial Government had assured them in return that it "fully acknowledged the reciprocal obligation of defending every portion of the Empire with all the resources at its command". These declarations had a decided tendency to clear the air; the Canadian delegates believed that they would be "gratifying to many devoted subjects of Her Majesty throughout British America, whose fears have been excited by the language too often heard of late years on the subject of Colonial Connection."[3] Furthermore, however slight the conference's achievement as regarded defensive organization, it was completely successful

---

[1] See the much-emended draft in *ibid.*, 144.
[2] Cardwell to Monck, June 17, 1865: G, 174, p. 54. Published in *Papers relating to the Conferences . . . between Her Majesty's Government and a Deputation from the Executive Council of Canada . . .* (Canadian parliamentary document, 1865), 9; and also in the similar paper (*P.P.*, 1865, cd. 3535, vol. XXXVII) presented to the Imperial Parliament.
[3] Report to Lord Monck, dated July 12, 1865: *Papers relating to the Conferences*, 3.

in its relation to Confederation, for henceforth the Imperial authorities used all their influence in the Maritime Provinces in the interest of the scheme. The Governor of Nova Scotia was replaced by Sir Fenwick Williams, who could be trusted to appreciate the military importance of union, and the governor of New Brunswick instructed to press the project to the uttermost.[1]

On the whole, therefore, the Canadian ministers returned home moderately well pleased. Galt wrote privately that the agreements made constituted " a termination, which I think will in some respects cause disappointment, but on the whole commends itself to my judgment."[2] The American war was over, and—encouraging sign!—the enormous Union army (it numbered more than a million men on May 1) was rapidly being disbanded; 640,000 men had been mustered out by August 7, and by November 15 more than 800,000.[3] The tension of the previous winter was eased somewhat. In August the Canadian Parliament met, and received the report of the mission to England.[4] It provided $480,000 for the militia; in accordance with the conference decisions, it was not asked for funds for fortifications,[5] nor was the million-dollar appropriation provided in the spring expended. The colony's military preparations proceeded on the lines already familiar—encouragement of the active volunteer force, and careful training of officers for the service militia.[6]

Nevertheless, while no definite menaces emanated from the Government of the United States, indications were not lacking of trouble of another nature; for the filibustering spirit was active again on the American side of the border, and was soon to produce those difficulties which the War Office had feared, as early as 1861, might follow upon the cessation of the Civil

---

[1] See Martin, " British Policy in Canadian Confederation," *C.H.R.*, XIII. Cf. Trotter, *Canadian Federation*, 131-32. The Imperial Government had, however, used its influence for federation even before the conferences, as Professor Martin points out.
[2] Galt to his wife, June 3, 1865: Skelton, 386.
[3] *Official Records, War of the Rebellion*: Series III, vol. V, p. 517.
[4] Pope, *Memoirs of Macdonald*, I, 287.
[5] Supply act, 29 Vict., cap. 2.
[6] By April 30, 1866, the military schools had issued 2,113 certificates: *Report on State of the Militia, 1866* (S.P., 1866, no. 4). The volunteers who had been enforcing the neutrality of the border were withdrawn in July, 1865: order in council, June 27, in S.P., 1869, no. 75, p. 74.

War.[1] The Fenian Brotherhood[2] now enjoyed its hey-day. With American feeling bitter against Britain, and discharged soldiers everywhere, there were capital opportunities for practitioners of unofficial war; and Irish-Americans were soon playing with the idea of striking at England through her possessions in America.[3] In November, 1865, a warning from the British Consul at New York led the Canadian Government to call out nine companies of volunteers for service at exposed points on the border, while the regular command took large precautions on its own account.[4] As the months passed, the Fenian danger—relatively slight, but yet immediate—dwarfed that of war with the United States; but this more terrible possibility always lurked behind the border troubles which the Fenians strove to foment.

At the end of 1865, the Fenian organization split. While one wing under John O'Mahony preached action in Ireland, the other under W. R. Roberts openly advocated the invasion of Canada. By spring, anxiety was running so high along the frontier, and such alarming reports were arriving, that the Canadian Government was moved to take dramatic action to meet the situation. On March 7 they called out 10,000 volunteers; and the troops and the public responded with an outburst of loyal feeling comparable to that at the time of the *Trent* affair.[5] Finding that the actual strength of the volunteer force was only about 20,000 men, the ministry ordered that it should be increased as speedily as possible to 25,000.[6]

These active measures were favourably noticed in Britain, even by *The Times*;[7] and when Sir John Michel, the Commander-in-Chief in North America, asked for two additional regiments from England, the request was promptly granted.[8] Shortly afterwards, the Canadian ministry called the situation

---

[1] See above, p. 119.   [2] See above, p. 164.
[3] Stacey, " Fenianism and the Rise of National Feeling in Canada at the Time of Confederation," *C.H.R.*, XII.
[4] Order-in-council in *C*, 184, p. 1. Michel to Cardwell, Nov. 13, 1865 (two dispatches) : *G*, 218, pp. 154–60. The consul's letters are in *G*, 236.
[5] The whole episode is described in " Fenianism and the Rise of National Feeling," as above.
[6] Order-in-council, March 10, 1866 : *E*, State Book A.C., p. 282.
[7] March 31, 1866.
[8] Michel to Monck, March 14 : *G*, 180 B, p. 196. Cardwell to Monck (confidential), April 7, 1866 (in answer to a confidential dispatch of March 15): *G*, 175, p. 196.

to the attention of the Imperial Government in a memorandum[1] which took a very serious view of it, and asked that armed vessels should be placed on the border waters. In consequence, the admiral of the station was authorized to employ his men and guns in local vessels on the Lakes, within the limits of the Rush-Bagot convention, and even to exceed those limits in case of emergency.[2]

Before any use was made of this permission, a crisis occurred. Excitement having subsided, the Canadian volunteers had been released from service; a threat against New Brunswick by the O'Mahony Fenians, early in April, came to nothing, save that the militia and volunteers of the Maritime Provinces were in part called out, and the scare helped to bring the province to approve Confederation in the election that took place immediately afterwards; but at the beginning of June the Roberts faction attempted an invasion of Canada on a comparatively large scale. It was ill-concerted, though several thousand filibusters were gathered at different points along the border; and no fighting took place except on the Niagara frontier, where a Fenian force under John O'Neill defeated a detached column of volunteers and then made good its escape.[3] We need consider these events only as they affected the military relations of Canada and the mother country.

In this crisis, the military effort of the province was of generous proportions. The whole volunteer force was called out, and the spirit of the population at large was reflected in very numerous applications to form new corps. The Government, arguing that it was "obviously better to accept . . . willing services . . . than to resort to the conscription provided by the Militia Act", authorized increasing the volunteers' strength to 35,000, the whole number permitted by the statute.[4] Advantage was now taken (a few days too late, unfortunately) of the Home Government's recent offer; steamers were hired on the St. Lawrence and the lakes, and promptly manned and armed by the Royal Navy.[5] The province supplied the vessels

[1] Council minute, April 7, 1866: *E*, State Book A.C., p. 351.
[2] Cardwell to Monck, with enclosures, April 28, 1866: *G*, 175, p. 300.
[3] Hamilton, "The Canadian Militia: the Fenian Raids," *C.D.Q.*, VI. Cf. *C.H.R.*, XII, 249-51.
[4] Order-in-council, June 21, 1866: *E*, State Book A.C., p. 558.
[5] Order-in-council, June 4, 1866: *ibid.*, p. 507. In the course of 1866 and 1867, 15 vessels in all were chartered by the Canadian Government for varying

FENIANISM AND FEDERATION

and the navigating crews, and the Navy the armament, fighting crews and working expenses.[1]

The actions of the Canadian Parliament, which met immediately after the raid, are revealing. It proceeded to vote, out of a total budget of only a little over $7,000,000, the sum of $1,897,085 for defensive objects.[2] While it is true that this appropriation included large sums already expended without legislative sanction for frontier protection and repelling the raid, it was nevertheless of unprecedented generosity. The actual shedding of blood by a few marauders had induced the legislature to expend with a will sums greater than those which a few years earlier it had refused to devote to insurance against invasion by a first-class military power.

The Imperial troops had, of course, shared with the volunteers the exertions of guarding the frontier (though it happened that the only fighting was done by the Canadians, and done rather badly); and the whole force was directed by the Imperial Commander-in-Chief. The raid caused Monck to have one regular regiment brought from Halifax to Canada,[3] and he decided to retain in the colony, for the time being, two regiments which in the ordinary course of reliefs would have left it that season;[4] but beyond this (save for suggesting that the force of artillery might well be increased) he asked for no aid from home. At his request, three small naval gunboats were sent to assist the vessels supplied by the local Government in policing the Lakes; but out of deference to the Rush-Bagot convention they were detained for some time at Kingston.[5]

Before August was out the face of events had changed. Reports of renewed Fenian activity led to a panic in Upper Canada.[6] The ministry hastily arranged to maintain a camp of observation on the Niagara frontier for the rest of the summer;[7] Monck ordered the gunboats to their stations on the

periods; the provincial expenditure on this service to Nov. 1, 1867, was $126,600: S.P., 1867–68, no. 37 (Information respecting Government gunboats).

[1] Monck to Carnarvon, Aug. 10, 1866: G, 220, p. 24.
[2] Supply act, 29–30 Vict., cap. 8.
[3] Monck to Cardwell, June 6, 1866: G, 465, p. 462.
[4] Monck to Cardwell, June 21, 1866: ibid., p. 480.
[5] Monck to Cardwell, June 22, 1866: ibid., p. 483; Monck to Carnarvon, with enclosure, Aug. 2, 1866 (G, 180 B, p. 206). [6] C.H.R., XII, 253–54.
[7] S.P., 1867–68, no. 28: Report of Colonel Wolseley on the camp at Thorold. Cf. Wolseley, Story of a Soldier's Life, II, 162–64.

Lakes ;[1] and, finally, he and Michel decided to use the cable just put in service across the Atlantic to ask for large regular reinforcements—three additional regiments of infantry and one of cavalry, and two field batteries. They were able to promise that the Canadian Government would provide barracks for the extra troops. They further declared that breechloading rifles for the whole regular force in Canada were " indispensably required immediately ".[2] Breechloaders had suddenly become something of a fetish, for the story—apparently unfounded[3]— had got about that the Fenians possessed these terrible weapons. The Canadian Government purchased 6,300 of them in the United States at this time of panic.[4]

These sudden requests took the Home Government by surprise.[5] Lord Carnarvon, Colonial Secretary in the new Conservative ministry, reminded Monck once more that British efforts could only be complementary to those of Canada, and observed that, except for the Imperial Government's confidence that the colony was ready to incur great sacrifices on its own account, they would have felt powerless to assist. As it was, they sent a force only less than that requested ; great exertions were made to embark two regiments of infantry, and the 13th Hussars with their horses, for Canada at once, and drafts amounting to 500 men, including 200 artillerymen, followed. As the government factories could not produce an immediate supply of the new Snider breechloader, an officer was hurriedly sent out to New York to buy such breechloading arms as could be obtained there for the regulars in Canada, while those of various patterns available in England were sent to the colony.[6] Considering these prompt measures, it seems hard to justify John A. Macdonald's writing to a correspondent, " You will

[1] Monck to Carnarvon, Aug. 18, 1866 : *G*, 220, p. 66. He took the responsibility, in the emergency, of doing so without waiting for final permission.
[2] Copy of cable sent Aug. 25, in Monck to Carnarvon, Aug. 27, 1866 : *G*, 220, p. 81.
[3] See the Adjutant-General's remarks in *Report on State of the Militia of the Province of Canada* . . . *1867*, p. 13 : S.P., 1867-68, no. 35.
[4] Monck to Carnarvon, Sept. 26, 1866 : *G*, 220, p. 98.
[5] Carnarvon to Monck (confidential), Sept. 12, 1866 : *G*, 180 A, p. 117.
[6] Carnarvon to Monck, Aug. 31, 1866 : *G*, 176, p. 302. In point of fact, the Sniders did get to Canada that autumn : " We went on working at the gun factory day and night—and, I am sorry to say, sometimes on Sundays— but we succeeded in sending out converted Sniders to every British soldier in Canada before the navigation closed." (*Hansard*, CLXXXV, 1456 : speech of General Peel, March 7, 1867.)

see that Her Majesty's Government has at last sent us out troops. They ought to have come out some time ago, and it was only after pressing remonstrances that they have been so sent ".[1] One wonders whether the Canadian Government (who always avoided asking for troops on their own account) had been importuning Monck to ask for them, and had previously found him reluctant.

In answer to expressions of surprise from Carnarvon, Monck explained that the suddenness of his requisition was the result of " the state of alarm and moral depression *within* the Province " which itself came on very suddenly ; and he remarked that the " moral results " of the home Government's compliance with his request satisfied him that he had done right in making it.[2] The arrival of the reinforcements raised the strength of the regular garrison to a figure not far short of the maximum attained at the time of the *Trent* affair ; the spring of 1867 found 11,923 officers and men in Canada, and 3,726 in the Maritimes.[3] If the Fenians had accomplished nothing else, they had saddled the British Government with great expense, and thwarted yet once more its desire to reduce the proportion of the army stationed in the colonies.

The new Conservative ministry was no more friendly to the existing colonial military system than the Liberals had been. The reinforcement of Canada led Disraeli (now Chancellor of the Exchequer) to write to the Prime Minister a letter which shows how little he rose above the prevailing pessimism on colonial subjects :

". . . We must seriously consider our Canadian position, which is most illegitimate. An army maintained in a country which does not permit us even to govern it ! What an anomaly !

" It can never be our pretence, or our policy, to defend the Canadian frontier against the U.S. If the colonists can't, as a general rule, defend themselves against the Fenians, they can do nothing. They ought to be, and must be, strong enough for that. Power and influence we should exercise in Asia ; consequently in Eastern

---

[1] Macdonald to R. J. Cartwright (private), Sept. 17, 1866 : Pope, *Correspondence of Sir John Macdonald*, 35.
[2] Monck to Carnarvon (confidential), Sept. 28, 1866 : G, 180 B, p. 224.
[3] *P.P.*, 1870, no. 254, vol. XLII. These figures are for April 1. On Oct. 5, 1866, Monck had informed Michel confidentially that he considered that conditions justified moving one of the regiments lately sent from England to another station, if necessary : G, 180 B, p. 227.

Europe, consequently also in Western Europe ; but what is the use of these colonial deadweights which *we do not govern ?*

" I don't regret what we did the other day about Canada, because the circumstances were very peculiar. A successful raid of the Fenians was not off the cards, which would have upset your untried Ministry, and might have produced an insurrection in Ireland ; and it was not fair to the Canadians, when, at the last, they were making some attempts at self-defence, to allow them to be crushed in the bud of their patriotism. But the moment the American elections are over, we should withdraw the great body of our troops, and foster a complete development of self-government.

" Leave the Canadians to defend themselves ; recall the African squadron ; give up the settlements on the west coast of Africa ; and we shall make a saving which will, at the same time, enable us to build ships and have a good Budget.

" What is more, we shall have accomplished something definite, tangible, for the good of the country. In these days, more than ever, the people look to results. What we have done about Canada is perfectly defensible, if it is not looked upon as a permanent increase of our Canadian establishments."[1]

England at this moment, as she surveyed the aspect of continental politics, was disturbed once more by fears for her own safety. With awful suddenness, the Seven Weeks' War had toppled Austria from her high place in Europe, and out of the powder-smoke of Sadowa[2] a new and terrible Prussia had arisen ; while the Emperor of the French was (as usual) an uncertain quantity. Men regarded the Prussian army with mingled fear and admiration, and Army Reform suddenly became a major issue in English politics. The *Spectator* voiced a general feeling :

" We, who pride ourselves on being a practical people, have never turned out such a military machine as that which has just laid Germany at the feet of King William, made Austria, for the first time in history, a non-German power, and dispelled, for the time at least, the dreams of France. . . . Austria has fallen mainly because of her flagrantly defective system, and we ought not to disregard the warning."[3]

---

[1] Disraeli to Derby, Sept. 30, 1866 : Monypenny and Buckle, *Life of Disraeli*, IV, 476–77. For a critical account of Disraeli as an Imperial statesman, see Morison, " The Imperial Ideas of Benjamin Disraeli," *C.H.R.*, I. The American elections here referred to are the congressional ones of the autumn of 1866.

[2] Fought on July 3, 1866.   [3] *Spectator*, Aug. 11, 1866.

Britain's great immediate military problems were those presented by a steady falling-off in recruiting (in 1866 the army was more than 6,000 below establishment) and the lack of any proper reserve force to strengthen the regular army at the outset of a war.[1] When Parliament reassembled in February, 1867, the Queen's Speech invited its consideration for these matters.[2] The recruiting difficulty was now solved, for the moment at least—chiefly by the simple expedient of adding twopence to the soldier's daily pay; but measures taken to provide the requisite reserve proved inadequate, and the final resolution of this problem was left to another adminstration.[3]

With the whole military organization undergoing searching examination, it was inevitable that the colonial garrisons should again become targets of criticism. They got their full share of attention in the legion of periodical articles which attested the magnitude of public interest in the question. There were some to point to the requirements of colonial defence as an additional argument for a better reserve system;[4] but there were more to urge the necessity of calling home the legions, and devoting the British Army to the defence of Britain. "We do not . . . want a very large standing army in this country", wrote the author of a series of papers in *Blackwood's*; "and we could do with a small one, were it not that India and the colonies act like running issues on our manhood. . . . Is it either necessary or becoming to tax the people of England, not in money only, but in what is of more importance—men—in order to give the appearance of military protection to States which may be loyal in their own sense of that term, but which are certainly not of the slightest benefit, socially or commercially, to the community from which they sprang?"[5]

---

[1] "Military Reform," *Fraser's Magazine*, Dec., 1866, states the situation at its worst.

[2] *Hansard*, CLXXXV, 5 (Feb. 5, 1867).

[3] Fortescue, *History of the British Army*, XIII, 532–37. Anxiety over the supply of men was reflected in an investigation by a Select Committee of the House of Commons into the possibility of employing portions of the native Indian army as colonial garrisons or using Asiatic troops for general service in suitable climates: *P.P.*, 1867, no. 478, vol. VII.

[4] e.g., the articles on "Military Reform" in *Fraser's* for December, 1866, and March, April, June and August, 1867: see especially the first of them.

[5] "The Army," *Blackwood's*, February, 1867. For similar views, cf. the following: "Home Defences" (*Macmillan's*, February, 1867); "The National Rifle Association" (*ibid.*, July, 1867); "The Reorganisation of the Army" (*Fraser's*, May, 1868).

The Canadian Confederation proposal had now reached the Imperial Parliament, in the shape of the British North America Bill and its annex, the Canada Railway Loan Bill, designed to authorize an imperial guarantee to aid in the construction of the Intercolonial Railway. To *The Times* (and many eminent British politicians were certainly of the same mind)[1] the primary importance of the whole project consisted simply in the opportunity which it seemed to present for relieving the mother country of her responsibilities in America. The great newspaper considered the guarantee scheme " unpleasant, and we may say suspicious " ; yet it thought it acceptable " if by enabling Canada to make this railway the Mother Country is to be held to have now fulfilled all its duties, and to be henceforth entirely at liberty to consult its own interests " :

" The first and most important of our duties will then be the speedy withdrawal of all British troops from the North American Continent. . . . As long as these troops are shut up during half the year in an almost inaccessible Province, and exposed at all times to an invasion, which their very presence tempts, the American Government has so many hostages, as it were, for British good behaviour. . . ."[2]

The reduction of the United States army, by 1866, to an establishment of 54,000 rank and file—a modest allowance, with the French still in Mexico and the Indians on the warpath from Canada to the Rio Grande[3]—had failed to allay English anxiety over the " perilous " situation of the troops in Canada. While the thorny questions that had arisen between the two nations during the Civil War (the greatest, of course, being that of the depredations committed by the *Alabama* and other Confederate cruisers fitted out in British ports) remained unsettled, war was never beyond the bounds of possibility ; and there were Englishmen ready to maintain that the " honour " of Britain would survive a hasty withdrawal of her forces to escape this menace, leaving her Canadian subjects to fight their own battles, but not the defeat of those forces by superior numbers. " The defeat of an armed police is vexatious ", declared a writer in *Fraser's*, " especially if it be followed by the

[1] See below, pp. 204–5.
[2] *The Times*, March 29, 1867.
[3] Ganoe, *History of the United States Army*, 306–09.

loss of a province. But the defeat of a single British regiment is a thousand-fold more serious. We lose in the first case territory, but not honour ; we lose in the latter both."[1] Not every critic went so far ; but many considered that, with Britain facing a threatening situation in Europe, the Canadian frontier was a most unfortunate weak spot in her military position.

Canada, in the meantime, was full of the stir of defensive preparation. Again the colony was full of regular troops, very widely distributed, the new regiments being quartered at Canadian expense.[2] The volunteer force, which had been only 19,600 strong in the spring of 1866, increased to 33,750 by the end of 1867, and its organization and equipment were much improved. The whole force was provided in 1867 with Sniders lent to the Colonial Government by the War Office. Arrangements were made for improved co-operation between regulars and volunteers in the event of another Fenian inroad ; but despite periodical alarms the attack did not materialize.[3]

In the midst of these events, the statesmanship of 1864 bore fruit. New Brunswick had been brought round to accepting Confederation by Imperial influence, Canadian money, and Fenian threats ;[4] Nova Scotia was given no chance to declare against it ; in the spring of 1867 the British North America Act was passed at Westminster ; and on July 1 Lord Monck was sworn at Ottawa as Governor-General of the Dominion of Canada. John A. Macdonald became a Knight Commander of the Bath, and was entrusted with forming the first Government of the new nation. That Government was to encounter many perplexing problems ; and the old problem of defence was not to be the least of them.

As might have been expected from the views expressed by Disraeli, the reinforcements of 1866 had not been long in Canada before the Home Government began to suggest reductions. In

[1] " The Reorganisation of the Army," *Fraser's Magazine*, May, 1868.
[2] The Canadian estimates for 1867-68 include $80,000 for buildings and $120,000 for barrack fitments : *S.P.*, 1867-68, no. 62. Quarters were provided at Brantford, Hamilton, Toronto, London and Ottawa : orders-in-council, Aug. 27, Oct. 8, Nov. 7, 1866 : *E*, State Book A.D., pp. 102, 216, 399.
[3] *Report on State of the Militia, 1867* (*S.P.*, 1867-68, no. 35), pp. 1-13. These observations apply to the volunteer force of the Province of Canada, which after July 1, 1867, became the Provinces of Ontario and Quebec. For a serious Fenian alarm in March, 1867, see *C*, 184, pp. 22 ff.
[4] Martin, " British Policy in Canadian Confederation," as above.

January, and again in March, of 1867, Sir John Michel, administering the government in Monck's absence, strongly discouraged such proposals.[1] Monck himself, on his return, was disposed to think that two battalions might be spared;[2] but as it was clear that there was still a Fenian menace, the Imperial authorities decided to defer taking any action.[3]

In the following year, however, they took a stronger line; whether the fact that the decline of Derby's health had left Disraeli in effective command of the ministry had an influence in this connexion is only a matter for conjecture. Canada was now briskly informed that it was proposed to withdraw three battalions of infantry from Ontario and Quebec.[4] The Dominion ministers' prompt protest got no support from the Governor-General. His information indicated, he said, that the Fenians would not be able to renew their attacks " in any considerable force ", and he added :

" The Govr. Genl. must also call the attention of the Council to the fact that there is not at present nor has there been for many months any portion of the local force of the Dominion on permanent duty and that he does not think it advisable for the Canadian Ministers to call on the Impl. Govt. to maintain in Canada a large Imperial force when they do not find it necessary to call out for duty any of the troops which are under their own control."[5]

Monck's chief personal task during his long administration had been to urge successive Governments to the assumption of larger defensive responsibilities, and now that British North America was at last united he seems to have felt more than ever justified in this attitude. But Confederation had not altered the views of the Canadian politicians. They would not be reconciled to the withdrawals, and even refused to give advice on the redistribution of the troops which they occasioned.[6]

Other matters vexed the military relations of mother country

[1] Michel to Carnarvon, Jan. 14, 1867, and March 18, 1867 : *G*, 221, pp. 33, 95.
[2] Monck to Buckingham (confidential), July 11, 1867 ; copy in *C*, 184, p. 38.
[3] Buckingham to Monck, July 27, 1867 : *ibid.*, p. 44.
[4] Buckingham to Monck, Feb. 22, 1868 : *G*, 558. Cf. Forster to G.O.C., Canada, Feb. 29, 1868 : *C*, 37, p. 102.
[5] Memorandum for the privy council, March 20, 1868 : *G*, 573 A, p. 52.
[6] Council minute, April 7, 1868 : copy in *C*, 37, p. 234.

FENIANISM AND FEDERATION

and Dominion. There was, for instance, a dispute arising out of the Colonial Secretary's attempt (which proved unsuccessful) to make Canada pay a share of the bills for the transport of troops by rail during the defensive operations of 1866.[1] The gunboat patrol also became an occasion of controversy. It had been customary, as already noted, for Canada to supply merely the vessels, while the Admiralty paid the working expenses and supplied the fighting crews. At the same time that the Duke of Buckingham (who had succeeded Carnarvon at the Colonial Office) announced the reduction of the garrison, he asked Monck's opinion of this arrangement; and the Governor-General hinted broadly that the whole expense might well be laid upon Canada.[2] Buckingham, of course, acted on this advice, and the Canadian Government again protested.[3] Probably because the navigation season was already open, the old arrangement was apparently allowed to continue during 1868.

The question of barrack accommodation was likewise causing friction. The Canadians took their stand on the fact that they had agreed to pay for quarters only for the reinforcements sent in 1866—which was true; and when the Home Government sought to obtain from them funds for improved quarters for troops previously in the colony, they refused.[4] These partial agreements had produced " a great increase of correspondence, continual differences of opinion as to pecuniary liability and consequent irregularity in the settlement of accounts ".[5]

In February of 1868 Buckingham, evidently anxious for a general housecleaning of military problems, brought up the fortification question again.[6] The Imperial authorities, he pointed out, had made much progress with the works at Quebec (where three new and powerful forts had appeared on Point

---

[1] Carnarvon to Monck, Nov. 30, 1866, with enclosure: *G*, 177, pp. 328–50. War Office to G.O.C., Canada, Aug. 26, 1867, and Gov. Genl's military secretary to G.O.C.'s military secretary, Nov. 5, 1867: *C*, 184, pp. 59, 71.
[2] Buckingham to Monck, Feb. 22, 1868: *G*, 558. Monck to Buckingham, March 14, 1868: *G, To Secretary of State, 1867*, p. 116.
[3] Buckingham to Monck, April 14, 1868: *G*, 559. Monck to Buckingham, June 2, 1868: *G, To Secretary of State, 1867*, p. 181.
[4] Monck to Buckingham, Aug. 26, 1868: *ibid.*, p. 245; and cf. enclosures in Buckingham to Officer administering government, Dec. 8, 1868: *G*, 561.
[5] Monck to Buckingham, July 23, 1868: *G, To Secretary of State, 1867*, p. 219.
[6] Buckingham to Monck, Feb. 22, 1868: *G*, 558. Published in *S.P.*, 1867–68, no. 63. On February 22, Buckingham sent to Canada dispatches on the strength of the garrison, the gunboat question, and the fortifications.

Lévis), but nothing had yet been done elsewhere in Canada. The Canadian Government, having undertaken in 1865 to address itself to the permanent defence of the country after Confederation, now showed an evident desire to avoid any imputation of shirking its obligations. In the second part of the first Dominion Parliament's first session, immediately after the receipt of this reminder, an Act[1] was passed authorizing the raising by loan, under guarantee of the Imperial treasury, of sums not exceeding £1,100,000 sterling for constructing works " for the defence of the City of Montreal and other cities and places west of Montreal, and . . . of the City of St. John, in the province of New Brunswick ".

At the same time, another Statute[2] set up a military system for the Dominion. It was largely a transcript of that of the old Province of Canada. The " Active Militia " was to be 40,000 strong, composed in effect of the existing volunteer corps. The formal obligation of universal service was retained; but it was to be resorted to in time of peace only if the number of the volunteers was insufficient, and in point of fact the conscriptive provisions of the law have never been invoked from that day to this—for the conscription enforced during the Great War was authorized by a special Statute. In practice, the law was a volunteer law only. But the volunteers of 1868 were more formidable, in almost every respect, than those of 1865; and with 40,000 of them on foot, efficiently armed and equipped and tolerably well-drilled, and now under unified control, the native defensive resources of British North America were more efficiently organized than at any previous period.

England was informed that Canada desired to obtain as soon as possible the authorization of the guarantee for the fortification loan.[3] The Imperial Government, however, now seemed to be in no hurry to meet the Canadians' views; and this issue became another occasion of misunderstanding. In the hope of reconciling the ideas of the Dominion and the mother country on the fortifications and the whole vexed question of defence in general, as well as on certain other matters, the Canadian Government, in the autumn of 1868, once more

---

[1] 31 Vict., cap. 41. [2] 31 Vict., cap. 40.
[3] Monck to Buckingham, May 27, 1868 : *G, To Secretary of State, 1867*, p. 175.

decided to send a delegation to England. Sir George Cartier, the Minister of Militia and Defence, and William McDougall were authorized to proceed thither and confer with the Imperial Government. But before their conversations had made any progress, they were interrupted by the fall of Disraeli's ministry.

Of that ministry's last acts, some had boded ill for the delegation's success. In October it ordered two more battalions home from Canada; and immediately afterwards Sir John Pakington, the Secretary of State for War, made the Dominion Government's attitude on the barrack question the occasion of an attack on the whole Canadian situation.[1] He recalled that prior to the outbreak of the American Civil War about 2,000 regulars had been considered a sufficient establishment for the Province of Canada. Since the reductions lately ordered would leave the force in Ontario and Quebec still more than 5,000 in excess of that of 1859, he suggested that it was deserving of serious consideration " whether, looking to our existing relations with the United States, and bearing in mind that the Elections in that Country are over,[2] and that the Fenian agitation may be presumed to be at an end, the Force in Canada would not admit of still further reduction ". Buckingham shared these views, and in a bald dispatch[3] informed the Dominion that it had been decided to reduce the garrison to 5,000 men in Ontario and Quebec, 2,000 in Nova Scotia, and 1,650 in New Brunswick. It was just at this moment that the Conservative Government resigned, having met defeat in a general election; and further policy became the concern of a Liberal ministry headed by William Ewart Gladstone.

. . . . . .

The first eighteen months of the Dominion of Canada's existence had signally failed to produce a solution of those military difficulties which had so long embarrassed the relations of the old Province of Canada with the mother country. On

[1] Lugard to Rogers, Nov. 17, 1868: copy in Buckingham to Officer administering government, Dec. 8, 1868: *G*, 561.
[2] General Grant had just been elected President; and an arrangement (later rejected by the United States) was being made for the amicable settlement of the *Alabama* dispute.
[3] Buckingham to Officer administering government, Dec. 8, 1868: as above.

the contrary, the divergence in viewpoint seemed more marked than ever. The year 1868 had seen a clear manifestation of the Imperial Government's desire to reduce its own responsibilities in Canada ; and it had demonstrated with equal clarity the determination of the colonial ministers to resist any diminution of the Imperial contribution towards the defence of British North America. A whole series of disputes over responsibility were in progress at the same time, and a stable settlement seemed very distant.

Though the past five years had produced a gradual and tangible expansion of Canadian military effort, there had been no corresponding diminution of the Canadian burdens of the British Army and the British taxpayer. Rather the reverse ; for in the Dominion's first year of life the Imperial expenditure in that section of it which had formerly been the Province of Canada was greater than ever. It amounted to £937,000, of which £806,000 was the cost of regular troops, £59,000 expenditure on fortifications, and £23,000 the cost of barracks.[1] For the previous year the total had been £864,000, and for the year before that £622,000. This enables us to judge the money value of the reinforcements sent to Canada in 1866. Even at the time of the *Trent* affair, the annual expenditure had been less—£737,000 in 1861-62, and £718,000 in 1862-63 ;[2] and in the period before the Civil War it had fallen as low as £166,000. Adding the cost of Nova Scotia and New Brunswick to that of Ontario and Quebec, we find that the Dominion at its birth was costing the mother country about £1,250,000 a year[3]—or more than $6,000,000 in Canadian money ; and this included only a small proportion of that part of the cost of the Royal Navy which might justly have been considered Canada's share.[4] As the Dominion was spending about $1,500,000 of its own

[1] This is for the financial year 1867-68.
[2] Although the force in Canada was smaller in 1867 than in 1862, the cost of the regular troops was higher. This was occasioned no doubt by their recent increase in pay, and perhaps in part also by changes in armament. The *Trent* affair caused the appearance of a very large item for " naval charges " in 1861-62—£322,000 for the whole of British North America. The cost of the regular troops for Canada that year was only £384,000 ; in 1862-63 this was almost doubled.
[3] The actual total for 1867-68 is £1,243,423.
[4] The allowances for " naval charges " included in these returns seem to refer only to the cost of shore establishments in the colonies and certainly do not represent the cost of the squadrons maintained on the coasts. The naval

annual revenue for defence,[1] Great Britain was carrying roughly four-fifths of Canada's military burdens.

This was the situation in a colony with a population of some three and a half millions, exercising (save only in the sphere of foreign policy) practically complete control over its own affairs, and commercially entirely independent of the mother country; yet for a score of years the Imperial Government had been striving to reduce the burden which the colonies imposed upon the British taxpayer. It was clearly impossible for these circumstances to perpetuate themselves; and now the end was to come soon, and swiftly.

activity on the Great Lakes raises this item, for Canada, to £82,762 in 1866-67, which might possibly include the cost (or part of it) of equipping and working the provincial gunboats. All the statistics of Imperial expenditure quoted above are from *P.P*, 1870, no. 80, vol. XLIX.

[1] Supply act, 31 Vict., cap. 31, provides $1,484,000 for militia and gunboats in 1867-68.

CHAPTER IX

CARDWELL CUTS THE GORDIAN KNOT

> "I am fully conscious of the great difficulties which surround the question . . . but I believe the time for parleying is past, and that the only safety lies in dealing with them without fear."
> —CARDWELL TO GLADSTONE, December 3, 1868.

IN December of 1868, a keen observer of English politics might have prophesied that the colonial garrison system was about to receive its long-delayed death-blow. Indeed, as he surveyed the personnel of the new Liberal ministry, he might (if he chanced to be a convinced Imperialist) even have had some apprehensions for the whole colonial connexion.

The Prime Minister himself had never disguised his dislike of the existing military arrangements in the colonies. We have seen Gladstone telling the Select Committee of 1861 that it was necessary for the colonies to learn self-defence if they were to develop into the great free communities which they might well aspire to become.[1] He had eloquently recapitulated these opinions in Parliament quite lately, declaring, "If Canada is to be defended, the main element and power in the defence must always be the energy of a free people fighting for their own liberties", and stating quite as definitely as *The Times* (though much less rudely) that his hope from Confederation was for the development in Canada of "more self-reliance, and more self-relying habits". It was, he said, in great part the fault of the mother country that in the past the people of British America had "to some extent separated the burdens of freedom from the spirit of freedom"; and now:

> "We have to bring about a different state of things. The best way to do it is to raise their political position to the very highest point . . . in order that with that elevated position their sense of

[1] See above, pp. 125-6.

responsibility may likewise grow. It cannot be too distinctly stated that it is in this light that we look upon the plan for uniting the Provinces of British North America."

He was careful to declare his belief that the unity of the Empire would not suffer by such a policy; that unity, he said, rested on far stronger foundations than " the expenditure of money through the means of little standing armies kept in the colonies ".[1]

He had colleagues in the new Government, however, who had not been so scrupulous in their utterances. The views of the Chancellor of the Exchequer, Robert Lowe, had changed since 1861 as little as his chief's; in fact, he repeated his own remarks of that period with some relish in the same debate in which Gladstone used the words just quoted.[2] Another distinguished Little Englander in the cabinet was John Bright, who had been prevailed upon to take the Board of Trade. His attitude was well known. He had declared that the separation of Canada from England would be for the good of both; he had strongly opposed on the floor of the House that vote for the fortifications of Quebec which Gladstone himself had resisted in the cabinet; and in a bitter speech on the Confederation proposal he had demanded that it be " clearly understood that the taxes of England are no longer to go across the ocean to defray expenses of any kind within the Confederation which is about to be formed ".[3]

As for the minister especially charged with the colonial department, Lord Granville—" Pussy " Granville—there is evidence that he had accepted the separatist doctrines more fully than most politicians of his day. " Our relations with North America are of a very delicate character ", he wrote in 1869. " The best solution of them would probably be that in the course of time and in the most friendly spirit the Dominion should find itself strong enough to proclaim her independence."[4] He disclaimed any present intention of seeking such a goal; yet he had already thrown out the suggestion

[1] *Hansard*, CLXXXVI, 749-57 (speech on the Canada Railway Loan Bill, March 28, 1867).
[2] *Ibid.*, 762. Cf. above, p. 125.
[3] *Ibid.*, CLXXXV, 1180-85 (Feb. 28, 1867).
[4] Granville to Russell, Aug. 28, 1869: Fitzmaurice, *Life of Earl Granville*, II, 22.

in an official (though confidential) dispatch to the Governor-General.[1]

This was not a group calculated to inspire confidence in the breasts of colonial politicians. It remains to consider the minister most important for our present purpose—the man who had gone to the War Office. Gladstone had entrusted to Edward Cardwell[2] the Herculean task of reorganizing the British Army. The choice was wise; for Cardwell was

"a public servant of the first order; not a political leader or a popular orator, but one of the best disciples of Peel's school; sound, careful, active, firm, and with an enlightened and independent mind admirably fitted for the effective despatch of business."[3]

He had, moreover, given careful consideration to the particular problems now confronting him. On the same day that Gladstone accepted office, Cardwell addressed to him a memorandum on the condition of the army.[4] The reformed Parliament, "resolved to obtain the greatest amount of efficiency at the lowest cost", would now, he thought, demand a sweeping reformation of the military system. "I doubt very much", he wrote, ". . . whether the time has not arrived when wide and extreme changes will be imperatively demanded, and will meet with less rude opposition than measures of a temporising and palliative character". One of the chief subjects on which an active policy would be required was:

"Recruiting; and this will raise the question whether service is to be for a long or a short period; whether there shall not be a very considerable change in the proportionate numbers of men serving in the Colonies and of those serving at home—with a special provision for India—whether after a short service in the first army, the soldier shall not pass into a second army, with gradations to the mere militia, etc., etc., and interconnection of all services."

Thus did Cardwell, before he had even received the seals of office, foreshadow the great reforms of his administration. It was clear that this forceful minister was moved by a new

---

[1] See below, p. 216. Mr. Knaplund suggests that Granville really had little interest in Colonial questions, and that his dispatches reflect the views of the Permanent Under-Secretary, Sir Frederic Rogers.
[2] See the article by Goldwin Smith in the *Dictionary of National Biography*; and (on this most important phase of his career), General Sir Robert Biddulph's *Lord Cardwell at the War Office*.
[3] Morley, *Life of Gladstone*, II, 359.
[4] In Biddulph, *op. cit.*, 249-54.

CARDWELL CUTS THE GORDIAN KNOT 207

spirit; and though "the world generally was inclined to smile at the notion of a lawyer, educated to the study of politics and of social problems, who assumed the garb of an army administrator, and, what was still worse, of an army reformer",[1] a revolution, no less, was impending in the affairs of the War Office.

With the colonial garrison problem Cardwell had previous first-hand acquaintance. As Colonial Secretary from 1864 to 1866, he had conducted the negotiations of 1865 with the Canadian delegates in a tone in which firmness was no less to the fore than friendliness. Firmness had been still more in evidence in his dealings with New Zealand. A Maori war had led to more than 10,000 troops being assembled there in 1864-65, and (incidentally) to serious disputes between the civil authorities and the Commander of the Forces. At the end of 1865, the Colonial Office initiated a policy of withdrawal; five regiments were brought home in 1866, and by 1868 only one was left.[2] Most striking of all, perhaps, Cardwell's tenure of the colonial department had seen the passage of the Colonial Naval Defence Act of 1865, designed to permit and encourage the formation of colonial naval forces.[3] This record boded ill for the garrison system.[4]

In 1868, moreover, there were special reasons for the adoption of a policy of colonial withdrawal. Gladstone had included in his campaign programme in the late elections a strong advocacy of retrenchment, attacking the Conservatives for having added £3,000,000 to the national expenditure,[5] and he considered the verdict of the constituencies a definite endorsement of his attitude in this respect.[6] Now the £3,000,000 increase had been mainly on account of the army; and it was clear that the two objects of economy (to which the Government was pledged) and increased military efficiency (which the public at home was demanding) could be reconciled only by reducing the expenditure for the army abroad.

[1] Lord Wolseley, in Ward, T. H., (ed.), *The Reign of Queen Victoria: a survey of fifty years of progress*, London, 1887, II, 199.
[2] Fortescue, *History of the British Army*, XIII, 509-12.
[3] *Annual Register*, 1865, 47-49.
[4] Cardwell's speech on the Army Estimates, March 23, 1868 (*Hansard*, CXCI, 93-4)—nine months before he took office under Gladstone—clearly reflects the strength of his conviction of the essentiality of large reductions.
[5] Gladstone's election address, *The Times*, Oct. 10, 1868.
[6] Speech at Greenwich, Dec. 22, 1868: *Annual Register*, 1868, 180-81.

Other considerations led to the same practical conclusion. The recent recruiting difficulties had forced upon the attention of Government the fact that the military question was one of men as well as of money. Cardwell's greatest problem was to provide a fully-trained reserve available at short notice to expand the regular army; and this he proposed to effect by substituting for the time-honoured arrangement by which a British soldier was understood to be a soldier practically for life, a system of "short service", under which enlistment would be for twelve years only, and the latter half of this period would be spent, not with the colours, but in the reserve, liable for service in emergency. This plan required for success a considerably greater annual supply of recruits even than that which had been obtained with such difficulty in recent years; and it was well understood that the disproportionate amount of time spent by British regiments on foreign service was one of the greatest deterrents to enlistment. The War Office, when Cardwell came to it, was still worried by the problem of reliefs; in 1867 the Duke of Cambridge had said that, when the regiments returning from New Zealand arrived, the situation would " very nearly, if not quite, have arrived at the point when the infantry will be one-third at home and two-thirds abroad ".[1]

Having decided that sweeping colonial reductions were a necessary preliminary to the great general scheme of army reorganization which had already formed itself in his mind, Cardwell lost no time in taking active steps. On January 9, 1869, he submitted to Gladstone another memorandum which proposed point-blank " to reduce the total force in the Colonies from 50,000 to 26,000 ". The regiments from the colonies would not be kept at full strength in the United Kingdom, but none would be disbanded; their full *cadres* would be maintained, ready to be filled up, in the event of trouble, from the reserve. Gladstone fully approved these principles.[2]

At a time when the Home Government was laying plans along these lines, it was natural that Cartier and McDougall, the Canadian delegates who had been sent to England, should find

---

[1] *Report from the Select Committee on Army (India and the Colonies)* : P.P., 1867, no. 478, vol. VII. Evidence of Duke of Cambridge, pp. 144–45.
[2] Biddulph, 26–28.

CARDWELL CUTS THE GORDIAN KNOT 209

themselves unable to obtain the satisfaction they desired on the defence question; and their negotiations on this point did not prove particularly pleasant. An illness of McDougall, combined with the change of government in England, delayed the real commencement of discussions until after the New Year of 1869. Granville aided the Canadians in reaching a satisfactory settlement with the Hudson's Bay Company (the acquisition of whose lands was one of their chief concerns); but on the defence problem he gave them little satisfaction. They pointed out that the Canadian Government had as yet had no answer to its representations (made almost a year before) respecting the guarantee for the fortification loan; and they strongly urged " the necessity of keeping and maintaining in the Dominion as large a force of Her Majesty's Regular Troops as possible ". Granville merely replied that these matters would in due course be dealt with in a dispatch to the Governor-General; and with this they had to be content.[1]

Lesser matters, relating to the armament of the militia, caused controversies, of which one especially was singularly petty and vexatious. The Enfield rifles, loaned to Canada by the Imperial Government, during the Civil War, to arm her volunteers, had now been replaced on the same generous terms by Snider breechloaders. Many of the Enfields, when returned to the Imperial stores, were found to be unserviceable; and in consequence bills for the small sum of £847 were presented to the militia department. Twice within six years the whole Canadian active force had been armed, wholly at the expense of the British taxpayer, with the most modern weapons, and the only payment demanded of the colonial treasury was this $4,000, due under the regulations; yet Cartier and McDougall strenuously objected to paying it, alleging—on grounds which were not given—that the damages resulted from wear and tear on active service.[2] Unfortunately for them,

---

[1] *Report* of Cartier and McDougall to the Governor-General, May 20, 1869: *S.P.*, 1869, no. 60, p. 2. It was a long time before the Canadians got an inkling of what was going on behind the scenes; Cartier believed that Granville and Cardwell sympathized with their point of view, and even after the Government's intentions had begun to leak out he maintained that his own and McDougall's representations had had a good effect (Cartier to Macdonald, Dec. 24, 1868, and Jan. 16 and 23, 1869: *M.P.*, " Sir George Cartier Papers," I, pp. 146, 158, 162).

[2] Cartier and McDougall to Rogers, March 23, 1869: *Report*, p. 3.

P

Sir Charles Windham (Michel's successor), had reported most categorically that they were caused by simple neglect;[1] and Cardwell insisted on the payment being made.[2] The dispute was one of those that leave a bad taste behind them.[3]

Cartier and McDougall, in fact, seem to have made a thoroughly unfortunate impression in England; for the new Governor-General, Sir John Young (afterwards Lord Lisgar) felt obliged to make explanations. "The two [ministers] you had on a visit", he wrote to Cardwell, "are about the least reasonable of all. Cartier as a Frenchman imbued with the modes and habits of French thought looks to H.M. Govnt for everything. McDougall, whom I have never seen, is reckoned a difficult person to deal with. So I do not wonder they pressed you."[4]

Young had taken over the administration of Canada at the end of 1868 from Lord Monck, who then retired after seven anxious years in the colony. He had not been a popular figure, but he had done valuable work in an unobtrusive fashion; the influence which he exercised on the Confederation project should in itself assure him a permanent place in the history of Canada. But his most constant concern was the development of the native defensive resources of Canada. It was a thankless task; yet at his departure he could reflect with satisfaction that the Dominion which he had helped to found was spending annually on her own defence nearly fifteen times as much as the Governments of British North America were accustomed to devote to that purpose at the time when he began his government amid the alarms of the *Trent* Affair.[5]

Young took up the problem where Monck dropped it. Almost his first task was to give private advice to the Imperial Government on its reduction projects. He estimated the force which it was desirable to maintain in the Dominion and Newfoundland at 6,400 all ranks, and found that this was not very different from that contemplated in the immediate plans of the War

---

[1] Windham to Sec. of State for War, Jan. 22, 1869: *ibid.*, p. 7.
[2] Lugard to Rogers, April 20, 1869: *ibid.*, p. 10.
[3] For another dispute, over the 31,000 Sniders in store in Canada as a reserve, which Cardwell threatened to remove unless the Dominion chose to purchase them, see *ibid*, pp. 3, 8, 10.
[4] Young to Cardwell (private), Feb. 15, 1869: copy, *G*, 573 A, p. 103.
[5] On Monck's views, see Stacey, C. P., "Lord Monck and the Canadian Nation," *Dalhousie Review*, XIV, July, 1934.

Office. He assumed that both Quebec and Halifax would continue to be Imperial stations, but that Canada would soon be required to pay for troops kept at such points as Montreal.[1] Finding his ministers in general " very reasonable ", he confessed himself disappointed when they handed him a minute of council protesting against any diminution of the regular force. Conversations with some of them had led him to infer that they were prepared to acquiesce in a larger reduction than that ordered by Buckingham at the end of the Conservative ministry. " But they appear ", he wrote, " to deprecate any further step in the direction of reduction—the fact is they do not wish to stand otherwise in the eyes of their constituents than as strenuous advisers of the retention of a large British Force."[2]

Both to Cardwell and Granville, Young expressed the opinion that the Fenian menace had more reality than it was generally credited with in England. As long as disbanded soldiers, " reckless and unemployed ", continued to swarm over the United States, there was, he thought, " room for apprehension and for precaution ".[3] John O'Neill, commander of the Niagara raiding party in 1866, had become president of the " Canadian " wing of the Brotherhood at the end of 1867, and there was no doubt of the sincerity of his desire to renew the attack ; the only doubt was as to whether he would be able to collect the necessary sinews of war.[4]

The views of the Canadian ministers had no effect on Cardwell. He introduced the Army Estimates for 1869-70 with a careful exposition of his policy. Boasting of a total net saving, over the previous year, of just under £1,200,000, he explained that this resulted mainly from his review of the colonial distribution of the forces. The colonies had cost the War Office more than £3,000,000 in 1868-69, but this year the bill would be down to £2,237,000. Drawing the distinction between genuine colonies and mere " stations for our fleet " (and Cardwell classed Halifax among these last), the expenditure on the former class—the only one on which large retrenchment was

---

[1] *Ibid.*
[2] Young to Granville (confidential), Feb. 18, 1869 : *G*, 573 A, pp. 100-03.
[3] *Ibid.*
[4] For O'Neill's activity, see the Canadian secret service reports in *M.P.*, " Fenians " and " McMicken Reports " series, *passim.*

possible—was cut from £1,643,000 to £1,070,000. This saving had been effected chiefly through reducing the estimated garrison of British North America from 16,185 men for 1868–69 to 6,249 for 1869–70.

The motion passed by the House of Commons in 1862, said Cardwell, represented what had since been " the settled policy of this country ". The policy had not been applied to Canada, " for remarkable and exceptional reasons, which reasons, however, have now ceased to exist " ; and reduction there had been initiated, not by the Liberals, but by the previous Government. He declared that his policy would strengthen rather than weaken the colonies :

" If, instead of calling upon your colonists to exert themselves and to rely on their own resources, you distribute forces among them in small divisions, you will paralyze their efforts without furnishing them with real strength. I believe that Canada, with 30,000 or 40,000 armed men of her own, occupies a stronger and more independent position than she ever did before. . . . The true defence of our colonies is that they live under the ægis of the name of England, and that war with them is war with England. You are strengthening and defending your colonies, and increasing the power of England, when you generate in every one of the settlements where the British name is known a spirit of British energy and self-reliance ; for you consolidate and concentrate the strength of the mother country for their defence in time of need."

He now reckoned upon having at home 61 battalions of infantry of the line, each of 560 men, whereas before there had been only 46 battalions on larger establishments. Declaring his desire for a short-service system, he urged the need of reducing the soldier's proportion of foreign service with that end in view ; the Duke of Cambridge had hoped that the time was at hand when the soldier could be assured one-third of his service at home, but Cardwell now spoke boldly for the principle that *half* his time should be spent in the United Kingdom.[1]

The reception accorded these estimates demonstrated once more the dissatisfaction of Parliament with the old colonial arrangements. The proposals for withdrawal encountered no real criticism whatever.[2] Indeed, Cardwell's comprehensive grasp of the essentials of Britain's military problem was already

---

[1] *Hansard*, CXCIV, 1111–1139 (March 11, 1869).
[2] See the debate, *ibid.*, 1139–75.

CARDWELL CUTS THE GORDIAN KNOT 213

so patent, and his approach so workmanlike, that criticism was disarmed, and he was able to thank the House for the " marked kindness " with which his statement had been received.[1] A few weeks later his policy received an important endorsement in the Lords. Lord Monck, free now to express his private views on the question which had occupied him so long in Canada, did not mince words :

" In justice to the colonies, and in order that they might be able to place themselves in a condition of self-defence, they should be explicitly informed that the withdrawal of troops now going on resulted . . . from deliberate policy ; and that in time of peace they must, under no circumstances, expect to see an Imperial soldier within their limits ; while in time of war Imperial troops will be handled and distributed solely with reference to Imperial strategical considerations, and will be sent to a colony in the event only of its becoming the theatre of the decisive contest of a war."[2]

That the Government was determined not to be lightly turned from its course was soon indicated. Another crisis had arisen in Anglo-American relations ; for the Johnson-Clarendon convention, concluded for the settlement of the *Alabama* question, had been rejected by the United States Senate after a sensational speech by Senator Sumner which estimated the American claims against England at an almost astronomical figure.[3] The fear of war revived ; and the Foreign Secretary, sending a summary of Sumner's remarks to the Queen, told her frankly :

" It is the unfriendly state of our relations with America that to a great extent paralyses our action in Europe. There is not the smallest doubt that if we were engaged in a Continental quarrel we should immediately find ourselves at war with the United States."[4]

Nevertheless, a question in the House of Commons as to whether " existing circumstances " had altered his plans concerning the Canadian garrison drew from Cardwell only the brief rejoinder that the order for withdrawal was being executed, " and it was not the intention of the Government to countermand it ".[5]

[1] *Ibid.*, 1173.
[2] *Ibid.*, CXCV, 1431 (April 23, 1869).
[3] Rhodes, J. F., *History of the United States*, VI, 336–41.
[4] Clarendon to the Queen, May 1, 1869 : *Letters of Queen Victoria*, second series, I, 594–95.
[5] *Hansard*, CXCVI, 747–48 (May 13, 1869).

Granville had sent to Canada an official intimation of the new policy in a dispatch[1] dated April 14, which took up all the outstanding defensive problems. In reply to the allegations of the Dominion Government that an exceptional amount of imperial assistance was due to Canada on account of her being exposed to danger from the Fenians, whose hostility to her was based purely on her connexion with Great Britain, Granville observed that the Imperial Government trusted that this annoyance, the product of the recent disbandment of large armies in the United States, was fast disappearing. Passing on to the question of the fortifications, and the late Canadian Act authorizing their construction under an Imperial guarantee, he wrote :

" Without anticipating any arrangements of detail. . . . I will only here say that the present Government are prepared to redeem the pledge of their predecessors, and will introduce into Parliament a Bill authorizing the contemplated guarantee.

" But they are also of opinion that the military and naval assistance hitherto given to Canada, under circumstances which they hope are now passing away, must at once be very largely reduced. . . .

" Halifax will be considered as an Imperial Station, and for its defence about 2,000 men will, for the present, be left in Nova Scotia.

" About 4,000 men will, for the present, be left in Ontario, Quebec, and New Brunswick. But this must be considered a temporary arrangement, and I am disposed to concur with Mr. Cardwell in the opinion that it will soon become unnecessary to maintain any British force in those Provinces, beyond what may be required for the training of the Militia and Volunteers and the maintenance of Schools of Instruction. The terms on which any of H.M.'s Regiments can be retained in the colony, for this or any other purpose, will be a matter for future consideration. "

All assistance would be given in the organization of local forces ; and the War Department would be ready to supply arms and stores, " when practicable ", at cost price. It was proposed to disband four companies of the Royal Canadian Rifles at once, and ultimately the whole regiment, unless Canada chose to assume the cost of maintaining it.

[1] Granville to Young : published in *S.P.*, 1871, no. 46, " Copies of correspondence with Imperial authorities on the subject of withdrawal of H.M. troops "—quoted hereafter as " Withdrawal Correspondence ".

CARDWELL CUTS THE GORDIAN KNOT 215

As to the naval forces on the Lakes, Granville, while hoping that it would soon be possible to reduce them on both sides within the limits of the Rush-Bagot convention, announced that the Imperial authorities were willing to replace their three gunboats on the border waters in 1869, and Canada might consider what further force was desirable—but (a large but), " Her Majesty's Government are of opinion that this must now be done entirely at the expense of the Dominion ". He added, with reference to a contrary argument advanced by the Canadians, a comment which, while justified by the facts, showed rather less than customary official politeness :

" With regard to the observations contained in the Report of the Committee of the Privy Council that Canada has no power to commission vessels of war, I would call your attention to the Colonial Naval Defence Act of 1865, which was intended to provide against that difficulty. The Council do not state in what respect it is found to be imperfect."

With this dispatch was enclosed an extract of a letter from Cardwell to Granville[1] outlining the proposed reductions. This, however, referred to the part played by the regulars in training the colonial militia and declared that the withdrawals would not " interfere with these arrangements " and that the troops used for this purpose " would be sufficient, in any emergency, to furnish the garrison of Quebec ". This seems to presage an intention of leaving a small Imperial force in central Canada ; but it will be observed that Granville hints broadly that even a force for training the militia will be left only on special terms.

When the dispatch was published in Canada, it was immediately remarked that with regard to the fortification project it showed " an entire change of views on the part of the Imperial authorities ". They were ready to guarantee a loan if the Colonial Government wished to fortify ; but they no longer urged it to do so.[2] And in point of fact Granville soon requested Young, confidentially, to ascertain discreetly whether his ministers were undertaking the scheme from conviction, or merely because they thought it was required by the Imperial

---

[1] In *ibid.*, pp. 4–6 ; dated Jan. 25, 1869
[2] Toronto *Globe*, June 16, 1869. This point was immediately taken up by the opposition in the Dominion Parliament : see the speech of Alexander Mackenzie, the Liberal leader, who had consistently opposed expenditure for fortifications, on June 17 : *ibid.*, June 25, 1869.

Government. "If the latter," he wrote, "it is very desirable that the undertaking should be abandoned, and I should be glad to have your opinion as to the mode in which such an opinion could be obtained from the Canadian Government, without laying Her Majesty's Government open to a charge of desiring to escape from the pledge which has been given."[1] Here we seem to have a distinct echo of the attitude of Gladstone and Bright when the fortifications were first spoken of.

A month earlier, Granville had sent to Young another confidential communication, dealing generally with the relation of Canada to the mother country. He stressed the fact that the Dominion was free to determine its own future; the Imperial Government had no desire to maintain the connexion between the two countries "a single year" after it became "injurious or distasteful" to Canada. And the dispatch concluded:

"You will . . . be good enough to bring to my notice any line of policy or any measures which without implying on the part of Her Majesty's Government any wish to change abruptly our relations, would gradually prepare both Countries for a friendly relaxation of them."[2]

Nearly twenty years before, Elgin had protested against the prevalence of such doctrine in the mouths of British statesmen; but its popularity had not declined, and now it had crept into an official utterance of the Colonial Secretary. An apologist of Gladstonian colonial policy hopes that this dispatch represented only Granville's personal views, and that the Prime Minister had not seen it.[3] Be that as it may, one cannot help remarking that the colonial military policy of the Gladstone ministry fits into the scheme of things which it envisages. The Canadians were right in perceiving a difference between the attitude of the old Palmerston Government and that of Gladstone's towards the defence of their country. The former (at least while Newcastle was at the Colonial Office—for after the advent of Cardwell the atmosphere is not quite the same)

[1] Dated July 10, 1869: *G*, 565 A, p. 72.
[2] Granville to Young, June 16, 1869: copy, Public Record Office MS., C.O., Canada, 43, 156; quoted in Knaplund, *Gladstone and Britain's Imperial Policy*, 98–99. Cf. above, p. 205.
[3] Knaplund, *ibid*.

CARDWELL CUTS THE GORDIAN KNOT 217

had for its central idea the provision of effective means for defending Canada against the United States—by the presence of Imperial forces, by urging and encouraging Canada to provide forces of her own, by suggesting programmes of defensive works. The central idea of the Gladstonian policy, on the other hand, seems to be simply the diminution of Imperial responsibility in America. We have just seen that the new ministry was far from considering that the American danger was at an end; yet they did not particularly press Canada to defensive exertions, and were even hesitant, looking before and after (as in this instance of the fortifications) in meeting the efforts she seemed ready to make. Their determination to remove the Imperial troops from Canada was fixed; but they betrayed no overmastering interest in whether Canada would provide other forces to replace them. This might perhaps be regarded as a manifestation of true liberal Imperialism, of the realization that the impulse of self-defence would be more effective (as Elgin had once said) " as the product of movements from within, not of pressure from without "; nor can it be doubted that the ultimate effect of the new policy was for the good of the Imperial spirit. On the other hand, it might be regarded—as most Canadians at the time regarded it—as simply a manifestation of indifference, tempered by timidity in the face of responsibility; and (considering the spirit and circumstances of the day, and the personnel of Gladstone's ministry) this view seems far from unnatural.

The news of the impending departure of the troops was certainly not welcome to the Canadian public, among which there was now no survival of the distrust which the reform party had felt towards the Imperial forces in the days of the fight for responsible government. Yet the opposition to Granville's proposals was not so fierce as might have been expected.[1] Though the Fenian agitation was still in progress, there had not been any actual aggression since 1866; and it was only under the shadow of an immediate menace that the people of the colony would interest themselves seriously in the means of defence. The leading journal of Canada greeted the

[1] His dispatch of April 14 was laid before the Canadian House of Commons by a message of June 11, and at once published in the Press, along with the report of Cartier and McDougall.

first rumours of the Cardwell policy with some complacency,[1] nor did it become disturbed when the official correspondence was made public—being prejudiced in favour of the Imperial ministry's proposals by their lukewarmness towards the fortification scheme, which it disliked on the score of expense, while the new plan was not interpreted as signifying complete withdrawal.[2]

More acute anxiety seems to have been generated in French Canada. The attitude of the French-Canadian Press suggests that there was foundation for Young's assertion that this section was particularly disposed to "look to Her Majesty's Government for everything"; and it was particularly sensitive to Granville's brusque tone. The radical *Rouge* journals turned the new policy to account as an argument for Canadian independence. *L'Ordre* of Montreal reported a dispute on this issue between one of these and a Conservative organ with the remark that the latter had a hard task in resisting the independence logic, and an accusation of mercenary spirit against England: "Ne va-t-elle pas jusqu'à nous marchander et la poudre et les accoutrements?"[3]

The Governor-General attempted to produce a better impression by a speech delivered at Quebec, in which he said:

"There are three reasons, the improbability of war, the necessity for economy in the public service so that taxes can be reduced, and superior advantages for drilling troops when congregated together, which have led to the recall of the troops from Canada; but let their presence be required here, and you may rely with confidence upon the assurance given in Mr. Cardwell's despatch of June, 1865, that the Imperial Government will be prepared to defend every part of the Empire with all the resources at its command." [*Loud cheers.*]

Doubtless remembering, however, what he had lately heard from Granville, he added that the Dominion was now "in reality independent": that it was for Canada's statesmen to decide whether to maintain the present connexion with England "or in due time of the maturity of the Dominion to change it for some other form of alliance."[4] This not only drew down the reproaches of the *Globe*,[5] but enabled *L'Ordre* to observe that,

---

[1] *Globe*, June 16, 1869.　　[2] *Weekly Globe*, April 16, 1869.
[3] *L'Ordre*, July 15, 1869.
[4] *Globe*, July 16, 1869. (The speech was delivered the previous day).
[5] *Ibid.*, July 21.

CARDWELL CUTS THE GORDIAN KNOT

while His Excellency's tactful phrases lacked " la rudesse qui distinguait à un aussi haut degré la récente dépêche du comte de Grandville [sic]", they came to much the same thing.[1] On the other hand, the Government journal in Montreal, *La Minerve*, which had been finding it hard to justify the new departures, was glad to make the most of Young's remarks, declaring:

" Ce discours . . . vaut infiniment mieux que la lettre du Comte Granville ; il la corrige, il l'excuse, il la fera oublier. . . . Disons à l'Angleterre que nous désirons lui continuer l'allégeance sous laquelle nous avons grandi, et elle sera prête à dépenser pour notre défense son dernier sou et sacrifier son dernier soldat ; c'est le représentant de Sa Majesté elle-même qui nous donne une telle assurance."[2]

Though the Canadian ministers, feeling that they had already made their views clear, made no direct answer to Granville's dispatch, they were soon involved in another series of military disputes with the Imperial authorities. These began with a criticism by Cardwell of the distribution proposed by Sir Charles Windham for the force remaining in Canada ; the minister particularly desired that Toronto, " an expensive and isolated position", should be abandoned.[3] Windham replied that this would have a bad effect upon the people of Ontario, and, by ending the existence of the military schools now at work in Toronto, upon the efficiency of the militia.[4] The Governor-General agreed ;[5] but Cardwell, afraid of " stationing Troops in small detachments in isolated positions . . . lest they should invite attack from Fenians or others in the United States in serious force, and be obliged to retreat ", practically told the General that he would leave troops in such positions on his own responsibility, and would be held answerable for their being properly supported in emergency by the local forces.[6] It required a second letter from Windham, representing that though he agreed with Cardwell's attitude from a purely military point of view, there were weighty political considerations on the other side, and that he could hardly take the heavy responsibility which Cardwell laid upon him,[7] to elicit from the

[1] *L'Ordre*, July 22.   [2] *La Minerve*, July 17, 1869.
[3] Lugard to G.O.C., Canada, Feb. 20, 1869 : *C*, 37, p. 194.
[4] Windham to Sec. of State for War, March 12, 1869 : *ibid.*, p. 201.
[5] Military secretary, Ottawa, to military secretary, Montreal, March 12, 1869 : *ibid.*, p. 210.
[6] Lugard to Windham (confidential), April 29, 1869 : *ibid.*, p. 239.
[7] Windham to Under-Secretary of State for War (confidential), June 4, 1869 : *G*, 565 A, p. 78.

War Office definite sanction " for a time " for the arrangements which he proposed.[1]

But in the meantime there had been a Fenian alarm, and the Governor-General, at the request of his ministers, had asked the assistance of the Commander of the Forces in defensive arrangements.[2] Remembering Cardwell's solemn warning, Windham now requested the Minister of Militia to call out 3,000 volunteers in Ontario and Quebec and place them at his disposal to support his detached posts. Cartier refused, on the ground that Parliament had voted no money for the purpose. This evasion (after all, troops had been called out without parliamentary authority several times during 1864-66) disgusted Windham, and he let it be known that he proposed to withdraw the garrison at Toronto. Immediately the Dominion Government took alarm. Sir John Macdonald called on Windham, declared that in its moral effect upon the people of that district such action would be " suicidal ", and assured him that " if more serious information should be received and be thought worthy of being reported " to him, the Government would call out and place at his disposal 3,000 volunteers ready for immediate service. Sir Charles then agreed to leave the troops in Toronto.[3]

This arrangement left the Canadian Government still the sole judges of the seriousness of any emergency ; and the promise of action if more information was sent to the General seems to have resulted merely in their avoiding, thereafter, sending him any information at all. It was one of the absurd features of the military situation in Canada that, although the Commander of the Forces was responsible, in case of attack, for the general defence of the country and the disposition of regulars and militia alike, nevertheless the whole intelligence service (by this time extremely efficient) which could afford information on the enemy's resources and plans was under the control of the civil government. The General received only such information as the latter chose to communicate.

To add to his troubles, the Canadian authorities, although

---

[1] Storks to G.O.C., Canada, Aug. 4, 1869 : *C*, 37, p. 251.
[2] Young to Granville (confidential), July 23, 1869 : *G*, 573 A, p. 156.
[3] For these episodes, see Windham to Sec. of State for War (confidential), Aug. 13, 1869 (*C*, 1287, p. 335) ; and Windham to Young, July 29, 1869 (*C*, 1319, p. 251).

CARDWELL CUTS THE GORDIAN KNOT

they had urged upon the Imperial Government the great importance of the gunboat service, had, nevertheless, when Granville insisted that the Dominion pay the whole cost of it henceforth, laid up in harbour the two remaining colonial armed vessels, without men aboard to replace those formerly supplied by the Royal Navy, and thus useless in any sudden emergency. This increased Windham's anxiety for his detachments, particularly for the single company in Fort Wellington, at Prescott on the St. Lawrence. Seconded by Young, he now requested Canadian support for this exposed post; but the Minister of Militia obstinately refused either to commission a gunboat on the river or to call out volunteers to support or relieve the garrison.[1] Windham was obliged to reinforce it from his own diminished regular force.

The Governor-General's patience with his advisers was now exhausted; and he proceeded to urge the Colonial Office, confidentially, to order the evacuation of Fort Wellington on a given date, giving the Canadians the definite alternative of taking over the fort or having it dismantled. " Otherwise ", he remarked, " we may be amused by a lengthy negotiation while this petty defenceless fort with its weak garrison is left exposed to insult ".[2] This somewhat unusual recommendation was scarcely necessary, for as soon as Windham's report of the events reached Cardwell the latter, in some disgust, strongly recommended the same course.[3] In October the whole Imperial force at Prescott was withdrawn, 200 regulars being replaced by precisely twenty-four Canadian volunteers. The Dominion Government had maintained throughout that Prescott was in no danger—that the Fenians would attack, not where there were only a few troops, but where there were none at all ;[4] but this exhibition of nonchalance seems almost excessive.

By this time, however, the situation was altering again. Militant Fenian preparations were reported. The Governor-General was decidedly anxious ;[5] and at last the ministers decided to commission the gunboats and call out volunteer gunners to man them. The step Windham had urged so long

---

[1] Windham to Sec. of State for War (confidential), Aug. 13, as above.
[2] Young to Granville, Aug. 13, 1869 : pencil draft, *G*, 573 A, p. 160. Copy, *Confidential Despatches 1867–1873*, p. 136.
[3] Cardwell to Granville, Aug. 26, 1869 : copy in *G*, 565 A, p. 126.
[4] Macdonald to Young, Aug. 13, 1869 : *M.P.*, private letter book 13, p. 94.
[5] Young to Granville (confidential), Oct. 14, 1869 : *G*, 573 A, p. 169.

was thus taken; and the General first learned of it through the newspapers! (Perhaps their promise to call out troops " if more serious information was received and thought worthy of being communicated " had been in the ministers' minds.) Windham lost no time in pointing out to the Governor-General that this procedure gave him the best possible grounds for complaint :

". . . As the entire Military Authority over all the Troops, whether Regular or Militia in the event of Canada being assailed, rests with the Genl. Officer in Command, I consider that he should be allowed to have a voice in all preparations for defence.

" Your Excellency is aware that I cannot divest myself of the responsibility which attaches to my Command nor of that which in the event of any disaster however small, whether to Regulars or Volunteers will be laid upon me by the Public both here and at home."[1]

The absurdity of the situation needed no further demonstration. Windham soon reported to London that he had received assurance of better information in future, and that the " countenance and support " of the Governor-General, which had never failed him, served as guarantees that he would get it.[2] It is clear that the two Imperial officials were allies in these disputes. Poor Windham, however, was done with all such squabbling. Going south on leave in an attempt at recruiting his failing health, he died at Jacksonville on February 2, 1870,[3] leaving to other men the arduous and vexatious task of military co-operation with the Canadian Government.[4]

The succession of episodes just narrated indicates that during 1869 that co-operation had suffered an all but complete breakdown. The Imperial determination to throw the cost of the naval defence of the border upon Canada had merely resulted in the border being left undefended. The hostility of the War Office towards allowing regular detachments to remain in isolated stations forced the Commanding General, when apprised of danger, to apply to the Canadian Government for support on two occasions; both these requests met with definite

[1] Windham to Young, Oct. 22, 1869 : *C*, 1319, p. 353.
[2] Windham to Sec. of State for War, Nov. 5, 1869 : *C*, 1287, p. 368.
[3] *Ibid.*, note, p. 404.
[4] The present writer has described the foregoing events in detail in " The Garrison of Fort Wellington : a military dispute during the Fenian troubles," *C.H.R.*, XIV.

refusals. Finally, when Fenian menaces led the ministry to take defensive action on their own account, they failed to inform the General either of their own measures or of the reasons for them. The Canadians were deeply vexed by the withdrawal policy, and considered the War Office's fears for Imperial detachments the product of unjustifiable timidity; they were as determined as ever to keep their military expenditure within narrow limits, and (above all) to avoid any action which could possibly be regarded as implying acceptance of an enlargement of the Dominion's defensive responsibilities. The Imperial Government, on the other hand, showed not only that anxiety for the safety of its troops in Canada which we have often seen before, but also a new resolution in its moves towards reducing its own Canadian commitments, and an increasing dissatisfaction with Canada's failure to display that more generous spirit which the English ministers thought should have accompanied the recent changes in her political condition. This series of irritating squabbles may be presumed to have exercised a very considerable influence upon the minds of Granville and Cardwell as they faced the problem of determining the line of their further policy in Canada.

The feeling which the Canadian administration showed in these disputes did not lead it, however, to countenance an extra-constitutional proposal made at this time for a protest against the new Imperial policy. It emphasized the correctness of its relations with Britain by refusing to accept the invitation of a group of persons in London, claiming to represent colonial feeling, who attempted to organize a demonstration with this object. These individuals suggested, in a circular letter to the Colonial Governments, dated August 13, 1869, that a conference of colonial representatives should assemble in the following February to discuss the new departures. The immediate origin of the proposal was serious difficulties which had arisen in New Zealand, where the Cardwell policy had appeared in the shape of orders for the removal of the last regiment from that colony, despite the fact that hostilities with the Maoris had again broken out, and in the face of the strongest representations from the local Government.[1]

[1] Fortescue, *History of the British Army*, XIII, 512–13; Rusden, *History of New Zealand*, chaps. XV and XVI; *P.P.*, 1868–9, no. 307, vol. XLIV

Granville, naturally enough, discouraged the scheme, and while the Gladstone Government undoubtedly was not popular with the colonies, the latter showed little disposition to present their grievances through such irregular channels. The Canadian answer was eminently discreet ; the ministers merely stated " that with every respect to the gentlemen who composed the meeting, and with due appreciation of their motives, the Committee do not think it fitting that the Canadian Government should appoint representatives to attend the proposed Colonial Conference, unless invited to do so by Her Majesty's Government."[1] Macdonald wrote to Sir John Rose in London, " I am . . . strongly inclined to believe that we ought to have nothing to do with it. We have no wrongs to complain of, we are quite satisfied with our position and relations with the Mother Country, and we have had a special understanding, since 1865, on all matters connected with those relations."[2] As regarded the organization of the Empire, Canada's great ideal (now that her political autonomy was secure) was simply the maintenance of the *status quo*.

It was not colonials only who were disposed to resist the policy of withdrawal ; some much greater personages were perturbed by it. The Queen told Lord Granville that it would reduce England " to the state of a second-rate power " ;[3] and at the end of 1869 her cousin, the Commander-in-Chief, finding that Cardwell now proposed the complete evacuation of central Canada, solemnly declared his belief that this course was dangerous. He was especially troubled by the prospect of the abandonment of Quebec, and suggested that by continuing to occupy that important post Britain would have the right to ask Canada to fortify Montreal, as was so desirable.[4] But it may be inferred from what we have already seen that such an

(Correspondence between the Colonial Office and the Governors of New Zealand), continued in no. 307, I, and in *P.P.*, 1870, cd. 83, vol. L.

[1] The documents relating to this affair, including the original proposal, Granville's dispatch, and the replies of Canada and other colonies, are in *P.P.*, 1870, cd. 24, vol. XLIX (Correspondence respecting a proposed conference of colonial representatives in London).

[2] Macdonald to Rose, Nov. 16, 1869 : *M.P.*, Private letter book 13, p. 438. Published in Pope, *Correspondence of Sir John Macdonald*, 102–05.

[3] Guedalla, P., *The Queen and Mr. Gladstone, 1845–1879*, London, 1933, 56.

[4] Memorandum dated Dec. 14 : Verner, *Military Life of George, Duke of Cambridge*, I, 396–99 ; and cf. the Duke's letter to Cardwell of the previous Aug. 3, *ibid.*, 394–96.

CARDWELL CUTS THE GORDIAN KNOT 225

argument had little force with the Gladstone ministry;[1] and in this, as in many other matters, the Duke of Cambridge was to find his judgment subordinated to that of the Secretary of State for War.

The exact motivation of the decision to push to extremes the policy of military withdrawal from Canada must be, in great part, a matter of conjecture, particularly as regards the effect of the uncertain relations subsisting with the United States. It has already been suggested that the very unsatisfactory state of military co-operation with Canada suggested the desirability of ending the whole situation which produced these disputes. Further, the reception of Cardwell's 1869 estimates must have encouraged him to believe himself on the right track with respect to English public opinion.

Active agitation against the colonial garrisons, moreover, was still in evidence. Adderley, who had been restricted in his utterances by being a member of the late Conservative ministry, was now a free agent once more. In the course of 1869 he published a lengthy work devoted to the thesis that the total abolition of the garrisons was desirable and would not endanger the unity of the Empire.[2] Nor had the commercial interest ceased to make itself heard. The Manchester Chamber of Commerce again made representations to the Colonial Office against the colonial tariffs, suggesting that " the injustice of this policy on the part of the Colonies is the more apparent when it is considered that the people of Great Britain and Ireland tax themselves for the support of the Imperial Army and Navy of which the Colonists enjoy their full share of benefit without contributing anything to the cost ". Granville reminded the memorialists that colonial tariffs were a matter for Colonial Governments, but as to defence they were assured that "his Lordship entirely concurs in the principle that Troops for Colonial, apart from Imperial purposes, should not be paid for by the British Taxpayer ", and that this principle was " in course of application to the Colonies ".[3]

[1] In the absence of evidence, it can only be suggested as possible that the ministry's small enthusiasm for the completion of the fortification scheme resulted in part from the apprehension that it might be utilized as an argument for the retention of Imperial forces in Canada.
[2] *Review of " The Colonial Policy of Lord J. Russell's Administration,"* by Earl Grey, 1853 ; and of subsequent colonial history.
[3] Enclosures in Granville to Young, June 4, 1869 : G, 564.

Q

Doubtless also the tense situation on the continent of Europe had its due effect. In any case, by the time the year 1870 began the Imperial Government had taken its decision—and it was in favour of much more drastic colonial reductions than (judging by his memorandum of January 9, 1869)[1] Cardwell himself had contemplated a year before. That scheme had proposed to leave 2,000 troops in Canada (apart from Halifax). It had listed the Dominion as a " contributing colony ", which may have indicated a hope that Canada might be prevailed upon to pay part of the cost of the garrison ; while the figure 2,000 suggests that Cardwell then had in mind merely a reduction of the force to the scale of 1860, and an adherence to the old Grey-Newcastle formula of Imperial occupation of fortified places. Now, however, the Grey ideal was definitely discarded. On February 12, 1870, Granville sent to the Governor-General a dispatch[2] describing the intentions of the Government. They would, he said, be expected by Parliament to carry out the reduction policy already announced ; but at the same time they were anxious to afford Canada all assistance in organizing for herself a suitable " Military and Naval power ". To this end they were ready (still) to recommend the fortification guarantee to Parliament ; but to meet possible objections they would be glad to know whether the Dominion still favoured the plan " and if so, how soon they are prepared to begin and carry out the proposed works ".

The future military arrangements were stated thus :

" The City of Halifax will be garrisoned . . . as an Imperial station.

" Besides supplying this force the Secretary of State for War is desirous of enabling your Ministers, if they should think it requisite, to retain in Canada the services of a small body of regular troops for the instruction of their Volunteers and Militia.

" With this view he would be ready to facilitate the formation of a Colonial Regiment . . . by enabling officers and men, now in the Dominion, to accept any offer made to them by the Government for the transfer of their services, and this even though an entire battalion were to volunteer as a Colonial Regiment, for service in Canada, the Head quarters and a small nucleus returning to this country on which the Regiment could be reformed. . . .

[1] In Biddulph, 28. Cf. above, p. 208.
[2] In Withdrawal Correspondence, p. 8.

" Besides the Halifax garrison, Her Majesty's Government propose to leave in Canada, for the present year, a battalion of infantry and one battery of garrison artillery.

" This force will be shortly concentrated . . . at Quebec. The regiment of Canadian Rifles will be disbanded.[1] The rest of the force now in Canada will be withdrawn.

" The barracks and fortifications finally vacated by Her Majesty's troops . . . will be handed over to Canada. . . . But it must be remembered that, if at any future period troops are sent to Canada at the request of the Local Government, or in furtherance of Colonial interests, the Dominion will be expected to provide them with barracks or lodging to the satisfaction of Her Majesty's Government. . . .

" You will take care to explain to your Advisers that the arrangements contemplated in this Despatch, and which are based on principles applicable not exclusively to the Dominion, but to the other self-governing British Colonies, are contingent upon a time of peace, and are in no way intended to alter or diminish the obligations which exist on both sides in case of foreign war."

At the same time the question of the militia arms was dealt with.[2] 43,000 rifles, chiefly Sniders, which had been issued on loan to the Canadian forces, were now made an unconditional gift to the Dominion. This was generous, but here Imperial generosity stopped abruptly. Cardwell had rescinded the regulations permitting loans to colonial forces. In 1868 Canada had requested the loan of 10,000 additional Sniders ; the request had been granted, but she had not then taken advantage of the permission. When the requisition was now renewed, she was informed that it could be complied with only under the terms of new regulations which demanded payment. Notice was also given that the reserve rifles then in Canada would eventually be returned to England unless the Dominion paid for them.

These decisions clearly represented a revolution. In 1854-56 and 1859-61 the Imperial garrison in Canada had been very small, but there had been no talk of removing it altogether ; above all, it had never occurred to Canadians that Imperial forces would cease to garrison the great fortress of Quebec. These, however, were the propositions now made. Except for

---

[1] This was carried out during the spring and summer of 1870.
[2] In another dispatch of the same date : Withdrawal Correspondence, p. 9.

the naval station on the east coast, the Queen's uniform was to disappear from Canada. And close examination of the dispatches revealed in them an alarming air of finality, reflecting an evident determination to effect as complete a severance as possible between the military systems of Britain and Canada, and in particular to relieve the British taxpayer from any liability whatever for that of the Dominion. Grey in 1851 had suggested that Imperial troops in excess of the force determined upon by the War Office might be left in Canada if the local Government would pay the cost of them. Even this arrangement is not countenanced by Granville's dispatch.[1] Canada may enlist British regulars, but they must be formed into a wholly distinct corps, for which Britain will have no responsibility. Nor is she ever again to be responsible for the armament of the colony's troops. Arms provided in future will be provided for cash and become colonial property; there will be no more petty disputes with obstinate colonial ministers over bills for damage.

The decision for the immediate abandonment of Quebec seems the least comprehensible element in this scheme, and certainly seemed so to Canadians at the time. That fortress had just undergone large alterations designed to make it one of the strongest positions in existence—the three new forts at Lévis, on which so much English money had been spent,[2] were in fact not yet quite complete; everything had indicated an apparent intention of making it a solid Imperial *pied-à-terre* in North America. The avowed object of the new fortifications had been to afford sure protection for the British garrison of Canada. They had moreover been part of a general joint scheme of Canadian defence, and as the Duke of Cambridge had pointed out, the complete withdrawal of Imperial forces would assuredly make it more difficult to induce Canada to proceed with her share.

Certainly the Government was not free from apprehension

---

[1] For a definite declaration by Granville against this principle, see his speech in the Lords on March 7, 1870: *Hansard*, CXCIX, 1342. And Cardwell discouraged a suggestion of General Lindsay that Canada might pay the cost of an Imperial regiment: Lugard to Lindsay, Sept. 24, 1870 (Withdrawal Correspondence, p. 60).

[2] The original estimate of £200,000 had been increased to £245,000 in the estimates for 1869–70: *P.P.*, 1868–9, no. 39, vol. XXXVI.

of American hostility, for the *Alabama* claims still remained unsettled, a constant danger. Talk of the peril to the small garrison of Canada, and assertions that the presence of redcoats was an incentive, rather than a discouragement, to attack either by Fenians or by the United States Government, were still abroad. The Imperial Government had always regarded its force in America as a self-reliant entity wholly responsible for its own defence, preferring not to reckon upon the assistance it would receive from local forces over which Whitehall could exercise no direct control; and the recent Prescott episode must have tended to confirm it in this attitude. Cardwell's insistence on concentration indicates that the Government was not uninfluenced by the croakers at home. It is perhaps no very wild conjecture to suppose that the ministry saw no middle course between maintaining in Canada a force large enough to be capable of defending itself for a time at least, and withdrawing the troops altogether. Had a small detachment been left merely to " show the flag ", as the naval phrase goes, a sudden emergency would have seen Britain obliged either to reinforce it (a repetition of those episodes which had foiled the reduction policy so often during the past twenty years) or to withdraw it in shameful haste; while those apprehensive publicists whom we have frequently quoted would shiver to see it constantly exposed to the risk of " disgrace " at the hands of superior American forces.

From the Canadian point of view, the one redeeming feature of the Imperial Government's programme was its declaration that in the event of foreign war it would hold itself bound by the same strong obligations as before—those obligations formally acknowledged after the conferences of 1865. (The cynic may remark, if he chooses, that it could not well have avoided making this declaration—for Sir John Young had only recently solemnly repeated those assurances in his speech at Quebec.) The ultimate responsibility of Britain thus remained undiminished. But the withdrawal of the entire garrison in time of peace relieved the mother country of very considerable expense; and undoubtedly many Englishmen believed that the departure of the last Imperial redcoat from central Canada would materially enhance the probability of permanent peace along the Empire's North American frontier.

CHAPTER X

THE END OF THE OLD ORDER

" Your young, gay countries north and south, we feel we own 'em too,
For they was made by rank an' file. Good-bye—good luck to you!"
—KIPLING, *The Parting of the Columns.*

UNDER almost any circumstances, the drastic proposals for the future military relations of Britain and Canada which the Imperial Government advanced early in 1870 would have elicited a vigorous protest from the Canadian administration. At that particular moment, however, there were elements in the situation of the new Dominion which led its rulers to regard these projects with special disfavour and even with grave apprehension.

It was not merely that the relations of Britain and the United States were still a matter of anxious speculation, nor that the Fenian O'Neill was known to be unremittingly active on the other side of the border in collecting war material for an attack on Canada. These things in themselves would have occasioned resistance to the new Imperial policy, but there were even more definite causes for anxiety. First, confidential information concerning the attitude of the United States administration which reached the Canadian Government heightened the apprehensions bred by the general situation. Senator Sumner had followed his alarming speech of April, 1869, with another in September urging the cession of Canada to the United States as a means of settling the *Alabama* claims. He believed that the annexation should be procured by none but peaceful means ; but there were others—notably Senator Chandler—who openly and loudly urged annexation by force.[1] And just at the time when these opinions were being loudly aired, word came to

[1] See Adams, " The Treaty of Washington," in *Lee at Appomattox and other Papers*, 145-56 ; Pierce, *Memoir and Letters of Charles Sumner*, IV, 413, 636-38 ; *The Works of Charles Sumner*, XIII, 98-130.

THE END OF THE OLD ORDER

Ottawa of disturbing expressions used by the American Secretary of State, Hamilton Fish.

At the beginning of 1870, private conversations were in progress on the *Alabama* question between Fish and Edward Thornton, British minister at Washington, in which the former referred to the possibility of the cession of Canada, and the latter observed that to negotiate on that basis was not practicable.[1] But Fish went further. On January 8 Thornton wrote to Lord Clarendon that the American had asked him " to ascertain whether Her Majesty's Government would offer any objection to a free vote being taken in Canada, or in any portions of it, whether the people desire to join the United States or not, and stated his conviction that if the vote were taken a large majority, nine-tenths he said of the people, would vote for Annexation ".[2] It is not surprising that when a copy of this letter reached Ottawa, Sir John Macdonald " viewed the announcements made in it as of the utmost gravity ", and caused his colleagues to submit on the matter a confidential memorandum which " walked into Fish at the rate of a hunt ".

Sir John Young wrote home :

." There is not so far as I know anything bearing the semblance of a political party in the Country which attempts to recommend itself to public favour by advocating the Annexation of Canada to the U.S. or the desirability of separation from England and independence.

" Mr. Fish is reported by Mr. Thornton to have sd. that he is informed that nine-tenths of the Canadians are in favour of independence or it may be he means annexation. All I have been able to observe points to the contrary conclusion.

" It is curious if it be as Mr. Fish asserts—for the expression of opinion is perfectly free—and yet the views Mr. Fish thinks of such extensive prevalence find no expression amongst a population outspoken enough on all other topics about which they feel any concern. . . . The legal maxim, de non apparentibus et non existentibus eadem est ratio, seems not inapplicable in reply to Mr. Fish's assertion."[3]

---
[1] Adams, *The Treaty of Washington*, 157–60.
[2] This is the version given by Sir John Macdonald : Macdonald to Rose, Jan. 26, 1870 (*M.P.*, Private letter book 13, p. 960 ; and cf. Long, M. H., " Sir John Rose and the Informal Beginnings of the Canadian High Commissionership," *C.H.R.*, XII). I have not found Thornton's own letter. A slightly different version of it is given in the Governor-General's dispatch quoted below.
[3] Young to Granville (confidential ; draft), Jan. 22, 1870 : *G*, 575 A, p. 6.

No student of the contemporary Canadian Press can doubt that the Governor-General's view was just. Nevertheless there existed in the Dominion a small group of men who—basing their argument largely upon the prevalence of lukewarmness towards the colonial connexion in Great Britain—had lately spoken out in favour of the eventual independence of Canada. Of these, Alexander Galt was the most eminent; it was his belief that the cultivation of such a sentiment was the only means of preventing the absorption of Canada by the United States. There were also some obscure annexationists, who attempted to turn the independence movement to account and got snubbed by Galt for their pains.[1]

Macdonald's view of the agitation was very definite : " This is simply nonsense. British America must belong either to the American or British System of Government. It will be a century before we are strong enough to walk alone ".[2] But it was alarming to find these opinions of small minorities regarded by the responsible officials of the neighbouring country as dominant forces in Canadian life. Such misconceptions might be dangerous.

The most immediately perilous feature of Canada's situation at the outset of 1870 was, however, the state of affairs on the western plains. During the past year she had, as we have seen, arranged to acquire from the Hudson's Bay Company those vast territories over which its authority had, with the advance of settlement across the American lands adjacent, become more and more difficult to maintain. But the *Métis*—the French-Canadian half-breeds who were so important a part of the small population of the Red River Settlement—were alarmed by the prospect of the transfer. Fearing injurious consequences against which no one had troubled to reassure them, they offered armed resistance to Canadian authority. The Company had no means of maintaining order; in October, 1869, the *Métis* prevented William McDougall, who had been appointed Lieutenant-Governor, from entering the territory; and a provisional government, headed by the eccentric Louis Riel, was set up at Fort Garry. The rebels were in complete control of

[1] Skelton, *Life of Galt*, 437–64.
[2] Macdonald to Dr. Carrall, of British Columbia, Sept. 29, 1869 : *M.P.*, Private letter book 13, p. 209.

THE END OF THE OLD ORDER 233

the little settlement in the Red River valley ; and that settlement was separated from the head of Lake Superior by five hundred miles of rugged wilderness, which could be traversed only in canoes or small boats navigating a long succession of lakes and rivers, and was freely said to be impassable by troops.

To the settlements across the border, on the other hand, the door stood open, for the British territories were separated from the United States only by an imaginary line upon the prairie With American public opinion still incensed against Britain, and an active filibustering organization, alert for an opportunity of injuring British interests, at work in the United States, the dangers of the situation were unbounded. In point of fact, one Fenian, W. B. O'Donoghue, became a member of Riel's Government and played a bold lone hand with the object of detaching the western territory from the British Empire ; and the danger of a stroke by filibustering forces, to set up an annexationist *régime* and create a situation of which, it was to be supposed, the United States Government would not be loath to take advantage, was only too obvious. The fate of the great west, and with it the whole destiny of British North America, hung in the balance.

Macdonald was fully convinced that Washington was casting sheep's eyes at the North-West. At the end of January, 1870, the managing director of the Grand Trunk Railway informed him that a business conversation with the president of the Northern Pacific had led him to believe that the United States authorities were offering special encouragement to that project in the hope that it would " maintain the present attitude of Riel and his party " and prevent Canada from getting the Hudson's Bay territory.[1] Macdonald replied :

" It is quite evident to me, not only from this conversation, but from advices from Washington, that the United States Government are resolved to do all they can, short of war, to get possession of the western territory and we must take immediate and vigorous steps to counteract them."[2]

It was while the Dominion was confronting this dangerously

[1] C. J. Brydges to Macdonald, Jan. 26, 1870 : *M.P.*, " C. J. Brydges ", p. 231. In Pope, *Correspondence of Macdonald*, the date is one day wrong.
[2] *Correspondence of Macdonald*, 124.

uncertain situation, with the possession of a country of continental proportions and immense potential wealth at stake, that the intimation reached Ottawa that the Imperial Government proposed to remove the whole of its troops from Canada. That it caused alarm goes without saying.

Pending the receipt of a draft of the fortification guarantee bill, which had been promised, the Canadian Government did not however send an official reply to Granville's dispatch. Their immediate attention was centred upon ensuring the co-operation of the Imperial Government in any military action that might prove necessary in the west. Macdonald observed with dismay the apparent disposition of both the Colonial Office and the Hudson's Bay Company to throw upon Canada the whole responsibility for meeting the difficulty, and his ministry in consequence refused to accept the transfer of the territories until order was restored.[1] By January, the Dominion Government was making tentative preparations for an expedition ; and the news of the hallucinations of Mr. Secretary Fish made the assistance of the Imperial authorities, in Macdonald's opinion, more than ever essential.[2] Early in February, he explained his views at some length to his Government's confidential representative in London :

" As I have already stated, I think it of the utmost importance that any force sent should be a mixed one of Regulars and Canadian Militia.

" Canada is strong enough to enforce her authority there unaided, but, in the first place, so long as the North West remains under the Hudson's Bay Government, and does not form a portion of the Dominion, we have, of course, no power to send any expeditionary force beyond our own Country. . . . And, in the second place, the sending of some of Her Majesty's troops there will show the United States Government and people that England is resolved not to abandon her Colonies, or is indifferent to the future of the Great West.

An opinion has been widely disseminated through the United States, and has, *we know*, got possession of the mind of the President and his Cabinet, that England wants to get rid of the North West if possible, and will not willingly raise her voice or her hand to retain it.

[1] Macdonald to McDougall, Dec. 12, 1869 : *M.P.*, Private letter book 13, p. 712.
[2] Macdonald to Rose, Jan. 26, 1870 : as above.

THE END OF THE OLD ORDER

" A mixed force will also show that England and Canada are acting in complete accord & unity in the retention of British North America under British Sovereignty."[1]

In the meantime, the new colonial military policy had at last produced some protest in England. The Government there had apparently anticipated some controversy over their drastic programme for 1870-71 ;[2] and it now materialized in an attack by the Conservative ex-Colonial Secretary, Lord Carnarvon, who was certainly moved by an Imperial enthusiasm such as was found in few statesmen of his day. When he found that the withdrawal was to be complete, he expressed his sense of the dangers of this course in a letter to Macdonald,[3] and a few days later was on his feet in the House of Lords, assailing Granville not only for his policy but also for the " harsh terms " and " severe logic " with which he had announced it to the colonies. There were, said Carnarvon, " whispers abroad that there is a policy afoot to dismember the Empire " ; and he made a passionate appeal against narrow and ungenerous behaviour :

" If the object of our whole national life is to become the mere workshop of the world, to give no hostages to Fortune, to run no risks, to incur no liabilities, but merely to accumulate money, well ; but no nation, more than any individual, can afford to live a selfish life, wrapping itself up in its own miserable interests. . . . For my own part, I see with dismay the course which is now being taken— a course at once cheeseparing in point of economy and spendthrift in point of national character."[4]

Granville, obviously nettled, declared that he could find no incivility in his own dispatches, adding, " and if logic is to be used at all, a little rigour is not, in my opinion, a bad thing ". He denied by implication (conveniently forgetting his confidential dispatch to Young) that there was any policy of dismemberment abroad, and with (perhaps) sounder sense than he himself realized, remarked that the withdrawal of two or three thousand troops from Canada would scarcely be sufficient to destroy " those strong feelings of attachment " which united

[1] Macdonald to Rose, Feb. 5, 1870 : *M.P.*, Private letter book 13, p. 1022.
[2] Marindin (ed.), *Letters of Frederic Lord Blachford*, p. 278.
[3] Carnarvon to Macdonald, Feb. 10, 1870 : *Correspondence of Macdonald*, 125-26.
[4] *Hansard*, CXCIX, 193-213 (Feb. 14, 1870).

the two countries. Carnarvon had hinted that the withdrawal was perhaps influenced by " some misgiving of yourselves and your own future conduct, if you come into disagreeable relations with the United States ". Granville said that while he believed the Americans hoped to possess Canada, they did not expect to gain it by conquest ; but he added significantly that in any case " the presence of some two or three thousand red-coats . . . would rather excite them, as a red flag excites a bull, than exercise any deterrent or preventive influence ". And the fact that the Canadians had not sent an official protest against the withdrawals of 1869 enabled him to represent them as compliant—which he certainly knew they were not.[1]

The Government still stood to its guns. Cardwell's second year's estimates again showed a diminution of expenditure—amounting to more than £1,100,000 as against the previous year. He estimated the colonial garrisons for 1870–71 as aggregating only 23,941 men—almost entirely for the naval stations ; in 1868–69 the figure had been 49,650. There would now be 68 infantry battalions at home, as against 46 in 1868–69 ; 105 batteries of artillery, as against 96 ; 19 cavalry regiments, as against 16.[2] The opposition made no very fierce resistance ; Sir John Pakington regretted that the withdrawal was to be so complete, but did not commit himself too deeply ;[3] no other member of the Commons really joined issue with Cardwell on the colonial question.

The Imperial Government, however, was not so obdurate as not to temper the effect in Canada of the announcement of the withdrawal by intimating about the same time that, subject to arrangements being made to its own satisfaction, it would permit a detachment of regulars to participate in the proposed expedition to Red River. " I am very glad of this ", wrote Macdonald. " Even if the force does not go, the agreement of England to co-operate with us will be immensely satisfactory to us, and show that England has no intention of abandoning her colonies."[4] Lieutenant-General the Hon. James Lindsay arrived from England, to replace the dead Windham, with special instructions regarding the proposed withdrawal and the

---
[1] *Ibid.*, 213–21.
[2] *Ibid.*, 1158 ff. (March 3, 1870).
[3] *Ibid.*, 1190 ff.
[4] Macdonald to Rose, Feb. 23, 1870 : *Correspondence of Macdonald*, 127.

western enterprise. The ministry continued to hope that force would not be necessary; the French Catholic half-breeds of the North-West did not lack sympathy among the French Catholics of Quebec, and there was danger of trouble on the prairies having echoes nearer home. But the arrival of news of the judicial murder by Riel of Thomas Scott, an Ontario man who had opposed him, was a strong indication that only forcible dispossession of the insurgents could afford a satisfactory solution.

A serious Fenian scare in April added to the Dominion Government's worries. Their excellent intelligence service informed them that John O'Neill was determined to make an attack to secure his reputation against the attacks of opponents within his organization. In consequence, 6,600 volunteers were called out and the gunboats fitted for service;[1] these preparations led O'Neill to abandon his scheme for the moment.[2] But this alarm drew from Sir John Macdonald the most bitter condemnation of Imperial military policy that he ever penned. Seeing that Carnarvon might be useful, he answered his letter in the strongest terms:

"We are glad to know that we have in you a friend—I may almost say a friend in need—for we greatly distrust the men at the helm in England who cannot, I fear, be considered as appreciating the importance of maintaining the Empire as it is, intact.

"We indulge the belief here, however, that Messrs. Bright, Lowe, and Gladstone (shall I add Lord Granville ?) are not true exponents of the public opinion of England. We may perhaps be obliged to appeal from the Government to the people of England.

"The withdrawal of the troops from Canada is, I think with you, a most unwise and short-sighted proceeding. At this moment we are in daily expectation of a formidable Fenian invasion, unrepressed by the United States Government, and connived at by their subordinate officials. And we are at the same time called upon to send a military force to restore order in Rupert's Land. Her Majesty's Government have been kept fully informed of the constant threats from the Fenian body for the last five years, and they have been especially forewarned of the preparations for the present expected attack. And yet this is the time that they choose to withdraw every

---

[1] Young to Granville (confidential), April 9, 1870: *G,* 575 A, p. 30. Cf. the orders-in-council of April 9 and 11, and the Adjutant-General's report of April 8, in *C,* 184, pp. 165, 168, 172.

[2] Young to Granville (confidential), April 28, 1870: *G,* 575 A, p. 37.

soldier from us, and we are left to be the unaided victims of Irish discontent and American hostility, caused entirely by our being a portion of the Empire. We must, however, bear it as best we may, and we intend, with God's blessing, to keep our country, if we can, for the Queen against all comers."[1]

The tone was somewhat extravagant, and the letter was doubtless consciously designed to encourage Carnarvon in his agitation; but the circumstances of the day go far to justify and explain it.

Preparations for the Red River expedition were in train. General Lindsay's instructions specified that it should be undertaken by a regular detachment " not exceeding 200 Infantry and a small force of Artillery, in company with a larger body of Canadians "; and it was particularly laid down that the regulars should leave the Red River territory not later than the end of September.[2] On April 11 the Governor-General cabled the Colonial Office that Canada would accept the transfer of the territories at once if the movement of troops was settled upon, and that she would pay " any reasonable proportion " of the cost of the operation, " say three-fourths ".[3] In the course of the next month there was much bargaining between the two Governments, for the Imperial authorities made strict stipulations. Witness their telegram of April 23:

" Troops may advance on following conditions. First. If Rose is authorized to pay £300,000 [to the Hudson's Bay Company] at once and Her Majesty's Government is at liberty to make transfer before end of June. Second. If Her Majesty's Government pays only expense of British Troops not exceeding 250 and Canadian Government the rest, sending not less than 500 trained men. Third. Canada to accept decision of Her Majesty's Government on disputed points of Settlers Bill of Rights. Fourth. General Lindsay to be satisfied with Military arrangements.[4] "

Later it was agreed that the Imperial contingent should be increased, Canada still undertaking to pay three-fourths of the

---

[1] Macdonald to Carnarvon (private), April 14, 1870: *Correspondence of Macdonald*, 132–34.
[2] Rogers to Under-Sec. of State for War, March 23, 1870: copy, G, 569 A, p. 42.
[3] G, 575 A, p. 31 (secret).
[4] Holland, for Granville, to Young (confidential): G, 569 A, p. 67. Delegates from Red River had presented demands on behalf of the population there.

THE END OF THE OLD ORDER 239

whole cost.¹ On May 4–5, Young cabled that Rose would be instructed to pay the money and that the transfer might be made before the end of June; while arrangements had been made with the Red River delegates for the erection of the settlement into a full-fledged province.² On the 6th the Colonial Office replied that the troops might proceed.³

In Canada, Lindsay had been striking snags. He found the Canadian Government dilatory from the beginning.⁴ As late as the first week in May, they had made no arrangements for chartering steamers for the expedition, and they objected to his undertaking to do so. "The necessity for going twice to Ottawa to spur on the Authorities, and the difficulty towards the end of a busy session, of getting the Government to attend to my business . . . have prevented my reporting to you earlier", he wrote to Cardwell on May 27.⁵ The ministers, in point of fact, continued to the very end to hope that the expedition might not be necessary.⁶ However, and despite the fact that Sir John Macdonald was stricken down by illness on May 6, and that this led to fears that the French party might prevail in the Government, the movement took place; the first detachment reached the head of Lake Superior on May 25.

The difficulties of Anglo-Canadian co-operation, however, were not altogether over. The able Commander of the expeditionary force, Colonel Garnet Wolseley, after his return to England published in *Blackwood's*⁷ an anonymous account of

[1] Cable, Young to Granville, April 28: *G*, 575 A, p. 39. Answer, Rogers to Young, April 30: *G*, 569 A, p. 71.
[2] Cables, *G*, 575 A, pp. 40–42.
[3] Rogers to Young, *G*, 569 A, p. 23.
[4] Cf. Macdonald to Cartier, April 18: *M.P.*, Private letter book 14 (private).
[5] *C*, 1287, p. 439: published in *P.P.*, 1871, cd. 298, vol. XLVIII: Correspondence relative to the recent expedition to the Red River Settlement. Cf. report of Assistant Controller Irvine, *P.P.*, 1871, cd. 391, vol. XLVIII.
[6] Macdonald to Young (private), May 4: *M.P.*, Private letter book 14, p. 157.
[7] "Narrative of the Red River Expedition: by an Officer of the Expeditionary Force." Three articles, Dec., 1870–Feb., 1871. Apart from the fact that Wolseley was a previous contributor to *Blackwood's*, the authorship is indicated as follows: first, in Canada he was generally understood to be the writer (cf., e.g., Hamilton, J. C., *The Prairie Province*, Toronto, 1876, 129–31); secondly, the account of the operation in Wolseley's much later book, *The Story of a Soldier's Life*, is a mere paraphrase of this one, with the controversial material omitted. See particularly the story of his adventure at the Slave Falls. Wolseley was much abused for these articles in Canada, and it was alleged that he had been piqued by the failure of the Dominion Government to make him Lieutenant-Governor of Manitoba.

the operation which spared the Canadian Government and its agents no criticism. The English officers, it appears, thoroughly distrusted the Canadian politicians, and unpleasant rumours went the rounds:

". . . The Ottawa authorities had announced that the road from Thunder Bay to Shebandowan Lake [the first stage of the journey beyond Lake Superior] would be fit for traffic before the end of May; whereas by that date not more than thirty miles of it were finished, and many miles were still uncut through the primeval forest. A rumour got abroad among the regular troops that the Canadian authorities were not very anxious to hasten the operation, lest by doing so they might make it possible for the regulars to get back before the winter set in; and every one knew that the Dominion Ministry was most anxious that they should be kept at Fort Garry for at least a year."

On the other hand, as the Minister of Public Works was a French-Canadian and said to be " favourably inclined to Riel ", " men of a suspicious turn of mind began to say that the fact of there being no road ready for our advance was part and parcel of a political scheme whereby the departure of the Expedition might be stopped altogether ".[1]

Nevertheless, the enterprise was a complete—and bloodless —success. The force of 750 Canadians and 450 regulars reached Fort Garry on August 24, and Riel fled at its approach. Regulars and militia had worked together in a most friendly spirit, co-operating better than their Governments. The Canadians stayed to garrison Fort Garry, but the Imperial troops, most of whom belonged to the 1st battalion of the 60th Rifles, immediately took the back trail for the east.[2] It was certainly true that the Dominion Government would have been glad to see them remain in Manitoba; and Sir John Young concurred in the suggestion of the Roman Catholic prelate of the district that a detachment be left there during the winter. But the Colonial Secretary would have nothing to do with the scheme. He wrote:

" Bishop Taché's letter seems to imply that the continued presence of Imperial troops will be required to counterbalance Canadian in-

---

[1] *Blackwood's Magazine*, vol. CIX, p. 52.
[2] For the events of the expedition, see Huyshe, *The Red River Expedition*, and Wolseley's *Story of a Soldier's Life*, II.

fluence, and in some way to control the action of the provincial administration.

"But when the authority of the Dominion has been duly established in Manitoba, the responsibility for all internal measures will rest with the Colonial Government, and it appears to Her Majesty's Government that any attempt on their part indirectly to interfere with the local administration would be unjustifiable, and would by weakening the authority of the Dominion tend to produce those disorders which Bishop Taché apprehends."[1]

The argument was a sound one, though it probably did not tell the whole story of the Imperial Government's reluctance to have its troops remain in the west. The advent of autumn found the whole Imperial force back in eastern Canada. But their summer's work had been fruitful in the highest degree. A new province had been added to the Dominion; and Wolseley's brilliant march had practically ended the danger that the great plains would be lost to Canada.

In the meantime, the whole question of the garrison of Canada had again been argued between Ottawa and Westminster. Macdonald was absent from the Canadian councils during this period, but it may be doubted whether his presence would greatly have altered the Canadian position. As soon as the western expedition was on its way, a memorandum drawn up by Sir George Cartier was sent to London in answer to Granville's announcement of the complete withdrawal of the troops. It was a strong protest, based in part upon the uncertain western situation, and still more upon the fact that the Fenian Brotherhood, a body "organized, not against Canada, but against the Imperial government", was (contrary to the hopes expressed by Granville) still in full activity. The Dominion ministry urged that, if the Imperial policy were irrevocably determined upon in other respects, Quebec at least should continue to be occupied by regular troops from England. They reiterated that they were ready to proceed with the construction of fortifications; and they formally recorded their satisfaction at the assurance that Britain's obligations towards Canada in time of war remained unaltered, recalling in detail the exchange of sentiments on this point during the conferences of 1865.[2]

[1] Kimberley to Young (confidential), Aug. 30, 1870: G, 569 A, p. 106.
[2] Memorandum of May 19, 1870: Withdrawal Correspondence, p. 65.

This statement had barely started on its way towards London when an episode took place which had the melancholy effect of embittering the controversy. On May 25, 1870, John O'Neill attempted his long-threatened raid. It was the last throw of a desperate man, and only a fraction of the Fenian organization participated in it. The day before the attack, some 13,500 militia were called out and " in a very quiet and rapid manner " occupied all threatened points along the border.[1] The regular force in the country was already greatly reduced; but the Canadian military organization of 1870 was better able to stand on its own feet than that of 1866. When O'Neill's men crossed the border near Franklin, Vermont, they came under fire at once, and at once fled; the Fenian chief himself was arrested by a United States marshal. Another attack on May 27 had a similar result.[2] But this new aggression inevitably caused great excitement in Canada, and public attention was suddenly directed to the new Imperial military policy.

In the Canadian Press the raid produced a flood of attacks upon the United States for tolerating Fenianism, and only less bitter strictures upon Great Britain for her failure to induce the Americans to take active steps against it. The latter grew in intensity as news came of British official thanks to Washington for its enforcement of the neutrality laws, and of praise accorded the United States Government by English newspapers. The week after the raid, the Toronto *Weekly Globe* carried three leading articles attacking the United States, and two attacking Britain.[3] The Imperial Government's attitude towards the employment of its troops in the Red River expedition came in for its share of scorn; the conditions under which they served, as described by Granville to the House of Lords,[4] seemed to the *Globe* to smack more " of a Yankee ' dicker ' than of British statesmanship "; and one can appreciate its feelings when it found that *The Times* was justifying the use of Imperial troops in the west with the sententious reflection, " The British

---

[1] *Report on the State of the Militia . . . for . . . 1870*: S.P., 1871, no. 7, pp. 6–7; cf. Col. Robertson-Ross to Minister of Militia, May 25, 1870, in C, 184, p. 185. The information received from the intelligence service enabled these dispositions to be made in time.
[2] *Report on State of the Militia for 1870*, pp. 70–79.
[3] June 3.
[4] *Hansard*, CCI, 251–53 (May 5, 1870).

THE END OF THE OLD ORDER 243

Parliament is now called upon to intervene for the last time in the affairs of the American Continent ".[1]

The news of the raid had led Carnarvon to bring the question of the troops up once more in Parliament. Granville stated in reply to his questioning that orders had been sent to suspend the withdrawal process during the actual emergency, but no longer.[2] The *Globe* greeted this announcement with bitter sarcasm;[3] and a little later another debate, in which the aged Lord Russell violently assailed the colonial policy of the Gladstone ministry and protested against the evacuation of Quebec,[4] led it to complain of the unsatisfactory state of the colonial relationship in general.

" The Colonies are well content with their position—they gain great advantages from their connection with Britain . . . *but they want a clear understanding as to their duties on the one hand, and the obligations of the Mother Country on the other*. They want such a settlement as will put a stop to the insolent reproaches that are constantly coming to them from English Statesmen and writers that the Colonies are a burden to Great Britain, that they are useless to her, that they only cling to her in hope of favours—and that she would get quit of them to-morrow could she do so with decency."

Canada's special position, with her vast area and small population, adjacent to a powerful and acquisitive neighbour, placed her, in the opinion of the newspaper, "beyond the scope of the ordinary colonial argument ". " Is it expected ", it asked, " that on this handful of people shall be thrown the defence and development of this half-continent ? . . . And what could be more monstrous than the boasting avowal that every soldier is to be withdrawn from the Red River enterprize in the month of October coming ? Is it for Imperial purposes or local purposes that those great North-Western Territories are to be opened up to settlement ? "[5]

Unquestionably the views of the Canadian ministers were not very different from those of the *Globe*. Unquestionably also, they feared the influence of the great opposition journal, and sought to protect themselves against the accusation that they

---
[1] *Weekly Globe*, June 10, 1870.
[2] *Hansard*, CCI, 1462 ff. (May 27, 1870).
[3] *Weekly Globe*, June 17, 1870.
[4] *Hansard*, CCII, 451 ff. (June 20, 1870). See also Carnarvon's further attack on the withdrawal, *ibid.*, CCIII, 703 ff. (July 22).
[5] *Weekly Globe*, July 8, 1870.

had failed to urge the Canadian point of view upon the home Government.[1] Seeking to obtain a modification of the Imperial policy, they first besought the Governor-General to suspend the withdrawal beyond the actual duration of the raid; he refused, and the Colonial Office approved the refusal, but afterwards made the small concession of giving orders that the Rifle Brigade should not sail until the 60th returned from Red River.[2] The Dominion Government now had recourse to their old expedient in extremity; they decided to send a special mission to London. Alexander Campbell, the Postmaster-General, was instructed to proceed thither and confer with the Colonial Office on the withdrawal of the troops, the fortification question, the Fenian situation, and the vexed problem of the fisheries, which had caused much international friction since the abrogation of the Reciprocity Treaty.[3] He was "to endeavour to induce Her Majesty's Government to take prompt action" in these matters in accordance with the views of the Dominion ministry.

On reaching England, Campbell found his business delayed by a reorganization of the cabinet caused by the death of Lord Clarendon, the Foreign Secretary. Granville was appointed to the Foreign Office, and Lord Kimberley succeeded him at the Colonies. To Kimberley, then, Campbell made his representations in a series of interviews. He expressed "some anxiety" on the continued delay over the Fortification Guarantee Bill, and was informed that it was going before Parliament at once. On the question of "the withdrawal of the Imperial troops and the relations of Canada to the Empire", it is well perhaps to quote his report:

"I submitted . . . that when the Confederation of the several Provinces of British North America was suggested, it was agreed on all sides that it was a matter of both Imperial and Colonial Policy, that Canada felt assured in carrying out the scheme that it would have the advantage of the moral and material support of the Empire. We had undertaken the task, and so far, carried it

[1] Young to Granville (confidential), draft, June 7, 1870: G, 575 A, p. 54.
[2] Young to Granville (cable; confidential), June 8, 1870: *ibid.*, p. 59. Same to same, June 9, *ibid.*, p. 60. Rogers, for Granville, to Young (confidential), June 13: G, 569 A, p. 94. Same to same, June 17: Withdrawal Correspondence, p. 17.
[3] Young to Granville, June 9, June 11, July 6, 1870: Withdrawal Correspondence, pp. 24–25.

THE END OF THE OLD ORDER 245

out successfully, but at very considerable sacrifice, and a sacrifice that was likely to be continuous. There was a growing feeling in Canada of distrust in the disposition of the Imperial Government to give us that support to which we thought ourselves entitled. It was somewhat difficult to point out the exact grounds which had occasioned this feeling, but generally it proceeded from the tone adopted by public men, and particularly by members of the Government, in reference to Colonial and Canadian topics. . . .

"Lord Kimberley said that his attention had been called to the feeling of distrust to which I had referred, but that he thought nothing had been done by the British Government to afford any grounds for it. . . . The Government did not wish to interfere with the freedom of Canada's future, but so long as she chose to remain connected with the Empire, so long under all circumstances of foreign aggression was the Empire bound to maintain the Union, but in internal affairs it was the duty of Canada to protect herself.

"I said that we had for many years undertaken the maintenance of the internal peace of the country, but that we did not consider the Fenian invasion an internal trouble, but one proceeding from Imperial causes. . . . I urged that it would re-assure the public feeling in Canada very much if the garrison at Quebec were to be maintained: we did not ask this on account of the number of men which might be placed there, but because their presence would be to us a symbol of the sovereignty of the Empire. Quebec was an Imperial fortress, and the maintenance of the garrison of Her Majesty's troops there would be looked upon as indicating the determination in England to maintain the existing relations, and would have the most useful effect on public feeling in Canada. . . . I added that the French-Canadian population regarded with particular disfavour the withdrawal of the troops. . . .

"Lord Kimberley said that the matter had been repeatedly and very fully considered, and that the decision that had been arrived at was not likely, he thought, to be departed from, but my representations should be considered."[1]

The Canadian Government, indeed, found it difficult to believe that the regulars were really to leave Quebec, which had been an Imperial fortress since 1759. They were slow in responding to General Lindsay's suggestions connected with the details of withdrawal and the necessary replacement of the Queen's troops by some permanent Canadian force. On June 3 he was informed that:

[1] Campbell's report to the Governor-General, Sept. 10, 1870: *ibid.*, pp. 26–29.

"... the Dominion Government expect, almost as a certainty, that on the representations made ... the withdrawal of the troops, if it should take place, will not be on the scale ... at first contemplated, and that Quebec will be permanently garrisoned by Her Majesty's regular troops. If the expectations of the Dominion Government are realized, of which they have little doubt, with regard to the *only partial* withdrawal of the troops, and the establishment of a permanent garrison at Quebec, a great part of the instructions given to the Lieut. General Commanding, will have to be postponed for future consideration and action."[1]

These hopes were utterly disappointed. One of Granville's last acts at the Colonial Office had been to send a swift reply to Cartier's memorandum, refusing to consider a permanent Imperial occupation of Quebec.[2] Kimberley's dispatch in answer to Campbell's representations was to the same effect.[3] Both spoke as though allowing one battalion of foot and one battery of artillery to remain at Quebec over the winter of 1870–71 were a considerable concession ; yet this arrangement had been contemplated in Granville's original dispatch of the previous February.[4] The accumulated difficulties of the year 1870, and the entreaties of the Dominion Government that even a small force should be left at Quebec, not so much for its military value as for its importance as a symbol of Imperial unity, had in fact failed to alter the policy of the Gladstone ministry in any essential. Under these circumstances an attempt which has been made at representing the decision not to remove the entire force during 1870 as evidence of the devotion of that ministry to the Imperial idea[5] seems a trifle forced.

Inevitably, the effect of this policy upon Canadian public opinion was not in the direction of breeding increased confidence in the Imperial Government. When the autumn of 1870 finally found only one regular battalion left in central Canada, the *Globe*, while more temperate now than at the height of the Fenian excitement, made the situation the text for a severe

[1] Futvoye (Deputy Min. of Mil.) to Gov.-Gen.'s military secretary, June 3, 1870 : *ibid.*, pp. 74–75.
[2] Granville to Young, June 23, 1870 : *ibid.*, p. 18.
[3] Kimberley to Young, July 27, 1870 : *ibid.*, pp. 18–19.
[4] If the wording of Granville's dispatch leaves any doubt, it seems resolved by the instructions to Lindsay, which mention " the Regiment which is to remain at Quebec during the winter " : Rogers to Under-Sec. of State for War, March 23, 1870 : G, 569 A, p. 42.
[5] Knaplund, *Gladstone and Britain's Imperial Policy*, 138.

condemnation of the English Liberals. It was glad to find the *Daily News*, the reputed organ of Gladstone's Government, attacking those who accused that Government of anti-colonialism; but it pointed out that there were grounds for the accusation.

" The fact remains that without a broad declaration of an anti-Colonial policy, there are among the members of the present Government very influential persons who are at heart opposed to the Colonial connection, and who, by their policy, have actually endangered that connection. . . .

" The *Daily News* maintains that Mr. Gladstone and his colleagues have done all that was needed to maintain the colonial connection. We do not think that the withdrawal of all the troops in Canada, with the exception of one regiment, was the act of men friendly to the colonial connexion. Without injury to the British taxpayer, but with great service to the connection two or three thousand men might have been left to garrison the chief cities of the North American Colonies. We do not say that this is a necessity. We can certainly dispense with the troops; but it would have been desirable, as a concession much desired by the people of this country, and as a means of connecting more closely the Dominion with the Mother Country. . . . Mr. Gladstone once said in the House of Commons that he desired to adopt a policy which would be acceptable whether the Colonies became independent or not. That is not the policy which is desired by the people of this country. We wish the Imperial authorities to say that they value the connection; that they are averse to see it broken up, and that they are willing to do everything in their power to prevent it."[1]

During the summer, however, events on the continent of Europe had lessened the possibility of a concession to Canadian feeling. Though there had been alarming tension between France and Prussia since 1866, the outbreak of war at the middle of July came with startling suddenness. Once more, England trembled for her own safety—(" No one can tell what we may not be forced into ", wrote the Queen to Gladstone)[2]—and the alarm increased when *The Times* published the secret French proposals for the annexation of Belgium, made to Prussia three years before and now communicated to the newspaper by Bismarck. The Government was now forced to regret

---
[1] *Weekly Globe*, Oct. 14, 1870.
[2] On July 16: *Letters of Queen Victoria*, second series II, 37.

its reduction in the total strength of the army. Plans were made for sending an expeditionary force to defend Belgian neutrality; 20,000 additional men were hastily voted for the army, and a vote of credit of £2,000,000 was obtained from Parliament.[1]

As the war passed to its swift conclusion, and Prussian efficiency triumphed once more, England saw only multiplied reasons for looking to her defences. The panic that had begun in fear of French designs on Belgium continued after France's downfall from fear of her opponent. Sir William Butler has left an animated description of those days:

" There had never been so many armies in England. There was a new army, and there was an old army; there was an army o militia, an army of volunteers, and an army of reserve; there were armies on horse, on foot, and on paper. . . .

" It was a time when everybody had something to do with military matters, everybody on the social ladder, from the Prime Minister on the topmost round to the mob-mover on the lowest.

" Committees controlled the army, Departments dressed it, Radicals railed at it, Liberals lectured upon it, Conservatives condemned it, Peers wrote pamphlets upon it, Dukes denounced it, Princes paraded it, and every member of Parliament who could put together half a dozen words with tolerable grammatical fluency had something to say about it."[2]

The inexorable development of Bismarck's policy from 1864 to 1870, and its complete and terrible success, left Englishmen wondering whether it had yet reached its final stage. " Few will deny ", wrote a nameless author in *Macmillan's* of October, 1870, " that the Danish war might have been stopped by firm action on our part; we scolded; we did not act, because we could not, we were not ready. From that Danish war flowed the Austrian war. . . . From the Austrian war flowed the French war. For what follows the French war Are we ready ? " And in the following May *Blackwood's* published a work of fantasy entitled *The Battle of Dorking: Reminiscences of a Volunteer*.[3] It represented the sad reflections, set down in the twentieth century, of an Englishman who had fought in the

[1] *Ibid.*, 46–47, 53–54; Biddulph, *Lord Cardwell at the War Office*, 62–65.
[2] *The Wild North Land*, 1–2.
[3] Vol. CIX, pp. 539–72; later published in separate form. The author appears to have been Col. Chesney, a frequent contributor to various magazines on military topics.

THE END OF THE OLD ORDER 249

ranks of the half-trained volunteers who went down to defeat before the disciplined legions of Germany when the latter invaded Britain. Some of the causes of the *débâcle* were thus outlined :

" First, the rising in India drew away a part of our small army ; then came the difficulty with America, which had been threatening for years, and we sent off ten thousand men [!] to defend Canada—a handful which did not go far to strengthen the real defences of that country, but formed an irresistible temptation to the Americans to try and take them prisoners. . . . The fleet was scattered abroad : some ships to guard the West Indies, others to check privateering in the China seas, and a large part to try and protect our colonies on the Northern Pacific coast of America, where, with incredible folly, we continued to retain possessions which we could not possibly defend. America was not the great power forty years ago that it is now ; but for us to try and hold territory on her shores which could only be reached by sailing round the Horn, was as absurd as if she had attempted to take the Isle of Man before the independence of Ireland. We see this plainly enough now, but we were all blind then."

The vigour with which these prophecies were canvassed demonstrated the reality of the British public's apprehensions.[1] And with such opinions circulating widely, there was less hope than ever of a reversal of the new colonial military policy. The domestic defence of Britain was the great problem of the moment ; and Cardwell's concentration scheme was pushed to completion without deference to the criticisms of it which made themselves heard both at home and in the colonies.

Nevertheless, these criticisms served an eminently useful purpose. Echoing the universal shout of protest from beyond the seas, the agitation in England against the Liberal colonial policy had attained respectable proportions. In the House of Commons, it is true, there was little or no opposition ; but in the Lords, Carnarvon assailed the new arrangements bitterly and repeatedly, and Russell brought to the support of the colonial viewpoint the prestige of an ex-Prime Minister.[2] General Sir William Denison, a veteran colonial governor, took

---

[1] For their reception, see *Annual Register*, 1871, Part I, p. 308.
[2] See above, pp. 235, 243. For Russell's views, see his *Recollections and Suggestions*, 198–204 ; cf. Carnarvon's letter to him, Jan. 16, 1875, in Gooch, G. P. (ed.), *The Later Correspondence of Lord John Russell*, London, 1925, II, 378.

the field against what he described as an attempt " to isolate ourselves from our relations, and to inclose ourselves within the narrow limits of our own native land ".[1] The stir caused by the proposal for a colonial protest conference in London[2] likewise called attention to the situation and probably did some good. As the *Montreal Gazette* put it, the object of this movement had been rather to urge the Imperial authorities to leave the Empire alone than anything else. " It was to prevent untoward movement on the part of the present Imperial Government, that the colonists felt called upon to act. In this they have been entirely successful ".[3]

In the English Press, the element hostile to the new policy got a fair hearing. *The Times* published a series of letters in this vein written by Sir John Rose over the signature " Colonist "[4] (though they had no effect on the views of *The Times* itself).[5] *Blackwood's* opened its pages to a fierce assault on Granville, based on his attitude to Canada at the time of the Fenian raid, and quoting liberally from the *Globe*.[6] That the various criticisms had not been without effect seems indicated by the attitude of that very moderate journal, the *Spectator*, at the time of Granville's translation from the Colonial to the Foreign Office. His colonial administration, it declared, had been " utterly bad—so bad as to imperil the Empire ; but it has been bad because based on a wrong idea, not bad because of any incapacity in the Secretary himself. On the contrary, he has been most firm in an injurious course, most adroit in securing the wrong end, most lucid in his exposition of erroneous facts, most dignified in his display of contempt for our most valuable friends ".[7]

It had, in fact, been demonstrated that Imperial feeling, in addition to being so strong in the colonies, was not without some strength at home, and that an anti-colonial policy might not be without its risks. The lesson had its effect. We have

---

[1] *Two Lectures on Colonization*, 18.   [2] See above, pp. 223-4.
[3] *Montreal Gazette*, Feb. 11, 1870.
[4] *The Times*, Jan. 18, 19, 20, 1870. See Long, " Sir John Rose and the . . . Canadian High Commissionership ", *C.H.R.*, XII, and *Montreal Gazette*, Feb. 4, 1870.
[5] *The Times*, Jan. 18, 1870 (leading article).
[6] " Canada : the Fenian Raid and the Colonial Office," *Blackwood's*, Oct., 1870 ; vol. CVIII.
[7] *Spectator*, July 2, 1870.

THE END OF THE OLD ORDER

seen that Granville had a definite inclination towards a policy of gradual dismemberment of the Empire—an inclination which seems to have been pretty widely known or suspected. Yet in the course of the controversy the Gladstone ministry, despite its formidable personnel of separatists, and in the very act of putting an end to one of the chief physical manifestations of the unity of the Empire, found itself obliged to disavow this policy publicly and repeatedly, and to make declarations of allegiance to the Imperial tie.

In Canada, during 1870, the transfer of Imperial property to the Dominion had accompanied the withdrawal of troops. The buildings and fortifications formerly occupied by the regulars at Toronto, Kingston, Isle aux Noix and Ottawa were handed over,[1] and by the end of September the little force remaining in what had been the Province of Canada was concentrated at Quebec. A request, fostered by Lindsay, that two companies might be stationed during the winter at Ottawa, the capital city, had met with a curt refusal from Cardwell.[2] During the same months an arrangement was gradually arrived at for the purchase by Canada of a great miscellany of reserve military stores,[3] in addition to those handed over to her as gifts.

Two points arising during these negotiations suggest the desire of the British Government to be quit of immediate responsibility for the future defensive organization of Canada. General Lindsay in one of his memoranda had made reference to the need of consideration for the naval side of Canadian defence. This led the militia department to rejoin that Cardwell in his famous dispatch of June 17, 1865, had stated that it would as a matter of course be the duty of the Imperial Government to undertake the naval defence of the colony.[4] When Cardwell heard this, he lost no time in writing to Lindsay as follows:

". . . Whatever obligations that despatch acknowledges on the part of the Imperial Government, it was not intended to exonerate the Government of the Dominion from any responsibility for taking

---

[1] See the various reports of Col. Wily to the Minister of Militia, Withdrawal Correspondence, pp. 80–109.
[2] Lugard to Lindsay, May 26, 1870: *ibid.*, p. 39.
[3] See the correspondence on the subject in *ibid.*, pp. 22, 30, 42–52, 81–88, 94, 110–12.
[4] Futvoye to Gov.-Gen.'s military secretary, June 3, 1870: *ibid.*, p. 74.

a share in its own naval defence, either by carrying into effect the provisions of the Colonial Naval Defence Act, or otherwise. On the contrary, all the assurances given in the Despatch on the part of the Imperial Government, were given, as Sir George Cartier observes in his Minute of the 19th May :—

" 'On the reciprocal assurance given by the Canadian Ministers, then in London, that Canada was ready to devote all her resources, both in men and money, to the maintenance of her connection with the Mother Country.' "[1]

The other point arose in connexion with Canada's purchase of the reserve of Snider rifles then in the Dominion. The local Government suggested that, in the event of an improved rifle being adopted, they should be allowed to receive from the Imperial stores any number of the new arm in return for the same number of Sniders, " on payment of any difference in value, and on condition that the rifles to be exchanged are quite new ".[2] Cardwell refused to countenance any such arrangement.[3] It is clear that he was determined that henceforth no shadow of responsibility for the equipment of Canadian forces would fall upon the War Office.

In the spring of 1871, with only a remnant of Imperial forces left in the Dominion, the Canadian Government made a last attempt at influencing the policy of the Gladstone ministry;[4] but it had no more useful result than to postpone the final withdrawal to the late autumn of the year. In the course of 1871 the Imperial properties in the province of New Brunswick were handed over;[5] and as winter drew on, the time came to take over the historic establishment at Quebec, with its 181 guns and its three new forts at Lévis, as yet unarmed.[6] As these preparations were being made, news came of a final feeble attempt by John O'Neill to disturb the peace of Canada. He had made an attack on a Hudson's Bay post on the Manitoba

[1] Lugard to Lindsay, Sept. 24, 1870 : *ibid*, p. 60.
[2] Deputy Controller to Lt.-Gen. commanding, July 21, 1870 : *ibid.*, p. 94.
[3] Kimberley to Lisgar, Jan. 9, 1871 : *ibid.*, p. 22.
[4] Lisgar to Kimberley, April 20, 1871 : *G, To Secretary of State, 1870*, p. 140. I have failed to find the text of the memorandum accompanying this dispatch; and the Historical Section of the Canadian General Staff have kindly searched for it, but likewise without result. It may perhaps be assumed that the Canadian ministers in it made further representations for delay.
[5] *Report on State of the Militia for 1871* (S.P., 1872, no. 8), pp. 208–09.
[6] One of the three, still unfinished, was retained temporarily by the Royal Engineers. *Ibid.*, p. 209.

THE END OF THE OLD ORDER

border, but had been arrested by United States forces before he could advance further. It was decided to reinforce the weak garrison of Fort Garry; but this time it was a purely Canadian force, 200 strong, that took the arduous trail that Wolseley had blazed. They set out on the edge of winter, and after an extremely difficult yet rapid march entered Fort Garry on November 18.[1] The success with which this little enterprise was carried through seemed to afford encouragement for the future of the Canadian forces, now left at last without the aid and support which for more than a century they had received from the Imperial army.

For while the second Red River expedition was toiling across the frostbound wilderness, the final act in the story of Quebec as an Imperial fortress had been played out. The old city said good-bye to the English soldiers with no feigned regret. It was peculiarly fitting that the last Imperial troops to occupy the citadel should have been a battalion (the First) of the 60th Rifles; for not only had that celebrated regiment been raised in the old American Colonies, but it had been with Wolfe in 1759, and thus had formed a part of the first British force to occupy Quebec. It was fitting, too, that units of those ubiquitous corps, the Royal Engineers and the Royal Artillery, should have remained to the last.

On the afternoon of November 11, 1871, the troops marched out for the last time from the citadel above Cape Diamond. To the strains of *Good-bye, Sweetheart, Good-bye* and *Auld Lang Syne*, the column swung through the narrow streets to St. Andrew's Wharf. There, amid the good wishes and regrets of a great crowd which had assembled to see the last of them, the soldiers embarked on the transport *Orontes*, which was to bear them to Halifax; and as the trooper dropped down the great river, an era in the history of Canada came to an end.[2]

That was a sad day for Quebec; one newspaper[3] showed its feelings by displaying on its premises the British flag at half-mast. Yet by that time the Dominion in general had become resigned to the loss of the troops, and the final episode did not

---

[1] Stacey, "The Second Red River Expedition, 1871," *C.D.Q.*, VIII.
[2] Toronto *Leader*, Nov. 13, 1871; *Weekly Globe*, Nov. 24; *Canadian Illustrated News*, Nov. 25. Cf. Butler, *Annals of the King's Royal Rifle Corps*, III, 287.
[3] The *Mercury*: *Leader*, Nov. 13.

attract as much attention as might have been expected. The sentiments of the Toronto *Leader* were probably fairly typical :

" In Canada all sorts of calamities were expected to follow the withdrawal of the Imperial troops, but we can say that the loss—if loss it can be called—has not been felt by any section of the country. We may regret that this link of attachment is broken, but never, never will Canadians say that our allegiance is a whit endangered because of the departure of the Imperial soldiers."[1]

Certainly no great apprehension of catastrophe resulting from the absence of troops was evidenced in the measures taken by the Dominion to replace the Imperial garrisons. The fact is that (as we have clearly seen in the Red River negotiations and in the request for a permanent garrison at Quebec) the Dominion Government had valued the presence of the Queen's soldiers less as a purely military resource than as a visible imperial link—a notice to the world in general, and the United States in particular, that Great Britain stood behind Canada. And by the end of 1871 even this was a matter of less immediate importance than before ; for Canada's hold on the great west was now fairly secure, and the signing of the Treaty of Washington, providing for the peaceable settlement of the *Alabama* question, had gone far to resolve the difficulties that had beclouded the relations of Great Britain and the United States for so many years. The Canadian people, as little disposed as ever to think of defensive preparation in time of peace, would not have consented to burden themselves with the upkeep of a regular army, and John A. Macdonald wrote to several correspondents that no such project was entertained.[2] With the confidence typical of a thoroughly unmilitary people, the *Globe* declared : " Canadians can dispense with a standing army because they possess the best possible constituents for a defensive force in themselves. The finest soldiers are men whose own stake and interest in the conflict impel them to respond to a call to arms."[3]

In accordance with such views, the Government put on permanent duty only the very smallest number of men that could possibly exercise supervision over the forts and arma-

---
[1] *Leader*, Nov. 16, 1871.
[2] e.g., to Wm. Cayley, Oct., 28, 1870 : *M.P.*, Private letter book 14, p. 338.
[3] *Weekly Globe*, Aug. 26, 1870.

ments newly committed to its charge, and it waited until the last moment to do so. Only on October 21, 1871, did the *Gazette* publish organization orders for two small batteries of garrison artillery, to amount together to not more than 240 gunners.[1] A considerable period was to elapse before the declining efficiency of the militia brought the Canadian authorities to the point of realizing that the presence of some body of regular troops was necessary to the health of the citizen force;[2] and it was longer before the militia developed into a homogeneous, self-dependent army. This, however, is not the place to relate its history.

The ultimate fate of the famous Jervois fortification scheme must be briefly noticed. That (as Granville suspected) the Dominion Government had not been greatly devoted to it, is certainly true;[3] but the ministry went on with the arrangements in order, presumably, to indicate that Canada was ready to fulfil her part of the joint defensive scheme and so give Britain no excuse for withdrawing her aid. But after the Treaty of Washington the apparent need for the fortifications had largely disappeared. Ultimately, in 1873, an arrangement was arrived at whereby the Imperial guarantee for a fortification loan was converted into one for a transcontinental railway, the original sum being augmented by £2,500,000 in compensation for Britain's failure to obtain from the United States satisfaction for the damage inflicted on Canada by the Fenian raids.[4] Montreal is unfortified to this day, and likely to remain so.

. . . .

It seems curious that historians of the British Empire have not made more of the revolution—for such it was—wrought by Cardwell and his colleagues in its military arrangements. The colonial garrison system, which went back to the days of the

---

[1] *Ibid.*, Oct. 27, 1871.
[2] This is pointed out in *Memorandum on the Militia System of Canada*, Ottawa, 1873, by Lt.-Col. Fletcher, military secretary to the Governor-General; and Sir John Macdonald had become fully aware of it by 1878: Pope, *Correspondence*, 239-42 (Macdonald to Northcote, May 1, 1878).
[3] See the very interesting letter, Macdonald to Lisgar, Jan. 22, 1872 (" most private and confidential "): *M.P.*, private letter book 17, p. 112.
[4] See *P.P.*, 1872, cd. 539, vol. XLIII, continued in the same volume in cd. 541 and cd. 557; and the further continuation in *P.P.*, 1873, vol. XLIX, cds. 702, 750 and 774. The Bill authorizing the guarantee is no. 159 in *P.P.*, 1873, vol. I.

Seven Years' War and which had been so vastly extended after the Napoleonic Wars that only a small proportion of the army paid by the British taxpayer was ever seen in the United Kingdom, was ended almost at a stroke during the years 1869-71. The alleviation of the mother country's military burdens in respect of colonies possessing large powers of self-government was, we have seen, no new idea; it had been a point of major concern with the very Colonial Secretary who gave responsible government to Canada, and successive administrations thereafter, without distinction of party, had striven to effect it. The end which they pursued unsuccessfully for twenty years Cardwell attained in three; though he aroused much ill-will in the process.

From the self-governing colonies about the globe, the troops came home. The Canadian withdrawal was only a part of Cardwell's project, though a most important part. The little colony of Newfoundland next door lost its 300 men, despite the almost piteous pleadings of its Government and legislature.[1] New Zealand, we have remarked, relinquished its last regiment amid heartburnings. The Australian colonies, which had been accustomed to pay for the maintenance of imperial troops, were prepared to continue to do so if assured that the troops would remain there permanently, and not be withdrawn to meet emergencies elsewhere; the assurance was not forthcoming, and from there too the redcoats sailed for home.[2] At the Cape, very large reductions were effected, responsible government being almost forced upon an unenthusiastic people at the same time.[3] By 1873, the Colonial Office could boast that in the colonies possessing responsible government there was no Imperial expenditure except for purely Imperial purposes.[4] The Cardwell broom had swept clean; and the work was not destined to be undone.

To the Imperial military system the value of the achievement was incalculable. Enlistment in the British Army ceased to

---

[1] See copies of the pertinent correspondence in *G*, 569 A, pp. 3-8; and cf. Toronto *Weekly Globe*, April 22, 1870.
[2] Rusden, *History of Australia*, III, 274-75.
[3] *P.P.*, 1870, cds. 181, 181—I and 181—II, vol. XLIX, and 1871, cd. 459, vol. XLVII (Correspondence respecting the affairs of the Cape of Good Hope). See Theal, *History of South Africa from 1795 to 1872*, IV, 86-92, 134-49.
[4] *Hansard*, CCXIV, 1526-30; speech of E. H. Knatchbull-Hugessen, March 7, 1873.

THE END OF THE OLD ORDER

be equivalent to a sentence of transportation. Since Cardwell's time the British soldier has put in approximately half his service in the United Kingdom; generally speaking, each infantry regiment has a battalion at home and a battalion abroad. With the popularity of the service thus enhanced, the short-service system was made possible, and short service in its turn permitted the formation of a proper reserve. At the same time, the concentration of battalions at home not only increased the security of the heart of the Empire—on which, in the last analysis, the safety of the colonies likewise depended—but it also made it possible to dispatch from England to any threatened point, at short notice and without straining the organization, a respectable expeditionary force. The ease with which, in the last decades of the nineteenth century, strong armaments were rapidly sent to the Sudan, was in notable contrast to the painful process of collecting a striking force for the Crimea in 1854.

It was primarily from the viewpoint of this improved military efficiency that Cardwell regarded his colonial projects; but their success had large consequences in other directions. We have seen the determined resistance of the colonies to the removal of the troops, and the irritation aroused by the brusqueness with which Granville enunciated the new policy. It seems clear that the thing might have been far more tactfully done; it is difficult, for instance, to see why one battalion should not have been allowed to remain a few years longer at Quebec, out of deference to Canadian feeling. It has been remarked that the motives of the Gladstone ministry's colonial policy are not entirely obvious. Yet the fact remains that, despite this uncertainty and despite all local vexations, the abolition of the colonial garrisons proved in the end, past all peradventure, an invaluable boon to the unity of the Empire.

Briefly, it put an end to the one concrete grievance which the British taxpayer and his representatives in Parliament could present against the overseas empire; and the removal of that grievance infinitely strengthened the whole Imperial structure. We have observed the strength of anti-colonial opinion in England through a great part of the nineteenth century, and have seen that the separatists, in season and out of season, urged one pre-eminent argument against the colonial connexion : the fact that the colonies were a source of very tangible expense to the mother country, whereas there was no evidence that they brought her any tangible utilitarian advantage which she could not have obtained from them had they been independent countries. No other weapon in the armoury of the anti-imperialists had a fraction of the effectiveness of this one. More than £4,000,000 for colonial expenditure in the annual British budget of the 'sixties—£1,250,000 for the Dominion of Canada alone in the first year of its existence— these were ineluctable facts ; and almost the whole of this expenditure was for military defence. The Cardwell policy practically wiped out these charges, except for those that could definitely be claimed as serving purposes imperial rather than local, and essential to the interests of England and her commerce ; and in so doing it cut the ground from under the feet of the Little Englanders.[1]

It was not altogether a coincidence that the same years that saw the end of the colonial garrison system saw also the beginning of the decline of anti-imperialism in England, the beginning of the rise of a new pride of empire which was soon to carry all before it. Other forces, it is true, were at work to produce these results. Imperialism had never died out in England, as the considerable protests made against the harsh appearance of the withdrawals in 1870 demonstrated. Public dissatisfaction with the supposedly anti-colonial policy of the Gladstone ministry was, apparently, sufficiently widespread to impress that matchless opportunist, Benjamin Disraeli—he of the " colonial deadweights which *we do not govern* "—with the belief that it might be turned to account ; and in 1872, in his famous Crystal Palace speech,[2] he suddenly appeared as the champion of the liberal Imperial spirit which those protests represented. A few months later, the poet laureate voiced similar sentiments in verses which had their origin in a more than usually brutal utterance of *The Times*[3] with respect to Canada :

[1] cf. *The Times*, Oct. 25, 1872 : ". . . the military expenditure on the Colonies proper is now less than a million sterling. . . . Contrasting this with the frightful sums previously lavished, we may congratulate the country on being in the fair way of removing the chief, if not the only, difficulty which besets the maintenance of a Colonial Empire."

[2] June 24 : Kebbel, *Selected Speeches of . . . the Earl of Beaconsfield*, II, 523-35.   [3] Leading article of Oct. 30, 1872.

THE END OF THE OLD ORDER

> "That true North, whereof we lately heard
> A strain to shame us ' keep you to yourselves ;
> So loyal is too costly ! friends—your love
> Is but a burthen : loose the bond, and go.'
> Is this the tone of empire ? here the faith
> That made us rulers ? . . .
>   The loyal to their crown
> Are loyal to their own far sons, who love
> Our ocean-empire with her boundless homes
> For ever-broadening England, and her throne
> In our vast Orient, and one isle, one isle,
> That knows not her own greatness : if she knows
> And dreads it we are fall'n."

Nevertheless, it may be questioned whether, without the effect of the withdrawals themselves, this spirit could have made the steady progress which it did make from this time onwards. When once the colonies could no longer be effectively represented (as Goldwin Smith had represented them in 1862) as " parasites ", clinging round the trunk of the English oak and " feeding upon its life " ; when once money from the slim purses of English taxpayers had ceased to be poured out for strictly colonial purposes—the way was open for the new sentiment to move freely and generously. By 1872 this state of things had in fact been brought about by Cardwell and his colleagues. Paradoxes are dangerous ; but one is tempted to say that it was those very " anti-imperial " acts with which the Conservative leader taxed the Liberals[1] that made Imperialism a safe horse for Disraeli himself to ride, and that the fact that there were no longer any grounds for plausible allegation of an unfortunate connexion between colonial loyalty and the English tax-rate made it far easier for an Englishman to thrill to Tennyson's elevated strain.

And indeed the ultimate adoption, in one fashion or another, of the policy which Cardwell put into effect with so little ceremony in 1869 and 1870 had long been inevitable. The colonial military expenditure had been a sore point with parliamentarians of divers schools for a generation and more ; no other issue joined together so many politicians whom the dubious divinities that govern Westminster had put asunder. The

---

[1] It must be observed that Disraeli was careful not to specify these acts, or commit the Conservatives to a reversal of the Liberals' military policy.

point needs no elaboration. The radical anti-imperialist Cobden found himself, on this matter, agreeing with the liberal imperialists, Molesworth and Adderley ; the democratic Bright stood for once shoulder to shoulder with Robert Lowe, that inveterate hater of popular government. It is perhaps a matter for wonder that the demand was so long resisted.

The demand, after all, was essentially a just one. Successive Governments in Britain were doubtless right in maintaining that it was not feasible to apply to all the colonies one uniform rule ; that it was proper that where (as in the case of Canada) a colony's membership in the Empire exposed it to special risk, it should be considered as entitled to special Imperial consideration ; nevertheless, it is abundantly clear that, in the political development of the colonies, the assumption of responsibility lagged woefully behind the assertion of privilege. When it was a matter of extending their legislative independence, they proved prompt and daring innovators ; but when the mother country sought to prevail upon them to take up the burdens of free governments as well as their rights, they clung stubbornly to the conservative position, unwilling to have the old imperial system tampered with or any new precedent established. On the question of military responsibility their attitude was one of passive resistance ; their history during the first decades of responsible government is the tale of one long rearguard action against successive attempts of the Imperial authority to shift to their shoulders some portion of its own heavy defensive burdens.

This resistance was not merely selfish. It proceeded in great part from a genuine lack of conviction, in the minds of the people of these unmilitary communities, of the need for the maintenance of an expensive military organization in time of peace. Canada, at least, valued the presence of Imperial forces less as a reinforcement to her immediate military strength than as a political advantage—a visible symbol of Imperial unity in an age of doubt, and an intimation to the world at large that to attack Canada was to attack Great Britain. It was largely from fear that the final withdrawal would be interpreted in other countries as evidence of a desire on Britain's part to terminate this relationship that Canada resisted the proposal with such resolution.

THE END OF THE OLD ORDER

Nevertheless, though there might be little sense in expecting Canada to keep up at her own expense armaments on a scale drawn to meet the requirements of English military opinion—requirements which the people of the colony could not have been convinced were justified—there was equally little in burdening the English taxpayer with Canadian defences conceived upon a scale which Canadians themselves did not regard as necessary. The most sensible plan was to ordain that in time of peace each unit of the Empire should maintain its own military organization at its own charges, keeping up as much or as little as its convictions dictated; each Government to pay its own piper and call its own tune. This was, in effect, just what Cardwell did. The scheme was not an ideal solution for the strictly military problem of Imperial defence, but it was politically just. When the first irritation in the colonies had died away, it left no part of the Empire nursing against any other part a grievance arising from Imperial defensive arrangements; and thus it paved the way for the advance of that generous spirit of Imperial confidence and co-operation which was itself to be the Empire's stoutest stay in its hour of trial.

By 1870 any idea of the possibility of Imperial troops being used to coerce the colony had passed so completely out of the minds of the people of Canada that they could have no feeling but regret at the soldiers' departure. The redcoats had been, in general, popular with all classes; and in the upper ranks, particularly, the military officers had been welcome ornaments of the exiguous society of the small colonial cities of those days. Not a few of them had married Canadian wives. The removal of the garrisons snapped a tie that had contributed to the social unity of the Empire; for each British regiment had been a little section of the mother country set down on a distant shore. Yet when one considers how long the troops had been a familiar and agreeable feature of Canadian life, it is curious how little difference their departure made. They went, and Canada was sorry; but she was soon reconciled to their absence.

The "colonial" period of Canadian history was ending; a period of larger national development lay ahead. And at this moment the Imperial army, to which Canada had owed so much in the epoch that was drawing to a close, passed quietly out of her scheme of things. Indeed, its work in British North America was done. The little colonies which it had shielded in their weakness had grown with time into a continental state; and the destiny of the young Dominion lay in its own hands, and in the secret will of God.

.   .   .   .

Cardwell's work closed another chapter in the history of the difficult question of Imperial defence. To say that it solved that problem would be to make a false claim; no completely satisfactory solution has yet been found. But it was Cardwell's achievement to abolish the most immediately troublesome aspect of it—the burden of taxation imposed upon the mother country by the colonial garrisons. In doing so he did a real service to the cause of Imperial unity (whether he and his colleagues of the Gladstone ministry fully realized it or not); and it can scarcely be doubted that the defensive position of the Empire as a whole was much improved by the reform of the British Army to which he considered the recall of the colonial detachments a necessary preliminary. Other questions remained to be faced by later administrators. In particular, the question of a contribution by the self-governing colonies to naval defence (though Cardwell himself had not neglected it) was not grappled with until the twentieth century.

We have remarked at some length upon the probable contribution of the abolition of the colonial garrisons to the growth of a freer imperial association and a new Imperial enthusiasm. That new spirit worked more and more strongly as Queen Victoria's long reign drew towards its close; and before the Queen died events had occurred which would have astonished the men of 1860—for the colonies, which once had leaned so heavily upon the mother country, and had been reviled as parasites upon her resources, were freely sending contingents of formidable fighters to augment her armies struggling in South Africa.

A more terrible test of the Imperial tie was soon to come. Nobody, at midsummer of 1914, could have predicted that, four years later, the Dominion of Canada would have raised more than half a million soldiers; that they would have proved their value in combat with the proudest troops of continental Europe; and that they would be sweeping across France, during the final days of the bitterest struggle that war-ridden land had ever known, as the spearhead of the victorious armies of the Empire. It may not be altogether fanciful to consider these achievements fruits, in some sort, of those new responsibilities which Canada accepted so hesitantly in 1871; nor to regard them as returns, tardy yet not ungenerous, for the protection which the mother country had afforded her in the days of her weakness.

*

AUTHORITIES

A. MANUSCRIPT

THIS study is based primarily upon documents in the great collection of historical manuscripts in the Public Archives at Ottawa. The " G " Series in particular has been heavily drawn upon. The folios which have supplied material are listed below.

I. SPECIAL COLLECTIONS.
    (a) *The Grey-Elgin Correspondence.*
The private letters that passed between Lord Grey as Colonial Secretary and Lord Elgin as Governor-General of Canada, 1847-52. The collection comprises mainly the following material, arranged chronologically :
    Letters of Lord Grey : 2 vols.
    Letters of Lord Elgin : 5 vols.
    Miscellaneous Papers, Elgin-Grey : 1 vol.

    (b) *The Macdonald Papers.*
The private papers of Sir John A. Macdonald, first Prime Minister of the Dominion. The collection amounts to more than 500 volumes, arranged topically and chronologically. The following series have been drawn upon for the present study :
    " C. J. Brydges " : 1 vol.
    " Fenians " : 7 vols.
    " Governor-General's Correspondence " : vol. I.
    " McMicken Reports " (secret police material) : 12 vols.
    " Militia and Defence " : 2 vols.
    " Private Letter Books " : especially vols. V, IX, XI, XII, XIII, XIV, XVII.
    " Railways " : vol. I.
    " Sir George Cartier Papers " : vol. I.
    " Visits to England " : vol. I.

II. " C " SERIES (MILITARY PAPERS).
  (See Cruikshank, E., *Inventory of the Military Documents in the Canadian Archives :* Ottawa, 1910.)
Volume
  35   Army Miscellaneous, 1832-46.
  37   Army Miscellaneous, 1864-70.

266   CANADA AND THE BRITISH ARMY

Volume
184   Fenians, 1865–70.
316–17   Military Aid at Riots, 1800–45 and 1845–54.
364   North-West, 1855–63.
482   Ordnance and Engineers, 1864.
523   Posts and Barracks, 1846–54.
769   Royal Canadian Rifles, 1840–42.
787   Royal Canadian Rifles, 1869–70.
1287   English Correspondence, 1868–70.
1304   Canadian Correspondence, 1848–49.
1305   Canadian Correspondence, 1849–50.
1319   Canadian Correspondence, 1869–70.
1343   English Correspondence, 1861–63 (Halifax).
1671   Trent Affair, 1861 (from Central Registry, Halifax).
1672   Fenian Raids, 1866 and 1870.

III. "E" SERIES (EXECUTIVE COUNCIL MINUTES, ETC.).

State Book
W.   1861.
A.A.   1864.
A.B.   1864–65.
A.C.   1865–66.
A.D.   1866–67.

IV. "G" SERIES (GOVERNOR-GENERAL'S CORRESPONDENCE).

Volume
121–22   From Secretary of State for the Colonies, 1845.
146   From Secretary of State, 1854.
153   From Secretary of State, 1857.
157   From Secretary of State, 1858.
160   From Secretary of State, 1859.
165   From Secretary of State, 1861.
166   From Secretary of State, 1861.
167   From Secretary of State, 1862.
168   From Secretary of State, 1862.
171   From Secretary of State, 1864.
172   From Secretary of State, 1864.
173   From Secretary of State, 1865.
174   From Secretary of State, 1865.
175   From Secretary of State, 1866.
176   From Secretary of State, 1866.
177   From Secretary of State, 1866.

AUTHORITIES

Volume
- 180A   From Secretary of State, "Secret and confidential despatches, 1856–66".
- 180B   To Secretary of State, "Secret and confidential despatches, 1856–66".
- 218   To Secretary of State, 1865.
- 219   To Secretary of State, 1866.
- 220   To Secretary of State, 1866.
- 221   To Secretary of State, 1867.
- 236   From H.M. Minister at Washington, 1865.
- 347   From Secretary of State, 1866 : British Columbia.
- 451   From Secretary of State, 1847–49.
- 460   To Secretary of State, 1843–46 (Copies).
- 461   To Secretary of State, 1846–51 (Copies).
- 462   To Secretary of State, 1851–56 (Copies).
- 463   To Secretary of State, 1857–61 (Copies).
- 464   To Secretary of State, 1861–63 (Copies).
- 465   To Secretary of State, 1864–66 (Copies).
- 532   From Secretary of State, 1850–52.
- 558   From Secretary of State, 1868.
- 559   From Secretary of State, 1868.
- 561   From Secretary of State, 1868.
- 562   From Secretary of State, 1869.
- 563   From Secretary of State, 1869.
- 564   From Secretary of State, 1869.
- 565   From Secretary of State, 1869.
- 565A   From Secretary of State, "Secret and confidential despatches, 1867–69".
- 566   From Secretary of State, 1870.
- 569A   From Secretary of State, "Secret and confidential despatches, 1870".
- 573A   To Secretary of State, "Secret and confidential despatches, 1867–69".
- 575A   To Secretary of State, "Secret and confidential despatches, 1870".

Also the following unnumbered volumes :
"To Secretary of State, 1867" (actually 1867–68). Copies.
"To Secretary of State, 1869" (actually 1869–70). Copies.
"To Secretary of State, 1870" (actually 1870–72). Copies.
"Confidential Despatches, 1867–1873" (to Secretary of State : Copies).
"From H.M. Minister at Washington, 1869–71."

Correspondence of the Governor-General's Secretary : bundles 11,316 and 11,392.

B. PRINTED SOURCES

I. OFFICIAL PUBLICATIONS.

(a) *Great Britain.*

Hansard's Parliamentary Debates . . .
(" New Series ", commencing with the accession of George IV, and " Third Series ".)

Parliamentary Papers, House of Commons :

1817, no. 162, vol. IV : Second report from the select committee on finance. (Cf. *Annual Register*, 1817, pp. 320–37).

1834, no. 570, vol. VI : Report from select committee on the colonial military expenditure.

1835, no. 473, vol. VI : Report from select committee on the colonial military expenditure.

1849, no. 224, vol. XXXIV : General abstract of the colonial expenditure of Great Britain for 1843–44 and 1846–47.

1849, no. 239, vol. XXXIV : Return of all the colonies, specifying form of government, amount of military force employed in each during the past five years and its cost, and the amount of colonial military force.

1849, no. 499, vol. IX : Second report from the select committee on army and ordnance expenditure.

1850, no. 662, vol. X : Report from the select committee on army and ordnance expenditure.

1851, no. 564, vol. VII : Report from the select committee on army and ordnance expenditure.

1851, cd. 1344, vol. XXXVI : Correspondence relating to the civil list and military expenditure in Canada.

1855, cd. 1871, vol. XXXVI : Despatches from Governors of British colonies transmitting addresses and resolutions on the subject of war with Russia. Continued in the same volume : no. 63, cd. 1888, cd. 1940, cd. 1983.

1859, session 1, no. 240, vol. XVII : Return of the cost of the several colonies, at the expense of the British Exchequer, from 1853 to 1857, inclusive.

1859, session 2, no. 114, vol. XVII : Return of average amount during the last five years of military forces maintained in each colony at the expense of the British Exchequer, and of those maintained in each colony at the expense of its own exchequer.

1860, no. 282, vol. XLI : Copy of report of the committee on expense of military defences in the colonies.

1861, no. 423, vol. XIII : Report from the select committee on colonial military expenditure. (The most important single document in the history of the Colonial military question. Valuable appendices).

AUTHORITIES

1862, no. 73, vol. XXXVI : Return of the strength and cost of troops in the British colonies for the years 1835 and 1858, and return of the population and chief statistics of the colonies in 1838 and 1858.

1862, cd. 3061, vol. XXXVI : Copies or extracts of correspondence between Her Majesty's Government and the Governor-General of Canada in reference to the militia bills proposed and passed in the Canadian Parliament.

1863, no. 147, vol. XXXVIII : Return of area, population, revenue, debt and commerce of each British colony and possession in the year ended on 31st December, 1860, and amount of Imperial expenditure for colonial services in the year ended on 31st March, 1861.

1864, no. 345, vol. XXXV : Return of regiments, etc., borne on strength of Imperial army serving in British North America, New Zealand, and the Cape of Good Hope.

1865, no. 460, vol. XXXII : Return of sums paid out of the Imperial treasury during 1862, 1863 and 1864 for objects connected with the defence of Canada ; and sums expended by the Colonial Government during 1862, 1863 and 1864 for the same objects.

1865, cd. 3434, vol. XXXVII : Letter to the Secretary of State for War with reference to the defence of Canada, by Lieutenant-Colonel Jervois, R.E., C.B., Deputy-Director of Fortifications.

1865, cd. 3535, vol. XXXVII : Papers relating to the conferences which have taken place between Her Majesty's Government and a deputation from the Executive Council of Canada appointed to confer with Her Majesty's Government on subjects of importance to the Province.

1867, no. 478, vol. VII : Report from the select committee on Army (India and the Colonies).

1867, cd. 3785, vol. XLVIII : Correspondence respecting the recent Fenian aggression upon Canada.

1868–69, no. 307, vol. XLIV : Correspondence between the Colonial Office and the Governors of New Zealand. Continued in same volume, no. 307, I.

1870, cd. 24, vol. XLIX : Correspondence respecting a proposed conference of colonial representatives in London. Continued in same volume, cd. 51.

1870, no. 80, vol. XLIX : Return of the annual cost of the several colonies of the British Empire at the expense of the British Exchequer, in continuation of paper no. 240, of session 1, 1859. (Covers 1858–59 to 1867–8, inclusive. Very useful).

1870, cd. 83, vol. L : Further papers relative to the affairs of New Zealand.

1870, no. 180, vol. L : Memorandum of the Hon. W. Gisborne, Colonial Secretary of New Zealand, being a reply to Lord Granville's despatch of the 7th October, 1869, relative to the withdrawal of the Queen's troops from the colony.

1870, no. 181, vol. XLIX : Correspondence regarding the establishment of responsible government at the Cape of Good Hope, and the withdrawal of troops from that colony. Continued in same volume, no. 181, I, and no. 181, II.

1870, cd. 185, vol. XLIX : Despatch from Earl Granville to Governor General Sir John Young, respecting the recent Fenian raid into Canada.

1870, no. 254, vol. XLII : Return showing the effectives of all ranks of each arm of the service actually stationed in the several colonies and garrisons abroad, and in India, in each year, 1860 to 1869. (Very useful).

1870, no. 367, vol. XLIX : Copy of an act of the Canadian legislature for raising a loan of £1,100,000 for constructing fortifications.

1871, no. 52, vol. XLVIII : Return of the cost of the several colonies of the British Empire at the expense of the British Exchequer for 1868-69, in continuation of paper no. 80, of session 1870.

1871, cd. 298, vol. XLVIII : Correspondence relative to the recent expedition to the Red River Settlement, with journal of operations. (Maps to illustrate are cd. 324 in same volume.)

1871, cd. 391, vol. XLVIII : Report on the Red River expedition of 1870 by Assistant Controller Irvine, with preface.

1871, cd. 459, vol. XLVII : Correspondence respecting the affairs of the Cape of Good Hope.

1872, cd. 539, vol. XLIII : Correspondence with the government of Canada in connection with the appointment of the Joint High Commission and the Treaty of Washington. Continued in same volume, cd. 541 and 557.

1873, bill 159, vol. I : A bill to authorise the commissioners of Her Majesty's Treasury to guarantee the payment of a loan to be raised by the Government of Canada for the construction of public works in that country, and to repeal the Canada Defences Loan Act, 1870.

AUTHORITIES

1873, no. 75, vol. XL : Returns of small arms, ordnance, and other stores handed over to the Dominion of Canada in free gift, and of stores transferred on payment ; also, descriptive statement of all forts and of all other military and public buildings transferred to the Government of the Dominion without payment.

1873, no. 367, vol. XL : Returns of the numbers of the regular forces maintained for service in the United Kingdom for each year since the year 1800.

1873, cd. 702, vol. XLIX : Further correspondence with the Government of Canada in connection with the Treaty of Washington. Continued in same volume, cd. 750 and 774.

Confidential Documents :

Copy of a Report to His Grace the Duke of Wellington . . . relative to His Majesty's North American Provinces by a Commission of which M. General Sir James Carmichael Smyth was President. . . . 1825. Lithographed.

Report of the Commissioners Appointed to Consider the Defences of Canada. 1862.

Report on the Defence of Canada and of the British Naval Stations in the Atlantic. . . . Part I. Defence of Canada. By Lt.-Col. W. F. D. Jervois, Feb., 1864.

Report on the Defence of the British Naval Stations in the North Atlantic ; together with Observations on the Defence of New Brunswick, &c. By Lt.-Col. Jervois, Jan., 1865.

Memorandum by the Defence Committee on the Report of Lieutenant-Colonel Jervois on the Defence of Canada. May 17, 1865.

(b) *British North America.*

Parliamentary Documents of the Province of Canada (1841–67) :

Journals of the Legislative Assembly of the Province of Canada. . . .

Parliamentary Debates on the Subject of the Confederation of the North American Provinces, 3rd Session, 8th Provincial Parliament of Canada. Quebec, 1865.

Report of the Commissioners Appointed to Investigate and Report Upon the Best Means of Re-organizing the Militia of Canada, and Upon an Improved System of Police. Quebec, 1855.

Report of the Commissioners Appointed to Report a Plan for the Better Organization of the Department of the Adjutant General of Militia, and the Best Means of Reorganizing the Militia of This Province, and to Prepare a Bill Thereon. Quebec, 1862.

Papers Relating to the Conferences which have taken place between Her Majesty's Government and a Deputation from the Executive Council of Canada, appointed to confer with Her Majesty's Government on the Subject of the Defence of the Province. 4th session, 8th Parliament of Canada, 1865.

The Annual *Report on the State of the Militia* in the *Sessional Papers.*

Parliamentary Documents of the Dominion of Canada:

Dominion of Canada. Parliamentary Debates. (First published 1870.)

Sessional Papers :

The annual *Report on the State of the Militia.* Especially those for 1867 (S.P., 1867-68, no. 35), 1870 (1871, no. 7), and 1871 (1872, no. 8).

1867-68, no. 28 : Report of Colonel Wolseley on the camp at Thorold.

1867-68, no. 37 : Information respecting Government gunboats for the years 1866 and 1867.

1867-68, no. 63 : Copies of correspondence between the Imperial Government and the Government of the Province and Dominion of Canada on the subject of colonial military expenditure. (Begins in June, 1862.)

1869, no. 60 : Fortifications and defence, arms, etc. (Report of Sir G. Cartier and W. McDougall on their mission to England.)

1869, no. 61 : San Juan Island, Fenian claims, fisheries. (Further report of Cartier and McDougall.)

1869, no. 75 : Return of copies of all correspondence with the Imperial Government relating to the outlay incurred by Canada in defence of the frontier of the United States in 1863-64, and also arising out of the threatened Fenian invasion subsequently, as constituting a claim for indemnity against the United States. Copies of all correspondence, orders in council, and documents relating to representations made by the Government of Canada relating to the rebellion of the Southern States.

1871, no. 46 : Correspondence with the Imperial authorities since Jan. 1, 1869, on the withdrawal of Imperial troops and transfer of fortified places. (Return to addresses of the Senate [May 10, 1870] and the House of Commons [Feb. 17, 1871].)

Statutes of Canada (Province and Dominion). Published in annual volumes.

AUTHORITIES

Confidential Document :
Report on the Defence of Canada. By Lt.-Col. W. F. D. Jervois, Nov. 10, 1864. (To the Canadian Government.)

II. NEWSPAPERS AND PERIODICALS.

(Magazine and review articles are in general noticed separately, under their own titles, under *Books and Articles*).

(a) *Great Britain.*
The Annual Register.
The Economist.
The Saturday Review.
The Spectator.
The Times.

(b) *Canada.*
The British Colonist (Toronto).
The Canadian Illustrated News (Montreal).
The Examiner (Toronto).
The Gazette (Montreal).
The Globe (Toronto). Daily and weekly.
The Herald (Montreal).
The Leader (Toronto).
La Minerve (Montreal).
The Mirror (Toronto).
L'Ordre (Montreal).
The Transcript (Montreal).

(c) *United States of America.*
The Albion (New York).
The New York Herald.
The New York Times.
The New York Tribune.

III. BOOKS AND ARTICLES.

(Periodical articles are here shown with their titles in inverted commas ; works published separately have their titles in italics. Works referred to in the text merely incidentally are in general not included.)

(a) *Contemporary, or Nearly Contemporary Works.*

Both the reminiscences of contemporaries, and collections of contemporary documents, are in general included in this list, even though published at a comparatively recent time.

T

Adderley, (Sir) Charles (1st Baron Norton). *Letter to the Right Hon. Benjamin Disraeli, M.P., on the Present Relations of England with the Colonies. New edition.* . . . London, 1862.
— *Review of " The Colonial Policy of Lord J. Russell's Administration ", by Earl Grey, 1853 ; and of subsequent colonial history.* London, 1869.
Anonymous. " Are We Ready ? " *Macmillan's Magazine,* XXII : Oct., 1870.
— " The Army ". *Blackwood's Magazine,* CI : 3 articles, Feb. to April, 1867.
— " The Battle of Dorking : Reminiscences of a Volunteer ". *Blackwood's,* CIX : May, 1871. Later published separately.
— *Canada and Invasion.* Canadian pamphlet : 1863 (?).
— " Canada : the Fenian Raid and the Colonial Office ". *Blackwood's,* CVIII : Oct., 1870.
— " Canada—Our Frozen Frontier ". *Blackwood's,* XCI : Jan., 1862.
— " The Defence of Canada ". *Blackwood's,* XCI : Feb., 1862.
— " The Defences of England ". *Macmillan's,* XXII : Sept., 1870.
— " On the Government Scheme of Army Reform ". *Blackwood's,* CVII : April, 1870.
— " Home Defences ". *Macmillan's,* XV : Feb., 1867.
— " Military Reform ". *Fraser's Magazine,* LXXIV–LXXVI : 5 articles, Dec., 1866, and March, April, June and August, 1867.
— " Our National Insurance ". *Macmillan's,* XX : June, 1869.
— " The National Rifle Association ". *Macmillan's,* XVI : July, 1867.
— " The Re-organisation of the Army ". *Fraser's,* LXXVII : May, 1868.
Beaconsfield, Benjamin Disraeli, Lord. *Selected Speeches of . . . the Earl of Beaconsfield.* (Ed.) T. E. Kebbel. London, 1882 : 2 vols.
Bell, K. N., and Morrell, W. P. *Select Documents on British Colonial Policy, 1830–1860.* Oxford, 1928.
Bernard, Mountague. *A Historical Account of the Neutrality of Great Britain during the American Civil War.* London, 1870.
Blachford, Lord. *Letters of Frederic Lord Blachford, Under-Secretary of State for the Colonies, 1860–1871.* (Ed.) G. E. Marindin. London, 1896.
Bright, John. *Speeches on the Public Affairs of the Last Twenty Years.* London, 1869.
Broome, F. N. " The Crisis in New Zealand ". *Macmillan's,* XX : Sept., 1869.

AUTHORITIES

Burgoyne, Sir John. *The Military Opinions of General Sir John Fox Burgoyne.* . . . (Ed.) G. Wrottesley: London, 1859.

Bury, Viscount (7th Earl of Albemarle). *Exodus of the Western Nations.* London, 1865: 2 vols.

Butler, Sir William. *The Great Lone Land.* . . . London, 1873: 4th ed.

— *The Wild Northland.* New edition, New York, 1922; first published, 1873.

Cairnes, J. E. " Our Defences: A National or a Standing Army ? " *Fortnightly Review,* XV: Feb., 1871.

Cartwright, Sir Richard. *Reminiscences.* Toronto, 1912.

Chesney, C. C. " Our Panics and their Remedy ". *Macmillan's,* XXIII: April, 1871.

Clode, C. M. *The Military Forces of the Crown; their Administration and Government.* London, 1869: 2 vols.

Cobden, Richard. *The Political Writings of Richard Cobden.* (Ed.) Sir L. Mallet, London, 1878; also other editions.

— *Speeches of Richard Cobden, Esq., M.P.* . . . *Delivered During 1849.* London, 1850 (?).

— *Speeches on Questions of Public Policy by Richard Cobden, M.P.* (Ed.) J. Bright and J. E. T. Rogers, London, 1870: 2 vols.

— *The Three Panics: An Historical Episode.* London, 1862: also in *Political Writings.*

Coffin, W. F. *1812: The War, and Its Moral: A Canadian Chronicle.* Montreal, 1864.

Denison, G. T. *The National Defences; or, Observations on the Best Defensive Force for Canada.* Toronto, 1861.

— *Soldiering in Canada.* London, 1900.

Denison, Sir William. *Two Lectures on Colonization.* Richmond, 1870.

Doughty, A. G. (ed.). " Notes on the Quebec Conference, 1864." *Canadian Historical Review,* I: March, 1920.

Duncan, Francis. *Our Garrisons in the West; or, Sketches in British North America.* London, 1864.

Durham, Lord. *Report on the Affairs of British North America.* (Ed.) Sir C. P. Lucas: Oxford, 1912: 3 vols.

Egerton, H. E., and Grant, W. L. *Canadian Constitutional Development.* . . . *Selected Speeches and Despatches.* . . . London, 1907.

Ford, W. C. (ed.). *A Cycle of Adams Letters, 1861–1865.* Boston and New York, 1920: 2 vols.

Grey, 3rd Earl. *The Colonial Policy of Lord John Russell's Administration.* London, 1853 : 2 vols.

Headley, J. W. *Confederate Operations in Canada and New York.* New York and Washington, 1906.

Howe, Joseph. *The Speeches and Public Letters of Joseph Howe. . . . New and Complete Edition.* (Ed.) J. A. Chisholm : Halifax, 1909 : 2 vols.

Hurlbert, J. B. *Britain and Her Colonies.* London, 1865.

Huyshe, G. L. *The Red River Expedition.* London, 1871.

Lewis, Sir George Cornewall. *Letters of the Right Hon. Sir George Cornewall Lewis.* . . . (Ed.) Rev. Sir G. F. Lewis : London, 1870.

— *An Essay on the Government of Dependencies.* Oxford, 1891 : originally published 1841.

Lysons, D. *Parting Words on the Rejected Militia Bill.* Quebec, 1862.

Malan, C. H. " The Recruiting Difficulty." *Fortnightly,* V : July 1, 1866.

Martin, R. M. *History of the Colonies of the British Empire. . . . From the Official Records of the Colonial Office.* London, 1843.

Merivale, Herman. " The Colonial Question in 1870." *Fortnightly,* XIII : Feb., 1870.

— *Lectures on Colonization and Colonies.* . . . London, 1841–42 : 2 vols. Reprinted, 1 vol., 1861 ; new ed., Oxford, 1928.

Mill, James. " Colony." Article in *Supplement to the Encyclopædia Britannica,* vol. III, 1819.

Molesworth, Sir William. *Selected Speeches of Sir William Molesworth . . . on Questions Relating to Colonial Policy.* (Ed.) H. E. Egerton, London, 1903.

Macdonald, Sir John A. *Correspondence of Sir John Macdonald.* . . . (Ed.) Sir J. Pope, Toronto, 1921 (?).

M'Culloch, J. R. *A Descriptive and Statistical Account of the British Empire.* . . . London, 1854 : 4th ed., 2 vols.

Panmure, Lord. *The Panmure Papers, being a Selection from the Correspondence of Fox Maule, Second Baron Panmure.* . . . (Ed.) Sir G. Douglas and Sir G. D. Ramsay. London, 1908 : 2 vols.

Parnell, Sir Henry (1st Baron Congleton). *On Financial Reform.* London, 1830.

Russell, Earl (Lord John). *The Later Correspondence of Lord John Russell, 1840–1878.* (Ed.) G. P. Gooch : London, 1925 : 2 vols.

— *Recollections and Suggestions, 1813–1873.* London, 1875.

AUTHORITIES

Russell, Sir William H. *Canada: Its Defences, Condition, and Resources. Being a Third and Concluding Volume of " My Diary North and South."* London, 1865.

Sala, G. A. *My Diary in America in the Midst of War.* 2nd ed., London, 1865 : 2 vols.

Shortt, A., and Doughty, A. G. *Documents Relating to the Constitutional History of Canada, 1759–1791.* Ottawa, 1918.

Sinclair, Sir John. *The History of the Public Revenue of the British Empire.* . . . 3rd ed., London, 1803–04 : 3 vols.

Smith, Goldwin. *The Empire. A Series of Letters Published in " The Daily News ", 1862, 1863.* Oxford and London, 1863.

Smyth, Sir James Carmichael. *Precis of the Wars in Canada from 1755 to the Treaty of Ghent in 1814.* . . . London, 1826 : " printed by desire of His Grace the Master-General, for . . . official people only " ; published, 1862.

Sumner, Charles. *The Works of Charles Sumner.* Boston, 1874–83 : 15 vols.

Trollope, Anthony. *North America.* New York, 1862.

Victoria, Queen. *The Letters of Queen Victoria.* First series (ed.) A. C. Benson and Viscount Esher, London, 1908 : 3 vols. Second series, (ed.) G. E. Buckle, London, 1926 : 2 vols.

Walrond, Theodore (ed.). *Letters and Journals of James, Eighth Earl of Elgin.* . . . London, 1872.

Wellington, Duke of. *Despatches, Correspondence, and Memoranda of Field Marshal Arthur Duke of Wellington.* . . . (Ed.) Second Duke of Wellington : London, 1867–80 : 8 vols.

Wolseley, Viscount. " Narrative of the Red River Expedition, by an Officer of the Expeditionary Force." *Blackwood's,* CVIII–CIX : Dec., 1870–Feb., 1871. (See above p. 239, *n.*).

— *The Story of a Soldier's Life.* Westminster, 1903 : 2 vols.

(b) *Later Works.*

Adams, Charles Francis, Jr. " The Treaty of Washington : Before and After." In *Lee at Appomattox and Other Papers.* Boston and New York, 1902.

Adams, E. D. *Great Britain and the American Civil War.* London, 1925 : 2 vols.

Allin, C. D., and Jones, G. M. *Annexation, Preferential Trade, and Reciprocity.* . . . Toronto, 1912 (?).

Beer, G. L. *British Colonial Policy, 1754–1765.* New York, 1907.

— *The Old Colonial System, 1660–1754. Part I . . . 1660–1688.* New York, 1912 : 2 vols.
— *The Origins of the British Colonial System, 1578–1660.* New York, 1908.
Begg, Alexander. *History of the North-West.* Toronto, 1894–95 : 3 vols.
Biddulph, Sir Robert. *Lord Cardwell at the War Office. A History of His Administration, 1868–1874.* London, 1904.
Bodelsen, C. A. *Studies in mid-Victorian Imperialism.* Copenhagen, 1924.
Brebner, J. B. " Joseph Howe and the Crimean War Enlistment Controversy between Great Britain and the United States." *Canadian Historical Review,* XI : Dec., 1930.
Buckingham, W., and Ross, G. W. *The Hon. Alexander Mackenzie, His Life and Times.* Toronto, 1892.
Burt, A. L. *The Old Province of Quebec.* Toronto and Minneapolis, 1933.
Butler, Lewis (and others). *The Annals of the King's Royal Rifle Corps.* London, 1913–32 : 5 vols.
The Cambridge History of the British Empire. Vol. I : *The Old Empire from the Beginnings to 1783.* Vol. VI : *Canada and Newfoundland.* Cambridge, 1929–30.
The Cambridge History of British Foreign Policy, 1783–1919. New York, 1922–23 : 3 vols.
Chambers, E. J. *The Canadian Militia, a History of the Origin and Development of the Force.* Montreal, 1907.
Channing, E. *History of the United States.* New York, 1905–25 : 6 vols.
Childe-Pemberton, W. S. *Life of Lord Norton (Rt. Hon. Sir Charles Adderley, K.C.M.G., M.P. . . .)* London, 1909.
Egerton, H. E. *A Short History of British Colonial Policy.* London, 1897.
Fawcett, Mrs. —. *Life of the Right Hon. Sir William Molesworth. . . .* London, 1901.
Fitzmaurice, Lord Edmond. *The Life of Granville George Leveson Gower, second Earl Granville, K.G.* London, 1905 : 2 vols.
Fortescue, Sir John. *A History of the British Army.* London, 1899–1930 : 13 vols.
Ganoe, W. A. *The History of the United States Army.* New York, 1924.

Hamilton, C. F. *Defence, 1812–1912*, in Shortt and Doughty (eds.), *Canada and Its Provinces*, VII. Expanded in a series of articles in *Canadian Defence Quarterly*, 1928–31 : see especially " The Canadian Militia : from the Crimean War to 1861 " (VI : Oct., 1928) and " The Canadian Militia : from 1861 to Confederation " (VI : Jan., 1929). (Probably the best single account of Canadian military development).

Hardinge, Sir Arthur. *Life of Henry Howard Molyneux Herbert, Fourth Earl of Carnarvon, 1831–1890.* Oxford, 1925 : 3 vols.

Historical section of the Canadian General Staff (eds.). *A History of the Organization, Development and Services of the Military and Naval Forces of Canada from the Peace of Paris . . . to the Present Time.* Vols. I–III, 1763–84, Ottawa, 1919–21.

Howay, F. W. *The Work of the Royal Engineers in British Columbia, 1858 to 1863.* Victoria, 1910.

Keith, A. B. *Responsible Government in the Dominions.* Oxford, 1912 : 3 vols. 2nd end., 1928 : 2 vols.

Kennedy, W. P. M. *The Constitution of Canada, an Introduction to its Development and Law.* Oxford, 1922.

Kingsford, William. *The History of Canada.* Toronto and London, 1887–1898 : 10 vols.

Knaplund, Paul. " E. G. Wakefield on the Colonial Garrisons, 1851." *Canadian Historical Review*, V : Sept., 1924.

— *Gladstone and Britain's Imperial Policy.* London, 1927.

Landon, F. " The Trent Affair of 1861." *Canadian Historical Review*, III : March, 1922.

Long, M. H. " Sir John Rose and the Informal Beginnings of the Canadian High Commissionership." *Canadian Historical Review*, XII : March, 1931.

Lucas, Sir Charles. *The Empire at War.* Oxford, 1921 : 5 vols. (Vol. I is a survey of the problem of Imperial defence to 1914, and probably the most useful publication in this field.)

— *History of Canada, 1763–1812.* Oxford, 1909.

Martin, Chester. " British Policy in Canadian Confederation." *Canadian Historical Review*, XIII : March, 1932.

— *Empire and Commonwealth, Studies in Governance and Self-government in Canada.* Oxford, 1929.

Martineau, John. *The Life of Henry Pelham, Fifth Duke of Newcastle, 1811–1864.* London, 1908.

Maxwell, Sir Herbert. *The Life of Wellington. . . .* London, 1900 : 3rd ed., 2 vols.

Monypenny, W. F., and Buckle, G. E. *The Life of Benjamin Disraeli, Earl of Beaconsfield.* London, 1910–20 : 6 vols.

Morison, J. L. *British Supremacy and Canadian Self-government, 1839–1854.* Glasgow, 1919.

— *The Eighth Earl of Elgin, a Chapter in Nineteenth-century Imperial History.* London, 1928.

— " The Imperial Ideas of Benjamin Disraeli." *Canadian Historical Review*, I : Sept., 1920.

Morley, John. *The Life of Richard Cobden.* London, 1881 ; 2 vols.

— *The Life of William Ewart Gladstone.* London, 1903 : 3 vols.

Morrell, W. P. *British Colonial Policy in the Age of Peel and Russell.* Oxford, 1930.

Macdonald, Helen G. *Canadian Public Opinion on the American Civil War.* New York, 1926.

Mackenzie, A. *The Life and Speeches of Hon. George Brown.* Toronto, 1882.

New, Chester W. *Lord Durham.* . . . Oxford, 1929.

Newton, Lord. *Lord Lyons : a Record of British Diplomacy.* London, 1913 : 2 vols.

Osgood, H. L. *The American Colonies in the Eighteenth Century.* New York, 1924 : 4 vols.

— *The American Colonies in the Seventeenth Century.* New York, 1904–07 : 3 vols.

Pierce, E. L. *Memoir and Letters of Charles Sumner.* Boston, 1877–93 : 4 vols.

Pope, Sir Joseph. *The Day of Sir John Macdonald.* Toronto, 1915 : *Chronicles of Canada* series.

— *Memoirs of the Right Honourable Sir John Alexander Macdonald.* . . . London, 1894 : 2 vols.

Prowse, D. W. *A History of Newfoundland.* . . . London, 1895.

Rusden, G. W. *History of Australia.* Melbourne, 1897 : 3 vols.

— *History of New Zealand.* Melbourne, 1895 : 3 vols.

Schuyler, R. L. " The Climax of anti-Imperialism in England." *Political Science Quarterly*, XXXVI : Dec., 1921.

— " The Recall of the Legions : a Phase of the Decentralization of the British Empire." *American Historical Review*, XXVI : Oct., 1920.

— " The Rise of Anti-Imperialism in England." *Political Science Quarterly*, XXXVII : Sept., 1922.

Shortt, A., and Doughty, A. G. (eds.). *Canada and Its Provinces: a History of the Canadian People and their Institutions.* Toronto, 1914-17 : 23 vols.

Skelton, O. D. *The Life and Times of Sir Alexander Tilloch Galt.* Toronto, 1920.

Smith, G. B. *The Life and Speeches of the Right Hon. John Bright, M.P.* London, 1881 : 2 vols.

Stacey, C. P. "British Military Policy in Canada in the Era of Federation." *Canadian Historical Association, Report of the Annual Meeting . . . 1934.*

— "Fenianism and the Rise of National Feeling in Canada at the Time of Confederation." *Canadian Historical Review*, XII : Sept., 1931.

— "The Garrison of Fort Wellington : a Military Dispute during the Fenian Troubles." *Canadian Historical Review*, XIV : June, 1933.

— "The Second Red River Expedition, 1871." *Canadian Defence Quarterly*, VIII : Jan., 1931.

Theal, G. M. *History of South Africa from 1795 to 1872.* London, 1889 : 5 vols.

Todd, Alpheus. *Parliamentary Government in the British Colonies. Second edition, edited by his son.* London, 1894.

Trotter, R. G. *Canadian Federation, its Origins and Achievement.* . . . Toronto and London, 1924.

Underhill, F. H. "Canada's Relations with the Empire as seen by the Toronto Globe, 1857-1867." *Canadian Historical Review*, X : June, 1929.

Upton, Emory. *The Military Policy of the United States.* Washington, 1907 : 2nd imp.

Verner, Willoughby. *The Military Life of George, Duke of Cambridge.* London, 1905 : 2 vols.

Walpole, Sir Spencer. *A History of England from the Conclusion of the Great War in 1815.* London, 1878-86 : 5 vols.

— *The History of Twenty-five Years.* London, 1904-08 : 4 vols.

Whitelaw, W. M. *The Maritimes and Canada before Confederation.* Toronto, 1934.

Whitton, F. E. *The History of the Prince of Wales's Leinster Regiment (Royal Canadians).* . . . Aldershot, 1927 (?) : 2 vols.

Williamson, J. A. *A Short History of British Expansion.* London, 1930 : 2nd ed. : 2 vols.

Wrottesley, G. *Life and Correspondence of Field Marshal Sir John Burgoyne, Bart.* London, 1873 : 2 vols.

ADDITIONS TO LIST OF AUTHORITIES, 1962

(BOOKS AND ARTICLES)

Contemporary Documents.

Doughty, Arthur G. (ed.). *The Elgin-Grey Papers.* Ottawa, 1937 : 4 vols.

Ramm, Agatha (ed.). *The Political Correspondence of Mr. Gladstone and Lord Granville, 1868-1876.* London, 1952 : 2 vols. (Royal Historical Society, Camden Third Series, vols. LXXXI-LXXXII.)

Later Works.

Allen, H. C. *Great Britain and the United States: A History of Anglo-American Relations, 1783-1952.* London, 1954.

Armstrong, F. H. "The First Great Fire of Toronto, 1849." *Ontario History,* LIII : September, 1961.

Baldwin, J. R. "The Ashburton-Webster Boundary Settlement." *Canadian Historical Association, Report of the Annual Meeting . . . 1938.*

Brebner, John Bartlet. *North Atlantic Triangle: The Interplay of Canada, The United States and Great Britain.* New Haven, 1945.

Bourne, Kenneth. "British Preparations for War with the North, 1861-1862." *English Historical Review,* LXXVI : October, 1961.

Childers, Spencer. *The Life and Correspondence of the Right Hon. C. E. Childers, 1827-1896.* London, 1901 : 2 vols.

Corey, Albert B. "Canadian Border Defence Problems after 1814 to their Culmination in the 'Forties." *Canadian Historical Association, Report of the Annual Meeting . . . 1938.*

— *The Crisis of 1830-1842 in Canadian-American Relations.* New Haven, 1941.

Creighton, Donald. *John A. Macdonald: The Old Chieftain.* Toronto, 1955.

— *John A. Macdonald: The Young Politician.* Toronto, 1952.

D'Arcy, William. *The Fenian Movement in the United States, 1858-1886.* Washington, 1947.

Davis, Harold A. "The Fenian Raid on New Brunswick." *Canadian Historical Review,* XXXVI : December, 1955.

Galbraith, John S. *The Hudson's Bay Company as an Imperial Factor, 1821-1869.* Berkeley, 1957.

ADDITIONS TO LIST OF AUTHORITIES, 1962 283

Gluek, Alvin C., Jr. "Imperial Protection for the Trading Interests of the Hudson's Bay Company, 1857-1861." *Canadian Historical Review*, XXXVII: June, 1956.
— "The Riel Rebellion and Canadian-American Relations." *Canadian Historical Review*, XXXVI: September, 1955.
Harrop, Angus J. *England and the Maori Wars.* London, 1937.
Hitsman, J. Mackay. "Please Send Us a Garrison." *Ontario History*, L: Autumn, 1958.
— "Winter Troop Movement to Canada, 1862." *Canadian Historical Review*, XLIII: June, 1962.
Horan, James D. *Confederate Agent: A Discovery in History.* New York, 1954.
Kerr, D. G. G., assisted by Gibson, J. A. *Sir Edmund Head, A Scholarly Governor.* Toronto, 1954.
Laws, M. E. S. *Battery Records of the Royal Artillery, 1716-1859.* Woolwich, 1953.
LeCaron, Henri [Beach, Thomas]. *Twenty-Five Years in the Secret Service: The Recollections of a Spy.* London, 1892.
MacCallum, Duncan. "Some Aspects of Defence in the Eighteen Fifties in New South Wales." *Royal Australian Historical Society Journal and Proceedings*, XLIV: July, 1958.
Maxwell, Sir Herbert. *The Life and Letters of George William Frederick, Fourth Earl of Clarendon.* London, 1913: 2 vols.
McInnis, Edgar W. *The Unguarded Frontier: A History of American-Canadian Relations.* New York, 1942.
Nevins, Allan. *Hamilton Fish: The Inner History of the Grant Administration.* New York, 1936.
Schuyler, R. L. *The Fall of the Old Colonial System: A Study in British Free Trade, 1770-1870.* London and New York, 1945.
Shippee, Lester Burrell. *Canadian-American Relations, 1849-1874.* New Haven, 1939.
Stacey, C. P. "The Backbone of Canada." *Canadian Historical Association, Report of the Annual Meeting . . . 1953.*
— "Britain's Withdrawal from North America, 1864-1871." *Canadian Historical Review*, XXXVI: September, 1955.
— "The Fenian Troubles and Canadian Military Development, 1865-1871." *Canadian Historical Association, Report of the Annual Meeting . . . 1935.*
— "Halifax as an International Strategic Factor, 1749-1949." *Canadian Historical Association, Report of the Annual Meeting . . . 1949.*
— "The Hudson's Bay Company and Anglo-American Military Relations during the Oregon Dispute." *Canadian Historical Review*, XVIII: September, 1937.

— " The Military Aspect of Canada's Winning of the West, 1870–1885." *Canadian Historical Review*, XXI : March, 1940.
— *The Military Problems of Canada.* Toronto, 1940.
— " The Myth of the Unguarded Frontier, 1815–1871." *American Historical Review*, LVI : October, 1950.
— " A Note on the Citadel of Quebec." *Canadian Historical Review*, XXIX : December, 1948.
— " The Withdrawal of the Imperial Garrison from Newfoundland, 1870." *Canadian Historical Review*, XVII : June, 1936.
Stanley, George F. G. *Canada's Soldiers.* Revised ed., Toronto, 1960.
Stewart, Charles H. (comp.). *The Service of British Regiments in Canada and North America : A Résumé.* Ottawa, 1962 (mimeographed).
Tylden, G. " The Royal Canadian Rifle Regiment, 1840 to 1870." *Journal of the Society for Army Historical Research*, XXXIV : June, 1956.
Waite, Peter B. *The Life and Times of Confederation : Politics, Newspapers, and the Union of British North America.* Toronto, 1962.
Way, R. L. " The Topographical Aspect of Canadian Defence (1783–1871)." *Canadian Defence Quarterly*, XIV : April, 1937.
Winks, Robin W. *Canada and the United States : The Civil War Years.* Baltimore, 1960.

Page 19. The comment here on the Webster-Ashburton treaty of 1842 now strikes me as naïve. The treaty did not, of course, condemn the winter communication between the Maritime ports and Quebec to follow " a very roundabout route ". What it did do was to preserve, by a very narrow margin, the one and only existing overland route, that by the St. John and Madawaska valleys and Lake Temiscouata. This route was itself roundabout, but it would have been severed by the acceptance of the American boundary claim, which would have thrown the Madawaska valley and Lake Temiscouata into the United States. The preservation of that route was a far more vital British interest than the mere matter of withdrawing the border as far as possible from the St. Lawrence in the area where it parallels that river—where even to-day the boundary is not crossed by a practicable road for 100 miles. British soldiers advising the government emphasized the importance of pushing the border back from the St. Lawrence ; Ashburton, acting under instructions, did have some success here (by comparison with the award of the King of the Netherlands of 1831), though he himself thought it more important to protect the Temiscouata route by getting land south of the St. John in the Madawaska Settlement. He had a very clear view of the vital elements of the situation—clearer than the generals' ; and it seems evident that, given the material earlier British statesmen had left him to work with, he could not have got a better bargain than he did. Historians have shown surprisingly little appreciation of the significance of the Temiscouata route in this boundary dispute ; many books contain maps supposedly illustrating this question which do not show the route at all. The matter is briefly discussed, and some of the most important references cited, in the present writer's " The Backbone of Canada, " *Report* of the Canadian Historical Association, 1953.

Page 73. The last of the local forces raised after the rebellion were not actually disbanded until the spring of 1850 ; in 1848 the British Government authorized the continuance of the " Provincial Force " (three troops of cavalry and one company of coloured infantry) for two years from April 30, 1848. Elgin greatly regretted the decision to do away with the cavalry : " For my own part I would rather part with two [regular] Regiments. The young farmers who enlist in this corps make excellent soldiers with very little training. . . . " But the decision to disband it was maintained. See Grey to Elgin, Jan. 14, 1848, and Dec. 22, 1849, *G*, 451, pp. 130, 588 ; and Elgin to Grey, Jan. 29, 1948, *G.E.C.*

Page 74. The statement that " the great grievance—the cost of the regular garrison of Canada—remained untouched " perhaps needs qualification. In 1850 the number of battalions of infantry of the line in Canada, which had been eight in 1848 and 1849, was reduced to six. However, since the battalions' establishments were increased, the actual reduction in strength was small. See *P.P.*, 1850, no. 662, vol. X (Report from the select committee on army and ordnance expenditure), Appendix 10, p. 770.

Page 154, note 5. I have attempted to expand the suggestion concerning the fashion in which " the uncertainty of the situation in America hampered Britain's action in Europe, and *vice versa* " in " Britain's Withdrawal from North America, 1865–1871," *Canadian Historical Review*, September, 1955.

Page 216. The publication of the correspondence of Gladstone and Granville has thrown new light on the background of Granville's notorious dispatch of June 1869. It is evident that Gladstone did *not* see the dispatch before it was sent, but there had been rather extensive discussion (apparently verbal as well as written) between the two men on the general question, and on May 29, 1869, the Prime Minister called Granville's attention to a dispatch which Gladstone, as Colonial Secretary, had sent Lord Cathcart in 1846, laying down distinctly that Britain did not " impose British connection upon the Colony. " Gladstone's recollection was that this dispatch went to the Queen and received " a rather decided expression of approval by the Prince. " This 1846 dispatch became the basis of Granville's of 1869, which quotes it at length. But the sting in the tail—the order to Sir John Young to report any measures which might prepare the two countries for a " friendly relaxation " of relations—was evidently Granville's own contribution. He wrote to Gladstone, " There is a phrase at the end . . . which would make it unwise to publish it at present." Gladstone's note to Granville, May 29, 1869, and Granville's to Gladstone, January 25, 1870, are items 59 and 195 in Agatha Ramm, ed., *The Political Correspondence of Mr. Gladstone and Lord Granville, 1868–1876* (2 vols., London, 1952). Gladstone to Cathcart, No. 14, Feb. 3,

NOTES ADDITIONAL TO THE TEXT 287

1846, is in Public Archives of Canada, RG 7, G 1, vol. III. Granville's dispatch to Young is in C.O. 42-678 (microfilm in Public Archives of Canada) ; the date is June 14, 1869 (not June 16 as in Knaplund). Sir John Young appears to have carefully impounded this dispatch, and it never got into the Canadian records.

Page 228, n. 2. The final cost of the three Lévis forts to the British Government was reported in 1872 as £249,456. See *C*, 1419, p. 65.

Page 240. It was only the advanced guard of Wolseley's force that reached Fort Garry on August 24.

Page 251. The regular garrison was withdrawn from Bytown (Ottawa) in 1853, though a party of enrolled pensioners was stationed there from 1854 to 1858 ; see documents in *C*, 31 and *C*, 503. However, after the government of the Province of Canada moved to Ottawa in 1866 it was again considered desirable to station troops there ; in that year of Fenian threats the Canadian ministers were willing to pay for renting and fitting up barracks for them (above, page 197). A regular garrison sometimes exceeding 500 men was maintained in the city from 1866 until 1870 (documents in *C*, 545). " Earnscliffe, " the house later owned by Sir John A. Macdonald, which is now the official residence of the British High Commissioner, served as the military hospital, 1869–70 ; see [Norman Reddaway] , *Earnscliffe* (London, Commonwealth Relations Office, 1955).

General. More might be said of the various forms of " aid to the civil power " rendered by the British troops in Canada. There is a reference (page 23) to their assistance in quelling riots. There were a good many such incidents, not least in turbulent Bytown ; see, for instance, the report of Major F. R. Thomson, R.E., on the part played by a company of the 60th Rifles in terminating a serious disturbance there on July 13, 1846 (*C*, 317). There was seldom much disorder after the troops appeared on the scene. The absence of any real civil police was the chief reason for these troubles. In this case Thomson wrote, " I am firmly convinced that one energetic Magistrate with temper & firmness, and less than a dozen constables, would have put an end to the disturbance ... even when at its height, without the intervention of the Military." In February 1850 we find the Royal Canadian Rifles being called upon to support the Revenue Department in searching the town of Aylmer East for smuggled goods (Report by Major F. W. Clements, Feb. 19, 1850, *C*, 318).

There were other forms of aid. In Toronto's great fire of 1849 the arrival of the troops when the local fire fighters were becoming exhausted was credited by the firemen themselves with saving the city from destruction : " The Brigade feel had it not been for the timely arrival and assistance of the military in seconding their endeavours on that wild night of woe, Toronto would not now stand as it does " (see F. H. Armstrong, " The First Great Fire of Toronto, 1849, " *Ontario History*, September, 1961). One of the last services of the troops in Ottawa was an unusual one : a large detachment of the Rifle Brigade was employed at the beginning of March 1869 in digging out a St. Lawrence and Ottawa Railway train which was stuck in snowdrifts outside the capital. William Pittman Lett, city clerk and doggerel bard, celebrated the occasion in verse (see *Ottawa Citizen*, weekly edition, Mar. 12, 1869). The departure of the imperial regiments removed a force to which the people and authorities of the communities in which they were stationed had learned to turn with confidence in many sorts of local emergency.

INDEX

ADDERLEY, (Sir) Charles (Lord Norton), 81, 260; on colonial military expenditure (1860–61), 113, 118–19; on Canada, 128, 140, 155; pamphlet (1862), 139, 142; book (1869), 225
Alabama Claims, 196, 213, 229, 230–31, 254
Annexation Manifesto (1849), 75
Ashburton, Lord, and treaty, 19, 285
Australia, Grey's policy towards, 66–7; military contribution, 86–7, 90–1, 112; troops withdrawn, 256
Aylmer East, Quebec, 287

BAGOT, Sir Charles, 22
Barracks, proposals for contribution, 72, 73, 74, 104; provided by Canada (1866), 192, 197, 199
Battle of Dorking, The, 248–9
Baxter, W. E., 128–9
Bentham, Jeremy, 30
Bermuda, 122, 161
Brantford, Ontario, 197
Bright, John, 34, 61, 62, 237; colonial views, 205
British Columbia, 118
Brown, George, opposes the Militia Bills (1855), 94; (1856), 101–2; in England (1862), 141–2; (1864), 168; coalition, 157; speech on Federation, 174; mission to England (1865), 177, 184
Buckingham, Duke of, 199, 201
Buller, Charles, 40
Burgoyne, Sir John, 59, 185
Bury, Viscount, 179–81
Butler, Sir William, 248
Bytown, *see* Ottawa

CAMBRIDGE, Duke of, 160, 185, 208; opposes evacuation of Quebec, 224–5, 228
Campbell, (Sir) Alexander, mission to England (1870), 244–5, 246
Cape of Good Hope, military problems, 43, 44, 45, 67, 85, 90; large withdrawals, 256

Cardwell, Edward (Lord), policy towards Canada as Colonial Secretary, 156, 160–1, 167 ff.; conferences with Canadian ministers (1865), 181 ff.; programme as Secretary of State for War (1868), 206–8; estimates (1869), 211–12, (1870), 236; on distribution of troops, 219–21; his achievement, 255–9, 262
Carleton, Sir Guy (Lord Dorchester), 8
Carnarvon, Lord, 140, 192–3; attacks Granville's policy, 235, 253, 249
Cartier, (Sir) George E., 134, 177, 181; mission to England (1868–9), 201, 208–10; refuses to call out militia (1869), 220–1; memorandum on troop withdrawals (1870), 241
Cathcart, Lord, 21, 66
Cecil, Lord Robert (Lord Salisbury), 155
Civil War (U.S.), chaps VI and VII, *passim*; outbreak, 117; progress, 149, 152, 165; peace proposals, 170–1; conclusion, 178
Clements, Major F. W., 287
Coalition ministry (1864), 157
Cobden, Richard, 26, 34, 56, 72, 77, 81, 111; views on colonies, 35–8, 46, 48–9, 61; pacifist agitation, 58, 62; Elgin on, 71; Canadian annexationists on, 75; views on Quebec fortifications, 173; death, 173
Colonial Conference, proposed (1869–70), 223–4, 250
Commission on defences of Canada (1825), 14; (1862), 147–8
Commission on Militia (1854–5), 92 ff.; (1862), 130 ff.
Committee, departmental, on defences in colonies (1860), 111–13
Concentration proposal (Quebec and Montreal, 1864), 155 ff., 161
Confederate plots in Canada, 152–3, 163–4, 181

U

290 INDEX

Confederation, *see* Federation
Conference, Anglo-Canadian (London, 1865), 175–8, 181 ff.
Corn Laws, 25, 47, 68
Crimean War, 89 ff., 114

DENISON, Sir William, 124, 249
Denmark, war in (1864), 154
Disraeli, Benjamin (Lord Beaconsfield), criticizes reinforcement of Canada (1861), 119, 139; on Canadian garrison (1866), 193–4, 197; government orders reductions, 198, 102; falls, 201; Crystal Palace speech (1872), 258–9
Dorion, A. A., 102, 148
Durham, Lord, 40; *Report on Affairs of British North America*, 18–19, 24–5

" Earnscliffe " (Ottawa), 287
Elgin, Lord, chap. IV, *passim*, 25, 48, 51, 67, 146, 216; on garrison in 1847, 23; difficulties as Governor-General, 64, 68; correspondence with Grey on garrison, 68 ff.; policy towards it, 71, 74, 78–9; relations with Grey, 67, 69, 85; advice to Newcastle (1853), 87; results of policy, 88; leaves Canada, 92; criticizes reinforcement (1856), 99–101; regrets disbandment of provincial cavalry, 285–6
Examiner (Toronto), 83–4
Expenditure, Canadian, on defence (1854), 88; (1855), 91, 94, 97; (1856), 102; (1857–9), 108, 112; (1861–2), 143; (1863), 150; (1864), 151, 164; (1865), 188; (1866), 191; (1867), 197, 202–3; (1868), 210; (Nova Scotia), 152
Expense of colonial garrisons, in earliest times, 3; (1834–5), 39; (1846–7), 42–3; (1857–8), 112; (1859–60), 127; reduction (1869–71), 211, 236; in Canada (before 1812), 11; (1838–41), 18; (1843–4), 20; (1847 and 1853), 88; (1859–60), 128; (1860–62), 137; (1867), 202, 258

FEDERATION, beginnings, 157, 162; Quebec conference, 165; debates in Canada, 174–5; in England, 196; Dominion organized, 197; military results, 198, 200, 201–3

Fenian Brotherhood, 164–5; activity and raids (1865–6), 189 ff.; later rumours, etc., 191–3, 197, 211, 217, 221, 237, 241; raid (1870), 242–3; (1871), 252–3
Filibustering, 17, 95, 119, 188
Fires, military assistance at, 287–8
Fish, Hamilton, 231, 234
Foley, M. H., 94, 142, 143
Fort Garry (Winnipeg), garrisoned (1846–8), 21; (1857–61), 118; 240, 253, 287
Fortifications, Conservative and Whig policies on differ, 65–6; in Canada, projects of 1819 and 1825, 14–15; of 1862, 148; Jervois programme (1864), 162, 166; discussions (1865), 185 ff.; loan (1868), 200; change in Imperial policy, 215; results in Canada, 215, 218, 255; fortifications in Australia, 67; in England, 111; in U.S., 153, 161
Fort Wellington, Prescott, 221, 229
France, fear of (1840–52), 57 ff.; (1859–61), 110–11
Franco-Prussian War, 247–8
Free Trade, adopted, 47; effect on colonial situation, 48–9; Grey on, 64–5
French-Canadians, and military service, 9, 133–4; *Trent* Affair, 123; on troop withdrawals, 218–19, 245

GALT, (Sir) Alexander T., opposes Militia Bill (1855), 94; tariff (1859), 108–9; on Militia Bill (1862), 133; mission to England (1865), 177, 181 ff.; independence movement, 232
Garrison of British North America, strength of (1767), 8; (before 1812), 10–11; (1819, 1835), 13, 15–16; (1838), 17–18; (1843), 20; (1851–2), 85; (1855), 90; (1858), 106; (1859), 111; (1861), 118; (after *Trent* Affair), 122; (1864), 154; (1867), 193
Gettysburg, Battle of, 149, 152
Gladstone, William Ewart, views on colonial defence, 45, 125–6, 204–5; objects to fortifying Quebec (1865), 171; forms Government (1868), 201; its personnel, 204–7; its colonial policy, chaps. IX and X, *passim*, 215–17; Sir John Macdonald on, 237; discussion with Granville on relations with Canada, 286

INDEX

Globe (Toronto), 94, 142, 217–18, 254; on Militia Bill (1862), 132, 134–6; on troop withdrawals (1870), 242–3, 246–7
Godley, J. R., 112, 124
Granville, Lord, 209, 224–5, 237, 244; colonial views, 205–6, 216; dispatches on troop withdrawals, 214–15, 218–19, 226–7; criticized, 235–6, 250; on " friendly relaxation " of relations, 286
Great Eastern, 118
Grey, Lord, chap. IV, *passim*, 25, 50–1, 101; fear of Cobdenites, 48; 72–3; on defence of England, 58–9; colonial views, 64–5; Australian policy, 66–7; correspondence with Elgin on Canadian defence, 68 ff.; dispatch (March, 1851) on Canadian garrison, 79 ff.; its reception, 83–4; retirement, 85

HALIFAX, founded, 5; citadel, 14–15; fortifications (1865), 161; importance, 86, 128, 211; garrison remains, 214, 226
Hamilton, Ontario, 197
Hardinge, Viscount, 55
Head, Sir Edmund, chap. V, *passim*, 89, 92, 114, 146; on raising troops in Canada, 95, 105–6; defensive preparations (1855–6), 98; on military contribution from Canada, 103–5; on volunteer system, 107, retirement, 120
Herbert, Sidney (Lord Herbert of Lea), 89, 124–5, 156
Holton, L. H., 94
Howe, Joseph, on Militia Bill crisis (1862), 142, 145
Hudson's Bay Company lands, 9, 175–6, 209, 232
Hume, Joseph, 33, 38, 77, 113; colonial views, 33–4, 46, 49, 61; letter to W. L. Mackenzie, 82
Huskisson, William, 32

INDIA, defence, 42; reliefs, 54, 55; Mutiny, 105–6, 111
Isle aux Noix, 14–15, 103, 251

JERVOIS, (Sir) William F. D., first report on Canada, 160–1; second visit and report, 162, 165–7, 171, 177; discussions, 167 ff., 182, 185; fate of scheme, 255

KIMBERLEY, Lord, 244–6

Kingston (Ontario), 80, 90, 102, 105, 122, 251; fortifications, 14–15, 21, 166

Lett, W. P., 288
Lévis forts, 170, 177, 199–200, 228, 252, 287
Lewis, Sir George Cornewall, colonial views, 50, 117, 129, 141
Lindsay, Lt.-Gen. Hon. James, 236, 238, 239, 251
London, Ontario, 160, 197
Lowe, Robert (Lord Sherbrooke), and *The Times*, 47; colonial views (1861), 125; on Quebec fortifications (1865), 172; in Gladstone ministry, 205, 237
Lysons, Col. D., 130, 132

MACDONALD, (Sir) John Alexander, Minister of Militia Affairs (1861), 122; on Militia Commission (1862), 130, 146; introduces Militia Bill, 132–4; return to power, 153–4; coalition, 157; on defence problem (1865), 177; mission to England (1865), 177, 184 ff.; heads first Dominion Government, 197; and Sir C. Windham, 220; on annexation and independence, 231–2; on Red River, 233 ff.; letter to Carnarvon, 237–8; illness, 239, 241; other refs., 192–3, 224, 254, 255
Macdonald, John Sandfield, forms ministry (1862), 142–3; military policy, 143, 144–6; new militia laws (1863), 149–50; falls, 153
MacDougall, Gen. Sir Patrick L., 114 *n*.
McDougall, William, 201, 208–10, 232
McGee, Thomas D'Arcy, 152
MacNab, Sir Allan, 92, 95
Madawaska route, 121, 285
Maine boundary dispute, 16, 19–20, 285
Maritime Provinces, x, 85–6; strength and cost of garrison, 13, 15–16, 20, 42–3, 85–6, 128; local expenditure (1858), 112; volunteers, 118; local forces (1863–5), 152; and Federation, 181, 187–8, 197
Matapedia Road, 121, 150
Merivale, Herman, 50, 124
Merritt, W. H., 101
Metcalfe, Sir Charles (Lord), 22

INDEX

Michel, Sir John, 189, 192, 198, 210
Military schools, 149–51, 157, 170, 188
Militia Acts (Canada), (before 1812), 11 ; projects (1845–6), 23 ; Act (1855), 93–4 ; (1856), 101 ; (1859), 107–8 ; (1862), 143 ; (1863), 149–50 ; (1864), 151 ; (1868), 200
Militia Bill (1862), 132 ff., 151
Mill, James, 30–1, 33, 39
Mills, Arthur, 113, 123, 129
Molesworth, Sir William, 40, 77, 109, 113 ; agitation against colonial garrisons, 40–2, 44, 46, 49, 56, 260 ; debate in 1851, 81–2
Monck, Lord, chaps. VI, VII and VIII, *passim*, 120, 122, 123, 191–2, 193, 197 ; *Trent* Affair, 120 ff. ; on defeat of Militia Bill (1862), 134–5 ; dealings with Sandfield Macdonald, 143–4, 148 ; on Militia laws (1863), 150–1 ; concentration scheme (1864), 156–7 ; coalition, 157 ; advice to ministers (1865), 176 ; on troop withdrawals (1868), 198 ; retires, estimate, 210 ; speech in Lords (1869), 213
Montreal, garrison (1849), 73 ; fortification projects (1825), 14 ; (1862), 148 ; (1864), 167–8, 169 ; postponed, 187 ; loan, 200 ; scheme lapses, 255

Napoleon III, 57, 60, 62, 89, 110–11, 194
Naval Defence and Expenditure, 42, 136, 153, 161, 185–6, 190–1, 202, 251–2, 262 ; Colonial Naval Defence Act (1865), 207, 215, 252 ; gunboat controversy (1868–9), 199, 215, 221
Navigation Acts, reform, 32 ; repeal, 47, 64
New Brunswick, rejects Federation, 175 ; posts handed over (1871), 252 ; *see* Maritime Provinces
Newcastle, Duke of, 156, 216 ; on Canadian tariff, 108–9 ; on garrison (1861), 124, 126–7 ; on Canadian militia policy, 144
Newfoundland, 9, 13, 15, 20 ; troops withdrawn, 256
New Zealand, military problems, 43, 44, 46, 66–7 ; troops withdrawn, 207, 223, 256
Nova Scotia, *see* Maritime Provinces

O'Neill, John, 190, 211, 230, 237, 242, 252–3

Ordnance lands, transferred, 91, 96–7, 102
Oregon dispute, 20–1, 23, 66
Ottawa (city), 197, 251, 287–8

Pakington, Sir John, 201, 236
Palmerston, Lord, 53, 60, 110–11, 113 ; reinforces Canada (1856), 99 ; (1861), 119 ; Militia Bill crisis (1862), 141 ; defence of Canada (1865), 171–2 ; contrast with Gladstone's policy, 216
Panmure, Lord (Fox Maule), 56, 78 ; on reinforcing Canada (1856), 99, 100–1
Parnell, Sir Henry, 33
Peel, Sir Robert, on Canada (1844), 24 ; Free Trade, 25, 47 ; reliefs, 55–6
Penetanguishene, 85, 91
Pensioners, enrolled, 80, 91, 97–8, 102, 287
Police, troops as, and aid to civil power, 16–17, 23, 73 ; volunteers, 101 ; proposed police force (1855), 93 ; lack of, 287

Quebec, fortifications (1820), 14, 15 ; (1862), 148 ; (1864), 161–2, 166, 170 ; discussions in Parliament, 171–3 ; progress, 199–200, 228 ; withdrawal of troops, 227–8, 241, 245–6, completed (1871), 252–3

Railway, Halifax–Quebec, 81, 183, 196 ; transcontinental (guarantee), 255
Rebellion in Canada (1837), 17 ; expense, 43
Reciprocity Treaty, 164, 174–5
Recruiting troubles, 195
Red River Insurrection, 232 ff. ; Expedition, 236, 238–40
Regiments :
  Guards, 3, 17, 20, 121, 149, 154
  Military Train, 121, 154
  Rifle Brigade, 244, 288
  Royal Artillery, 121, 253
  Royal Canadian Rifles, 20, 90, 106, 111, 118, 214, 227, 287
  Royal Engineers, 118, 121, 252, 253
  13th Hussars, 192
  60th Regt (King's Royal Rifle Corps), 118, 240, 244, 253, 287
  71st, 77
  96th, 122
  100th (Royal Canadian), 95, 105–6, 114

INDEX 293

Reliefs, for troops abroad, 52 ff., 208, 212
Reserve problem, 195, 208
Resolution of Commons on defence of self-governing colonies (March, 1862), 129–30, 212
Revolution, American, 6–7; results, 26–7
Rideau Canal, 14, 15, 103, 162
Riel, Louis, 232, 233, 237
Riots, military assistance at, 23, 287
Roebuck, J. A., 126, 140–1
Rose, Sir John, 234, 250
Rush-Bagot Convention, 148, 153, 164, 173, 190, 191, 215
Russell, Lord John (Earl), 17, 21, 25; on defence of England, 59, 60; of colonies, 78, 82; attacks troop withdrawals (1870), 243, 249

St. Albans Raid, 163–4
Select Committees:
  On Finance (1817), 38
  On Colonial Military Expenditure (1834–5), 15, 38
  On Army and Ordnance Expenditure (1849–50), 77–8
  On Colonial Military Expenditure (1861), 113–14, 123–8
  On Army (India and the Colonies) (1867), 195, 208
Seven Weeks' War, 194
Sicotte, L. V., 143, 148
Sinclair, Sir John, 30
Smith, Adam, 29, 31, 34
Smith, Goldwin, 137, 139, 259
Smith, Robert Vernon (Lord Lyveden), 48–9, 77, 171
Snider rifle, 192, 197, 209, 227, 252
Sumner, Senator Charles, 213, 230
Sydenham, Lord, 22

Tariff (Canada, 1859), 108–10, 126–7, 129, 141
Temiscouata, Lake, 121, 285
Tennyson, Lord, 62, 110, 258–9
Thomson, Major F. R., on riot at Bytown, 287
Thornton, (Sir) Edward, 231

Times, The (London), 110, 140, 142, 152, 155, 189, 250, 258; colonial views (1849–51), 47, 49; on Canadian Militia Bill (1862), 137–8; on Canadian Federation, 179, 196
Toronto, 103, 106, 122, 197, 251, 287–8; memorial from citizens (1864), 158–9; proposed evacuation (1869), 219–20
Trent Affair, 111, 120–3, 128, 202

United States Army, 11, 116; increase (Civil War), 131, 188; reduction, 188, 196

Victoria, H.M. Queen, fears for Canada (1865), 172; on troop withdrawals, 224
Volunteer force (Canada), inception, 93, 96–8, 101–2; after *Trent* Affair, 131–2; (1864), 151; increase (1866), 189, 190; (1867), 197; after Federation, 200
Volunteer movement (England, 1859), 110–11

Wakefield, Edward Gibbon, 40; on garrisons, 45–6
War of 1812, 11–13, 116
Washington, Treaty of (1871), 254–5
Wellington, Duke of, on defence of Canada, 14–15; on reliefs (1827), 53–4; on defence of England (1846–7), 58–9; death, 61
West Indies, 10
Williams, Sir Fenwick, 119, 122, 155–6, 188
Windham, Sir Charles, 210, 219–22
Wolseley, Garnet (Lord), 121, 123, 239, 240–41

Young, Sir John (Lord Lisgar), chaps. IX and X, *passim*, 210, 215–16, 239, 240; on Canadian ministers, 210–11; on military co-operation (1869), 220–2; speech at Quebec, 218–19, 229; on annexation talk, 231; impounds Granville dispatch, 287

PRINTED IN GREAT BRITAIN BY
LOWE AND BRYDONE (PRINTERS) LIMITED, LONDON, N.W.10

www.ingramcontent.com/pod-product-compliance
Lightning Source LLC
Chambersburg PA
CBHW020355080526
44584CB00014B/1030